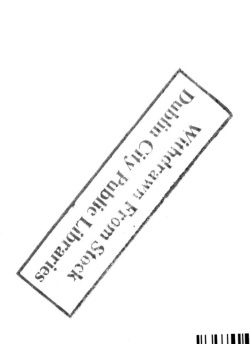

D1422424

The Catholic Church and the Northern Ireland Troubles, 1968–1998

The Catholic Church and the Northern Ireland Troubles, 1968–1998

MARGARET M. SCULL

School of Political Science and Sociology, NUI Galway

OXFORD
UNIVERSITY PRESS

OXFORD
UNIVERSITY PRESS

Great Clarendon Street, Oxford, OX2 6DP,
United Kingdom

Oxford University Press is a department of the University of Oxford.
It furthers the University's objective of excellence in research, scholarship,
and education by publishing worldwide. Oxford is a registered trade mark of
Oxford University Press in the UK and in certain other countries

First Edition published in 2019

Impression: 1

Published in the United States of America by Oxford University Press
198 Madison Avenue, New York, NY 10016, United States of America

British Library Cataloguing in Publication Data
Data available

Library of Congress Control Number: 2019937229

ISBN 978-0-19-884321-4

Printed and bound by
CPI Group (UK) Ltd, Croydon, CR0 4YY

Acknowledgements

A first book is no small undertaking and would have been impossible without the kindness and generosity of a great number of individuals. These paragraphs can in no way measure up as a proper way of thanks, but it must suffice for now. To begin I thank my PhD supervisors Ian McBride and Alana Harris for their guidance throughout the researching and writing of my doctoral dissertation which has formed the basis of this book. I owe a great deal of thanks to my dissertation examiners, Niall Ó Dochartaigh and Simon Prince, for their detailed advice throughout. In addition, I must thank the anonymous OUP reviewers for their insightful comments. A number of people have kindly discussed areas of my work with me at length, including Jennifer Altehenger, Máire Braniff, John Brewer, Christopher Dillon, David Edgerton, Richard English, Gladys Ganiel, Thomas Hennessey, Dianne Kirby, George Legg, Carmen Mangion, Maria Power, F. Stuart Ross, Simon Sleight, Richard Vinen, and Tim White. This book would not have been possible without Kelly Cronin and Cathal Nolan. Both helped to shape me as a scholar.

Furthermore, I must highlight my appreciation for the individuals who kindly agreed to be interviewed for this book, including Mgr Raymond Murray, Fr Joe McVeigh, Fr Des Wilson, Fr Bobby Gilmore, Bishop Pat Buckley, Dr Geraldine Smyth OP, and Fr Gerry McFlynn. I was also able to speak to the late Bishop Edward Daly before his passing and I am incredibly grateful for his insight. I would like to express my gratitude to Brian Feeney, Laurence McKeown, and Danny Morrison who also agreed to be interviewed. The staff at the following diocesan archives kindly granted permission to quote from their material: Arundel and Brighton, Birmingham, Derry, Dublin, Liverpool, Salford, Southwark, and Westminster. Also, Roddy Hegarty and everyone at the Cardinal Tomás Ó Fiaich Memorial Library and Archive in Armagh, who generously assisted me with the archive's holdings. Furthermore, I am grateful to the Irish Research Council, the Moore Institute at NUI Galway, the Royal Historical Society, and the British Association of Irish Studies as all provided funding for the research that has gone into this book.

My gratitude goes out to Alison Garden, Caroline Magennis, and Margot Mache. I am thankful for their advice, guidance, and friendship. I appreciate the support of my in-laws, my four sisters, and especially my mother Barbara Scull, who has been steadfast in her belief in me, even if greatly bemused at times. Finally, to my husband, Andrew Harrison, who has been unwavering in his patience and kindness. This work would not have been possible without his support and encouragement.

This book is in memory of my late father, William 'Bill' Scull, who inspired me to follow my passion.

Table of Contents

List of Figures

List of Abbreviations

AAW	Archives of the Archdiocese of Westminster
ABDA	Arundel and Brighton Diocesan Archive
AMP	Archbishop McQuaid Papers
BDA	Birmingham Diocesan Archive
CAIN	Conflict Archive on the Internet
CCP	Cardinal Conway Papers
CIC	Churches Industrial Council
CO.	County
CRC	Christian Renewal Centre
CS (gas)	Type of Tear (gas)
CTOMLA	Cardinal Tomás Ó Fiaich Memorial Library and Archive
DeDA	Derry Diocesan Archive
DCAC	Derry Citizens' Action Committee
DDA	Dublin Diocesan Archive
DFA	Department of Foreign Affairs
DUP	Democratic Unionist Party
FAIT	Families Against Intimidation and Terror
FCO	Foreign and Commonwealth Office
FDFP	Fr Denis Faul Papers
GFA	Good Friday Agreement, also known as the Belfast Agreement
HMG	Her Majesties' Government
ICC	Irish Council of Churches
ICCL	Irish Council for Civil Liberties
ICJP	Irish Commission for Justice and Peace
ICPO	Irish Commission for Prisoners Overseas
IRA	Irish Republican Army
INLA	Irish National Liberation Army
LAA	Liverpool Archdiocesan Archive
Mgr	Monsignor
MP	Member of Parliament
NIA	The National Archives of Ireland, Dublin
NICRA	Northern Ireland Civil Rights Association
NIO	Northern Ireland Office
NISRA	Northern Ireland Statistics Agency
NUI	National University of Ireland
Official IRA	Official Irish Republican Army (Officials)
PREM	Records of the Prime Minister's Office
Provisional IRA	Provisional Irish Republican Army (Provisionals)
RAC	Relatives Action Committee

Rev	Reverend
RFPC	Relatives and Friends of Prisoners Committee
RUC	Royal Ulster Constabulary
SaDA	Salford Diocesan Archive
SCS	Special Category Status
SDA	Southwark Diocesan Archive
SDLP	Social Democratic Labour Party
SF	Sinn Féin
SSCP	Sr Sarah Clarke Papers
STOP	Stop Terror Oppression and Pain
TD	Member of Parliament (Ireland)
TNA	The UK National Archives, Kew
UDA	Ulster Democratic Alliance
UDR	Ulster Defence Regiment, locally recruited force supporting the RUC
UFF	Ulster Freedom Fighters
UUP	Ulster Unionist Party
UVF	Ulster Volunteer Force

Introduction

'Religion from Rome, Politics from Home'?

'One learned, quite literally at one's mother's knee, that Christ died for the human race and Patrick Pearse for the Irish section of it.'[1]

Tom Fee was born in 1923 in Cullyhanna.[2] He spent his formative years in Camlough, Co. Armagh, where his schoolmaster father raised him and his brother, as a single parent, after his mother passed away. The family owned a car, a rarity in the community, and the boys excelled in school. From a young age, Fee knew he wanted to join the prestigious priesthood and set off for the national Roman Catholic seminary for Ireland at St Patrick's College, Maynooth.[3] After his ordination in 1948, and a brief stint as an assistant priest, Fee became a young faculty member at Maynooth where he taught on many aspects of clerical training during the 1950s, specializing in modern history. But Fee was destined to take a different path from those who preceded him. As the conflict in Northern Ireland flared, dominating the Irish and British social, political, and religious landscape for decades to follow, Fee's nationalist views took hold. These politics led him to adopt the Gaelic version of his name and, by the time he became President of Maynooth in 1974, he was known as Tomás Ó Fiaich (see Appendix). For a religious leader to hold such views, and regularly vocalize his want for a united Ireland, proved controversial. The blatantly sectarian, outrageous political cartoon on the cover of this book, discussed in greater detail in Chapter 3, was one such outcome.

Under his tutelage, and the influence of the Second Vatican Council, Maynooth broke with tradition, rejecting teaching in Latin in favour of courses mainly taught in English and Irish.[4] Radical new courses on 'the role of priest in society' were added to the seminary curriculum, reflecting a new vision for the priesthood and an updated ecclesiology.[5] However, these changes were not the result of one man's

---

[1] Eamonn McCann, *War and an Irish Town* (London, 1993), 65.
[2] Chapter title reference: K. Theodore Hoppen, *Ireland since 1800: Conflict & Conformity* (London, 1989), 160–5.
[3] The Roman Catholic Church will henceforth be referred to as the Catholic Church throughout.
[4] Tom Inglis argues that before Vatican II, documents were written in Latin to deliberately hide Church business from the laity; Tom Inglis, *Moral Monopoly: The Rise and Fall of the Catholic Church in Modern Ireland* (Dublin, 1987), 45.
[5] *Kalendarium: Collegii Sti Patritii*, (Dublin, 1975–76), 51.

actions: the national seminary for Ireland was adapting to changing times, when the country's priests were needed not only for rites of the Church but also to act as leaders in social justice movements, representing families, communities, and ideas. Ó Fiaich would leave Maynooth to become the Archbishop of Armagh and later join the College of Cardinals, having spent twenty-five years developing his ideas in the seminary. Ó Fiaich's journey reflects a wider truth, explored throughout this study, about the power of individuals within the institutional Catholic Church and their role during the conflict in Northern Ireland. Tom Fee's evolution to Tomás Ó Fiaich, with his entrenched nationalist sympathies, was not an isolated occurrence. Similarities can be found in the stories of many other Church figures who were either thrust into the wider public gaze through their actions, or who seized the initiative to forward their interpretation of what their work should be in a period of conflict, struggle, violence, and upheaval, thus defining a new era for the Church and its role in Northern Ireland.

Maynooth was the epicentre of Irish Catholic theological thought. A significant number of priests who passed through its halls and began their clerical journeys in Co. Kildare would go on to play major roles in peace and reconciliation initiatives during the Troubles, the euphemistic name for the conflict in Northern Ireland. The list of seminary students and those recently ordained in the college's annual *Kalendarium* constitutes a catalogue of individuals who would go on to work as prison chaplains, community organizers, parish priests, and school teachers: all positions of social influence. Most of the Irish Catholic bishops served on the Board of Directors and many priests acted as lecturers on their way to becoming bishops.[6] Maynooth priests had a 'home grown' feel: a special knowledge of Irish history, thanks to their curriculum which included the subject extensively; and a respect for Irish Catholicism deeply rooted in Irish nationalism. Priests' time at Maynooth shaped their pastoral and theological viewpoints, which became apparent in their work in Northern Ireland during the conflict. The evolution of the seminary between the 1940s and the 1970s reflected a changing priesthood, and one that reacted to the conflict differently over time.[7]

Maynooth, while undoubtedly the primary influence on the clergy, was not the only source of new ideas. Returning missionaries were also key to this evolution in religious thought. These influences were most keenly felt within the clergy who did not study at Maynooth. The five other seminaries in Ireland were exposed to external ideas through the large number of missionaries.[8] All of priests interviewed as part of this study recounted having a cousin, friend, or neighbour who

---

[6] The hierarchy will refer to Catholic Church bishops, archbishops, and cardinals in Northern Ireland.

[7] Anthony Akinwale, 'The Decree on Priestly Formation, *Optatam Totius*' in Matthew Lamb and Matthew Levering (eds.), *Vatican II: Renewal with Tradition* (Oxford, 2008), 237–9.

[8] The clergy will refer to diocesan and religious priests in Northern Ireland unless otherwise specified.

came back from their mission trips filled with different perspectives on the world. Liberation theology, a term coined in 1971 by the Peruvian priest Gustavo Gutiérrez, found its way to Ireland through missionary work and global media. It is an interpretation of Christian theology which emphasizes a concern for the experience of the poor and oppressed. Liberation theology divided the Church, with conservative bishops fearing it a 'Trojan horse' for Communism.[9] Only a handful of Irish priests and women religious professed adherence to this new theological perspective and other European theological influences such as the worker-priest movement, which spread throughout France and Italy during the 1940s and 1950s, advocating for a left-leaning clergy living alongside their parishioners.[10] However, as Marianne Elliott has noted, the Irish Catholic Church left little room for innovation among its priests. For example, the Bishop of Down and Connor refused to send priests abroad, fearing foreign influences.[11] In the North, as Maurice Hayes has argued, priests were drawn from closed communities and educated 'in a sort of enclosed clerical hothouse' before returning to their communities with greater overarching status.[12] Clerical attitudes on a national level in Northern Ireland throughout the period of the conflict were constant, despite the influence of Maynooth for gradual reform. Nevertheless, there were changes on a diocese-by-diocese basis, as will be explored throughout this study.

This study critically analyses the influence of the Catholic Church in mediating between paramilitary organizations and the British government during the Northern Ireland Troubles from 1968 to 1998. It contends that the role of the Church, especially in its attempts to resolve the conflict, lessened over time because of a wide range of factors. These include a gradual weakening of clerical authority and the changing nature of the conflict itself. Additionally, this study explores the different roles assumed by the clergy and their bishops in response to the conflict. As the public face of the Irish Catholic Church bishops shouldered more responsibility, were more accountable, and garnered far more criticism than their priests who had greater freedom of action and opinion. Of course, viewpoints on, and responses to the conflict can be influenced by an individual's background, upbringing, location, and parochial experience. Equally, the response of the English and Welsh Catholic Church to the conflict often diverged from that of the Irish Catholic Church.

---

[9] *Irish Catholic*, 4 Feb. 1993; 'An Irish liberation theology: Learning from the Universal Church', Joseph McVeigh, Catholic Church and Irish Diaspora Conference, (London, 2014); Breifne Walker, 'The Catholic Church in Ireland—adaptation or liberation?', *The Crane Bag*, 5 (1981), 77–8.

[10] Arthur Marwick, *The Sixties: Cultural Revolution in Britain, France, Italy and the United States, c.1958–c.1974* (Oxford, 1998), 34; Gerd-Rainer Horn, *The Spirit of Vatican II: Western European Progressive Catholicism in the Long Sixties* (Oxford, 2015), 61–82.

[11] Maurice Hayes, *Minority Verdict: Experiences of a Catholic Public Servant* (Belfast, 1995), 117.

[12] Marianne Elliott, *The Catholics of Ulster* (London, 2000), 466–7.

D. George Boyce has called Catholicism 'one of the essential ingredients of Irishness'.[13] When Catholic emancipation did not come swiftly after the Act of Union in 1800–1801, R.V. Comerford argues it resulted in the creation of a 'modern nationalist movement in which Irish nationality was reinvented with Catholicism as its key identifier'.[14] The Catholic Church supported Catholic emancipation and it appeared to work in tandem with most nationalist groups throughout the nineteenth century. Yet the twentieth century relationship between elements of Irish nationalism and the Catholic Church as an institution is quite revealing of, at times, blatant animosity between the two groups.[15] Regardless of this division, the majority of unionists in Northern Ireland believed 'Catholic equalled Nationalist'.[16] This study seeks to address the place of the Catholic Church in this conflict and examine whether Catholicism was still one of those essential ingredients in the 1970s, 1980s, and 1990s.

Traditionally, priests have occupied a special place at the heart of Irish Catholic communities. Under the hierarchical organization of the Church, bishops were accountable to Rome, priests accountable to bishops, and the laity accountable to their priests.[17] Priests had contact with their congregation not only through the religious sacraments and at moments of great joy, like baptism, confirmation, and marriage, but as well in times of sadness, aiding the sick, and presiding over funerals. The priest was not simply a moral and spiritual advisor in this quasi-confessional state, but was consulted on political, economic, and social issues.[18] Priests' involvement in Irish politics had lessened after the Civil War ended in 1923, and while they still urged parishioners to vote with their Christian conscience, their presence in encouraging rebellion had diminished.[19] The priest remained a respected person in Catholic communities and, sometimes begrudgingly, acknowledged for their appeals for non-violence in Protestant neighbourhoods. The Northern Ireland Troubles proved the Home Rule adage from the 1880s: 'Religion from Rome, politics from home' mostly to be true. Throughout the conflict, Catholics listened to theological perspectives promulgated from the pulpit but privately voted for whoever they wished, evidenced in the minority who voted for Sinn Féin (SF) after the 1981 hunger strikes. Even in the early 1970s, when Richard Rose asked in his substantive survey 'if you wanted advice on a political question, who would you go to for help?', he found that only 16 percent of Northern Catholics would approach their priest: most preferring a lawyer, physician, or politician.[20] By the time of the 1994 ceasefire and clerical child abuse

---

[13] D. George Boyce, *Nationalism in Ireland* (London, 1982), 360.
[14] R.V. Comerford, *Ireland: Inventing the Nation* (London, 2003), 108.
[15] Boyce, *Nationalism*, 317–18.   [16] Comerford, *Ireland*, 117.
[17] Inglis, *Moral Monopoly*, 44.   [18] Inglis, *Moral Monopoly*, 47.
[19] See Dermot Keogh, *The Vatican, the Bishops and Irish Politics 1919–1939* (Cambridge, 1986).
[20] See Richard Rose, *Governing without Consensus- An Irish Perspective* (London, 1971) in Gerald McElroy, *The Catholic Church and the Northern Ireland Crisis, 1968–86* (Dublin, 1991), 10.

revelations, priests' seemingly automatic role as men of integrity and morally upright and scrupulous advisors had been tarnished irreversibly. The conflict began with deference to clerical authority but ended with a greatly diminished quotient.[21] In 1968, the Irish Catholic Church was reeling from the effects of the Second Vatican Council. It would take years to implement these changes, with the laity only taking a larger role within the Irish Church in the 1980s. The Irish Catholic Church was changing structurally throughout the conflict because of outside factors, including Vatican directives and growing western European secularization.[22]

There is a propensity in the historiography to prioritize certain explanations when evaluating the causes and motivations for the conflict. Historians grapple with its origins, favouring one specific value or motivator as creating and continuing the violence. In 1995, John McGarry and Brendan O'Leary argued religion was not the main driver, claiming if 'socio-economic inequalities, cultural or national differences, inter-state relations...must be of secondary or no importance...We will argue that those who think the conflict is based on religion are wrong.'[23] Marxist political theorists and sociologists have ignored religion altogether in their analyses. Conversely, Frank Wright and Steve Bruce earlier provided excellent studies on the centrality of religion.[24]

Likewise, while Protestant churches are frequently grouped together as a subject for analysis, key distinctions remain between their viewpoints and experiences.[25] Steve Bruce has argued for a case of Irish exceptionalism concerning secularization; namely that unlike the rest of Europe, Ireland clung to religion until the late 1960s.[26] Class also has a crucial role to play in shaping experiential realities: a working-class boy on the Shankhill does not have the same concerns as a Malone Road housewife. The violence and bloodshed in Northern Ireland cannot be explained as a conflict rooted purely in tensions over class, gender, or religion, but rather through a complex interplay of multiple factors. This older (and politically invested) historiography, with its desire for a definitive, mono-causal explanation of the origins of the conflict, disregards the fact these causes interact. Part of this impetus to assert the explanatory certainty of one attribute over

[21] A 1968 poll conducted among young people age seventeen to twenty-four in Northern Ireland found that Catholics chose priests as the most well respected occupational group. See McElroy, *Catholic Church*, 10.

[22] However, Steve Bruce challenges this notion of secularization in Ireland; Steve Bruce, 'History, sociology and secularisation', in Christopher Hartney (ed.), *Secularisation: New Historical Perspectives* (Newcastle upon Tyne, 2014), 190–1.

[23] John McGarry and Brendan O'Leary, *Explaining Northern Ireland: Broken Images* (Oxford, 1995), 171–2.

[24] See Frank Wright, *Northern Ireland: A Comparative Analysis* (Maryland, 1987) and Steve Bruce, *God Save Ulster! The Religion and Politics of Paisleyism* (Oxford, 1986).

[25] See Eric Gallagher and A.S. Worral, *Christians in Ulster* (Oxford, 1982).

[26] Steve Bruce, 'Secularization and the impotence of individualized religion', *Hedgehog Review*, 8 (2006), 38.

another may stem from a partisan need to deal with the past: to demonstrate historians have a role in shaping a post-conflict society.[27] For the Troubles, all history is 'public history' and the nexus between memory and history returns its salience. Therefore explanations of the conflict have been fought over and 'colonized' by those who experienced the conflict.

Class plays a major role in this study when examined alongside religion, ethnicity, and masculinity. Priests as an exclusively male, educated group, were construed as 'superior' within their lay communities. Partition served to 'restore the clergy to positions of political dominance'.[28] This began to change but the financial costs of training and joining the priesthood were still relatively high. Scholarships existed to aid able, less financially fortunate students to study at Maynooth, but the price was still too steep for many. In 1940, a £30 deposit of half tuition fees and 'other fees' needed to be paid before guaranteeing the student entry for that year. Students 'nominated to a free place' were still required to pay a £13 deposit.[29] Therefore, priests were generally better off than their parishioners. Class and educational divisions developed between members of the hierarchy and the clergy as well. Wealthier priests who received a more rigorous, often grammar school, education and had family connections, climbed higher and faster.[30] This became less of a problem by the late 1980s and early 1990s as priestly ordinations had dropped. Seminarians were more difficult to come by so the bureaucratic climb mattered less. Class divisions within the clergy influenced their differing approaches to the conflict to a certain extent. In the 1960s, a more heterogeneously-classed group of clergy emerged, conflicting with the hierarchy because of their different parochial experiences in the post-Vatican II Church, rather than purely as a result of class differences.

A second, and arguably more influential, factor is the power of personalities (see Appendix for individual biographies). Key individuals played crucial roles in altering how the Catholic Church responded to the conflict. When the conflict began, Cardinal William Conway was Archbishop of Armagh (see Appendix). Conway was a quiet man who had lectured at Maynooth in the 1940s and 1950s and was theologically conservative. His successor in 1977, Ó Fiaich, was just one of many individual priests who had a major impact on the conflict. The push and pull between Ó Fiaich and Bishop Cahal Daly of Down and Connor (see Appendix) in the 1980s, which will be discussed in Chapter 4, remains but one example of how disparate personalities could collectively shape the Church's response. Daly succeeded Ó Fiaich as Archbishop of Armagh after the latter's unexpected death in 1990, once again altering the position of the hierarchy in response to the

---

[27] Ian McBride, 'In the shadow of the gunman: Irish historians and the IRA', *Journal of Contemporary History*, 46 (2011), 690–1.

[28] Oliver Rafferty, *Catholicism in Ulster 1603–1983: And Interpretative History* (London, 1994), 3.

[29] *Kalendarium: Collegii Sti Patritii*, (Dublin, 1940–41), 248.

[30] Elliott, *Catholics of Ulster*, 466–70.

conflict. The power of subjectivities and opinions cannot be limited to members of the hierarchy, as many priests became household names in the North, leaving a lasting mark on conflict resolution. While many of these priests had the same goal—an end to the violence—their methods, public personas, and theological and pastoral approaches brought them into conflict with Protestant clergy, unionists, and paramilitaries, as well as each other.

The traditional narrative of the Church in the Troubles has focused solely on the Irish Catholic Church.[31] This study broadens our collective understanding by introducing analysis of the English and Welsh Catholic Church. Ecumenical relations and endeavours in England were separate and differently framed to those in Northern Ireland. Therefore, this study employs a mixed method approach. The Irish Catholic Church's response to the conflict must be viewed as an entangled history. The existing histories, which will be discussed in the next section, merely evaluate in a somewhat circumscribed fashion the reaction of the Irish Catholic Church to the conflict.[32] This approach is partial and overly parochial; the Provisional Irish Republican Army (IRA) had a bombing campaign in England, and the English and Welsh Catholic Church was frequently asked for their thoughts on the excommunication of IRA members. It is futile to study the Troubles in terms of national narratives, as the conflict spilled over national borders. For an entangled history, as Margrit Pernau argues: 'Every transfer is a two-way process, which influences not only the sender but the receiver'.[33] Comments on the conflict by English bishops directly impacted upon the perception of, and the reaction to, the Irish Catholic Church. This is not simply a comparative history, as Jürgen Kocka acknowledges, because these units of comparison 'cannot be separated from each other'.[34] English bishops' opinions on suicide and excommunication differed from their Irish counterparts causing confusion among the laity: this directly impacted upon the ability of the Irish Catholic Church to mediate the conflict. The Churches' close proximity and the Irish diaspora in Britain led to frequent interactions. Examining how the Catholic Churches responded to the conflict reveals differing approaches on either side of the Irish Sea.

This study argues it is crucial to evaluate the intertwined relationship between the Irish and English and Welsh Catholic Churches in relation to the conflict in Northern Ireland. If historians focus only on the Irish Catholic Church's

---

[31] Oliver Rafferty, Gerald McElroy, Marianne Elliott, Tom Inglis, and Mary Kenny, whose works are discussed below, focus their studies to the Irish Catholic Church; Elliott, *Catholics of Ulster*; McElroy, *Catholic Church*; Inglis, *Moral Monopoly*; Rafferty, *Catholicism in Ulster*; Mary Kenny, *Goodbye to Catholic Ireland* (Dublin, 2000).

[32] See McElroy, *Catholic Church*; Elliott, *Catholics of Ulster*; Kenny, *Goodbye to Catholic Ireland*; Rafferty, *Catholicism in Ulster*; Inglis, *Moral Monopoly*.

[33] Margit Pernau, 'Whither conceptual history? From national to entangled histories', *Contributions to the History of Concepts*, 7 (2012), 4.

[34] Jürgen Kocka, 'Comparison and beyond', *History and Theory*, 42 (2003), 41.

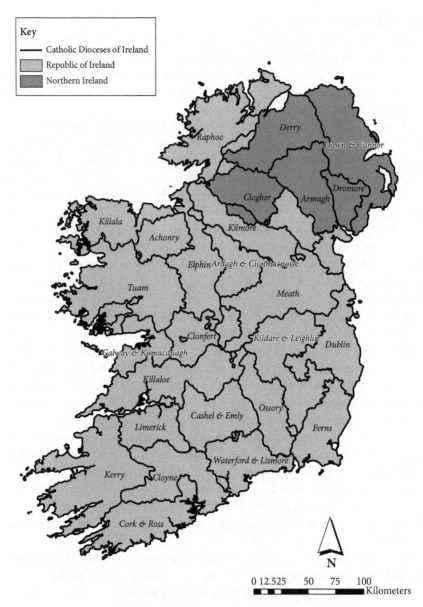

Figure 1 Map of Catholic Church Diocese Boundaries
Source: Eoin O'Mahony.

responses to the conflict, (see Figure 1 for diocesan boundaries, which do not directly overlap with the Irish border), they miss out on a fuller history of the role of religious institutions in the conflict. As will be explored, the English and Welsh hierarchy disagreed with the Irish hierarchy on IRA funerals, excommunication, and the status of Irish prisoners. British newspapers reported these squabbles, especially during the 1980-81 hunger strikes.[35] If the Church could not agree, how could it shape opinions of the faithful? There were also Catholic British Army soldiers stationed in Northern Ireland. Their actions and, at times, their deaths forced wider Catholic Churches to respond to the conflict.

Sources and their Limitations

Accessing diocesan archives in Ireland has often proved challenging to historians. Many files from the period are yet to be made available to scholars. As a result, this study has supplemented Irish sources with English diocesan archival material. Dioceses across these islands generally keep a one-hundred-year rule from the date of a priest's death, leaving many of the relevant papers unavailable. Documents concerning the hierarchy, however, are regulated differently. The Irish Catholic Church often releases documents relating to a particular bishop thirty years after his death. The English and Welsh Catholic Church operates a thirty-year rule from the date that documents were created. In some cases, more sources have become available earlier at a bishop's discretion.[36] English diocesan archives have therefore proved fruitful for this study with a majority of correspondence between the Irish and English and Welsh bishops available until 1988.

British and Irish government archives have been quarried extensively for this study. These documents reveal relationships between Church leaders and British and Irish government officials on a variety of issues, including: perceptions of clerical authority; political and pastoral tensions among bishops and clergy members; and a measure of government thought concerning the nature of the Catholic Church in the conflict. The National Archives of Ireland, Dublin, operates a thirty-year rule, while The National Archives, in Kew, Surrey, is moving from a thirty-year rule towards a twenty-year rule concerning UK government documents.[37] Generally speaking, while Irish government officials demonstrated much more reverence for Catholic Church leaders, British politicians and civil servants handled bishops and priests with a degree of suspicion and scepticism.

This study benefits from oral testimony from priests, bishops, politicians, women religious, and former paramilitaries, which has helped to fill vital gaps left by incomplete or closed archives. This has provided otherwise inaccessible and

---

[35] See Margaret Scull, 'The Catholic Church and the hunger strikes of Terence MacSwiney and Bobby Sands', *Irish Political Studies*, 31 (2016), 282–99.

[36] At the time of publication, only four boxes of Cardinal William Conway's documents were released to the Cardinal Tomás Ó Fiaich Library and Archive (CTOMLA). Most of Cardinal Ó Fiaich's papers should be released in 2020.

[37] At the time of submission, the National Archives of Ireland (NAI) had released files until 1986. The UK National Archives (TNA) had opened documents concerning Northern Ireland until 1988.

illuminating personal insights into the conflict and was supported by ethics clearance.[38] In particular, my interviews among clergymen and women, as well as bishops, revealed a group divided on many issues. Existing broadcast interviews supplemented this material, allowing for analysis of perspectives of deceased or unwilling interviewees.

An Appendix details biographical information of the important clerical figures in the conflict. Such a list, a kind of *personae dramatis*, did not exist previously and features well-known public hierarchy figures and lesser-known members of the clergy. This Appendix is itself an original scholarly contribution to our knowledge as many of these figures have not been subject to separate scholarly works or have entries in the Dictionary of National Biography.

From 2014 until 2018, Dr Dianne Kirby and PhD student Briege Rafferty conducted group interviews with women religious involved in the conflict.[39] There were more women religious than priests or bishops in the Irish Catholic Church. Kirby and Rafferty's forthcoming publications will change existing narratives of the Church's role in the conflict by incorporating the perspectives of this often silent majority.[40] The conflict affected women religious as well. In addition to emotional trauma suffered by many, Sr Catherine Dunne died as result of her injuries following a roadside bombing in July 1990.[41] Three exceptions are Sr Sarah Clarke, Sr Genevieve O'Farrell, and Dr Geraldine Smyth OP (see Appendix) whose perspectives are analysed throughout. Tom Inglis described women religious as the 'silent, solid foundation of modern Irish Catholicism',[42] working on peace projects and fundraising for Catholic refugees. The release of Kirby and Rafferty's findings and the gradual opening of religious order archives will create opportunities for thorough study of women religious' parochial, grassroots, and often unrecognized roles in the conflict. As a consequence of Kirby and Rafferty's study and justified concerns about duplication, fewer women religious were willing to be interviewed for this study.

This study relies on a mixed method approach, incorporating contemporary newspapers, oral history testimonies, memoirs, and religious and government archival research. The British and Irish Catholic newspapers consulted included:

---

[38] King's College Research Ethics Committee Ref: REP/13/14–10 and National University of Ireland, Galway Ref: 18-Sept-22.

[39] http://globalsistersreport.org/column/justice-matters/conversations-between-sisters-belfast-regarding-%E2%80%98-troubles%E2%80%99-25581

[40] Briege Rafferty and Dianne Kirby, 'Sisters in the "Troubles", *Doctrine and Life*, 67:1, (January 2017), pp. 2–12; *Sisters of the Troubles*, BBC News World Service, 25 March 2018, https://www.bbc.co.uk/programmes/p0623s43. Rafferty and Kirby were also a part of this BBC radio programme. Rafferty's doctoral thesis is entitled '*Caught in the crossfire: Catholic religious sisters and the Northern Ireland Troubles 1968–2008*'.

[41] 'Revisiting the Past: Catholic Religious Sisters and the Conflict in Northern Ireland', Briege Rafferty, *Writing the Troubles*, 19 Nov. 2018, https://writingthetroublesweb.wordpress.com/2018/11/19/catholic-religious-sisters/

[42] Inglis, *Moral Monopoly*, 52.

the liberal progressive *The Tablet*; *The Universe*, which had the largest readership; the mainly British-focused *Catholic Herald*; and the Irish-focused *Irish Catholic*. These papers provided readers with specific information on the Catholic Church in both Britain and Ireland, often reporting statements by the hierarchy in full. *The Tablet* openly voiced criticism and regularly featured articles by priests with more revolutionary ideas. Whereas *The Universe*, *Catholic Herald*, and *Irish Catholic* did not deviate from traditional theological teachings and advocated more conservative political positions. Analysing a range of Catholic newspapers help give us an understanding of how religiously-minded Irish and British Catholics were informed about the wider conflict, thus adding another dimension to this study.

Despite the publication of memoirs by political figures, few studies analysing the historical importance of autobiographical accounts exist. One of the few examples is Stephen Hopkins' book which identifies the impact republicans had in shaping a 'public history' narrative through their publications. However, Hopkins excludes memoirs by religious figures.[43] At times, clergy members unhappy with the choices of the institutional Catholic Church have used memoirs to air grievances with the leadership, for example Fathers Joe McVeigh, Des Wilson, and Pat Buckley (see Appendix).[44] In other instances, memoirs have raised awareness of areas of contention and those in the Catholic community who sought to enact change. One example is the activism of Sr Clarke, through her work with Irish prisoners in Britain.[45] As with oral history, memory and personalized perspectives play a role in such publications and as such must be carefully interrogated. Like all sources, memoir material is best triangulated with other sources in the course of its critique. Even when the narratives in memoirs do not correlate or reinforce written evidence, they are still useful to evaluate perspectives.

These source materials collectively form the first critical study of the Irish, and English and Welsh Catholic Churches throughout the conflict. They allow an analysis of the complex interactions of belief, religious authority, and politics across three decades. Sources in diocesan archives often privilege the hierarchy's perspective and this study acknowledges this starting point and institutional perspective. As will be discussed further, an in depth analysis of laity views has not been possible despite their importance to the Catholic Church structure as a whole.[46]

---

[43] Stephen Hopkins, *The Politics of Memoir and the Northern Ireland Conflict* (Liverpool, 2013).

[44] Pat Buckley, *A Thorn in the Side* (Dublin, 1994); Joseph McVeigh, *Taking a Stand: A Memoir of an Irish Priest* (Cork, 2008); Desmond Wilson, *A Diary of Thirty Days – Ballymurphy – July–December, 1972* (Belfast, 1973); Desmond Wilson, *The Chaplain's Affair*, (Belfast, 1999); Desmond Wilson, *The Way I See It*, (Belfast, 2005).

[45] Sarah Clarke, *No Faith in the System: A Search for Justice* (Dublin, 1995).

[46] For studies of the Catholic laity during the conflict, see Elliott, *Catholics of Ulster*, 371–428.

Historiography

Ian McBride argues historians have long sought to dispel the myths that have sustained the Provisional IRA. Despite many historians of the conflict coming from Northern nationalist or unionist backgrounds 'very few could be described as unionist or nationalist historians'.[47] Their writings, fashioned from their lived experiences, have played a key 'role in reshaping the public discourse on Northern Ireland'.[48] Perhaps unsurprisingly, the origins of the conflict have received significant academic attention primarily framed by an adjudication of whether the Troubles were rooted in sectarian or ethno-nationalist tensions.[49] By including discussion of the Catholic Church as a religious actor without engaging in this overworked debate, this study deciphers the multifaceted role of the Catholic Church throughout the conflict.

The Catholic Church's position and influence within Irish Catholic communities was far wider reaching than any statistical analyses of Mass attendances could ever show. The Church effectively created its own state by assisting with housing, controlling education, and creating opportunities for leisure. The institution traditionally acted as guardian for its followers, and thus provided a self-help tradition in Derry—as elsewhere—remaining closely connected to Catholic religious life.[50] Catholics in Belfast shared a similar connection to the Church. A 1969 survey conducted among Protestants and Catholics in East Belfast showed Catholics 'had warmer feelings for their church than for any other organization, group, political party, or political leader'.[51] There were Catholic hospitals, schools, and voter registration, which all relied on lay volunteers and Church funds. The Church also supported the Credit Union movement, which was 'Catholic in origin' according to Derry branch treasurer, John Hume.[52] As a result, the Church spoke to class issues and developed a precedent for providing Catholics with financial aid in Northern Ireland. Moreover, the Church's emphasis on education, especially after the 1947 Education Act, was another route for Catholic social mobility. Through insisting on segregated religious education, the Church secured control of that vital aspect of parishioners' lives.[53] However, disagreement over education existed within the Church, with accusations that the more conservative hierarchy preferred grammar schools by individual priests and women religious

---

[47] McBride, 'In the Shadow of the Gunman', 690.

[48] McBride, 'In the Shadow of the Gunman', 690.

[49] McBride, 'In the shadow of the gunman', 701; McGarry and O'Leary, *Explaining Northern Ireland*, 250.

[50] Elliott, *Catholics of Ulster*, 466.

[51] See Malcolm Douglas Jr, *Conflict Regulation vs. Mobilisation: The Dilemma of Northern Ireland*, PhD Thesis, Columbia University, 1976 in McElroy, *Catholic Church*, 10.

[52] *Derry Journal*, 14 Feb. 1961 in Simon Prince and Geoffrey Warner, *Belfast and Derry in Revolt: A New History of the Start of the Troubles* (Dublin, 2011), 21.

[53] Edward Daly, *Mister, Are You a Priest?* (Dublin, 2000), 119.

like Sr Genevieve O'Farrell of St Louise's Comprehensive School in West Belfast, who advocated for rigorous education at all levels.[54] As pertains to higher education, priests pressed for a university in Derry, although this action failed.[55]

In Derry, priests worked to alleviate housing pressures. Father Anthony Mulvey (see Appendix) worked with politicians and community activists, like Hume and Paddy Doherty, to found the Derry Housing Association (DHA).[56] The DHA attempted to alleviate housing pressures by taking over buildings and converting them into flats with reasonable rates. Housing associations like this were vital by the 1960s as a chronic housing shortage meant many Catholics were being pushed out of Derry city centre.[57] Therefore, in controlling religious and community resources, and social interactions for Northern Catholics, the differential between those who were practising Catholics and those who saw themselves as culturally Catholic was increasingly undefined.

The theory that the conflict was based on ethno-nationalist tensions has been a prevailing one. John McGarry and Brendan O'Leary are the main champions of this approach, arguing ethnicity was the catalyst of the Troubles. Yet their idea that ethnicity is fixed and unchanging, built on inherited cultural difference, is reductionist at best.[58] McGarry and O'Leary argue against cultural explanations of the conflict promoted by Marianne Elliott, Ruth Dudley Edwards, Roy Foster, and Oliver MacDonagh.[59] They downplay religion as an active, salient, and operational factor, preferring to see it as a marker of socio-economic and ethnic difference between communities.

In contrast, Joseph Ruane and Jennifer Todd offer a more convincing analysis. They argue Northern Ireland has an 'evolving system of relationships' which help reinforce each other.[60] For Ruane and Todd, the origins of the conflict can be found at the intersections of religion, ethnicity, ideology, and colonialism. In other words, the Troubles were rooted in centuries of community division formed by political and social inequalities. Ruane and Todd challenge the idea of the 'grand narrative' yet their analysis places the origins of discontent as far back as the sixteenth and seventeenth centuries. Ethnicity is just one facet of this narrative.[61] The authors create an argument based on the situational as well as longitudinal:

---

[54] John Rae, *Sister Genevieve* (London, 2001), 111–13.
[55] *Derry Journal*, 2 Feb. 1965 in Prince and Warner, *Belfast and Derry*, 24–5; Interview with Mgr Raymond Murray, 11 Feb. 2014.
[56] Prince and Warner, *Belfast and Derry*, 21.
[57] Prince and Warner, *Belfast and Derry*, 22–3.
[58] McGarry and O'Leary, *Explaining Northern Ireland*, 250.
[59] McGarry and O'Leary, *Explaining Northern Ireland*, 227–30.
[60] Joseph Ruane and Jennifer Todd, *The Dynamics of Conflict in Northern Ireland: Power, Conflict and Emancipation* (Cambridge, 1996), 8.
[61] See Joseph Ruane and Jennifer Todd, 'The roots of intense ethnic conflict may not in fact be ethnic: categories, communities and path dependence', *European Journal of Sociology*, 45 (2004), 209–32; Joseph Ruane and Jennifer Todd, 'Path dependence in settlement processes: Explaining settlement in Northern Ireland', *Political Studies*, 55, 2007, 442–58.

the perfect storm of historical difficulties mixed with religion, politics, and ethnicity which could only have happened in Northern Ireland at that particular time and historical moment. This makes it difficult to compare the origins of the Troubles with that of other twentieth-century nationalist conflicts. In an interview with the author, ecumenical expert Dr Geraldine Smyth OP echoed these sentiments: 'The cultural factors, the historical factors that get explained away, are all put into a religious basket.... "They worship Mary", "They do everything the Pope tells them", or "They don't have any sacraments"... We wrote each other off based on mutual ignorance.'[62] Equally, Richard Bourke's work on the differences of political sovereignty and democracy as the origins of the conflict marked an important development in the field.[63] He dismisses the ethno-national approach, as 'downplay[ing] the role of politics in the formation of allegiance'.[64] Instead, he argues the conflict was a contest 'over the meaning of popular sovereignty'.[65] Bourke has challenged the primacy of ethnicity as an explanatory device for conflict.[66] What is absent from Bourke's work though is an analysis of how religion and ethnicity work in tandem with politics specifically in the context of Northern Ireland.

An innovative perspective comes from Claire Mitchell. She challenges the historiographical consensus of religion as merely an ethnic marker providing a name for a community identifier. In her sociological study, Mitchell confronts the argument of religion being 'seen as a kind of lazy shorthand for deeper divisions' when it comes to conflict in Northern Ireland. Instead, she writes: 'Religion gives meaning to group identities in a variety of ways'.[67] There is no straightforward link between politics and theology; but religious values, institutions, and rituals 'construct ideas about self and other in an uncertain and divided political situation'.[68] Mitchell's work is an important intervention that chimes with the approach of this study. She analyses how religion matters in Northern Ireland and her core argument is that it derives social and political significance from five intertwining and supporting dimensions. Firstly, religion is a marker of social difference, maintained through separate community functions such as education, lack of intermarriage, social networks, and leisure activities.[69] Secondly, religious ideas and symbols 'help constitute group identities', leading to differences between

---

[62] Dr Geraldine Smyth OP interview, 3 Dec. 2018.

[63] Richard Bourke, *Peace in Ireland: The War of Ideas* (London, 2003).

[64] Richard Bourke, 'Languages of conflict and the Northern Ireland Troubles', *Journal of Modern History*, 83 (2011), 550.

[65] Bourke, 'Languages of Conflict', 549.

[66] Richard Bourke, 'Antigone and after: "ethnic" conflict in historical perspective', *Field Day Review*, 2 (2006), 168–94.

[67] Claire Mitchell, *Religion, Identity, and Politics in Northern Ireland: Boundaries of Belonging and Belief* (Aldershot, 2006), 1–2.

[68] Mitchell, *Religion, Identity, and Politics*, 2.

[69] Mitchell, *Religion, Identity, and Politics*, 5–6.

nationalist and unionist policies.[70] Thirdly, the practice of religion helps to construct these separate communities: coming together to participate in baptisms, marriages, and funerals to shape the social consensus of each group.[71] Fourthly, each community develops their identity in response to the other, for example Protestants seeing themselves as hardworking as opposed to 'lazy' Catholics.[72] And finally, that religious institutions are 'politically influential', a concept this study also employs.[73] Resonating with Mitchell's approach, this study places importance on the understanding of how religion shapes identity in post-Second World War Europe.

The idea that the conflict was sectarian in nature is now rarely championed. Indeed, broader histories of the conflict published in the last twenty years have generally excluded the role of religious institutions. The otherwise informative *Talking to Terrorists: Making Peace in Northern Ireland* (2009), by John Bew, Martyn Frampton, and Iñigo Gurruchaga, barely acknowledges the impact of religious institutions, except to briefly mention Fr Alec Reid's role (see Appendix) in bringing together John Hume and Gerry Adams.[74] Similarly, Richard English's richly detailed *Armed Struggle: The History of the IRA* (2003) evaluates the IRA's use of bishops as negotiating pawns with the British government, but the wider impact of the Church in the conflict is omitted.

Of course, this work benefits from those which have come before. The work of Marianne Elliott, Oliver Rafferty, Tom Inglis, Mary Kenny, Maria Power, Gerald McElroy, John Brewer, Francis Teeney, Gareth Higgins, and Gladys Ganiel have all provided influence and guidance. However, through analysis of one religious institution during the conflict, paying a careful study to the men and women within that institution as well as the policies of the institution itself, this work takes the wider debate forward.

The most closely related study is Gerard McElroy's *The Catholic Church and the Northern Ireland Crisis, 1968–86* (1991). However, McElroy's sociological work relies predominantly on newspaper reports, anonymous interviews, and survey data, as most diocesan archival material was unavailable at that time. Nevertheless, McElroy's anonymous clerical survey data, collected through a 1986 postal questionnaire remains crucial for this study, providing views of the larger clerical class not previously documented in Irish Church history.[75] This data reveals wider trends, especially concerning clerical generational shifts. Broadly speaking, it reveals aged priests remained subservient, while younger priests

---

[70] Mitchell, *Religion, Identity, and Politics*, 1, 78, 142.
[71] Mitchell, *Religion, Identity, and Politics*, 2, 24.
[72] Mitchell, *Religion, Identity, and Politics*, 2, 101.
[73] Mitchell, *Religion, Identity, and Politics*, 1–20.
[74] John Bew, Martyn Frampton and Iñigo Gurruchaga, *Talking to Terrorists: Making Peace in Northern Ireland and the Basque Country* (London, 2009), 113–16.
[75] McElroy, *Catholic Church*, 1.

challenged authority. Furthermore, according to McElroy's figures, younger priests were less likely to support a united Ireland. It is important to note, however, that McElroy's survey only had a 36.9 percent response rate from the Catholic clergy, with secular priests less likely to participate than those in religious orders.[76]

While these figures provide a foundation and questions for this study, McElroy's conclusions concerning the role of the hierarchy remain underdeveloped. He argues the clergy were more critical of the state than the hierarchy, and that the bishops were divided.[77] Yet he does not trace the evolution of priests' and bishops' opinions over the course of the conflict. In contrast, this study shows how the Catholic Church hierarchy evolved from supporting politicians to outright condemnation of violence once the political situation deteriorated. McElroy overreaches when he argues the signing of the Anglo-Irish Agreement (AIA) in 1985 was as a result of Bishop Cahal Daly's insistence that peace would not come with a united Ireland.[78] Little evidence supports this insight. The hierarchy played no role in the AIA and the British government largely disregarded Daly and the New Ireland Forum's claims in 1983–84. Therefore, despite exploration of the role of clergy, McElroy treats the actions of the hierarchy dismissively, failing to offer any interpretation of the bishops' difficult position or to trace the evolving nature of their responses.[79] This study stresses the Irish hierarchy were constrained in their ability to act; partly because of wider non-Irish Catholic Church pressure. Finally, McElroy's text is limited to the Irish Catholic Church and ends in 1986 which is problematic in terms of offering an overview of the entire conflict.

Oliver Rafferty provides an overarching view of the Church in Ireland over three centuries in *Catholicism in Ulster, 1603–1983* (1994). His chapters before the conflict provide an orientating foundation for this study. Written while the conflict raged, Rafferty views it as sectarian rather than economic, and focuses his work not only on the institutional Church but the role of the Catholic laity living as part of a minority community.[80] Rafferty argues: 'The seeds of northern Catholic discontent, its unease with itself and the tenacity of its attachment to Catholicism were sown in the Ulster Plantation of the early seventeenth century'.[81] Unfortunately, Rafferty's text stops short of crucial turning points for the Catholic Church and Catholics in Northern Ireland, namely the impact of the New Ireland Forum, the AIA, the rise of SF, and the 1994 ceasefires. By extending his timeline, this study is able to elaborate on the lasting effects of the 1981 hunger strikes on Irish politics, and on the relationship between the institutional Church and republicans. It also allows for discussion of the decline of clerical authority,

---

[76] McElroy, *Catholic Church*, 198–9. [77] McElroy, *Catholic Church*, 90–133.
[78] McElroy, *Catholic Church*, 63–4. [79] McElroy, *Catholic Church*, 139–40; 188–93.
[80] Rafferty, *Catholicism in Ulster*, 1–5. [81] Rafferty, *Catholicism in Ulster*, 1.

which Rafferty identifies as beginning in the 1980s. An update of this text would greatly add to the literature on the topic.

Similar to Rafferty's *longue durée* study of the Church in Ireland, Marianne Elliott's *The Catholics of Ulster* (2000) remains one of the most well-researched texts on Catholics in general and the conflict more broadly. Tracing the history of Catholics in the North back to the plantation period, Elliott uncovers the development of the trope of Catholic victimhood in Northern Ireland. Her study is not an examination of the Church, but rather of Catholicism, avoiding theology but engaging with spirituality. In terms of the conflict, Elliott describes the position of the Catholic Church as 'an unenviable one'.[82] No matter how vociferously Church leaders condemned violence, they were either seen to be betraying Catholics by speaking out at all, or conversely, not being tough enough by refusing to excommunicate paramilitaries. Elliott interrogates the integral relationship between class and the Catholic laity. Similarly this study evaluates the institutional Church through this lens. However, Elliott's work is chiefly concerned with exploring a more abstract sense of Catholic identity whereas this study actively engages with the institutional, theological, and lived responses to the conflict.[83]

Two other broader studies focusing on the Irish Catholic Church in the modern period, Tom Inglis' *Moral Monopoly: The Rise and Fall of the Catholic Church in Modern Ireland* (1987) and Mary Kenny's *Goodbye to Catholic Ireland* (1997) are useful.[84] Inglis' work is a rigorous academic study covering the evolution of the institutional Church in the nineteenth and twentieth centuries, while Kenny appeals more to the general reader and mainly focuses on twentieth century Irish Catholics. Both analyse the relationship between the Catholic Church and the Irish government after partition. Whereas Kenny provides a chapter discussing Catholicism, identity, and the Troubles, Inglis sidesteps the conflict entirely, and remains focused on the South. These studies provide important context for the socio-cultural state of the post-conciliar Irish Catholic Church in the Republic at same time as the Troubles, with the slow decline of Church influence over politicians and parishioners alike. However, by excluding any direct discussion of the impact the conflict had on the Republic, both authors disregard the national, united Church hierarchy and structures and therefore the effect of the conflict on Southern Catholics. Nevertheless, both works help situate this study into a wider narrative of decline of Catholic Church influence throughout Ireland. As such, I chart the processes that Steve Bruce explores elsewhere,[85] and their eventual application in the Irish context.

---

[82] Elliott, *Catholics of Ulster*, 472. [83] Elliott, *Catholics of Ulster*, xxxviii.

[84] Inglis published an updated version of the book in 1998 to evaluate the impact of clerical child abuse revelations on the Catholic Church.

[85] See Steve Bruce, *God Save Ulster*; Bruce, 'History, sociology and secularisation'; Bruce, 'Secularization and the impotence of individualized religion'.

Maria Power's historical survey expertly analyses the practical and academic shift from theological discussion confined to Church elites that characterized 1980s solution attempts, to the community-based, grassroots social work strategies of the new millennium.[86] Power's approach examines all facets of religious institutions in the conflict, from local initiatives to national strategies. However, her work is limited to the Irish churches, excluding the impact of wider Church movements and the religious Irish diaspora. Nevertheless, her rich archival explorations and interview materials add depth to the study and her conclusions about the way inter-community dialogue could progress in a post-conflict Northern Ireland chime with the current political landscape. Power argues both Protestant and Catholic churches initially responded to the conflict through hierarchical, elite theological interventions before eventually turning to grassroots, community-based activism with an evolving focus on community relations.[87]

Alongside these historical studies, sociologists have started to assess religious institutions and the conflict. An overarching theme of *Religion, Civil Society, and Peace in Northern Ireland* (2013), by John Brewer, Gareth Higgins, and Francis Teeney, centres on the failure of institutional Protestant and Catholic churches to bring about peace and reconciliation.[88] They argue the Northern churches viewed violence as the immediate problem but tended to treat it as a local process 'resisting an all-Irish dimension'.[89] The authors argue the churches' impact was indirect: through their resistance to ecumenical strategies, integrated education, and their 'perpetuation of negative stereotypes of "the other"'.[90] The text does not hold back in its criticisms, which on occasion are overly partisan. For example, on aspects of integrated education, the authors refer to the Catholic Church's rigid stance but fail to acknowledge the doctrinal importance of a religious education for Catholic children.[91] Many Catholics in the North of Ireland felt little trust towards the state with its exclusionist attitude towards Catholic employment and housing. Nevertheless, the study provides a compelling sociological framework on the forms of Church ecumenism and community building considered in this study. Acknowledging Power's arguments, the authors' ideas on active and passive,[92]

---

[86]   Maria Power, *From Ecumenism to Community Relations: Inter-Church Relationships in Northern Ireland 1980–2005* (Dublin, 2006).

[87]   Power, *From Ecumenism to Community Relations*, 3–6.

[88]   Brewer also co-wrote *Ex-Combatants, Religion and Peace in Northern Ireland* (2013) with David Mitchell and Gerard Leavey, which elaborated on the thoughts of former paramilitaries on religion and its role in the conflict.

[89]   John Brewer, Gareth Higgins, and Francis Teeney, *Religion, Civil Society, and Peace in Northern Ireland* (Oxford, 2013), 1.

[90]   Brewer, Higgins, and Teeney, *Religion*, 3.   [91]   Brewer, Higgins, and Teeney, *Religion*, 3.

[92]   Active peace-making is a commitment to peace by attempting to create opportunities for peace versus passive peace-making's 'idealistic commitment but lacking in application'; Brewer, Higgins, and Teeney, *Religion*, 4.

positive and negative,[93] and social and political peace-making[94] provide helpful leads for exploring varied actions of Catholic and Protestant institutions and individuals.[95] The authors argue the churches' strengths were in societal peace processes after the Good Friday Agreement (GFA), and that before this the churches acted more as a barrier against peace. Their sociological frameworks, used critically, and the extensive interviews collected, provide useful framings to which this study adds texture, with a focus on historical causation.

More recently, Gladys Ganiel's *Transforming Post-Catholic Ireland: Religious Practice in Late Modernity* (2016) explores the dynamic religious landscape across the island. In defining 'post-Catholic', Ganiel explains 'the religious landscape of the island of Ireland has changed from one in which the Catholic Church commanded a monopoly of religious, social, and political power, to one in which the Catholic Church is one option among many in a mixed, post-Catholic religious market'.[96] Despite these other religious alternatives, the Irish Catholic Church still maintains some of its legacy of Inglis' 'moral monopoly'. Ganiel's findings reveal the Irish, both North and South, have an almost obsession with discussing the Catholic Church. Her forthcoming work *Unity Pilgrim: The Life of Fr Gerry Reynolds, CSsR*, will further illuminate the role the Fr Gerry Reynolds and the Clonard Monastery played in the peace process.

Nukhet A. Sandal's *Religious Leaders and Conflict Transformation: Northern Ireland and Beyond* (2017) is a political science study looking at 'the impact religious actors have on the politics of peace and conflict'.[97] Sandal draws her source material from published speeches and declarations, in addition to some interview material. At times the study overwhelming relies on *The Belfast Telegraph*, *The News Letter*, *The Irish News*, and *The Irish Times*, putting aside regional and religious publications, interviewees, and viewpoints.[98] Sandal argues religious actors form an epistemic community, which has its own special ability for conflict resolution and peace building in Northern Ireland.[99] Through their intensive religious training, these religious actors 'capture the subtleties of human security, trauma healing, and reconciliation'.[100] Sandal uses Northern Ireland as a case study and applies her theory of religious epistemic communities to other

---

[93] Positive and negative peace-making builds on Johan Galtung's 1964 definitions. Negative peace-making works to end violence while positive peace-making works towards establishing principles of justice and equality; Brewer, Higgins, and Teeney, *Religion*, 4.

[94] Societal peace processes are slower initiatives to help heal relationships between groups, political peace processes focus more on the state; Brewer, Higgins, and Teeney, *Religion*, 4.

[95] An excellent work which compliments this text is R. Scott Appleby's *The Ambivalence of the Sacred: Religion, Violence, and Reconciliation* (2010).

[96] Gladys Ganiel, *Transforming Post-Catholic Ireland: Religious Practice in Late Modernity* (Oxford, 2016).

[97] Nukhet A. Sandal, *Religious Leaders and Conflict Transformation: Northern Ireland and Beyond* (Cambridge, 2017), 2.

[98] Sandal, *Religious Leaders*, 18.   [99] Sandal, *Religious Leaders*, 6, 13–15.

[100] Sandal, *Religious Leaders*, 7.

contemporary conflict societies, including South Africa, Burma, Poland, Sierra Leone, Rwanda, Nicaragua, and El Salvador. Sandal infrequently engages with the major texts—Power, Elliott, Rafferty, and McElroy, for example—which could have added a richer historical perspective. For example, engaging with Power's idea that religious communities evolved from ecumenism to community relations would further expand on Sandal's definition of exclusive and inclusive public theologies.[101] Nevertheless, this is an important study adding to our overall understanding of religious actors during the conflict and demonstrates the increasing amount of scholarship on religious actors and their role in peace building in the contemporary period.

To date, little has been written on the relationship between the Church and the politically nationalist Social Democratic and Labour Party (SDLP). McElroy and Elliott have explored the Church's relationship to militant republicanism but there is not yet any extensive investigation of the SDLP in the same context. As background, I have examined literature generated through a political science lens. However, most of the existing treatments fail to discuss, in an extended fashion, the relationship of the SDLP with the Church. Other than a brief mention of Fr Alec Reid's role in bringing together Hume and Adams, there is little or no consideration of the Catholic Church in the prevailing monographs on the SDLP. Gerard Murray and Jonathan Tonge mention the Church in *Sinn Féin and the SDLP: From Alienation to Participation* (2005), but only briefly, and with no sustained analysis of its central role.[102] They certainly do not engage with the Church's relationship with the party. Ian McAllister's *The Northern Ireland Social Democratic and Labour Party: Political Opposition in a Divided Society* (1977) also fails to address the constitutive and enduring relationship between the SDLP and Catholic priests and bishops.[103] P. J. McLoughlin *John Hume and the revision of Irish nationalism* (2010) engages most with the involvement of Reid during the Hume-Adams talks, but fails to account for why Reid's religious vocation allowed him to act as mediator. Murray's earlier publication *John Hume and the SDLP* (1988) also lacks analysis on Hume's relationship with the Church.[104] Barry White's *John Hume: Statesmen of the Troubles* (1984) discusses Hume's faith, but it too ignores Hume's meetings with leading Church figures and notes: 'There is little piety about the SDLP leadership'.[105]

This omission of the Catholic Church from the historiography on the SDLP is not unsurprising. In his study, McElroy concludes that despite the shared interests

---

[101] Sandal, *Religious Leaders*, 8.

[102] Gerard Murray and Jonathan Tonge, *Sinn Féin and the SDLP: From Alienation to Participation* (London, 2005), 1, 30, 36, 107–12, 162–71.

[103] McAllister does so briefly on integrated education; Ian McAllister, *The Northern Ireland Social Democratic and Labour Party: Political Opposition in a Divided Society* (London, 1977), 63.

[104] Gerard Murray, *John Hume and the SDLP* (Dublin, 1998).

[105] Barry White, *John Hume: Statesman of the Troubles* (Belfast, 1984), 208.

and goals of the Church and the SDLP, since Irish priests chose 'not to intervene in the electoral process in Northern Ireland' the SDLP was seen as a 'secular party'.[106] Rafferty agrees, noting the SDLP was rhetorically determined not to be 'susceptible to clerical influence'.[107] However, throughout the party's history, militant republicans attempted to tarnish the SDLP leadership claiming it was completely under the influence of the Church, and taunted its members for their middle class and otherwise religious nature.[108] Indeed, in *Personal Views: Politics, Peace and Reconciliation in Ireland*, Hume himself points out unionist concerns of Catholic Church domination of the South, viewing the Republic's relationship with the Church as 'sectarian' and tacitly differentiating the SDLP's relationship with the institution.[109] However, by excluding the Church, these monographs miss a crucial opportunity to explore the critical role of religion and religious institutions in the political manoeuverings throughout the conflict.

In addition to synoptic texts on the Troubles, this study employs microstudies on specific, shorter intervals and events within the conflict.[110] While none of these works focus specifically on the Catholic Church, they enrich this study and provide an excellent analysis of some key moments in the conflict. Edited collections, journal articles, and populist monographs have also informed this analysis. Harold Wells and Gregory Baum's *The Reconciliation of Peoples: Challenge to the Churches* (1997) helped to place this topic in a wider framework of religion in conflict during the modern period. Martin Dillon's *God and the Gun: The Church and Irish Terrorism* (1997) is a sensationalist work on religion in the conflict, full of unnamed interviewees. However, it supplies useful anecdotes which, when treated with caution, can illuminate the personal experiences of everyday priests in the conflict. The Methodist Reverend (Rev) Norman Taggart's *Controversy, Conflict, Co-operation: The Irish Council of Churches and 'the Troubles' 1968–1972* (2004) delivers participant and observer insight into the early conflict, when the ecumenical attitude of the Irish Council of Churches (ICC) and their relationship with the Catholic Church were greatly tested. Taggart worked part-time as the ICC secretary during this period.[111] At the start of the conflict, ecumenism was viewed as controversial and those who participated in such organizations ran the risk of threats and abuse.[112] Taggart believes meetings between the ICC and the

---

[106] McElroy, *Catholic Church*, 189.   [107] Rafferty, *Catholicism in Ulster*, 3.

[108] *An Phoblacht*, 7 Dec. 1977; *Irish Press*, 25 Jan. 1985.

[109] John Hume, *Personal Views: Politics, Peace and Reconciliation in Ireland*, (Dublin, 1996), 65.

[110] Simon Prince and Geoffrey Warner's *Belfast and Derry in Revolt* (2012), Niall Ó Dochartaigh's *From Civil Rights to Armalites: Derry and the Birth of the Irish Troubles* (1997), and Thomas Hennessey's *The Evolution of the Troubles* (2007) all provide an excellent background for the period between 1968–72. More specific works on the period of the prison protests in Long Kesh/Maze Prison remain some of the most detailed scholarship and David Beresford's *Ten Men Dead: The Story of the 1981 Hunger Strike* (1987) engages with priests and bishops as political actors.

[111] Norman Taggart, *Conflict, Controversy and Co-operation: The Irish Council of Churches and 'The Troubles' 1968–1972* (Dublin, 2004), 13.

[112] Taggart, *Conflict*, 17.

Catholic Church during this period formed the beginnings of ground-breaking inter-church dialogue.[113]

The combination of these vast, complex but partial literatures, all with a critical viewpoint in respect of religious actions during the conflict, provide a robust and multifaceted foundation for this study. I build upon this knowledge and expand upon multiple lines of the debates concerning the origins of the Troubles, and the role of a religious institution in a multifaceted and prolonged conflict. At times, these earlier studies include archival material that is no longer accessible, or interviews with participants who have since died, and they therefore remain crucial, both analytically but also substantively.

Structure

This study follows a chronological format, with the chapters organized thematically by timeframe. The first chapter evaluates the Catholic Church and the evolution of the conflict from a peaceful civil rights movement to violence, from October 1968 until the Official and Provisional IRA ceasefires in 1972. It argues that while the clergy and bishops remained mostly united, the bishops delayed reaction to intern-ment and consequent growing politicization of the clergy acted as a precursor, or first fissure of discontent, to the escalating tensions between the clergy and hier-archy. Discontent between these groups continues in Chapter 2, which analyses the bloodiest years of the conflict, from 1972 to 1976, in which there appeared to be no solution in sight. Some in the clergy became more vocal in their condemnation of perceived British government and Army injustices towards Catholics, while the bishops continuously condemned paramilitary, but not state, violence.

Chapter 3 focuses exclusively on the protests in Long Kesh/Maze Prison, beginning with the removal of special category or 'political' status for IRA prisoners in 1976 and culminating with the 1981 hunger strikes. It argues the 1981 hunger strikes mark a turning point in the relationship between the Church and repub-licans, with the mistrust between the institutional Church and SF intensifying and becoming irreparable. Chapter 4 contends that despite the best efforts of Cardinal Ó Fiaich to reach out to Catholics who support SF, he became the lone voice of the hierarchy in these attempts. This chapter examines the Church's reaction to the rise of SF. Analysis focuses on the institutional Church and grassroots clergy who were more united in the long-standing efforts to free the Birmingham Six, Maguire Seven, and Guildford Four. This chapter also argues the clergy began to take over grass-roots ecumenical efforts during this period, epitomized through the Remembrance Day bombing in 1987 and Gibraltar killings. Bishop Edward Daly's (see Appendix) banning of republican paramilitary funerals in Derry constituted another challenge to republicanism from the institutional Church. Finally, Chapter 5 sets out the

---

[113]   Taggart, *Conflict*, 95, 110–13.

importance of individual, grassroots priests in mediating dialogue between republicans, the SDLP, and the Irish government. The role of the Church in the Republic of Ireland had changed by the 1990s, and its part in Northern Ireland's peace process correlates with its reduced societal influence, concluding with the GFA.

In conclusion, casting forward to the same-sex marriage referendum in 2015 and the repeal of the eighth amendment in 2018, this study diagnoses the decline in Church moral authority in the Republic of Ireland, leading to a near collapse in its public influence. As well as drawing together the lines of analysis explored throughout, the conclusion also identifies further fruitful avenues of inquiry for future study of religion in the conflict.

There is a longstanding conflation in Ireland between religion, nationalism, and politics. While the Catholic Church was initially suspicious of the Home Rule movement in the 1870s, by 1884 the bishops supported the movement,[114] and unionists therefore feared Home Rule as 'Rome Rule'.[115] However, Limerick Bishop Thomas O'Dwyer understood it was better to 'bend with the wind' and 'keep the people attached to [the Church]', by working with leading parliamentary nationalists to 'draw the line between politics and religion'.[116] In 1921, Irish nationalist politician Joseph O'Doherty revived the cry 'we'll take our religion from Rome, but our politics from home' in response to perceived interference by the Vatican concerning violence in Ireland.[117] The title of this introduction takes inspiration from this adage, casting forward to the beginning of the conflict. Over time, religion and politics were both reconfigured and became more inflected and refracted through a regional lens. The 1980-81 hunger strikes and the division between the bishops over whether this was suicide act as one instance of a divergence between the Irish Church and Vatican stance. The Vatican position on suicide evolved after Vatican II meaning individual Churches increasingly made their own decisions and interpreted what the 'signs of the times' meant in their own context.

This same concept applies to republican paramilitary funerals, as seen by an English bishop denying a Requiem Mass to the IRA's James McDade in Coventry, but an Irish bishop granting a religious funeral in Derry. By comparing the Irish Church reactions to the conflict with that of the English and Welsh Catholic Churches, we see both politics and religion increasingly came from 'home'. Yet global changes, through international scrutiny and intervention simultaneously, and somewhat paradoxically, also assumed unprecedented importance.

---

[114] Joseph Coohill, *Ireland: A Short History* (Oxford, 2005), 98–101; Hoppen, *Ireland since 1800*, 160–5.

[115] Animosity between republicans and the Irish bishops grew during the 1880s and 1890s. The Irish bishops condemned nationalist leader Charles Parnell after his affair with the married Katharine 'Kitty' O'Shea was revealed in court proceedings; Coohill, *Ireland*, 105; Marcus Tanner, *Ireland's Holy Wars: The Struggle for a Nation's Soul 1500-2000* (London, 2001), 255–62.

[116] Hoppen, *Ireland since 1800*, 163.   [117] Keogh, *The Vatican*, 66–8.

1

'From Civil Rights to Armalites'

By August 1968, civil rights organizers had grown frustrated at their lack of progress. It had been eighteen months since the Northern Ireland Civil Rights Association (NICRA) was formed with little to show for their efforts.[1] To elevate their cause, NICRA attracted an estimated 2,000 people to march from Coalisland to Dungannon on 24 August. The Northern Irish communist activist, Betty Sinclair, praised the 'peaceful' action.[2] Another civil rights march was scheduled for 5 October 1968. Although smaller, this march would have a very different ending.

At the time, however, the Irish Catholic Church was preoccupied with education. Church reaction to the civil rights movement remained muted. The Northern bishops were worried by British government education policy changes, and 'the motives underlying Stormont's October 1967 White Paper on education'.[3] They feared for the ties between Catholics and their mother Church. The Church had created its own statelet for the North, providing Catholics with alternative leadership. As a result, the Church's reaction to one of the most important days in modern Irish history was muted.

A handful of priests did work to calm and disperse rioters at the 5 October march. In addition, the Archbishop of Armagh and Primate of All Ireland, Cardinal William Conway, implored politicians to acknowledge the riots' societal roots, stating: 'They grow out of the frustration of ordinary people who want houses and a fair chance of a job and equitable representation'.[4] Conway argued social, economic, and political reform would prevent future violence. These early responses to the conflict, revealing enduring and differing approaches of the clergy and hierarchy, would be repeated in the coming decades. Where priests

---

[1] Chapter title reference: Niall Ó Dochartaigh, *From Civil Rights to Armalites: Derry and The Birth of the Irish Troubles* (Basingstoke, 2005).

[2] Simon Prince, '5 October 1968 and the Beginning of the Troubles: Flashpoints, Riots and Memory', *Irish Political Studies*, 27 (2012), 396.

[3] Under this Bill, Catholic schools would gain 'maintained' status, increasing their grant funding in exchange for the Local Education Authority nominees sitting on the Catholic school management committees; Simon Prince, *Northern Ireland's '68: Civil Rights, Global Revolt and the Origins of The Troubles* (Dublin, 2007), 37–8.

[4] Cardinal Tomás Ó Fiaich Memorial Library and Archive (CTOMLA), Cardinal Conway Papers (CCP), 18–18 1968 Press Releases, 15 Oct. 1968.

and women religious provided immediate assistance within their communities, the hierarchy's often delayed response focussed on wider and more general issues beyond localized concerns. For Eamonn McCann, one of the 5 October march organizers: 'Religion and politics were bound up together, were regarded, indeed, as being in many ways the same thing'.[5] Therefore, few were surprised as the Church became embroiled in the escalating conflict.

This chapter argues that, despite their differing approaches, between October 1968 and June 1972, the episcopacy and clergy often spoke with one voice. Explicit clerical dissent towards hierarchical leadership remained limited. The clergy and hierarchy shared a common goal: to denounce British injustices and keep the peace. Violence, whether state or paramilitary, was condemned. However, not all in the Catholic community accepted this message. This divergence of opinion would lead to a widening gulf between Church and laity, partly around their differing assessments of peace-making.

This period reflects the emerging republican criticism of the Catholic Church. Previously, Irish freedom was synonymous with 'the freedom to be Catholic', a concept which the IRA continued after partition.[6] Yet with a perceived increase in police brutality and the subsequent emergence of a more militant generation of IRA supporters, the importance of this Catholic sentiment faded. This was emphasized by the introduction of new leadership in the Provisional IRA by the late 1970s. Indeed, when the Church attempted to keep the peace at the expense of a republican paramilitary campaign, it too became a barrier to freedom and an oppressor. In tandem with a broader move in 1968, republicans shifted the aims of the civil rights movement from 'equality' to 'liberation', from both the British and the Church. The hierarchy were the target of more public attacks than the clergy because bishops were more recognizable as faces of an institutional, remote, and distant Church. For example, in *War and an Irish Town*, McCann chastises Bishop William Philbin (see Appendix) for persuading Belfast Catholics to remove their barricades in September 1969. As British Army Land Rovers drove through Belfast, Philbin 'perched incongruously in his robes in the passengers' seat'.[7] McCann failed to mention Fr Padraig Murphy, an administrator of St Peter's parish, who travelled with the bishop and had coordinated this undertaking with the British Army.[8] Where Philbin faced republicans' derision, Murphy remained unscathed. In shaping his narrative, McCann creates an artificial dichotomy between the views of priests and bishops during this early period of the conflict. In reality, the actions of the clergy and hierarchy often demonstrated similar views.

Nevertheless, republican criticism of the Church was not entirely focused on the episcopacy. Anti-clerical sentiment came easily to young republicans. Articles

---

[5] McCann, *War and an Irish Town*, 69.   [6] McCann, *War and an Irish Town*, 69.
[7] McCann, *War and an Irish Town*, 127.   [8] *Irish Catholic*, 18 Sep. 1969.

published in the *An Phoblacht* newspaper after 1970 frequently criticized the clergy as a whole, while still publishing articles from individual priests critical of the British state. Irish republican criticism of priests can be viewed as part of the rise in anti-clericalism throughout western Europe. However, Irish Catholics still regularly attended Mass: a survey in 1973–74 revealed 90 percent went once a week, with 80 percent receiving Holy Communion.[9] In France regular Mass-going dropped from well over 20 percent in the 1950s to less than 15 percent by the end of the 1960s.[10] Anti-clericalism had different drivers in continental Europe then in Ireland. Regular contributors to *An Phoblacht* included Fathers Brian Brady, Denis Faul, and P.F. Malone. Other articles commented on the 'courage' of Fr Des Wilson in exposing Catholic British Army chaplains as 'spies and touts'.[11]

This chapter uses case studies examining the reactions of priests and bishops to the civil rights movement, internment, Bloody Sunday, and the re-emergence of the IRA. In addition to the Irish Catholic Church, it explores the reactions of the English and Welsh Catholic Church as the IRA initiated a bombing campaign in England. Individual clerics emerged in this period who subsequently shaped Church response throughout the entire conflict, including Fathers Brian Brady, Denis Faul, Des Wilson, and Bishop Cahal Daly (see Appendix). As relatively young men, their voices—and later dissent—demonstrate the power of individuals in shaping an institutional Church response.

Civil Rights Movement

The October 1968 demonstration established the tendency of a small number of priests to act as mediators and seek to diffuse tensions, rather than protest. McElroy argues priests' role as march peacekeepers protected the civil rights movement in Northern Ireland as non-violent protest.[12] Throughout 1968, the Church remained quiet on civil rights grievances. Not until 5 October did civil rights become a topic of conversation at bishops' houses, because their focus was on education reform.[13] Privately though, priests and women religious observed and discussed civil rights, although few became public, active campaigners.[14] The hierarchy was also deeply concerned about state funding for Mater Hospital. As violence continued at these marches, the Church welcomed Northern Irish

---

[9] Inglis, *Moral Monopoly*, 20–1.

[10] Maurice Larkin, *Religion, politics and preferment in France since 1890: Le Belle Époque and its legacy* (Cambridge, 1995), 198.

[11] *An Phoblacht*, Sep. 1973.   [12] McElroy, *Catholic Church*, 15–16.

[13] *The Irish Catholic* newspaper only begins to include articles on civil rights in Northern Ireland in July 1968. Overwhelmingly, the focus was on education policy for the 'Around the North' column.

[14] Rae, *Sister Genevieve*, 110–11.

Premier, Terence O'Neill's promise of reforms. This period between the 5 October 1968 march and the introduction of internment in August 1971 is framed by the consistency in clergy and hierarchy action. Fr Denis Faul was a lone operator voicing his discontent at the lack of action on reform as early as 1969.

The NICRA held a non-violent march in Derry on 5 October to protest against inequalities in housing, employment, and representation. The Home Affairs minister at Stormont, William Craig, banned the march but the NICRA proceeded as planned. Around 400 marchers joined the protest, revealing Derry did not yet have a strong civil rights movement. It was met with Royal Ulster Constabulary (RUC) brutality, which in turn rallied the wider nationalist community to the cause. Irish clergymen and women did not play a leading role in these marches unlike their American clergymen counterparts across the Atlantic.[15] Irish priests occupied a liminal position, acting both as insiders protesting for change, as well as outsiders, in their efforts to maintain the peace.

Following the Derry violence, some priests continued their active role in civil rights campaigning. The Derry Citizens' Action Committee (DCAC) organized many activities from October 1968 to April 1969. Although none of the elected DCAC officers were clergymen, the organization enjoyed favour with the Catholic Church. In his memoirs, Fr Edward Daly described his first civil rights experience, a DCAC mass sit-down in Guildhall Square, as 'a very powerful and moving moment'.[16] The attendance of priests at these events served an important purpose. Their peaceful participation in non-violent protest demonstrated to their parishioners that they should ask for civil rights. Continuing clerical deference and acknowledgement of the clergy's authority meant their approval of lay participation in these protests remained, for some, important. The Churches Industrial Council (CIC), an ecumenical organization made up of clergy from the Four Main Churches in Northern Ireland, also supported the DCAC.[17] This organization demonstrated an enactment of the Second Vatican Council's promotion of ecumenism through the document, *Unitatis redintegratio*.[18] On 21 October 1968, the CIC called for an impartial examination into claims of discrimination in housing and employment. The CIC's support gave credibility to the DCAC as its membership was not only Catholic.

A November 1968 civil rights march in Derry that O'Neill prohibited saw the clergy more involved. A delegation of Protestant and Catholic clergymen from the Derry Churches' Industrial Council met with O'Neill in Stormont to try and

---

[15] McElroy, *Catholic Church*, 20.   [16] McElroy, *Catholic Church*, 131.

[17] The Four Main Churches consisted of the Church of Ireland, Methodist Church, Presbyterian Church, and Catholic Church.

[18] Pope Paul VI, 'Unitatis redintegratio', 21 Nov. 1964. http://www.vatican.va/archive/hist_councils/ii_vatican_council/documents/vat-ii_decree_19641121_unitatis-redintegratio_en.html

convince him to lift the ban. O'Neill dismissed the idea.[19] The ban resulted in an inter-church gathering, with the Catholic Cathedral and Church of Ireland Cathedral staging a well-attended all-night vigil on the eve of the march.[20] It was the first major public act of ecumenical worship in the city, and *The Irish Catholic* reported it as 'a day of thanksgiving that their city had been spared bloodshed at the weekend'.[21] Daly noted that, despite initial awkwardness, the ecumenical service brought comfort to Protestants and Catholics.[22]

The service fostered further inter-church relations. Daly congratulated the Church of Ireland's Bishop of Derry, Charles Tyndall, for his courage. Tyndall responded by thanking Daly for his support and said: 'Whatever happens one feels that the Presence was with us that night'.[23] The 15,000-strong march did not erupt into violence despite some loyalists throwing rocks. Although Church of Ireland and Catholic Church leaders exchanged letters, these men did not release joint statements for another year. Looking toward 1969, Conway declared: 'The sooner justice comes—and is seen to come—the sooner lasting peace will be assured'.[24] To de-politicize his words, Conway framed civil rights as the 'hopes of ordinary people', in line with human rights concerns.[25]

Youth civil rights organization, People's Democracy, held another march on New Year's Day 1969 from Belfast to Derry. Various groups harassed the marchers with attacks becoming particularly vicious in Burntollet. News of the violence reached Derry, attracting march supporters to St Columb's Hall. Priests like Daly worked with John Hume and other civil rights stewards to diffuse the tension, to little avail. Sectarian riots ensued when clashing civil rights protestors met with loyalists led by the Rev Ian Paisley. Protestant and Catholic clergymen and women attempted to keep the peace between protestors and the mostly Protestant police force but failed. Perhaps an early indicator of their loss of influence as peacemakers in violent situations that spiralled out of control. This event led to CIC members establishing a semi-official committee to examine the underlying causes of the violence.[26] The committee of six clergymen included Fathers Denis Faul and Patrick Walsh, and the Revs Harold Allen, Eric Elliott, Eric Gallagher, and John Radcliffe. Committee discussions led to the creation of the 'Joint Group' in 1970 to further initiatives towards Irish ecumenism.

On 19 April 1969, the NICRA scheduled another civil rights march from Burntollet to Altnagelvin outside Derry. The Stormont government banned the march, prompting a sit-down protest inside the Guildhall. Protestors clashed with

---

[19] *Irish Catholic*, 21 Nov. 1968.   [20] *Irish Catholic*, 28 Nov. 1968.
[21] *Irish Catholic*, 21 Nov. 1968.   [22] Daly, *Are You a Priest?*, 132.
[23] Charles Tyndall to Edward Daly, 24 Nov. 1968 in Daly, *Are You a Priest?*, 133.
[24] *Irish Catholic*, 19 Dec. 1968.   [25] *Irish Catholic*, 19 Dec. 1968.
[26] The Irish Council of Churches (ICC) was originally founded in January 1923 as the United Council of Christian Churches and Religious Communions in Ireland. It was an all-Ireland body to represent the main Protestant churches; Louise Fuller, *Irish Catholicism since 1950: The Undoing of a Culture* (Dublin, 2002), 189.

loyalists led by Paisley, the RUC became involved, and the bloodiest rioting to date in the city occurred. Sammy Devenny, a politician and undertaker, was beaten so severely in his home by the RUC that he later died from his injuries. Mulvey and Daly arrived to help the family with priests attempting to calm the protestors. Daly said: 'I was as angry as the rioters at what was happening. There were times when one was severely tempted to join the rioters rather than attempt to quell them'.[27] As riots continued, it was clear the priests' message of non-violence was ineffective.

After the April 1969 march, Catholic priests and Protestant pastors organized for leaders of the Four Main Churches to jointly visit the poorest areas of Derry. Daly, Catholic Bishop of Derry Neil Farren (see Appendix), and Bishop Tyndall visited the Catholic Bogside and Protestant Fountain areas to examine meagre housing for the city's neediest.[28] People welcomed the church leaders. In this instance, the Protestant and Catholic clergy bridged the gap between their respective communities and episcopacies.

The hierarchy were slow to release public statements after the riots. A week after 5 October, Conway responded to a Protestant church leaders' pronouncement condemning discrimination.[29] Conway urged politicians not to see the march as purely political or worse, sectarian. He believed violence occurred because of social issues such as unemployment, discrimination, and poor housing conditions.[30] In his opinion, Catholics unanimously supported reform and there was a real desire for proactive response. Conway's pronouncement gave the civil rights movement legitimacy.

The hierarchy began releasing statements more quickly as marches continued to turn violent. After the November 1968 march, Conway appealed for calm.[31] As Christmas approached, Conway offered a seasonal reminder of the need for peace and goodwill. He reiterated the inequalities faced by Catholics in housing and employment, asking his congregation to 'pray to-day, therefore, for peace and for justice which is the foundation for peace'.[32] Perhaps Pope John XXIII's 1963 encyclical *Pacem in Terris*, addressed to all men of goodwill rather than solely Catholics, which advocated social harmony and equality, influenced Conway. The papal pronouncement observed that, when societies are built on the 'basis of rights and duties', people have a greater understanding of 'truth, justice, charity and freedom'.[33] Conway clearly framed the grievances of protestors in terms of equality and spoke to both Protestants and Catholics.

---

[27] Daly, *Are You a Priest?*, 144. [28] *Daily Express*, 26 April 1969.
[29] Taggart, *Conflict, Controversy and Co-operation*, 26–7.
[30] CTOMLA, CCP, 18-8-1 1968–72 Press Releases, 13 Oct. 1968.
[31] CTOMLA, CCP, 18-8-1 1968–72 Press Releases, 5 Dec. 1968.
[32] CTOMLA, CCP, 18-8-1 1968–72 Press Releases, 15 Dec. 1968.
[33] Pope John XXIII, 'Pacem in Terris', 11 April 1963. http://w2.vatican.va/content/john-xxiii/en/encyclicals/documents/hf_j-xxiii_enc_11041963_pacem.html

Bishop Neil Farren released a statement to be read at all Masses in his parish in response to loyalist attacks on the January 1969 People's Democracy march. Farren asked Derry Catholics to 'continue to act with... dignity and restraint'.[34] He promised to ask the authorities to 'consider the validity of the protests' which he called 'legitimate'.[35] When a strike was planned in response to the attack, Farren and Protestant church leaders pleaded with Derry workers not to participate, as it would damage the city's 'future chances of progress and job opportunities'.[36] Other bishops encouraged the NICRA branches to cancel any planned civil rights marches because of the heightened tensions.[37] Bishops across the North once again asked for restraint from Catholics and that they would seek justice through official and institutional means.

The January 1969 Burntollet incident sparked the first Northern Irish Catholic joint hierarchy statement of the conflict. Previously, the bishops joined together to release statements on wider issues in the North, including threats to Catholic education and the economy.[38] The Archbishop of Armagh and the Catholic Bishops of Derry, Clogher, Dromore, Kilmore, and Down and Connor drew attention to the decades of discrimination felt by Catholics in Northern Ireland. This group praised the non-violent actions of the civil rights movement, while it blamed individuals who 'were allowed to impede lawful and peaceful demonstrations with the threat or use of force'.[39] The language of the statement was deliberately vague, neither allotting blame nor explicitly suggesting the RUC allowed these individuals to disrupt peaceful marches.

This joint statement went on to praise the wisdom of the NICRA in cancelling a march in Strabane: the bishops noted the organization realized the 'harm that could be done to community relations' if the march occurred.[40] A brief portion of the statement praised the efforts of Protestants 'including leading Churchmen' who worked towards 'the cause of social justice'.[41] The shift in Vatican priorities after the Second Vatican Council to the issues of peace and socio-economic inequality was reflected in a series of teachings, including: *Mater et Magistra* (1961), *Pacem in Terris* (1963), and *Populorum Progressio* (1967). The term 'social justice' reflected Catholic Social Teaching and was a Vatican directive.[42] The declaration concluded by calling for government action. This joint statement demonstrated a shift in the hierarchy towards the use of stronger language in their statements concerning the security forces. They could no longer tiptoe

[34] Neil Farren Statement, 6 Jan. 1969 in Daly, *Are You a Priest?*, 140.
[35] *Irish Press*, 7 Jan. 1969.   [36] *Irish Press*, 9 Jan. 1969.
[37] *Irish Press*, 16 Jan. 1969.
[38] *Irish Catholic*, 25 Jan. 1968; 15 Feb. 1968; 11 July 1968; 8 Aug. 1968.
[39] CTOMLA, CCP, 18-8-1 1968–72 Press Releases, 20 Jan. 1969.
[40] CTOMLA, CCP, 18-8-1 1968–72 Press Releases, 20 Jan. 1969.
[41] CTOMLA, CCP, 18-8-1 1968–72 Press Releases, 20 Jan. 1969.
[42] Pope John XXIII, 'Pacem in Terris', 11 April 1963. http://w2.vatican.va/content/john-xxiii/en/encyclicals/documents/hf_j-xxiii_enc_11041963_pacem.html

around the issue, and parishioners looked to them to voice community concerns. As McCann notes, Catholics were taught from a young age 'to respect the authority of the church in all things'.[43] While the statement used more condemnatory language, the timing hindered its impact. Appearing two weeks after the Burntollet march, it did not prompt a change in political discourse. In this instance, the politics were from home while the religious context, and its reframing was driven from Rome.

The Church also became a strong link between Catholics in Northern Ireland and the Irish diaspora. 'Home' was a contested concept throughout the conflict. While unorganized at first, American Catholics lent support to the Irish civil rights movement through Church donations.[44] Bishop Farren acted as the go-between, transferring funds to civil rights organizers,[45] thus strengthening the bond between the Church and the campaign. In the early days of the conflict, American Catholics tended to keep their donations within the institutional Church. To access these donations, civil rights leaders needed close contact with Church leaders. This also gave the bishop discretionary power: if he disagreed with the movement, he could stop acting as intermediary. Therefore, civil rights organizations needed to pay deference to their bishop in order to receive crucial funds. As priests walked with the marchers,[46] hierarchy members held private pastoral visits and issued statements. When violence increased, however, the actions and the words of the clergy and bishops intensified, demonstrating the Church's condemnation of violence and the perception that more concentrated action was required.

Clerical Legitimacy

By the summer of 1969, a growing number of young Catholic men in the North no longer listened to the clergy. A key factor in the disintegration of this relationship was the fraught, contested, and increasingly divergent attitude towards masculinity. Conventional ideas of masculinity privileged the Irish nationalist hero, fighting against the 'invader' in a David versus Goliath battle, against the British state. Violence was synonymous with an accepted response to perceived injustice. Seamus Deane's novel *Reading in the Dark* traces this trope in Derry between 1945 and 1971 to explore ideas of Catholic masculinity and persecution by police, with deference shown to the Church through his characters' interactions with priests and bishops.[47] Traditional ideas of masculinity, such as being able to

---

[43] McCann, *War and an Irish Town*, 73.

[44] The Church also distributed donations raised from charity organizations in the Republic; *Southern Star*, 18 Oct. 1969.

[45] Ó Dochartaigh, *From Civil Rights to Armalites*, 52.

[46] *An Phoblacht*, May 1970.

[47] Seamus Deane, *Reading in the Dark* (London, 1997).

provide for a family, were also put under pressure in the latter half of the twentieth century because of high rates of unemployment among Northern Catholic men. Historian Sean Brady has argued: 'Men who did not fulfil the social and cultural expectations of masculinity...risked being marginalized'.[48] In addition, a violent section of rioters rejected priests who they felt did not fit with hegemonic ideas of masculinity and were not subject to the same pressures to provide and to adhere to societal norms. For some Catholic men, partition allowed them to play the role of victim and also cultivate a dissenting identity based on agency, opposition, and resistance to the British state. Their powerlessness in this situation compounded their victimhood, communicated and transmuted with grievances of previous generations. A small subset of Catholic men saw violent antagonism towards the state as the only available option.

Through their vow of celibacy, priests were already removed from these traditional ideas of masculinity. Parish priests were often older, with the average age of those appointed to this position being fifty-five.[49] The age gap often reflected a generational difference in opinion. The actions of these rioting men were in defiance of symbols of authority attempting to persuade them to go home.[50] While interviewees, in retrospect, expressed most of these specific tensions mentioned, these actions also speak to a wider narrative of youth revolt across Europe at this time.[51]

This lack of understanding between the two groups can be illustrated through the priests' response to violence in July 1969. Some young nationalist men clashed with Orangemen returning from a demonstration in Limavady. Fights between nationalists and the police followed, with Derry city residents phoning St Eugene's Cathedral asking for priests to calm the situation. Daly was among those who attended and witnessed teenagers looting shops. In his sermon the following morning, Daly called the youths' actions 'sheer hooliganism' that had 'no connection with civil rights or religion'.[52] Daly said the young people insulted the priests who attempted to reprimand them, indicating a shift in attitude towards generational deference and clerical influence, and that the conflict was spiralling beyond the control of the institutional Church.

By August 1969, it had become clear many young Catholic men no longer heeded their priests' advice. In the Bogside, for example, the time for preaching restraint had passed, and Daly noted even priests 'had given up on that

---

[48] Sean Brady, 'Why examine men, masculinities and religion in Northern Ireland?', in Lucy Delap and Sue Morgan (eds.), *Men, Masculinities and Religious Change in Twentieth-Century Britain*, (London, 2013), 224.

[49] Before becoming parish priests, young men who finished seminary acted as assistant chaplains and priests as well as schoolteachers; Inglis, *Moral Monopoly*, 46.

[50] Interview with Bishop Edward Daly, 2 June 2015.

[51] Interview with Fr Joseph McVeigh, 14 April 2014; Interview with Fr Desmond Wilson, 1 Sep. 2014.

[52] Daly sermon, 13 July 1969 in Daly, *Are You a Priest?*, 148.

particular effort'.[53] In his testimony to the Scarman commission Mulvey described 'a community in revolt'.[54] There were even allegations some young priests wore masks and threw petrol bombs alongside other rioters.[55] There is little evidence to support this claim but it promotes the idea that some younger members of the clergy shared the frustrations of their community. There are examples of priests becoming actively involved in the armed struggle. Fr Chesney, for instance, was a quartermaster in the South Derry Brigade of the Provisionals and was one of those responsible for the 1972 Claudy bombing, which killed nine and injured thirty.[56] Fr Patrick Fell's arrest and subsequent incarceration on charges of acting as an IRA commander in England provides another example, discussed further in Chapter 2.[57] At the same time a parish priest in Wolverhampton, Fr Michael Connolly, called on the Dublin government to provide guns for the IRA.[58] In an interview with the author, Bishop Edward Daly acknowledged divisions within the priesthood over republican violence but said 'very few' priests would have supported the IRA.[59] However, McCann claimed when a group of Derry rioters broke into Harrison's Garage on Williams Street to steal petrol, a priest endorsed the action 'as long as you don't take any more than you really need'.[60] Such instances challenge the notion that every priest condemned violence. At times, Daly said priests required their flock to protect them. For example, Daly recounted the time a large group of Catholics gathered to blockade a cathedral when it was rumoured a loyalist crowd were planning an attack.[61]

The rioters' dismissal of clerical authority demonstrates the intersection of the rejection of authority figures, more generally, with different ideas of masculinity. While priests still garnered the respect their communities in general, to a small subset of Northern Catholic men, these priests were out of touch. Of course, youth will often test authority at times of tension but the rejection of priests by many young men in the context of events in Northern Ireland is particularly noteworthy.

The British Army

Summer 1969 began with a lull in violence long enough for Cardinal Conway to release a statement against Marxism and its attractions for young people.[62] Civil unrest in France during May 1968 served as a backdrop to global unease. Kristin

---

[53] Daly, *Are You a Priest?*, 153.
[54] Scarman Report, p. 72 in Ó Dochartaigh, *Civil Rights to Armalites*, 106.
[55] Interview with Mitchel McLaughlin, a Sinn Féin member of Derry City Council and member of the IRA since 1966 in Ó Dochartaigh, *Civil Rights to Armalites*, 124.
[56] Brewer, Higgins, and Teeney, *Religion, Civil Society, and Peace*, 3.
[57] *An Phoblacht*, 2 Aug. 1974.   [58] *Irish Examiner*, 9 Nov. 1971.
[59] Interview with Bishop Edward Daly, 2 June 2015.
[60] McCann, *War and an Irish Town*, 117.   [61] Daly, *Are you a Priest?*, 155.
[62] CTOMLA, CCP, 18–18 1969 Press Release, 29 June 1969.

Ross argues May '68 was about more than just students or 'youth' revolt.[63] The worker-priest movement began in France and became the foundation from which left-wing and Marxist ideas spread among French and Italian priests.[64] The temporary cessation in violence in Ireland meant Conway could tackle religion's nemesis: communism.[65] Conway cautioned young people filled with 'a burning sense of justice' could turn to radical ideas—like Marxism—as a means to end discrimination.[66] In a July 1969 RTÉ radio interview, Conway warned again of young people's attraction to 'the concentration camp of Marxism'.[67] His statement was a crucial indicator of Church policy. The bishops' support of civil rights in 1968 and 1969 was, in part, a self-protective measure. The Old IRA was an organization with known Communist sympathies[68] so Conway's proclamation demonstrated a distancing from republicanism without naming the IRA explicitly.

On 12 August 1969, an Apprentice Boys' march in Derry resulted in three days of rioting. While trying to dispel the crowd, the RUC drove rioters into the Bogside before attempting to enter the Catholic stronghold. Bogsiders mobilized to prevent the police from entering, resulting in clashes between the RUC and hundreds of Catholics. Priests toured their parishes, calling for calm and attempting to reassure the elderly. In West Belfast, Sr Genevieve O'Farrell opened up St Louise's School as a temporary shelter for those Catholic families driven from their homes.[69]

Conway released his first statement on the 'Battle of the Bogside' on 14 August 1969. He entreated Catholics to avoid escalating the violence, both for community safety and to avoid damage to the civil rights campaign. Conway questioned the march's timing and why the RUC needed to enter the Bogside, where Catholics 'had been terrorized by some members of the police force on a number of earlier occasions'. The memory of which had not been forgotten.[70] This was the first time Conway specifically criticized the RUC as the level of violence forced the cardinal to draw attention to police brutality.

Following this statement, Conway began to receive threatening letters. Regular hate mail continued throughout the rest of his tenure as archbishop. An anonymous author accused Conway of partisanship: 'Far from being a Man of God you are a Republican politician who has banked on the troubles of the British people at the

---

[63] Kristin Ross, May '68 and its afterlives (Chicago, 2002), 2.

[64] Marwick, The Sixties, 34.

[65] The Irish Church's battle with communism discussed in Fuller, Irish Catholicism since 1950, 67–71; 213. Communist dictatorships silencing the Catholic Church and religion attacked were frequent topics in The Irish Catholic, see Irish Catholic, 9 May 1968, 6 June 1968, 27 June 1968.

[66] CTOMLA, CCP, 18–18 1969 Press Release, 29 June 1969.

[67] CTOMLA, CCP, 18–18 1969 Press Release, 31 July 1969.

[68] Cathal Goulding, Chief of Staff of the IRA and of the Official IRA after the split, was a known Marxist and his 'reading of Irish republicanism was certainly class tinged'; Richard English, Armed Struggle: The History of the IRA (London, 2003), 84.

[69] Rae, Sister Genevieve, 126–7.

[70] CTOMLA, CCP, 18-8-1 1968–72 Press Releases, 14 Aug. 1969.

moment enabling you and your Republican friends to get away with it'.[71] Conway had made himself vulnerable to accusations of pro-republican sympathies from unionist detractors who overlooked his genuine hopes for peace.

Violence had died down in Derry by the evening of 14 August but Catholic protestors in Belfast had rioted in solidarity. The IRA Belfast brigade had a new strategy: creating events rather than responding to them and attacking armoured police cars using petrol bombs and rifles. Most of the fighting in Derry occurred between the Catholic majority and the RUC. Yet, in Belfast Catholics were the minority, often living in communities sandwiched between Protestant areas. Violence in Belfast during the following days would take a viciously sectarian turn.

The Catholic hierarchy in Northern Ireland released a joint pronouncement on 23 August, naming the B Specials as an organization in which the Catholic community had no faith.[72] It rejected the Scarman inquiry implication that violence stemmed from armed insurrection. Further, the hierarchy said Catholic neighbourhoods in Belfast were 'invaded by mobs equipped with machine guns and other firearms'.[73] They made no mention of the IRA's weapons. Most important was the bishops' claim 'that a necessary pre-condition to any restoration of confidence on the part of the Catholic community must be an open recognition of these facts'.[74] This statement was a clear break from the earlier vague pronouncements of the episcopacy and a sign that the Church had officially entered the political arena. It was interpreted as a direct condemnation of the Stormont regime. The August 1969 riots also brought international press attention to the movement, as well as the renewed concerns of the Vatican. The International Conference of Catholic Charities, Caritas Internationalis, gave Archbishop John Charles McQuaid of Dublin (see Appendix) $5,000 for Northern 'refugees' displaced by the rioting.[75]

After the Battle of the Bogside, Conway and Philbin dined with British Home Secretary James Callaghan at the Conway Hotel, outside of Belfast. Also in attendance were a unionist Member of Parliament (MP), Protestant clergymen, civil rights organizers, and two Westminster MPs, brought together to 'thrash out their differences'.[76] The dinner was part of Callaghan's three-day visit to Northern Ireland to deal with the unrest. The invitation to Conway and Philbin, along with Protestant clergy, could demonstrate the British government's view of the conflict as sectarian rather than political, which Conway went to great lengths to refute.[77] Nevertheless, Paisley refused to participate because of the Catholic hierarchy's attendance, saying: 'We are at war in this province with the hierarchy of the

---

[71] CTOMLA, CCP, Anonymous to Conway, 15 Aug. 1969.
[72] Guardian, 25 Aug. 1969.
[73] CTOMLA, CCP, 18-8-1 1968–72 Press Releases, 23 Aug. 1969.
[74] CTOMLA, CCP, 18-8-1 1968–72 Press Releases, 23 Aug. 1969.
[75] Irish Catholic, 18 Sep. 1969.   [76] Guardian, 27 Aug. 1969.
[77] Observer, 31 Aug. 1969.

Roman Catholic Church and I will not be sitting down to eat dinner with the enemies of this province'.[78] Paisley also accused Callaghan of 'siding with' Catholics on the issue of discrimination.[79] Conway felt the talks were 'helping to bring both sides together'.[80] *The Times* described Callaghan's meeting with Conway as one of the 'most critical' of his visit.[81] The hierarchy could attempt to influence the British through private meetings which helped both parties formulate more refined policy stances.

Callaghan's visit was held against the backdrop of British Army troops arriving in Belfast. Edward Daly asserted that historians have overplayed the acceptance of British troops in Derry, as it was not pleasant 'to have helmeted soldiers in full battle-dress armed with machine guns at the end of your street'.[82] *The Irish Catholic* contemporaneously noted that 'the return of British troops to Derry's streets... is not welcomed by nationally-minded people.'[83] The rector of the Holy Cross Monastery, Fr Colm O'Donnell, appealed to the people of Ardoyne for calm, supported by the republican movement.[84] Catholics may have felt protected by the army's presence but they hoped it would be a short-term arrangement.

The situation in Northern Ireland remained tense and the hierarchy responded to this mood. Conway diagnosed the need for 'breathing space', for 'even a spark could produce an explosion'.[85] Dismissive of this injunction, the IRA's Cathal Goulding warned that the British Army would have to 'take the consequences' if soldiers participated in the oppression of Catholics.[86] The IRA's threat to the British Army proved a barrier to the breathing space Conway desired.

Yet, the following months did bring a lull in the violence, allowing the Church to focus on the roots of animosity between the communities. Conway spoke on the necessity for Catholics to pass on their faith to their children after Pope Paul VI released *Matrimonia Mixta* in March 1970. This clause resulted in anxiety about mixed faith marriages for both Protestants and Catholics. The establishment of the CIC in 1959, the first body in Ireland where Catholics and Protestants worked together for improvements in industry and employment, indicated some inter-church feeling. However, the Catholic Church would not compromise on mixed marriages. Conway sought to defuse sectarian violence by suggesting that often this type of conflict emerged when groups knew little about each other's customs.[87] The hierarchy needed to combat the perception that Catholic doctrine might fuel such segregation and tensions as many believed the teachings of canon

---

[78] *Times*, 29 Aug. 1969.   [79] *Guardian*, 28 Aug. 1969.
[80] *Guardian*, 29 Aug. 1969.   [81] *Times*, 27. Aug. 1969.
[82] Daly, *Are You a Priest?*, 162.   [83] *Irish Catholic*, 21 Aug. 1969.
[84] *An Phoblacht*, June 1970.
[85] CTOMLA, CCP, 18–18 1969 Press Release, 29 Aug. 1969.
[86] Public Records Office of Northern Ireland (PRONI), CAB/9/B/312/1, Aug. 1969.
[87] CTOMLA, CCP, 18–18 1970 Press Release, 29 April 1970.

law on mixed marriage and the confessional education of children exacerbated sectarian conflict.

The first joint Catholic and Protestant church leaders' statement on violence in Northern Ireland appeared on 30 May 1970. Leaders of the Four Main Churches came together to label the conflict political not sectarian. These men acknowledged divisions but wished 'to assert that these divisions are not primarily of a religious character'.[88] Rather, they maintained disparities between Catholics and Protestants were 'historical, political, and social' and religious differences were not the primary cause of unrest.[89] Releasing a joint statement at this time was significant as pressure against the churches remained high. Many politicians and British government officials publicly wondered why the churches could not contain their flocks. This statement acted as a buffer for the Four Main Churches, pushing the responsibility away from the churches. However, Conway's earlier comments on *Matrimonia Mixta* indicate he understood the Catholic Church teachings would be contentious. By reaching out to Protestants on the issue, Conway acknowledged that in some ways the divisions also occurred because of religious teaching seeking to maintain endogamy. Religious leaders from various Christian churches had an essential role to play in ending the violence and this reveals how central religious institutions were to the conflict, even if they were helpless to stop the fighting.

As leader of the Catholic Church, Conway was in a position of authority to speak to Stormont politicians. After the publication of the Macrory Report in June 1970, which reviewed local government, Conway met with Northern Ireland parliament member Brian Faulkner to discuss reforms.[90] In his memoir, Faulkner noted the 'one positive response' to the report was from the Catholic Church, as Conway appointed a chaplain to Stormont for the first time 'in recognition of our local government reforms'.[91] Unionist politicians welcomed the appointment, as indicating a 'formal recognition of Stormont as an institution of the Roman Catholic community'.[92] *The Guardian* called the appointment 'a major gesture of goodwill' by the Church.[93]

Fighting again erupted on the Lower Falls Road in July 1970. Conway requested the establishment of an impartial system of laws on 'a foundation for social justice for all'.[94] Newspapers in Northern Ireland, the Republic, and Britain agreed that Conway's statement lacked direction. Concerned citizens and outraged residents also made their views known in letters to the cardinal. One anonymous Dublin

---

[88] CTOMLA, CCP, 18–18 1970 Press Release, 30 May 1970.

[89] CTOMLA, CCP, 18–18 1970 Press Release, 30 May 1970.

[90] 'Review Body on Local Government in Northern Ireland 1970', Patrick A. Macrory, http://cain.ulst.ac.uk/hmso/macrory.htm

[91] Previously the Church had not employed a chaplain at Stormont, a small protest against the British; Brian Faulkner, *Memoirs of a Statesman* (London, 1978), 73.

[92] *Times*, 24 Dec. 1970.   [93] *Guardian*, 24 Dec. 1970.

[94] CTOMLA, CCP, 18–18 1970 Press Release, 5 July 1970.

writer felt 'sickened' by Conway's 'milk-and-watery approach to the injustices inflicted on the poorer members of the Catholic Church in the North', an approach the author believed lacked a convincing, pragmatic response.[95] British Catholics and Protestants alike claimed Conway had yet to speak on the conflict.[96] This incorrect perception grew from the fact many newspapers in Britain did not publish Conway's statements, leading many to write to the archbishop requesting him to voice his stance. Nevertheless, from 5 October 1968 until 1 August 1971, *The Times* reported on Conway's activities twenty-two times.[97] However, when he delivered a statement or sermon his words were often most briefly summarized rather than quoted. The General Secretary of the British Council of Churches, Anglican Bishop Kenneth Sansbury, wrote to *The Times* and noted this discrepancy in December 1968:

> Everyone recognises that in Ulster religion and politics are inextricably mixed. Yet in the present crisis, apart from one or two short references to comments made by Cardinal Conway of Belfast, the only religious leader I have seen quoted in the newspapers or interviewed on TV has been that rabble-rousing Ian Paisley. The views of responsible Church leaders have been passed over.[98]

Over this same period, *The Guardian* reported on Conway's activities related to the North twenty-three times[99] and published Conway's full statement once, in relation to the August 1969 violence.[100] Conversely, *The Daily Express* published only seven articles on Conway's statements during the same period.[101] The comparatively low level of coverage by all three newspapers meant that much of the general British readership would have been largely unaware of the cardinal's full pronouncements.

Conway routinely spoke against murders but did not identify the offenders, state or paramilitary. When the Provisional IRA shot and killed three off-duty Scottish soldiers on 10 March 1971, Conway received hateful letters asking him to denounce the IRA. The archbishop had released a statement that evening, declaring he was 'horrified at the news of this callous murder' but not naming the

---

[95]   CTOMLA, CCP, Anonymous to Conway, 8 July 1970.

[96]   CTOMLA, CCP, M.C. to Conway, 18 July 1970; CTOMLA, CCP, R.C.B. to Conway, 6 July 1970.

[97]   *Times*, 13 Oct. 1968, 2 Dec. 1968, 14 Dec. 1968, 28 April 1969, 20 Aug. 1969, 21 Aug. 1969, 22 Aug. 1969, 25 Aug. 1969, 26 Aug. 1969, 27 Aug. 1969, 29 Aug. 1969, 9 Sep. 1969, 13 Sep. 1969, 23 Sep. 1969, 31 March 1970, 22 April 1970, 22 May 1970, 29 June 1970, 8 July 1970, 13 Aug. 1970, 24 Dec. 1970, 11 Feb. 1971.

[98]   *Times*, 14 Dec. 1968.

[99]   *Guardian*, 2 Dec. 1968, 16 Dec. 1968, 9 Jan. 1969, 10 Jan. 1969, 24 Feb. 1969, 21 May 1969, 18 Aug. 1969, 25 Aug. 1969, 26 Aug. 1969, 27 Aug. 1969, 29 Aug. 1969, 12 Sep. 1969, 8 Oct. 1969, 14 Oct. 1969, 22 Oct. 1969, 3 April 1970, 13 Aug. 1970, 24 Dec. 1970, 16 Feb. 1971, 17 Feb. 1971, 26 Feb. 1971, 27 May 1971, 10 June 1971. *The Guardian's* affiliate newspaper *The Observer* published on the cardinal twice during this period; *Observer*, 24 Aug. 1969, 31 Aug. 1969.

[100]   *Guardian*, 25 Aug. 1969.

[101]   *Daily Express*, 26 April 1969, 19 Aug. 1969, 21 Aug. 1969, 27 Aug. 1969, 29 Aug. 1969, 30 Aug. 1969. 13 Aug. 1970.

perpetrators, possibly for fear of interrupting due process.[102] A similar statement appeared after the July 1971 shooting of two men in Derry and two soldiers in Belfast, where Conway declared those deliberately taking innocent life were committing a crime.[103] Both pronouncements lacked force and did little to quell the violence: they reveal Conway's initial reaction as one of caution. However, as the conflict intensified, Conway began to make serious accusations against the British government, the RUC, and the British Army, particularly following the introduction of internment in August 1971.

By contrast, in January 1970, republican efforts to shape the narrative of contemporary events highlighted the perceived inaction of the Irish Catholic Church in the press. Articles in the newly re-launched *An Phoblacht* newspaper allowed republicans to distribute their views across Ireland. In one article, Irish journalist and author Deasún Breathnach quoted theologian Fr John Mockey on the necessity for Christians 'to take part actively in protests'.[104] Breathnach argued the silence of any priest or bishop was tantamount to supporting injustice. A piece on the theology of violence examined the 'Just War' theory[105] and the ethics of protesting.[106] *An Phoblacht's* editors clearly felt applying 'Just War' theory to the conflict would appeal to a core readership supporting armed struggle and holding strong religious convictions.[107] In this way, some Irish Catholics might be thought comparable to their Italian counterparts, who gave formal allegiance to the Communist Party but held strong Catholic beliefs on contraception and divorce.[108] Initially published monthly and then fortnightly, the newspaper would later commission articles on injustice written by priests. However, condemning the inaction of the majority of clergy and hierarchy over state violence was its main concern. Nevertheless, individual priests, including SF member Fr Seán Kearney, Fathers Padraig Murphy, P.F. Malone, Sean McManus, Des Wilson, Denis Faul, Raymond Murray, and Brian Brady were among the few who did receive recognition for their work. Indeed, in a three-part series on the morality of the conflict, Breathnach also praised Fathers Fergal O'Connor Order of Preachers (OP), Austin Flannery OP, and Michael Sweetman Society of Jesus (SJ) for following 'the spirit of Vatican II' in supporting civil rights protestors.[109] O'Connor was a Dublin-based Dominican priest and scholar of political economy, while fellow Dominican Flannery was a social justice campaigner and editor of *Doctrine and Life*. Sweetman's contacts with republicans earned him the

---

[102] CTOMLA, CCP, 18-8-1 1968–72 Press Releases, 10 March 1971.

[103] CTOMLA, CCP, 18-8-1 1968–72 Press Releases, 15 July 1971.

[104] *An Phoblacht*, May 1970.

[105] In paragraphs 2302–17 of the *Catechism of the Catholic Church*, 'Just War' is defined as actions which constitute the just defense of a nation against an aggressor.

[106] *An Phoblacht*, June 1970.

[107] Later in the conflict Breathnach wrote on theology and the Church for *An Phoblacht*, but under his penname Dara MacDara.

[108] Marwick, *The Sixties*, 33–4.   [109] *An Phoblacht*, April 1970.

nickname the 'Commie Jesuit'.[110] For Breathnach, these priests were few and far between, as he lamented the minimal impact of Vatican II, and the newspaper continued to vilify the wider clergy and hierarchy as a whole.[111]

The Church responded tentatively and non-committedly in the early years of the conflict. The year 1968 began with Church's worries over education reform in the North and ended with concerns over police brutality and state injustice. The clergy and hierarchy shared one aim: to bring socio-economic reform to Northern Ireland and de-escalate the violence. The summer of 1971 and the coming months pushed some quarters of the clergy to a more radical stance while the hierarchy continued their condemnations of violence. As the bishops began denouncing the IRA by name, tension with republican paramilitaries increased and pushed the Irish bishops out of a strong and commanding negotiating position as the conflict became increasingly polarized.

Internment

The British government policy of internment without trial shook the Catholic community from its commencement on 9 August 1971. While Martin McCleery has argued the British policy was a success in detaining the correct paramilitaries, the brutality of the internment process impacted upon many.[112] It was a damaging psychological and physical tactic mainly targeting Catholic men. In a series of raids across Northern Ireland, the security forces arrested 342 people. Seventeen died within forty-eight hours: ten killed by the British Army. One of the deceased was Fr Hugh Mullan, shot by a British soldier while administering the last rites to a wounded man after riots in Ballymurphy. The Church was not immune to the heightened emotional atmosphere. Stories of men being taken in the early hours and beaten in front of their screaming wives and children were heard across the North. The evaluative term was 'injustice', and it passed from the lips of priests and bishops alike. The immediate Church reaction centred on the clergy comforting families. The hierarchy eventually condemned internment. As time passed, a handful of clergy wrote pamphlets raising awareness of internment. One of the largest protest actions by priests during the conflict culminated in a petition to the British government and a priest boycott of the 1971 census. Conway accused the British Army soldiers of brutality and repeatedly called for an end to internment as Catholic Church leaders met with government officials to end the policy.

---

[110] *Irish Press*, 7 Dec. 1970.
[111] *An Phoblacht*, Oct. 1970, Dec. 1970, April 1971, Nov. 1971, April 1972.
[112] Martin McCleery, *Operation Demetrius: and its aftermath: A new history of the use of internment without trial in Northern Ireland 1971–75* (Manchester, 2015), 44–7; 53–6; 82–4.

With a larger proportion of Catholics now imprisoned clergymen visited detainee centres to meet with the inmates. The Church had exercised spiritual ministry in prisons for centuries but internment brought non-prison chaplains into play. Internees were anxious to hear news from home and what was being done on their behalf. Priests organized meetings and events for the prisoners, including a concert at Long Kesh Internment Camp by volunteer Derry musicians.[113] These pastoral visits strengthened a handful of priests' relationships with those campaigning for civil liberties. Outside the prison, women religious like Sr Ita in West Belfast visited the families of the internees.[114]

Not every clergy member was seen as helping the internees, as was the case with Catholic British Army chaplains. Fr John Moran in an article for the *Catholic Gazette* journal discussed the difficulties of army chaplaincy and his experience at Aldershot Barracks, arguing: 'Any priest has the right to preach pacifism if he so wishes, but he has no right to do this whilst being sponsored by the Army'.[115] Other accusations that British Army chaplains would go out on patrol and or drink in pubs to gather intelligence against republicans also occurred.[116] Catholic army chaplains, often from outside Northern Ireland, found it much easier to separate their duties from their political ideals.

Two clergymen sought to raise awareness on a wider scale. Fathers Denis Faul and Raymond Murray (see Appendix) collected statements from internment raid witnesses and testimonies from internees. They published multiple pamphlets, with the proceeds going to the internees.[117] In an interview with the author, Danny Morrison named Faul as a 'hero' until the mid-1970s, for his work in exposing the cruelties of internment.[118] At a lecture in Dungannon, Faul decried internment as 'immoral' and against the teachings of the Church, noting: 'Men must raise their voices and use their pens to ensure the cessation of torture and the end of internment'.[119] McElroy observes that, while Faul was 'somewhat isolated in his views' compared to his clerical colleagues in 1969, the census boycott demonstrated the radicalization of the clerical community by 1971.[120] Not every priest went to such lengths to publicize grievances, with some contenting themselves with helping internees' families and visiting incarcerated men.

Faul gathered the signatures of 387 priests, upwards of 60 percent of the clergy in the North, for a November 1971 statement calling for a judicial inquiry into allegations of abuse of internees.[121] They forwarded this petition to political and

---

[113] Daly, *Are You a Priest?*, 183–4.   [114] Rae, *Sister Genevieve*, 159.
[115] John Moran, 'Priest in Uniform', *Catholic Gazette* (June 1972), 5.
[116] Wilson, *The Chaplains' Affair*, 5.
[117] Denis Faul and Raymond Murray, *The Hooded Men: British Torture in Ireland August, October 1971*, 1974; Denis Faul and Raymond Murray, *Long Kesh: The Iniquity of Internment August 1971–August 1974*, 1974.
[118] Interview with Danny Morrison, 29 April 2014.
[119] *Irish Catholic*, 21 Oct. 1971.   [120] McElroy, *Catholic Church*, 123.
[121] *Irish Catholic*, 11 Nov. 1971.

military figures and it was reported widely in the local press.[122] In support of the priests, the Northern bishops released a statement decrying state violence, through the use of 'interrogation in depth', and paramilitary violence.[123] The previous spring, twenty-seven Down and Connor diocese priests declared their intention to boycott the census after a young man was interned for shouting 'up the IRA', when young Protestant men who shouted 'up the UVF' (Ulster Volunteer Force) and 'to hell with the Pope' were not taken away by police.[124] Refusing to complete these government forms violated the law demonstrating these priests' disdain for British policies. While their bishop declined to comment on the boycott, the pro-nationalist *Irish News* supported the endeavour. In total, seventy-one priests, or approximately 11 percent of all Northern priests, boycotted the census.[125] The census boycott must be put in perspective, as these clergymen enjoyed support from high-ranking nationalist politicians like Gerry Fitt and groups including the Association for Legal Justice, the Campaign for Social Justice, and thirty-nine Catholic schoolteachers who also refused to complete the census. The priests' militancy rivalled that of the NICRA. *The Irish Catholic* reported these seventy-one clergymen encouraged others to fill in the census but 'resolved to make a personal protest in vindication of the right to justice and fair play'.[126] In a long tradition of census boycotting by other non-violent movements, these priests were contesting the treatment of Catholics as non-citizens whose basic civil rights had been infringed.

Eight of the priests refused to pay a £7 fine for failure to complete the census. Instead, they donated the money and legal costs to the Association for Legal Justice, making a statement outside the court that 'legalised brutality and torture, which accompany [internment], subverts humanitarian conventions'.[127] By not paying their fines, these priests faced mandatory jail sentences. The Catholic Minister for State in the Northern Irish Prime Minister's office, Dr G.B. Newe, approached Philbin and Mgr Arthur Ryan, offering to contribute towards the priests' fines. The RUC had already arrested one of the priests, Fr Gerald Park, but released him five hours later. On 31 January 1972, the eight clergymen released another statement, claiming Newe added 'insult to injury' by approaching their fellow priests to contribute towards the payment of their fine in order to deliberately 'undermine our protest'. Another of the protesting priests, Fr Malachy Murphy, of St Anne's, Derriaghy, was arrested but also soon released.[128] Government ministers claimed an anonymous source paid the fine saving the priests from imprisonment. Before these statements and boycotts, most clerical criticism towards the British came from individuals like Faul: easily dismissed by

---

[122] *Fermanagh Herald*, 6 Nov. 1971; *Irish Press*, 2 Nov. 1971; *Donegal News*, 6 Nov. 1971.
[123] *Irish Catholic*, 25 Nov. 1971.   [124] McElroy, *Catholic Church*, 124.
[125] McElroy, *Catholic Church*, 125.   [126] *Irish Catholic*, 6 May 1971.
[127] *Irish Times*, 26 Nov. 1971.
[128] *Irish Press*, 31 March 1972; *Irish Independent*, 3 April 1972.

Stormont as a lone, radical voice. Internment reveals the radicalization of a wider section of the clergy, and a continuing widening of the gulf between the hierarchy and some of the priests' actions.

The introduction of internment brought an upsurge in paramilitary recruitment. As McCann notes: 'The twenty-four hours after internment were the bloodiest Northern Ireland had known in decades'.[129] The death count alarmed the Church. Priests witnessed the death toll first-hand through last rites and funerals. Emotionally and physically, priests across Belfast and Derry were exhausted and had little outlet for their own grief. These priests often worked in groups: as one saw to the deceased, another would visit the family. They took shifts comforting the bereaved as well as supporting each other.[130] In September 1971, Fr Edward Daly witnessed his first death in the conflict and gave the last rites to fourteen-year-old Annette McGavigan, killed in the crossfire of British Army and IRA shootings. He recounted her mother screaming after he informed the family and remarked that her death 'had a considerable impact on me'.[131] The emotional toll that the escalation in killings wrought on the clergy galvanized them in their efforts against internment.

Internment saw priests' role as intermediaries between the British Army and paramilitaries grow. Priests carried messages between combatants and offered advice to both sides. One example concerns the removal of a defective bomb in Gartan Square, Derry in 1971. After attempting to bait the British Army with an explosive in a children's play area, the IRA grew concerned that the device would not detonate for its intended target but rather be triggered by children the next day. An IRA volunteer approached Daly and the politician Ivan Cooper to remove the bomb, which they did with great difficulty. A comparable event occurred in April 1969 when Fr Hugh O'Neill disarmed a bomb inside a church in Saintfield, County (Co.) Down.[132] Similar situations called for priests to remove bombs without revealing their informants to the British Army: a difficult position to be in with rumours of torture of internees.

Priests would often approach the British state directly on behalf of their communities. Increased rioting after internment forced priests to step in to calm the situation. For instance, Fr Martin Rooney, a parish priest in Creggan, telegrammed British Prime Minister Edward Heath during continuous rioting in early September 1971. He asked Heath to withdraw British troops from Creggan and evacuate the Blighs Lane post. Creggan was like a 'vast gas chamber' because of the massive amounts of Tear (CS) gas employed by the troops.[133] His efforts had little effect.

---

[129] McCann, War and an Irish Town, 149.   [130] Daly, Are You a Priest?, 175–6, 179–81.
[131] Daly, Are You a Priest?, 180.   [132] Irish Catholic, 1 May 1969.
[133] The UK National Archives, Kew (TNA), DJ/14/9/71.

Many Catholics were outraged by internment, with few outlets for their frustration. The tarring and feathering of young women in romantic relationships with British Army soldiers by a small minority of the Catholic community was one such reaction. It was thought that these women gave information resulting in the internment of some Catholic men. The Provisional IRA warned women against befriending or socializing with soldiers and those who defied them had their hair cut, were tied to lampposts, and were covered in tar.[134] Through this practice we see manifest violent constructions of Catholic masculinity and endogamy, written into the bodies of 'deviant' Catholic women. An *An Phoblacht* article defended the IRA, noting the practice was 'as old as the black and tan days' as when 'the IRA warn, they warn only once'.[135] Daly said, sadly, other Catholic women often joined in the shaming, helping to place a sign like 'Brit Lover' around their necks. Others stood by, as Seamus Heaney recounts in his poem 'Punishment': 'I who have stood dumb / when your betraying sisters, / cauled in tar, / wept by the railings' too nervous to intervene'.[136] The sympathetic British media attention Marta Doherty, of Derry, received, when the IRA tarred and feathered her before her wedding to a British soldier, contrasted with the silence after a British soldier shot and killed mother-of-six Kathleen Thompson around the same time.[137] While many in the Catholic community would disapprove of tarring and feathering, 'in the circumstances they could not reasonably be expected to take a very strong line on the matter'.[138] The expectations placed on priests were different and they held a moral obligation to help everyone, regardless of religion or position. There are numerous examples of priests releasing women who had been tied up when others in the community would not help for fear of IRA retaliation. In November 1971, Daly wrote to the *Derry Journal* calling the practice 'abominable and abhorrent' and arguing those who practised it 'had no right to call themselves Christians'.[139] Sr Genevieve O'Farrell on the Falls Road told her pupils not to speak with soldiers, but the young women's fear of being tarred and feathered meant that command was hardly necessary.[140] Conway also received shocked letters from Britain and the USA, appealing for him to make a statement against tarring and feathering.[141] The defenceless nature of the women added to the barbarity of these crimes. These letters often reflect on the reporting of the conflict outside of Ireland with *The New York Times* replicated stories appearing *The Times*, amplifying British commentary on the conflict.

---

[134] *Irish Independent*, 13 Nov. 1971; *Irish Press*, 4 May 1972.
[135] *An Phoblacht*, Feb. 1971.   [136] Seamus Heaney, 'Punishment', *North* (London, 1975).
[137] *Irish Independent*, 6 Nov. 1971.   [138] McCann, *War and an Irish Town*, 153–4.
[139] *Derry Journal*, Nov. 1971 in Daly, *Are You a Priest?*, 182.
[140] Rae, *Sister Genevieve*, 137.
[141] CTOMLA, CCP, M.C. to Conway 17 Nov. 1971; Faculty of St Cecilia High School to Conway, 12 Nov. 1971; M.R. and A.H. to Conway, 10 Nov. 1971.

The bishops commented on the increased violence in the aftermath of introduction of internment with growing alarm. A brief statement by Conway came on 10 August, calling on Catholics to control their feelings. On 31 August, Conway urged people to break the vicious cycle of 'injustice-violence-repression'.[142] Those who participated in destruction needed to 'pause and reflect before God' on the consequences of their actions.[143] As the violence raged, Northern bishops released a statement condemning paramilitary attacks; listing actions of IRA members and quoting their language ('who in his sane senses wants to bomb a million Protestants into a united Ireland?'). It was clear the bishops were speaking against the IRA specifically.[144] Yet why not name them? Possibly because of fear of attacks on the Church, the bishops' words being misconstrued by the press, or the risk of isolating Catholics who felt the IRA offered protection. Antagonism 'towards the Brits' was high thanks to internment.[145] To many Catholics in Derry's Bogside, the IRA was going to bring the unionist government to an end. Two further hierarchy statements in September 1971 condemned republican violence, but noted it grew out of a frustrated political situation. The bishops felt they needed to tread carefully as condemning the perceived protectors of the community could push Catholics further into the IRA's clutches. Reflecting on the early days of the conflict in 2015, Bishop Edward Daly said: 'If you're not with the IRA, you're against them, period'.[146] In another interview with the author, Danny Morrison recounted walking out of a Mass when Fr Brian Jones condemned IRA retaliatory violence in the early 1970s.[147]

The morality of internment became a major point of difference between the hierarchy and clergy. Conway was only willing to call internment 'a terrible power to give any political authority', while the majority of the clergy viewed the policy as evil and immoral.[148] The basis for the statement signed by the 387 priests condemning internment came from paragraph 27 of the Second Vatican Council's *Pastoral Constitution on the Church in the Modern World*, part of which was quoted in the priests' document. The pastoral urged 'everyone must consider his every neighbour without exception as another self, taking into account first of all His life and the means necessary to living it with dignity.' The priests believed internment denied that dignity.[149]

[142] CTOMA, CCP, 18-8-1 1968–72 Press Releases, 31 Aug. 1971.
[143] CTOMA, CCP, 18-8-1 1968–72 Press Releases, 31 Aug. 1971.
[144] CTOMA, CCP, 18-8-1 1968–72 Press Releases, 12 Sep. 1971.
[145] McCann, *War and an Irish Town*, 152.
[146] Interview with Bishop Edward Daly, 2 June 2015.
[147] Interview with Danny Morrison, 29 April 2014.
[148] McElroy, *Catholic Church*, 114.
[149] Pope Paul VI, 'Pastoral constitution on the Church in the modern world', 7 Dec. 1965, http://www.vatican.va/archive/hist_councils/ii_vatican_council/documents/vat-ii_cons_19651207_gaudium-et-spes_en.html

On 23 September 1971, the Ulster branch of the Association of Irish Priests called on the hierarchy to denounce internment as immoral. Here, we see the first fissures of division between hierarchy and clergy reactions to the conflict. In their 21 November 1971 statement 'Violence in Northern Ireland', the six Northern bishops condemned 'interrogation in depth' as 'immoral and inhuman' but did not judge internment itself as immoral.[150] Despite Vatican II, the Catholic community continued to rely heavily on their religious leaders for moral guidance—more so than their Protestant counterparts—and looked to their bishops to make moral judgements. A bishop denouncing internment as immoral would have strengthened middle-class Catholics' opposition to the policy; partly out of their loyalty to the Church. However, it is clear most working-class Catholics already despised internment, whether the hierarchy told them it was immoral or not. The Irish government had employed internment during the IRA's border campaign from 1956–62, which did not generate this clerical denunciation. Bishops declaring internment to be immoral may have brought more middle-class Catholics to this way of thinking, but those communities directly affected by internment, like the Bogside or areas in West Belfast, did not need persuasion to formulate their own judgments.

While the bishops in the North condemned the violence, the hierarchy in the South called for prayer and raised funds for internees' families. Archbishop McQuaid held a public Exposition of the Blessed Sacrament on 15 August 1971 at St Mary's Pro-Cathedral in Dublin. This Day of Prayer was held in 'reparation for the sins of injustice, hatred and revenge committed against God' and to ask God to grant peace in Northern Ireland.[151] McQuaid called for a Dublin-wide Sunday collection on 29 August to raise funds for refugees fleeing internment in the North.[152] McQuaid received letters requesting he help create peace in the North by arranging regular special devotions in the Dublin archdiocese.[153] The clergy and hierarchy in Northern Ireland appreciated McQuaid's call for a Day of Prayer and the generous donations to Catholics generated in dioceses in the Republic.[154] However, critics condemned McQuaid for speaking about internment but not about the murder of British Army soldiers.[155] Sisters in the Republic also helped refugee Catholics by making housing available in convents and schools for 1,650 mothers and children 'within a few hours'.[156] That number rose to 4,000 in the following days, with McQuaid sending a personal cheque for £1,000 to the

---

[150] 'Violence in Northern Ireland: Statement by the Northern Ireland bishops, 21 November 1971', *The Furrow*, 23 (1972), 60.
[151] Dublin Diocesan Archives (DDA), Archbishop McQuaid Papers (AMP), Press Statement, 10 Aug. 1971. DDA/AB8/B/XVIII/55/21
[152] *Irish Catholic*, 26 Aug. 1971.
[153] DDA, AMP, C.H. to McQuaid, 11 Aug. 1971. DDA/AB8/B/XVIII/55/24
[154] DDA, AMP, Bishop William Philbin to McQuaid, 13 Aug. 1971. DDA/AB8/B/XVIII/55/27
[155] DDA, AMP, Anonymous to McQuaid, 16 Aug. 1971. DDA/AB8/B/XVIII/55/29
[156] *Irish Catholic*, 26 Aug. 1971.

Irish Red Cross to aid the refugees. Funds from the South were often sent to Northern bishops to be distributed.[157] McQuaid praised their efforts, while calling for collections to raise funds for these displaced persons.[158] Dundalk and Drogheda took in other refugees, with Republic of Ireland Army accommodation used in Kilworth and Donegal.[159] Other members of the hierarchy in the South, including the Bishop of Ardagh and Clonmacnois, Cahal Daly, praised the Catholic Church's leadership in Northern Ireland. He applauded the bishops who 'no less courageously condemned the brutalities and inhumanities of the other violence which is military repression'.[160] In their support for the hierarchy in the North, the bishops of the Republic could make clear their own opinions on the conflict.

The Irish Episcopal Conference at Maynooth brought the Northern and Southern hierarchy together to discuss the violence caused by internment in September 1971. As one united caucus, they condemned the practice and presented it as part of a long line of injustices against Northern Catholics for the past fifty years. Yet they agreed force was 'not the answer'; a view shared by 'the overwhelming majority of the Irish people'.[161] The bishops claimed the use of internment 'with its violation of human rights' contributed to the continuing spiral of destructiveness. This pronouncement signalled the Irish Catholic Church, specifically the North and South hierarchy, were united and unequivocal on this issue.

The policy of internment forced the first public statement by Pope Paul VI on the conflict. He concluded it 'greatly aggravated' the situation in Northern Ireland and was 'greatly resented by some of the people'.[162] A week later, the Pope commented on the killing of seventeen-month-old Angela Gallagher in Belfast after a speeding car fired shots in the Falls Road area, blaming the violence for her killing but not a specific organization. Echoing the criticism of the hierarchy, when the Pope was accused of biased intervention the bishops deflected the insinuation by claiming the press did not report his whole statement, which 'was much more balanced' in its entirety.[163] Pope Paul VI spoke again on internment while addressing pilgrims at Castel Gandolfo, proclaiming the situation had worsened because of 'exceptional security measures which were strongly resented by at least part of the citizens'.[164] While the Pope's language was

---

[157] *Connaught Telegraph*, 18 May 1972.
[158] DDA, AMP, Press Statement, 22 Aug. 1971. DDA/AB8/B/XVIII/55/34
[159] *Irish Catholic*, 26 Aug. 1971.
[160] Address at Mohill, County Leitrim on 12 December 1971 in Cahal Daly, *Violence in Ireland and Christian Conscience: From Addresses given by Cahal B. Daly Bishop of Ardagh and Clonmacnois* (Dublin, 1973), 11.
[161] CTOMA, CCP, 18-8-1 1968–72 Press Releases, Irish Episcopal Conference Statement, 29 Sep. 1971.
[162] *Chicago Tribune*, 5 Sep. 1971.
[163] Archives of the Archdiocese of Westminster (AAW), He 1–475, J.W. to Heenan, 31 Aug. 1971.
[164] *Irish Catholic*, 26 Aug. 1971.

deliberately abstract concerning the toddler's death, here he blamed the British government. His statement on the conflict brought the policy of internment into the international spotlight and demonstrated Vatican support for the Irish bishops' efforts.

In conclusion, internment introduced considerable tension between the clergy and bishops. Clergymen and women played a more active role in negotiations between the British Army and the IRA, while also practically supporting bereaved families. The hierarchy felt compelled, even obliged, to use stronger language as the number of deaths and internees rose. Finally, the Vatican spoke out against the conflict. However, the bishops' condemnation of internment faded by the end of 1971, and it was not until Edward Daly became Bishop of Derry in 1974 that the issue became a priority for the hierarchy once again. At this point the Church, while still publicly focused on its abhorrence for the loss of human life, condemned internment and also countered that reactionary violence to this issue was rooted in real injustice. Yet, over the course of the conflict, the hierarchy would become more vocal in their criticism of paramilitary violence. While the bishops disagreed with British policies and discrimination towards Catholics, they could not condone republican violence and it became viewed as the greater sin.

Bloody Sunday

On 30 January 1972, the NICRA planned a march through Derry to protest against internment. The British Army shot at the crowds, killing thirteen unarmed Catholics; another man later died from his injuries. Six priests were on duty across the Bogside that day, witnessing the soldiers' fire. These clergymen were quick to condemn the British government on the scene, while the hierarchy released a statement that evening. Bloody Sunday and its violent aftermath of increased Provisional IRA bombing marked a turning point for the Catholic Church. However, it must be noted that the bishops only subsequently commented on a comparatively small number of instances where civilians were shot by the security forces.

Bloody Sunday took on symbolic importance in the history of the conflict. One of the most iconic images from the conflict is the photograph of the priest, Fr Edward Daly, waving a bloody handkerchief while others helped to carry critically wounded teenager Jackie Duddy (Figure 2). Seven clergymen acted to save victims and administer the last rites on that day, and they subsequently went on to promote knowledge of injustices done to Catholics in Northern Ireland in the following months. These priests were outspoken in their disapproval of the British Army, who they witnessed shooting unarmed civilians as they ran from the scene. Globally, Bloody Sunday connected the Catholic Church with the

Figure 2 Fr Edward Daly assisting Jackie Duddy during Bloody Sunday
Source: Photo courtesy of Fulvio Grimaldi.

conflict more than any instance before through photographs and television interviews of clergy condemning the British government.[165]

Before the civil rights march began that day many demonstrators attended Mass at St Eugene's Cathedral. Rumours circulated that British Army paratroopers would be stationed at the march, so Daly's homily appealed for attendees to remain calm. Priests often visited areas where marches occurred to reassure the elderly and immobile. This is why so many priests were already in the area when the gunfire began.[166] As the British Army started firing and bodies fell to the ground, Fr Mulvey waved a handkerchief at the soldiers in an attempt to stop the bullets and move the bodies to ambulances.[167] The priests administered the last rites to the waiting wounded before paramedics took victims to hospitals. That evening, clergymen and women gathered at St Eugene's Cathedral to pray for the victims as Catholics gathered to wait for the RUC to release the names of the deceased.

---

[165] Erika Hanna, 'Photographs and the "truth" during the Northern Ireland troubles', *Journal of British Studies*, 54 (April 2015), 480.
[166] Daly, *Are You a Priest?*, 189–91.   [167] Daly, *Are You a Priest?*, 196.

Shortly after, John Bierman of the BBC interviewed Daly who was visibly upset and shaken as he recounted a British Army soldier shooting a fleeing Jackie Duddy in the back. Further, Daly affirmed, 'there was no provocation whatsoever' for soldiers to shoot at the civilians rather than use the less severe methods of water cannons and Tear (CS) gas.[168] Daly did not shy away from these inflammatory words. This was a true condemnation of the British government which the international community had not previously heard from the clergy or hierarchy.

The day after the shootings, the seven priests who had witnessed the events gave a press conference at the City Hotel in Derry.[169] The men involved were mostly secular clergy, including Daly, Mulvey, Denis Bradley, Michael McIvor, Tom O'Gara, Joseph Carolan, and George McLaughlin. They reported 'the British Army were guilty of wilful murder' and accused the British Army of firing indiscriminately into a fleeing, unarmed crowd. They called the paratroopers 'trained criminals', arguing they differed from terrorists 'only in the veneer of respectability that a uniform gives them'.[170] However, these priests voiced a minority position as McElroy argues the majority of the Northern Catholic laity believed security force violence did not justify IRA actions.[171] Later, Daly spoke on the RTÉ programme *Seven Days* about Bloody Sunday before embarking on a speaking tour in the USA.[172] The priests' statement and Daly's subsequent interviews publicized Bloody Sunday and the conflict to an international audience. The politics of home were no longer confined to these islands.

Court proceedings led by Lord Widgery into the British Army's conduct proved divisive to both the Catholic community and clergy. Nationalists believed the tribunal would merely act as 'whitewash' to dismiss claims of misconduct against the army. The priests who witnessed Bloody Sunday remained divided about whether they should submit their testimonies as evidence, should the court call upon them, because of these fears of cover-up by a British government court. These dissenting clergymen held another press conference, describing why they had decided to contribute to the tribunal. They began by condemning the narrow focus, insisting 'every relevant piece of evidence should be admissible'.[173] However, their positions as priests made them feel it was important to have 'the truth about the events of January 30th put before the world'.[174] By condemning the British Army, the clergy publicly allied themselves with civil rights.

Cardinal Conway released a statement on the events of 30 January 1972 that very evening. He felt 'deeply shocked' by the 'first-hand account of a priest who was present at the scene'.[175] He revealed he had already telephoned British Prime

---

[168] https://www.youtube.com/watch?v=MQsr1buOCbc
[169] Daly, *Are You a Priest?*, 201–2.   [170] *Irish Times*, 1 Feb. 1972.
[171] McElroy, *Catholic Church*, 99.   [172] Daly, *Are You a Priest?*, 202.
[173] Press Statement, 17 Feb. 1972, Derry Diocesan Archives (DeDA) in Daly, *Are You a Priest?*, 208.
[174] Press Statement, 17 Feb. 1972, Derry Diocesan Archives (DeDA) in Daly, *Are You a Priest?*, 208.
[175] CTOMA, CCP, 18-8-1 1968–72 Press Releases, 30 Jan. 1972.

Minister Ted Heath demanding an investigation. Conway urged calm from the Catholic community, claiming that with an 'impartial and independent public inquiry' the 'world will be able to judge what has happened'.[176] He blamed the British authorities. *The Belfast Telegraph* reflected upon the immediate polarization of the two communities by dismissing the cardinal's statement as 'one-sided'.[177]

On 2 February, in St Mary's Church in Creggan, Bishop Farren led the Requiem Mass for the thirteen Bloody Sunday victims, with Conway also presiding.[178] Conway commented that on this day of mourning God asked his followers for 'love, not hatred—forgiveness, not revenge'. The IRA had already made sure of British Army and civilian deaths in retribution.[179] The following day, Archbishop George 'Otto' Simms of the Church of Ireland, the President of the Methodist Church in Ireland Rev Charles Bain, the Moderator of the Presbyterian Church in Ireland Rev J.M. Haire, and Conway released a joint Protestant-Catholic statement expressing an ecumenical stance. The leaders lamented that community tensions were being exacerbated by rapidly increasing violence and an unbalanced socio-economic situation. These, they said, were the main issues needing to be resolved. Yet their statement did not clarify who should undertake this task, just that Catholics and Protestants must 'stop and recognise the danger' of not understanding each other's point of view.[180] This reserved response caused fallout. In contrast to Conway's statement, it was ineffectual and anodyne. However, because of now entrenched resentment between Protestant and Catholic communities, any ecumenical, united gesture, no matter how small, held symbolic importance.

The international response to the hierarchy in Northern Ireland varied. Most individuals who wrote to Conway from Britain, and more specifically England, condemned his comments. One anonymous author addressed him as 'Hypocrite Conway', writing that the victims Conway referred to 'died through their own fault'.[181] This 'Bitter Protestant' understood that Catholics—the 'poor devils' who 'breed like animals'—were afraid of their priests.[182] Another who wrote from Hampshire criticized the provision of a Requiem Mass for the Bloody Sunday victims but not for the IRA murder victims.[183] Most often these individuals had probably not read the archbishop's statements but saw priests on television discussing Bloody Sunday. This led one Englishwoman, from Enfield, Middlesex to write:

---

[176] CTOMA, CCP, 18-8-1 1968–72 Press Releases, 30 Jan. 1972.
[177] *Belfast Telegraph*, 2 Feb. 1972.
[178] A fourteenth victim, John Johnston, survived the day but died six months later from his injuries.
[179] CTOMA, CCP, 18-8-1 1968–72 Press Releases, 2 Feb. 1972.
[180] CTOMA, CCP, Joint Catholic-Protestant hierarchy Statement, 3 Feb. 1972.
[181] CTOMLA, CCP, Anonymous to Conway, 2 Feb. 1972.
[182] CTOMLA, CCP, Anonymous to Conway, 2 Feb. 1972.
[183] CTOMLA, CCP, J.G.S. to Conway, 4 Feb. 1972.

Do you realise that the presence of Catholic priests in the forefront of all these troubles and their comments to the BBC newsmen is leading myself and other Catholics to the inevitable conclusion that they are actively encouraging these terrible situations?[184]

The presence of priests on television programmes brought new perspectives to those in Britain who were previously unaware of the hierarchy's statements on the conflict. Alana Harris has discussed the often conservative, conformist attitudes of Catholics in England, where they remained a religious minority. English Catholic opinion was often formulated by an educated, traditionalist middle-class elite and with the tumultuous history of Catholicism in England, they did not wish to antagonize their Protestant neighbours. The more outspoken clergy, perhaps with Irish diaspora congregations or themselves of Irish extraction, did not possess the same level of responsibility as their bishops, nor did they share the same public scrutiny. These priests could speak as individuals without the institutional commitment of their hierarchy counterparts. They also received less hate mail as their addresses were not widely known. Therefore, the bishops of Northern Ireland, and of England and Wales, bore the brunt of public frustration at the Church's position.

Conway's papers reveal at least fifteen English priests wrote to him to assure the cardinal that they said prayers for the deceased, but simultaneously to criticize the Church's response and the march itself as 'unlawful'.[185] Other priests were more proactive, suggesting different avenues for engagement after noting there was 'some need for action' but that politicians were likely to act too late.[186] Letters to the Archbishop of Westminster from this period suggest English priests did not question his judgement. Irish priests felt able to criticize English bishops but were more reserved when writing to their own. These letters provide early evidence of the weakening of the rigid hierarchical structure of Irish Catholic Church; a process that had been exacerbated by the reforms of the Second Vatican Council and the *Humanae Vitae* encyclical. Questioning one's bishop became more acceptable as the conflict continued.

Individuals who wrote to Conway from Northern Ireland had a more accurate understanding of his statements and they therefore criticized his lack of action, rather than his words. One Ballymurphy Catholic condemned Conway for speaking against Fr Denis Faul, who publicly denounced the laws forbidding marching, claiming that unlike Faul, Conway had not identified himself 'with the people in that struggle'.[187] This individual further criticized Conway for not visiting Long Kesh Internment Camp nor Armagh Prison. One former Belfast woman, who had

[184] CTOMLA, CCP, V.A. to Conway, 1 Feb. 1972.
[185] CTOMLA, CCP, J.M. to Conway, 31 Jan. 1972; CCP, W.P.J.F. to Conway, 7 Feb. 1972.
[186] CTOMLA, CCP, P.K. to Conway, Feb. 1972.
[187] CTOMLA, CCP, Anonymous to Conway, 3 Feb. 1972.

moved to Cork, beseeched Conway to lead the next civil rights march and join his people.[188] These Catholics called for action and public support, not platitudes and placatory sentiments.

Immediately after 30 January 1972, civil rights campaigners called for another march in Newry. The hierarchy received many mixed messages, as some Catholics wanted the bishops to join the marchers while others beseeched them to prevent the demonstration occurring. After Bloody Sunday, one wrote: 'The time for words has passed', respectfully requesting Conway 'to lead your people in a peaceful silent march to assert their right to walk in the streets of their cities'.[189] Conway did not take up this suggestion. Others warned of unionist violence against the march.[190] One correspondent claimed that if any priests were killed it would be the 'end of Christianity.'[191] The demonstration turned out to be a peaceful affair. After the march, Conway replied to one concerned Catholic:

> I have great hopes after today's peaceful demonstration in Newry. If only things were confined to this type of non-violent protest the world would be most impressed and justice would be achieved. But when people shoot men dead in front of their wives and children a good cause is dragged through the mud.[192]

Conway insinuated that while many supported the civil rights movement, when organizations like the IRA declared they sought justice for Catholics by murdering others, goodwill generated by peaceful events was lost. His fears were confirmed when the Official IRA bombed Aldershot Barracks on 22 February, killing seven soldiers. Conway expressed sympathy to the relatives of those who died, conveying his 'horror at the news of this foul crime'.[193]

By releasing statements condemning violence but not directly involving themselves in the peaceful civil rights movement, the bishops could not demonstrate full devotion to the cause. In March 1972, Conway released two written statements against violence yet did not commit himself to any public demonstration. Therefore, Bloody Sunday should be seen as a turning point for the Northern Catholic hierarchy. Following this event, the Catholic community in Northern Ireland began to shift their support behind their local priests in the fight against injustices, rather than looking to their bishops for leadership and endorsement. Institutional disillusionment among Catholics in Northern Ireland was a consequence of a perceived lack of action by the bishops.

The surge of violence after Bloody Sunday caused Prime Minister Heath to dissolve the Stormont Government. Both the clergy and hierarchy welcomed the

---

[188] CTOMLA, CCP, K.C. to Conway, 31 Jan. 1972.
[189] CTOMLA, CCP, B.M. to Conway, 2 Feb. 1972.
[190] CTOMLA, CCP, C.T. to Conway, 4 Feb. 1972.
[191] CTOMLA, CCP, Anonymous to Conway, 4 Feb. 1972.
[192] CTOMLA, CCP, Conway to F.D., 6 Feb. 1972.
[193] CTOMLA, CCP, 18-8-1 1968–72 Press Releases, 22 Feb. 1972.

end of the old regime, with priests in Belfast and Derry calling for the IRA to lay down their arms for negotiations. More than forty priests in Belfast stated: 'There is a choice to be made—a continuation of armed conflict or a cessation of it, followed by political action, discussion and negotiation...We feel that the choice must be for cessation of armed conflict on all sides.'[194] Fr Padraig Murphy, of St John's Parish in the Falls Road area of Belfast, claimed 95 percent of 'the people in the troubled areas now want peace'.[195]

With Bloody Sunday and the intensified Provisional IRA bombing campaign that followed, the Catholic Church 'began flexing its political muscles'.[196] The Church had always insisted killing was immoral and against God's will. However, sermons following IRA bombings were tempered by acknowledging paramilitary violence 'had its roots in real injustice'.[197] After the end of the summer 1972 Provisional IRA ceasefire, however, these balanced condemnations by the clergy slipped into what republicans perceived as one-sided denunciations of paramilitary violence.

Early signs of this politicized Church came with the death of nineteen-year-old British Army Ranger William Best, in May 1972. A Creggan native but stationed in West Germany, Best decided to spend his leave at home. Official IRA men warned the young soldier to leave twice, and he was finally picked up by an Official patrol unit to be taken in 'for questioning'.[198] When his body was found early the next morning, it sparked outrage. If Best had been an 'ordinary' soldier, his death would passed with little notice, but a community killing one of their own went too far as: 'He came home to see his mother'.[199] In response, 400 women, the 'Derry Peace Women', marched to the Official IRA headquarters in Meenan Square.[200] The Church called for a peace meeting at a school in Creggan, and RUC committee members, John Maultsaid and Frank McCauley, shared the platform with priests. The Church performed Best's funeral: a signal to republicans of a shift in the tides. Bishop Farren and twenty-five priests delivered the Requiem Mass, in stark contrast to the two priests assigned to fifteen-year-old Manus Deery, killed by a British Army sniper two days before. Best's funeral was an early example of what would become the phenomenon of the Requiem Mass and burial as a battleground between republicans and the Church. The soldier's high profile ceremony, compared to the teenager's illustrated the Church's differing reactions to paramilitary and state violence. The Official IRA were forced to refine their attitude towards the Church.

---

[194] *Irish Press*, 10 April 1972; *Fermanagh Herald*, 15 April 1972.
[195] *Irish Independent*, 10 April 1972.   [196] McCann, *War and an Irish Town*, 161.
[197] McCann, *War and an Irish Town*, 161.   [198] *Irish Independent*, 23 May 1972.
[199] McCann, *War and an Irish Town*, 161.
[200] David McKittrick, Seamus Kelters, Brian Feeney, and Chris Thorton, *Lost Lives: The Stories of the men, women and children who died as a result of the Northern Ireland troubles* (Edinburgh, 1999), 189.

Best's death and the Derry Peace Women reaction presented the Church with an opportunity to condemn the Officials. Fr O'Neill claimed the murder of Best was directly related to their Marxism; a political framework that O'Neill labelled an 'alien ideology'.[201] The Derry Peace Women and subsequent protests over Best's death provided the Church with clear evidence that the majority of the Catholic community did not support republican violence. Some young men may have been driven to rioting because of the climate around them but this did not reflect the entire Catholic community.

Partially because of Church pressure, the Officials called a ceasefire on 23 May 1972.[202] The Provisionals deemed this as the Officials caving in to Church pressure, and claimed no Provisional volunteers attended Sunday Mass or felt such 'hang-ups about Catholicism'.[203] The Church's reaction to Best's death demonstrated its increased politicization in the months after Bloody Sunday. This was magnified by the divided response of republicans. The Old IRA had a relationship with the Church, which was built on a shared history and struggle against English oppression. However, the IRA split saw the Provisionals dominant over the Officials which led to a rigid stance against the Church. By 1972, the Church did not have a coordinated approach towards the conflict. Frequent condemnations from bishops of paramilitary violence and their activity at funerals became commonplace for the rest of the conflict.

Republican criticism of the Irish and English Churches' actions over Bloody Sunday came much later. In an effort to demonstrate Church support for the British rather than their own people, An Phoblacht editors cited the Church's words and actions during Bloody Sunday as an instance of betrayal.[204] Over time, Bloody Sunday became a watershed event in republican memory, mobilized against the Church by republicans who used it in efforts to alienate people from the hierarchy. In a response to a letter to the editor in An Phoblacht, Ciarán Mac An Ailí wrote of the English bishops' silence: 'Not a letter of sympathy, or a wreath, much less attendance by a member of the English hierarchy at the mass funeral in Derry'.[205] This article followed an early piece discussing Irish bishops' double standard concerning paramilitary and state violence, asking: 'Are the bishops Irishmen?—or are they little Englishmen?'[206] Bloody Sunday became another instance in which the Church had failed its people for republicans. Yet for many in England, it was an example of the Church's collaboration with militancy.

---

[201] McCann, War and an Irish Town, 166.
[202] The Derry women and Catholic Church reaction to the killing of Best pushed the Officials to call for a ceasefire but it was just one instance of a further schism within the Official IRA; Bew and Gillespie, Chronology of the Troubles, 52.
[203] McCann, War and an Irish Town, 167.
[204] An Phoblacht, Nov. 1972; An Phoblacht, Sep. 1973.
[205] An Phoblacht, 18 May 1973.   [206] An Phoblacht, 2 May 1973.

With the exception of Bloody Sunday, the bishops only publicly commented on a very small number of civilian deaths by the security forces. Building on the data collected by Murray, McElroy noted that of 177 such deaths, 109 occurred in Belfast and thirty-five in Derry. Yet in all of these disputed killings, neither Farren nor Philbin 'expressed their concern…about the specific circumstances surrounding any of these shootings'.[207] Bloody Sunday, with its high number of causalities and media attention, forced the bishops to comment. While priests in many parochial settings reflected on civilian causalities, this silence from the bishops continued until Edward Daly became Bishop of Derry in 1974. Daly was relatively young when appointed at the age of forty and known for his frequent criticism of security forces shootings in his own diocese. Daly understood his community and their reaction to the conflict, as he had witnessed first-hand both state and paramilitary violence. Daly's appointment may have been strategic; a deliberate attempt to win back disillusioned Northern Catholics through the appointment of a recognizable figure. Certainly, his media experience, his strong leadership, and connection to the community, put him in stark contrast to his conservative predecessor.

After Bloody Sunday, with the growing IRA presence across the North, priests worked with communities in an attempt to protect possessions and livelihoods. The IRA often hijacked cars to move weapons and siphoned fuel from residents' vehicles to create petrol bombs. Priests helped Catholics locate their vehicles, although often enough the cars were damaged beyond repair. In June 1972 the priests at St Eugene's Cathedral spoke against these criminal acts at all Masses. In his memoirs Daly recounted these pronouncements had little practical effect, as 'few of those who were actively engaged in these activities were churchgoers'.[208] The Provisional IRA were also quick to declare their recruits did not regularly attend Church services. This assertion served the interests of both parties. The Church therefore could claim, as Daly did, that republican paramilitaries were not true Catholics. In contrast, the Provisionals could insist they were not under the thumb of their bishop. McCann nevertheless notes in his updated 1993 edition of *War and an Irish Town*, the desire for respectability the Provisionals possessed:

> In the Bogside throughout the Troubles few meetings of any campaign involving Republicans have passed without a proposal that a letter be written or a delegation selected to visit the Catholic bishop to ask for some message or gesture of support. It has not been uncommon for this suggestion to come from a Sinn Feiner who has not darkened a church door in ages.[209]

Even in these days of the conflict, some republican paramilitaries felt they needed the Church. Bishops lent gravitas, even legitimacy, to republican negotiations with

---

[207] McElroy, *Catholic Church*, 94–5.   [208] Daly, *Are You a Priest?*, 217.
[209] McCann, *War and an Irish Town*, 38.

the British. Individual priests acted as mediators and carried messages between organizations. Yet the Church condemnations of republican violence and republican responses to these statements left the relationship fractious. The battle for influence within Catholic communities continued until the 1990s.

By the time of the Officials' ceasefire in the summer of 1972, the Provisional IRA had openly declared their defiance of the Catholic Church. The Officials would fade in importance over the coming years. Therefore, the clergy's words from this point on would have little direct effect on ending violence unless they could address and isolate the Provisionals. Catholics mostly welcomed the introduction of direct rule from Westminster, as it recognized the failure of single-party rule in Northern Ireland. Direct rule was an aim of the civil rights movement, with NICRA chair Frank Gogarty stating in April 1969 reform could only come 'by the complete destruction of the Stormont regime and direct rule from either London or Dublin'.[210] Yet *An Phoblacht* warned its readers that direct rule was 'just the beginning', while the end of Stormont was a battle won, republicans had 'not yet won the war'.[211] The Church itself remained steadfast in its mission: end the violence and find peace. Appearing on BBC's *Panorama* on 27 March 1972, Conway explained Catholics 'passionately want this campaign of violence to stop'. For the first time, Conway directly condemned a member of the Provisional IRA, then Chief-of-Staff Seán Mac Stíofáin, who Conway believed had 'no right to tell the Catholic people of the Falls "No, you must go on. This agony of yours must be prolonged".'[212] This specific mention of Mac Stíofáin by the cardinal marked a turning point for the hierarchy, as they felt able to specifically name IRA Council members, even if they did not directly identify the IRA. The hierarchy's stance against republican paramilitaries now grew stronger and more condemnatory, contrasting with their earlier vague and placatory statements. The bishops' words began to acquire a more critical dimension in response to the even bloodier escalation of violence by the IRA. Politics from home required a reworked theology.

The hierarchy continued to make statements asking both Catholics and Protestants to redouble their prayers and actions for peace. On 31 March, Conway believed disaster could be averted in an ecumenical way through 'united prayer of a whole people'.[213] He released an almost identical statement on 10 April 1972,[214] and another on his return from India on 21 May.[215] Rather than make strong condemnations of the IRA's leader, as in his *Panorama* interview, Conway

---

[210] Frank Gogarty, 'The Development of the Civil Rights Movement and its Future Course', May 1969, PRONI, D/3253/3/11/5 in Prince and Warner, *Derry and Belfast*, 183.
[211] *An Phoblacht*, May 1972.
[212] CTOMLA, CCP, 18-8-1 1972 Press Releases, Panorama Interview, 27 March 1972.
[213] CTOMLA, CCP, 18-8-1 1972 Press Releases, 31 March 1972.
[214] CTOMLA, CCP, 18-8-1 1972 Press Releases, Panorama Interview, 10 April 1972.
[215] CTOMLA, CCP, 18-8-1 1972 Press Releases, 21 May 1972.

reverted to statements asking for peace and calling for prayer. Even a joint statement issued by leaders of the Four Main Churches requested prayers for peace, asking Christians to show their 'rejection of violence and their commitment to peaceful means'.[216] Fathers Hugh O'Neill and Martin Rooney worked with the Derry Peace Women in May 1972 to march on the streets and demand the IRA put down their arms but the hierarchy watched from afar, not attending these rallies but demonstrating their tacit support of peace through public prayer.[217] Conway commented in Portadown that 'the women of Derry have shown great moral courage' but he did not join them in their marches.[218] This lack of action by Church officials showed a significant degree of disconnect with everyday Catholic people, which reinforced the belief that the hierarchy was not proactively helping to achieve the ends demanded by congregations.

Despite Conway's lack of participation in peaceful demonstrations, the list of his sermons preaching peace sheds some insight into his plans. Between March and July 1972, the cardinal called for peace in seven different locations throughout Northern Ireland, from Moy to Kilmore, and once in Dublin.[219] By speaking at towns across the North, the cardinal understood the need to be seen to be engaging with Catholics throughout the country. He spread his message, and by doing so acknowledged the conflict challenged both rural and urban communities. Rather than making his statements from the comfort of Armagh Cathedral, which the cardinal had previously preferred, his itinerant preaching suggests an opening of the hierarchy to the conflict. Later however, as Conway's health declined, these tours ended.

Conway also commented on both the ceasefires by the Officials and the Provisionals in the summer of 1972. At a pastoral visit to Middletown, Conway welcomed the Officials' ceasefire and reflected it was 'the first glimmer of a new dawn of peace'.[220] A month later at Clonard Monastery, the seat of the Redemptorist Order in the heart of West Belfast and located between two strongly divided Catholic and Protestant areas, Conway focused on the Provisionals' ceasefire as his message for the day. Within his sermon the archbishop attested to Catholics' desire for 'an atmosphere in which peaceful initiatives may be able to melt away the root causes, both in history and in men's hearts'.[221] At this hopeful time, Conway reminded his priestly audience that 'responsibility must rest on everyone' for the 386 dead at that point.

---

[216] CTOMLA, CCP, 18-8-1 1972 Press Releases, Joint Protestant and Catholic Statement, 27 May 1972.

[217] *Irish Press*, 24 May 1972; *Irish Independent*, 24 May 1972.

[218] CTOMLA, CCP, 18-8-1 1972 Press Releases, 28 May 1972.

[219] CTOMLA, CCP, 18-8-1 1968–72 Press Releases, List of Statements by Conway from 1968 to 1972.

[220] CTOMLA, CCP, 18-8-1 1968–72 Press Releases, 30 May 1972.

[221] CTOMLA, CCP, 18-8-1 1968–72 Press Releases, 25 May 1972.

When both ceasefires failed, Conway released a brief plea asking those with power to bring these 'campaigns of violence and threats of violence to a speedy end'. His call fell on deaf ears.[222] Violence erupted in Northern Ireland in the summer of 1972, leaving many feeling helpless as to how to end the conflict. Both members of the clergy and the hierarchy continued to work towards peace, but they sought that goal in different, sometimes contradictory, ways.

The violent aftermath of internment and Bloody Sunday prompted the Church to condemn the British government, RUC, and IRA by name. At this point in the conflict, the bishops no longer felt the need to protect Catholics by not directly condemning the IRA. With the increased bombing campaign and the end to the ceasefire, with no immediate resolution in sight, the bishops could not allow themselves to look as though they supported the IRA in what was becoming an entrenched conflict. The hierarchy's shift from condemning state injustices to speaking out against the evils of the IRA marked a turning point in the Troubles. For the bishops, violence in their communities had become far more destructive than state injustices. And as a consequence, the IRA had become a greater threat to peace than the British government. The bishops' fears were not unfounded. The IRA would go on to kill more Catholic civilians than any other organization.[223] Those priests who still spoke out against British injustice and civilian deaths by security forces were now in minority within the Church. Protests, like the 1971 census boycott and the statement signed by 387 priests were not to be seen again in the conflict which had developed into a dispute of polarized opinions and entrenched positions.

Conclusion

From the outbreak of violence on 5 October 1968 to the end of the Provisional IRA ceasefire in July 1972, the Catholic Church's actions and pronouncements on the conflict changed considerably when viewed through the lens of its episcopal spokesmen. One instance saw a united response from both clergy and bishops: Bloody Sunday. This event united the priests and their pastoral leaders in their condemnation of the British Army and government's actions. Yet on all other instances, the clergy gave a more impassioned, involved, and pastoral response than their hierarchy counterparts, mostly because of their everyday parochial connections and interaction with Catholics in the North.

The clergy were slow to gain their voice during the early part of the conflict, perhaps as they believed, like many others, that the violence would not last nor escalate as it did. While they made many condemnations of violence, directed at

[222] CTOMLA, CCP, 18-8-1 1968–72 Press Releases, 10 July 1972.
[223] McKittrick, Kelters, Feeney, and Thorton, *Lost Lives*, 1477.

both the paramilitaries and the British Army, they realized their calls for calm proved ineffective by the time the government introduced internment. The next four years, until the removal of Special Category Status (SCS) in September 1976, saw the emergence of a group of clergymen and women actively campaigning for human rights and prison reform.

This key period defined how the Catholic hierarchy, under the direction of Cardinal William Conway, reacted to the Troubles. As the Primate of All Ireland, Conway steered the six Northern dioceses through the early storms, only effectively 'rocking the boat' during internment and Bloody Sunday by shaming the actions of the British Army and government. Despite numerous condemnations of violence, he did not specifically identify the IRA until after Bloody Sunday. It was a volatile and confused situation in which Conway needed to tread diplomatically. Regardless of which organization he condemned, someone was going to be unhappy with his leadership.

Increased communication between the hierarchy and clergy led to the bishops' statements becoming more informed and provocative. Instances of this alteration occurred on Bloody Sunday when the hierarchy, hearing priests' first-hand accounts from the scene, criticized the British government and Army directly. Possibly the lack of first-hand evidence in other cases prevented the hierarchy from making condemnatory statements against republican paramilitary organizations, as priests rarely spoke if they witnessed IRA killings.

The next chapter will examine the period after the Provisional IRA ceasefire in July 1972 until the removal of SCS in Northern Irish prisons in September 1976. The disconnect between the Catholic Church clergy and hierarchy would become far more acute in this period than at any time before. 'Bloody Friday' and Operation Motorman escalated the conflict to unprecedented levels, marking 1972 as the deadliest year of the conflict. The British government effectively introduced political prisoner status in June 1972 and, with the heightened number of imprisoned Catholics, priests, and women religious would spend much of the 1970s advocating for prisoners' rights.

2

'The Demands of Justice Must be Stated before the Words of Peace Find a Receptive Ground, 1972–1976'

In July 1972, the Secretary of State for Northern Ireland, William Whitelaw, introduced Special Category Status (SCS) for all prisoners convicted of Troubles-related offences in Northern Ireland.[1] This concession was part of a deal the Provisional IRA made with the British government during negotiations for a ceasefire in the summer of 1972.[2] As I argued in Chapter 1, persistent condemnations of paramilitary violence by both bishops and priests were one of many factors which pushed the Officials and then the Provisionals to call for a ceasefire. The prisoners now gained additional privileges as defined in the Geneva Convention for Prisoners of War, which meant that they could wear their own clothes and be exempt from prison work. Yet by 1 March 1976, the British government phased out SCS for all newly convicted prisoners. The years in between the introduction and abolition of SCS are acknowledged as the most violent in the conflict. This chapter seeks to evaluate the Catholic Church clergy and hierarchy's response to the increasing numbers of deaths throughout these tense years.

The Church faced difficulty in the months following Blood Sunday, with many young men and women joining the IRA.[3] Even Bishop Edward Daly, reflecting to the author at a distance of four decades, confessed that if he had been a young person at the time he did not know if he could have resisted enlisting.[4] Many young adults in the Catholic community ignored the calls for restraint by Cardinal Conway, Bishop Farren, and Bishop Philbin. Since the media and Protestant communities watched the words and actions of the hierarchy closely to indicate the Church's position on violence, these men confined their preaching to vague injunctions to 'Love thy Neighbour'. Yet by July 1972, bishops began to visit prisons in an effort to become more involved with prison communities. While their tepid statements against violence did not change during the 1972–76 period,

---

[1] Chapter title reference: CTOMLA, FDFP 1972, 'The necessity for a statement of the Church's teaching on the immorality of internment', 1972.
[2] McElroy, *Catholic Church*, 145.   [3] McCleery, *Operation Demetrius*, 53.
[4] Bishop Edward Daly Interview, 2 June 2015.

the hierarchy took further practical action between times in attempting to end the conflict.

Between summer 1972 and autumn 1976, more than 900 people died, making it the most deadly period of the conflict.[5] In combination with sectarian murders, the death toll rose because of the heightened campaign of paramilitary bombing. Like many institutions in Northern Ireland, the Troubles overwhelmed the Catholic Church. Both the clergy and hierarchy worked round the clock to make condemnations, fight injustices, minister to the sick, as well as hold funerals, and comfort families.

Throughout this chapter, I argue that relations between the clergy and hierarchy grew even more strained as a result of their differing approaches towards the conflict. In the previous period, the clergy focused their efforts on community work rather than publicly condemning violence and injustice until the introduction of internment. The clergy's public disapproval of what they perceived as the hierarchy's lack of conviction and co-ordination, especially towards British Army killings and British government policies, remained a continuous theme of the period. The rift between the more radical members of the clergy and the entrenched hierarchy divided the Church on a number of issues, including internment, sectarian murders, bombings, and the 1974–75 Provisional IRA ceasefire.

This chapter begins with a discussion of the Church's reaction to the breakdown of the Provisional IRA ceasefire in July 1972, which resulted in a series of intense bombings that lasted until the end of 1976. It continues by analysing the clergy and hierarchy's response to the growing number of sectarian murders followed by the growing politicization of the clergy. The chapter then considers the Church's response to internment after its initial introduction in August 1971, before evaluating the clergy's role in bringing about negotiations for the 1974–75 Provisional IRA ceasefire. It concludes with a discussion of the removal of SCS in March 1976, which set the stage for the blanket protest to begin in September 1976.

Breakdown of the July 1972 Provisional IRA Ceasefire

Thousands of bombings occurred during this heightened period of violence between 1972–76.[6] The clergy and the hierarchy both worked to bring lasting peace, albeit in very different ways. The clergy handled the day-to-day operations of the conflict, including ministering to the injured victims, repairing bombed

---

[5] Based on calculations from McKittrick, Kelters, Feeney, and Thorton, *Lost Lives*, 1473.

[6] Between 1972–76, there were 6,313 bombs planted and more than 3,750 explosions. Figures calculated from Bew and Gillespie, *Chronology of the Troubles*, 57, 76, 97, 109, 117.

churches, holding Requiem Masses, and working to rebuild the community. The hierarchy continued publicly to condemn each bombing. This period saw both the clergy and hierarchy attempt to keep pace with the onslaught of republican and loyalist paramilitary bombings.

While the hierarchy denounced the numerous explosions during this period, the clergy worked to build community relations. One such priest was Fr Seamus Shields, who created a community centre, the Magilligan Co-operative in Co. Derry. The centre, which opened in 1968 but grew in prominence by 1972, contained a zoo, café, and museum to bring tourism to a failing rural community.[7] Shields contacted Archbishop John Heenan in Westminster (see Appendix) to petition the cardinal for funds, for while his local bishop approved of the scheme, he needed to find the money elsewhere.[8] Shields' case illustrates attempts at a greater connection between the Irish and English and Welsh Catholic Churches throughout this difficult period. The English and Welsh Catholic Church would either raise funds for existing programmes in Northern Ireland or initiate their own aid organizations.[9] Shields' work with both the Protestant and Catholic community demonstrated grassroots efforts to build ecumenism, as well as improve the economy, by a small number of clergy members during the early stages of the conflict.

Priests also became more directly involved in dealing with the aftermath of the bombing campaign as they developed relationships with their parishioners. In his memoirs, Bishop Edward Daly recounted an incident where a Provisional IRA bomb exploded prematurely in a house on Meehan Drive in Derry. Three Provisionals had been assembling the bomb but only two bodies were found at the scene, leaving the community to question if one person had escaped the blast. Since the individual could have escaped, the Provisionals did not want to release all the names of the victims in case one was still alive and his/her cover blown. However, the parents of one of the suspected individuals, Jimmy Carr, were worried that their son may have been involved. Daly waited with the family throughout the day for news and then petitioned the authorities to view the remains of the two individuals at the morgue. Daly described the two bodies, barely recognizable in human form except for the buttocks of one victim, who wore red underpants.[10] The clothing confirmed the families' worst fears: that Carr was one of the deceased. Daly's intense and emotionally taxing commitment to his parishioners is an example of what many clergy members coped with on a daily basis, chiefly the effects of constant bombings on the community. Although, in this situation, the deceased was responsible for creating the bomb that killed him,

---

[7] *Manchester Guardian*, 14 Aug. 1971.
[8] AAW, HE 1-1-2, S.S. to Heenan, 14 Aug. 1972.
[9] Salford Diocesan Archives (SaDA) 636, M.J.F. to Bishop Thomas Holland, 1 Feb. 1974; SaDA 636, M.G. to Norman St. John Stevas, MP, 1972; SaDA 636, W.D.N. to Holland, 18 Aug. 1975.
[10] Daly, *Are You a Priest?*, 220–1.

Daly still ministered to the distraught family, as was his duty. The high number of priests in Northern Ireland meant that they would often be nearby when explosions occurred and many were the first on the scene to comfort the victims.[11] Priests helped their communities by administering last rites, identifying victims' bodies, and grieving with families. Therefore, priests witnessed first-hand the destruction of the bombing campaign, strengthening their passionate resolve to end the conflict.

The Northern hierarchy continued the policy of condemnatory statements after every bombing, regardless of its loyalist or republican origin. When the Provisional IRA ceasefire broke down on 10 July 1972, Conway released a statement that evening, appealing 'to all responsible for God's sake to have mercy on the innocent' and to end the violence.[12] The day before the official breakdown, British Army snipers killed Fr Noel Fitzpatrick along with four others during a shooting incident at the Springhill estate in West Belfast.[13] Conway sent Bishop Philbin a telegram with his prayers and sympathies following the 'tragic death' of Fitzpatrick.[14] Because of the bizarre circumstances surrounding Fitzpatrick's death, the hierarchy needed to tread carefully when condemning the death, so not to further the opinion held by some Protestants and Catholics that the Catholic Church was complicit in the violence.[15]

After the breakdown of the ceasefire, Conway met with the leaders of the Four Main Churches. While the group took no specific ecumenical action in the form of creating organizations or prayer weeks, they agreed that people coming together in prayer was the best solution. Unlike their earlier message in 1970, the leaders did not emphasize the non-religious element of the conflict. They kept their message brief, with vague promises to hold meetings in the future to decide the best way for 'the cause of peace to be fostered'.[16] In contrast, the Protestant church leaders' 1971 statement accepted internment as a necessary evil, forcing the Catholic bishops to phrase their statements carefully so as to not disrupt fledgling ecumenical endeavours.[17]

Visiting hierarchy members to the North from other countries became another increasing trend for the rest of the conflict. Cardinal Terence Cooke of New York visited Armagh to pray with Conway for peace on 21 July 1972.[18] Cooke was of Irish descent, his parents came from Galway, and earlier that year he organized

---

[11] McElroy calculates that there were 628 priests in Northern Ireland, both in dioceses and religious orders, in 1985. The estimated census for 1981 was 1,543,000. Roughly calculated, there was one priest for every 2,457 people; McElroy, *Catholic Church*, 196; Northern Ireland Statistics Agency (NISRA), 'Historic Population Trends', http://www.nisra.gov.uk/Census/Historic_Population_Trends_%281841-2011%29_NI_and_RoI.pdf

[12] CTOMLA, CCP, 18-8-1 1968–72 Press Releases, 10 July 1972.

[13] Rafferty, *Catholicism in Ulster*, 269.

[14] CTOMLA, CCP, 18-8-1 1968–72 Press Releases, 10 July 1972.

[15] Rafferty, *Catholicism in Ulster*, 272.

[16] CTOMLA, CCP, 18-8-1 1968–72 Press Releases, 11 July 1972.

[17] Rafferty, *Catholicism in Ulster*, 267.   [18] *Irish Press*, 20 July 1972.

a relief fund in his archdiocese for Northern Ireland.[19] American hierarchy members, particularly those with dioceses containing large numbers of Irish Americans, paid close attention to the conflict in Northern Ireland.[20] As discussed in Chapter 1, funds for the civil rights movement frequently came from Irish Americans and the Irish Catholic Church distributed this money. Cooke had been outspoken about the use of internment and, like his parishioners, felt shocked by the British government policy.[21] Over the years the connections between the American and Irish hierarchy members grew and resulted in the shipment of home-grown priests' pamphlets on Catholic injustices to the USA, strengthening the bond between Irish Americans and their counterparts in the North.[22]

Eleven days after the end of the ceasefire, on the day that would become known as 'Bloody Friday', twenty-two bombs exploded in Belfast City Centre, killing nine and injuring 130 people. Conway immediately responded with a statement deploring the explosions, stating his belief that both Catholic and Protestant Irish people shared his 'disgust and condemnation'.[23] Yet other than Conway's short pronouncement, the hierarchy did not comment further on the explosion. Republic of Ireland Taoiseach Jack Lynch asked for talks between the political leaders in Dublin and London and agreed with Conway's pronouncement: 'I am certain that this disgust and condemnation is shared by the overwhelming majority of Irish people, Catholic and Protestant.'[24] The NICRA called upon the Provisionals to end the violence, with Whitelaw also 'strongly condemning' the attacks.[25] A Protestant clergyman and father of one the victims, Rev Joseph Parker, took a slightly different approach and stated that: 'With God's help, we, too, can find the power to forgive and find the power to make a new Ireland.'[26]

The bombings increased during this period and, as they did, the hierarchy's condemnatory statements began to appear tokenistic and formulaic. Often they included a call to shared prayer, a belief that most Catholics did not support the IRA, a Gospel verse discussing endurance, and a statement on the individual bishop's abhorrence of violence. This formulaic response was a necessary reaction to the sheer number of explosions and the bishops needed to quickly condemn the bombings while also not alienating people in Catholic communities. The press expected the hierarchy to comment on an explosion immediately, sometimes before the bishop knew much about the details of the event. Yet, some bishops developed good relationships with the media, so this occurred less often in a

---

[19] CTOMLA, CCP, 18-8-1 1968–72 Press Releases, 19 July 1972.

[20] *Irish Examiner*, 23 Dec. 1974.

[21] Matthew Terence Peoples, 'The Catholic Church and the Northern Ireland Conflict', (University of Ulster MA Thesis, 2002), 23.

[22] Fathers Denis Faul and Raymond Murray regularly shipped their pamphlets to Irish American centres throughout the conflict.

[23] CTOMLA, CCP, 18-8-1 1968–72 Press Releases, 21 July 1972.

[24] *Irish Examiner*, 22 July 1972.   [25] *Fermanagh News*, 29 July 1972.

[26] *Irish Press*, 27 July 1972.

diocese like Derry.[27] Furthermore, the hierarchy's statements received less press attention as the conflict continued, as the media coverage of these atrocities grew, saturated, and then fatigued. As bombings became more of an everyday occurrence, column inches devoted to Northern Ireland also decreased, unless the bombings occurred on English soil or in the Republic.

Bombings in the Republic of Ireland garnered condemnation from the Church hierarchy both North and South. Throughout this period, the Provisional IRA, Official IRA, and loyalist organizations operated in Dublin.[28] At St Mary's Pro-Cathedral in Dublin, the Irish Catholic Church held a large Requiem Mass for the thirty-three victims of the UVF's Dublin and Monaghan bombings in May 1974. The bombing also killed one unborn, full-term child, which added to the tragedy in the eyes of the Church.[29] Archbishop Dermot Ryan of Dublin issued a statement similar to those released by Conway on the bombings, arguing that 'these attacks can only serve to demonstrate the contempt for the lives of innocent people' shown by the bombers.[30] Ryan acknowledged that it may be difficult to see God's divine providence in such attacks, but he urged all to pray to find strength for forgiveness. While Ryan lead the Mass, Conway telegrammed his condolences as he could not attend.[31] These attacks occurred less frequently than in Northern Ireland so they received more press attention and the hierarchy's statements were therefore more widely reported.

Unsurprisingly, bombings in England received the most attention from the English and Welsh Catholic Churches. By 1973, the Provisional IRA had extended its bombing campaign to Britain in an effort to increase public pressure on the government to withdraw from Northern Ireland. However, the bombings only occurred in England: the IRA did not bomb Scotland and Wales, as these were considered other 'Celtic' countries.[32] In 1974, the IRA on average planted a bomb on English soil once every three days, however many did not explode.[33]

On 5 October 1974, five people died in Guildford in bomb attacks orchestrated by the Provisional IRA, after they placed explosive devices in two pubs.[34] The Provisionals targeted these pubs because they were local haunts of British Army personnel. As the bombing occurred on English soil, Michael Bowen, then Bishop of Arundel and Brighton, released a condemnation almost immediately. Bowen also worked with the Mayor of Guildford to raise funds for the bereaved and

---

[27] Edward Daly, *A Troubled See: Memoirs of a Derry Bishop* (Dublin, 2011), 23.
[28] Hanley and Millar, *Lost Revolution*, 300–3.
[29] McKittrick, Kelters, Feeney, and Thorton, *Lost Lives*, 451.
[30] *Irish Times*, 18 May 1974.
[31] CTOMLA, CCP, 18-8-1 1974 Press Releases, 22 May 1974; Archbishop Dermot Ryan's personal papers will not be released until 2020.
[32] *BBC News*, 4 March 2001, http://news.bbc.co.uk/1/hi/uk/1201738.stm
[33] Brian Gibson, *The Birmingham Bombs*, (London, 1976), 50.
[34] Bew and Gillespie, *Chronology of the Troubles*, 95.

injured victims.[35] A message by Bowen was read at all Masses in the diocese on 13 October which stated that 'no cause can justify before God the planting of bombs with the intention of killing or wounding innocent people.' However, he asked the parishioners to pray to God to 'move the hearts of those engaged with violence'.[36] Even Pope Paul VI telegrammed his thoughts on the bombings, 'strongly condemning these and any act of violence' while adding his 'prayers of sympathy to the local authorities and those who have been bereaved'.[37] When a bombing occurred in an English diocese, the local bishop could condemn the actions and comment on the conflict without fear of damaging his relationship with the Irish hierarchy. An English bishop faced less public pressure from politicians, British or Irish government officials, Protestant church leaders, and the wider population. Often these English bishops had greater freedom of manoeuvre and their words were not analysed in the press in the same way as their Irish counterparts.

A month later on 14 November, James McDade, a British based member of the Provisional IRA, died when a bomb he attempted to plant at a Coventry telephone exchange exploded prematurely.[38] His death sparked even greater controversy when the Archbishop of Birmingham, George Patrick Dwyer, refused McDade a Catholic burial or Requiem Mass in his diocese.[39] Dwyer's forthright decision divided the Catholic community both in Britain and Ireland. Those who agreed with his actions sent Dwyer letters of praise and gratitude, like one woman from Hertfordshire, who blessed the Archbishop and thanked 'God at last someone in the Catholic Church . . . has a statement to make against wickedness'.[40] Others, like a woman from Cheshire, wrote that Dwyer's condemnation 'restored [my] faith'.[41] Many letters pushed the archbishop further, asking the hierarchy to excommunicate all IRA members. Yet around another half of the letters archived criticized Dwyer's decision. Some, like a woman from Belfast believed Dwyer 'had no right to refuse a Christian burial and Mass for this victim's soul', stating his actions were against the laws of the Church.[42] Others, like a man from Dublin, thought British injustices in Northern Ireland warranted McDade's actions, and he therefore should be given a Requiem Mass.[43] Dwyer also received a large number of anonymous hate mail for his decision. In the case of James McDade's funeral, it appeared Dwyer was stuck between a rock and a hard place. These letters were

---

[35] Southwark Diocesan Archives (SDA), D47.2, A.A.C. to Bowen, 14 Oct. 1974.
[36] SDA, D47.2, Bowen Pastoral Letter, 13 Oct. 1974.
[37] SDA, D47.2, Short Message Issued by the Catholic Information Office, 7 Oct. 1974.
[38] Bew and Gillespie, *Chronology of the Troubles*, 96.
[39] Birmingham Diocesan Archive (BDA), GPD-L-C4, Archbishop George Dwyer Statement, 17 Nov. 1974.
[40] BDA, GPD-L-C5, E. P. to Dwyer, 24 Nov. 1974.
[41] BDA, GPD-L-C5, I.B. to Dwyer, 23 Nov. 1974.
[42] BDA, GPD-L-C6, E.D. to Dwyer, Nov. 1974.
[43] BDA, GPD-L-C4, V.O. to Dwyer, 18 Nov. 1974.

strictly divided geographically: Irish writers disagreed with Dwyer's refusal while English writers congratulated the archbishop on this course of action. Bishops in Ireland and Britain therefore faced a fractured Catholic public on these issues.

A week after the failed Coventry attack, in the early evening hours of 21 November 1974, three bombs connected to two separate pubs and a bank in central Birmingham detonated.[44] Provisional IRA men issued an advanced warning to the security services around thirty minutes before the bombs were supposed to detonate, but it was too late: the bombs killed twenty-one victims and injured a further 182 people. The Birmingham Council of Christian Churches, which included leaders of the Catholic, Church of England, Presbyterian, and Methodist churches, stated that the bombers were 'motivated by malice and hatred', and hoped to 'spread fear and discord'.[45] The leaders worried that the anger caused by the bombings would extend to the substantial Irish community in Birmingham, many of whom were Catholic. The council stressed fellowship between all Christians, cautioning those against 'taking the law into their own hands'.[46] The statement included telegrams from the leaders of the Four Main Churches in Northern Ireland, who shared their 'horror and revulsion' at the 'frightful carnage'.[47] Six innocent men were wrongly convicted of the bombings and sentenced to life imprisonment in 1975. Eventually they were exonerated. These men became known as the Birmingham Six, and a campaign for their release lasted until 1991.[48] Dozens of members of the clergy and the hierarchy would privately and publicly campaign for their release throughout this period, which will be discussed in more detail in Chapter 4.

After 1976, the number of bombings greatly decreased. However, the clergy and hierarchy followed similar patterns of alliance laid out and well established by this time. Bombings by both loyalist and republican paramilitaries during this period were met with condemnation from both the clergy and the hierarchy. Since the bombings mainly occurred in the communities in which priests lived, rather than close to the bishops' houses or cathedrals, the clergy experience was different and more intimate than that of the hierarchy. Ultimately this lived experience tended to bring priests and their communities closer together.

Sectarian Murders

The summer of 1972 saw an increase in the number of sectarian assassinations in Northern Ireland. Both the clergy and hierarchy released condemnatory

---

[44] Bew and Gillespie, *Chronology of the Troubles*, 96.
[45] BDA, GPD-L-C4, Birmingham Council of Christian Churches Statement, 26 Nov. 1974.
[46] BDA, GPD-L-C4, Birmingham Council of Christian Churches Statement, 26 Nov. 1974.
[47] BDA, GPD-L-C4, Telegram from Church leaders in Northern Ireland, 22 Nov. 1974.
[48] English, *Armed Struggle*, 169–70.

statements of the murders but the priests also criticized the British government for not bringing the killers to justice. In comparison, the hierarchy felt unable to directly attack the British government's lack of action. Catholic priests wrote and distributed pamphlets both at home and internationally, hoping to raise awareness of the situation and highlight their concerns of possible collusion between British forces and loyalist paramilitaries.[49] Two of the most prominent pamphlet writers were Fathers Denis Faul and Raymond Murray. Anne Cadwallader discusses the importance of the pair in relation to their work as civil rights campaigners and activists.[50]

In April 1975, Faul and Murray published a booklet discussing an area between Portadown and Dungannon which was very rarely patrolled by British Army troops and where much sectarian crime occurred.[51] The pair accused the British Army and RUC of ignoring the sectarian murders of Catholics as 'a useful political weapon to crush the legitimate political aspirations of the Catholic community'.[52] Faul and Murray argued that the British government failed to acknowledge that there was a second campaign of violence in Northern Ireland being carried out by loyalists in order to focus solely on the actions of the IRA. Faul accused the British authorities of 'willful neglect'.[53] Their pamphlet included more than twenty examples of Catholics being murdered in this area between 1972–75, as well as letters sent to RUC, British Army, and government officials by the priests. An earlier pamphlet had exposed the British government's policy on sectarian murders. Whitelaw had claimed the RUC made 293 arrests over such killings in November 1972 but Faul and Murray highlighted that only one of those arrests was in relation to the assassination of a Catholic.[54] In 1974 Faul and Murray had also accused the Irish government of doing little to 'protect the legal rights of a minority in the North'.[55] There were consequences for the pair following from their activism. Faul, for example, claimed that the BBC had refused to allow him on television between 1971–74 and had referred to him and Murray as 'the IRA priests'.[56] As a consequence, Faul and Murray focused on achieving coverage through the international media and speaking to a non-British audience.[57]

---

[49] Anne Cadwallader, *Lethal Allies: British Collusion in Ireland* (Cork, 2013), 216–17, 274.
[50] Cadwallader, *Lethal Allies*, 34, 64.
[51] Denis Faul and Raymond Murray, *The Triangle of Death: Sectarian Assassinations in the Dungannon-Moy-Portadown Area*, April 1975.
[52] Cadwallader, *Lethal Allies*, 4.   [53] Cadwallader, *Lethal Allies*, 90.
[54] Denis Faul and Raymond Murray, *Whitelaws Tribunals- Long Kesh Internment Camp November 1972 to January 1973*, 1974.
[55] Cadwallader, *Lethal Allies*, 216–17.
[56] Faul and Murray Interviews in Peoples, 'The Catholic Church', 25; This thesis is the only source that asserts this claim. Murray did not discuss it in the interview with the author.
[57] CTOMLA, Fr Denis Faul Papers (FDFP) 1973–74, M.J.B. to Faul, 21 Nov. 1973; Interview with Mgr Raymond Murray, 11 Feb. 2014.

Faul and Murray were not the only priests hoping to raise awareness of sectarian murders. In an affidavit made in Dublin for the Commissioner of Oaths to the High Court, Fr Brian Brady of Andersonstown, said the lack of action was increasing fear and insecurity within the Belfast Catholic community. Brady believed British security forces 'were not making a real effort to track down the assassins' in contrast to their determined attempts to apprehend IRA members.[58] Brady's views were published in the Dáil Éireann newsletter, thus helping to spread the clergy's message outside of Northern Ireland. As the conflict continued, priests spoke at the USA Congress and the European Parliament to raise awareness of the killings.[59]

At home, priests continued to comfort bereaved parents and to work in teams to help the families as the level of violence increased. In one instance, loyalist gunmen killed two brothers: Brian and John Reavey, and a third brother, Anthony, died a month later from his injuries.[60] When the parish priest Fr Peter Hughes gave the brothers their last rites, another priest, Fr Con Malone, broke the news to their parents.[61] As discussed in Chapter 1, priests often shared the emotional and practical burdens of their work.

The hierarchy also condemned the renewed vigour of sectarian murders of Catholics in Northern Ireland. However, they tended to show far more restraint in their public statements. Instead, bishops often gave the homily at a Requiem Mass for a victim of a sectarian murder, highlighting the importance they placed on drawing attention to the 'second campaign' of violence against Catholics. Before the breakdown of the Provisional IRA ceasefire in 1972, Conway had already grown concerned at the rising number of sectarian murders after Bloody Sunday.[62] Equally, Conway was alarmed by a public that he felt 'tended to ignore the horrible assassinations'.[63] Conway worried that, unlike the outrage following the murder of three Scottish soldiers in March 1971, these deaths in July 1972 had drawn little public attention despite both incidents being 'gross violations of God's law'.[64] By November 1972, Conway condemned what he saw as a second campaign of violence by Protestant extremists. He hoped to bring attention to these killings as it was 'important for public opinion in Great Britain and throughout the world to realise that it exists'.[65] The hierarchy had previously played down the religious nature of the conflict, especially when they gathered with Protestant leaders from the Four Main Churches. However, it was now

[58] CTOMLA, FDFP 1974, Affidavit of Brian Brady, 5 Sept. 1973.
[59] Interview with Mgr Raymond Murray, 11 Feb. 2014.
[60] McKittrick, Kelters, Feeney, and Thorton, Lost Lives, 609–10.
[61] Cadwallader, Lethal Allies, 146–7.
[62] Rachel Kowalski, 'The role of sectarianism in the Provisional IRA campaign, 1969–1997', Terrorism and Political Violence, (2018), 658–660.
[63] CTOMLA, CCP, 18-8-1 1968–72 Press Releases, 6 July 1972.
[64] CTOMLA, CCP, 18-8-1 1968–72 Press Releases, 6 July 1972.
[65] CTOMLA, CCP, 18-8-1 1968–72 Press Releases, 14 Nov. 1972.

undeniable that some element of community violence influenced these murders.[66] Focusing on the period between August 1971 and December 1975, Sissel Rosland argued 'the construction of victimhood produced political truths'.[67] By drawing attention to these sectarian murders, the bishops' words added to the trope of Northern Catholic victimhood.

Conway continued his crusade into the summer of 1973. In his July statement, he highlighted a two-fold increase in the murder of Catholics since the previous summer.[68] He focused on the recent murder of Robert Clarke, a Catholic lorry driver from South Belfast, who was killed by the Ulster Defence Association (UDA)/Ulster Freedom Fighters (UFF), in retaliation for IRA murders as one UFF member claimed.[69] While his statement was reported locally, it did not interest the international press. Conway's frustrations grew and in November 1973 the cardinal pointed out that he had made numerous statements on the issue since May 1972 yet 'official' response remained muted. This was despite Conway's claim that the 'second campaign [was] carefully organised and planned'.[70] Conway said government attention to these sectarian murders was 'less than adequate' in the eyes of the Catholic community.[71] His words reveal his increased agitation at a lack of British government action and formal police investigations into the murders. However, unlike Faul and Murray, Conway failed in his aim to gain international coverage for his statements. As Niall Ó Dochartaigh has argued, international attention was key as the Catholic Church was strongly connected with ethnic Irish communities across the world but particularly in the USA.[72] World attention and politicized intervention from Irish Catholics abroad could help Catholics at home.

By the spring of 1975 sectarian murders were at a record high. On St Patrick's Day Conway spoke out in frustration, lamenting that 'brutal sectarian assassinations at the rate of three a week are no longer regarded as important news.' He went on to pray that this destruction of innocent lives would receive the media attention it deserved.[73] In April, the Armagh ecclesiastical diocese bishops further protested against the lack of reporting on the sectarian murders. Despite the relative absence of military conflict since February 1975, thirty people had now been killed with 'insufficient attention' devoted to the 'ghastly campaign'.[74] The bishops could not understand why 'in so many assessments of the situation it is

---

[66] Rafferty, *Catholicism in Ulster*, 270.

[67] Sissel Rosland, 'Victimhood, identity, and agency in the early phase of the troubles in Northern Ireland', *Identities: Global Studies in Culture and Power*, 16 (2009), 295.

[68] CTOMLA, CCP, 18-8-1 1973 Press Releases, 5 July 1973.

[69] McKittrick, Kelters, Feeney, and Thorton *Lost Lives*, 376.

[70] CTOMLA, CCP, 18-8-1 1973 Press Releases, 9 Nov. 1973.

[71] CTOMLA, CCP, 18-8-1 1973 Press Releases, 9 Nov. 1973.

[72] Niall Ó Dochartaigh, ' "Sure it's hard to keep up with the splits here": Irish American responses to the outbreak of conflict in Northern Ireland 1968–1974', *Irish Political Studies*, 10 (1995), 151–2.

[73] AAW, 18-8-1, CCP, 1975 Press Releases, 17 March 1975.

[74] Derry Diocesan Archive (DeDA), 'Statement by Northern Irish Hierarchy', 13 April 1975.

simply ignored'.[75] In April 1975, Conway accused the RUC of 'virtually ignoring' the eighty killings of Catholics in the previous three months and that the UVF 'openly boasted' of its murders.[76] Once again, the hierarchy used careful phrasing to avoid explicitly condemning the British Army or government, but it nevertheless drew attention to the lack of official comment on the growing number of sectarian murders.

At Christmas 1975, the leaders of the Four Main Churches released a public letter urging people in Northern Ireland to maintain hope for an end to violence. They asked Protestants and Catholics to cross sectarian boundaries 'in order to heal wounds'.[77] As an ecumenical statement, it placed no blame on any one particular group but instead focused on community aspects of prayer and fortitude. The churches could agree on very little other than prayer and hope being the best way forward to peace. The bishops also met with British govern-ment officials privately to voice their concerns. On 10 February 1976, Conway and nine other Catholic bishops met Prime Minister Harold Wilson at Downing Street. Conway asked where the UVF had acquired guns, to which Secretary of State for Northern Ireland, Merlyn Rees, replied 'Canada'.[78] Cadwallader argues Rees' response contradicts British Army's intelligence, 'which [revealed] that the main source of all loyalist weapons was the Ulster Defence Regiment (UDR)'.[79] This contradiction could reveal something of the British government's knowledge of collusion.

The English and Welsh Catholic hierarchy supported their Irish counterparts in condemning the sectarian murders, especially on St Patrick's Day, which became known as an annual day of prayer for Northern Ireland. Archbishop Heenan of Westminster rarely spoke publicly in the mid 1970s on account of his ill health. However, he did preach a sermon with the Irish ambassador present in which he spoke of the realities of sectarian assassinations. To many in England the conflict in Northern Ireland was remote; stories to be read in the newspaper rather than realities 'in terms of flesh and blood'.[80] Heenan urged mutual respect between all citizens of Northern Ireland. Since the conflict occurred outside his nation, Heenan avoided making direct statements and instead preached on the seemingly less complicated message of love.

After the 1972 IRA ceasefire ended in July, the Official and Provisional IRA had resumed their campaigns of violence. Representatives of the Provisionals held secret talks with a group of Protestant clergymen in Feakle, Co. Clare on 10 December 1974. According to Kevin Kelley the Provisional IRA had been 'putting out peace feelers through a small group of Protestant church

---

[75] DeDA, 'Statement by Northern Irish Hierarchy', 13 April 1975.
[76] Cadwallader, Lethal Allies, 274.   [77] DeDA, Conway to Edward Daly, 12 Dec. 1975.
[78] Cadwallader, Lethal Allies, 163.   [79] Cadwallader, Lethal Allies, 163.
[80] AAW, HE 1-1-2, Sermon by Heenan, 17 March 1974.

figures'.[81] Six days later, these Protestant clergymen met with Merlyn Rees. These developments lead to an IRA ceasefire that began on 22 December at midnight and was scheduled to end at midnight on 2 January 1975. However, the ceasefire lasted until 19 January and then resumed on 2 February for negotiations with the British government to take place. The Provisional IRA called a truce on 9 February, allowing for more open communication with the British government. The truce lasted until 23 January 1976. Both the Catholic clergy and hierarchy had worked privately to bring about the ceasefire and to prolong its duration, to various levels of success. Privately, mediator Brendan Duddy worried when meeting with Bishop Daly during the ceasefire the 'great lack of confidence' the Provisionals had in Daly to bring about any change,[82] revealing how little traction the hierarchy had with Provisional IRA at this time. The Catholic and Protestant clergy helped bring members of the republican paramilitary groups and hierarchy together, while the bishops spoke directly to the British government. By working together, the clergy and hierarchy helped organize and mediate within this period.

Redemptorist Brothers of the Clonard Monastery played a key role in negotiating the ceasefires between the Officials and the Provisionals by hosting talks at the monastery in 1972 and 1975. Danny Morrison recounted how in October 1975 the brothers urged republican paramilitaries of both organizations to 'amend their differences and not get in fights with each other'.[83] The monastery was a safe place for republicans of different organizations to meet. Clonard also played a pivotal role in negotiations between John Hume and Gerry Adams during the late 1980s and early 1990s, as we will see in Chapter 5.

As far as the British government was concerned, Harold Wilson and Merlyn Rees met with the leaders of the Four Main Churches in January 1975 during the ceasefire.[84] Wilson praised the Church leaders for planting 'a fragile tree (which one might call a Christmas tree) in the desert of terrorism' and asked how 'that tree could be watered and fostered'.[85] Conway cautioned that it was 'more difficult to keep the tree alive than it had been to plant it'.[86] Conway asked whether the situation could be helped if church leaders met with politicians in Northern Ireland to ask them to calm the situation and 'urged the Labour government to establish contact with' SF.[87] Rees warned against this tactic, believing the likes of Rev Ian Paisley would 'welcome an opportunity to reject such an approach'.[88]

---

[81] Kevin Kelley, *The Longest War: Northern Ireland and the IRA* (London, 1988), http://cain.ulst.ac.uk/events/truce/kelley88.htm

[82] NUI Galway, Hardiman Library, POL35-135–43, Brendan Duddy Diary Entry, 15 Jan. 1976.

[83] Interview with Danny Morrison, 29 April 2014.

[84] Conway; Archbishop George 'Otto' Simms; Rev Harold Sloan; and Rev Donald Fraser.

[85] TNA, PREM 15/515/3, Note of a meeting between Harold Wilson and church leaders from Northern Ireland, 1 Jan. 1975.

[86] TNA, PREM 15/515/3, 'Note of a meeting...'.

[87] S.C. Aveyard, *No Solution: The Labour Government and the Northern Ireland Conflict, 1974–9*, (Manchester, 2016), 63.

[88] TNA, PREM 15/515/3, 'Note of a meeting...'.

Such gatherings between the British government and the leaders of the Four Main Churches grew more commonplace as the conflict continued. However, it appears the impact these meetings had on British policy was minimal.

Bishop Edward Daly met with Merlyn Rees on 4 April 1975 at the Bishop's House in Derry. Daly described it as a 'heavy meeting' and he made four points in a subsequent press release.[89] Daly called for an end to internment, expressed concern over sectarian assassinations, denounced the court decision in the trial of Patrick McElhone's murder,[90] and cautioned against the return of a new campaign of violence.[91] After his consultation with Rees, a priest and layperson invited Daly to attend a secret meeting with members of the Provisional IRA leadership. They gathered at a religious house near Maynooth. Upon his arrival, Daly found Bishop Cahal Daly as well as Patrick Lennon, bishop of Kildare and Leighlin in attendance. At the meeting they discussed the 'ceasefire, internment, and the lack of British government response' to Provisional IRA demands.[92] The bishops received six proposals from the Provisionals to put to the British government, which Daly described as 'reasonable at the time'.[93] The Provisionals, whom Daly recounted as Dáithí Ó Conaill, Seamus Twomey, and J.B. O'Hagan, believed that the British government did not take their proposals seriously and that the Northern Ireland Office (NIO) civil servants were not passing on messages to Downing Street. Further, the Provisionals criticized the Catholic bishops for their lack of support.

Bishops Edward Daly and Cahal Daly travelled to Armagh the next day where they discussed the meeting with Conway. The cardinal assured the bishops he would get the documents directly to the Prime Minister. However, in his memoir Edward Daly admitted he did not know if Downing Street had responded to the Provisionals' proposals but he was 'confident that Cardinal Conway pushed the matter as far as he could'.[94] This meeting between three Catholic bishops and the Provisionals demonstrated that, at this stage, the Provisionals still believed the Catholic Church hierarchy held some political sway with the British government. On the whole, the Provisionals felt a lack of support from the hierarchy yet clearly decided that certain members could be counted on to act as mediators. As will be seen throughout the conflict, republicans continued to use some priests and bishops to negotiate with the British government and other nationalist politicians.

The ceasefire between December 1974 and February 1975, and the truce between February 1975 and January 1976 brought some stability to Northern

[89] Daly, *A Troubled See*, 46.
[90] A British soldier murdered McElhone while he was working on his family farm in Co. Tyrone on 7 Aug. 1974; McKittrick, Kelters, Feeney, and Thorton, *Lost Lives*, 470–1.
[91] Daly, *A Troubled See*, 46–7.   [92] Daly, *A Troubled See*, 48.
[93] Daly, *A Troubled See*, 48; These proposals included: the setting up of communications between SF and the security forces to avoid the spreading of false rumours of the ceasefire breaking down; allowing people under threat to carry firearms; ending internment; no restricting movement of peoples; withdrawing British troops to their barracks as the ceasefire continued.
[94] Daly, *A Troubled See*, 49.

Ireland. During the 1974–75 ceasefires, the Provisional IRA used the Catholic clergy and hierarchy, as well as Protestant clergymen, to communicate with the British government. Therefore they could claim they had made efforts to resolve peacefully the conflict. The clergy and hierarchy worked together to organize meetings between themselves, the British government and the IRA. Their efforts to both begin and maintain a ceasefire briefly united the clergy and hierarchy, with these months witnessing fewer priests condemning their own bishops for lack of action.

Growing Politicization of the Clergy

The early 1970s also witnessed the growing politicization of the clergy, some to a militant degree. As discussed in Chapter 1, more than seventy-one priests boycotted the census.[95] In November 1971, guided by Fr Denis Faul, 382 priests signed a petition asking for an impartial inquiry concerning allegations of prisoner torture after the introduction of the Special Powers Act.[96] Their militancy would only grow in the following years of heightened violence and their increased disappointment with the bishops' pronouncements continued well into the 1980s.[97] Chapter 1 revealed that Irish priests had signed a pledge and circulated it to newspapers on issues of internment and some of their counterparts in England did the same. In addition to this statement on civil rights, three years earlier, a group of English priests had used this form of protest to condemn the papal encyclical *Humane Vitae* in *The Times*.[98] In conjunction, these actions are symptomatic of a less deferential attitude to episcopal and papal authority. More than 100 priests in the archdiocese of Westminster also released their own statement on the conflict, with similar aims to that of their counterparts in Northern Ireland, pledging to work peacefully for civil rights in Ireland in December 1971.[99] These English priests writing on civil rights in Northern Ireland came from a variety of religious backgrounds, including religious orders and parishes.[100] However, what is clear is that more than half of the priests who signed this statement had Irish heritage, with these familial connections possibly influencing their stance. Their local archbishop, Cardinal Heenan, remained silent. As the clergy grew hardened in their stance on social justice issues, their militancy further isolated them from the hierarchy.

---

[95] McElroy, *Catholic Church*, 125.
[96] CTOMLA, Cardinal Ó Fiaich Papers 'Au Tuaisceart', 'We would like you to know', 1 Nov. 1971.
[97] McElroy, *Catholic Church*, 106.
[98] *Times*, 2 Oct. 1968.
[99] AAW, HE 1-1-2, Statement on Northern Ireland by Priests of the Diocese of Westminster, 31 Dec. 1971.
[100] They included one member of the Society of the Divine Saviour, more than twenty members of the Missionary Oblates of Mary Immaculate, Canons Regular of the Lateran, and more.

The Belfast clergy, in particular, grew increasingly disaffected with the leadership of Bishop William Philbin, who they felt was 'ill at ease in the street politics of north-east Ulster' and badly advised by his episcopal colleagues on his policy during the conflict.[101] In a farcical attempt to connect with his parishioners, Philbin published a translation of Greek poetry in 1973 that had little to do with the conflict.[102] Further, in 1974, he was the only hierarchy member to call on Catholics for unilateral support of the RUC and British Army. Oliver Rafferty diagnoses that this statement, coupled with Philbin's scholarly pursuits, exacerbated the distance between Church and people and put him at odds with his parishioners, who suffered greatly at the hands of the security forces during this period.[103] As many clergy grew closer to their own community through mutual experiences of checkpoints, bombings, and sectarian assassinations, others in the hierarchy became further distanced and more remote.

Many Catholics outside of Northern Ireland wrote to English bishops expressing concerns over the clergy's increasingly militant stance and public statements. A man from Cheshire wrote to Heenan in dismay about Irish priests criticizing the British Army on television, suggesting that clergymen 'should confine themselves to the spiritual side' of the conflict rather than the public domain.[104] Others, like a retired British Army Lieutenant based in Lisburn, but from England, believed that the actions of priests brought 'lasting discredit to the Church in general and the priesthood in particular'.[105] He wrote to Heenan rather than a bishop in Northern Ireland to air his grievances because he felt the Church there had 'no power and very little influence'.[106] A man from Surrey told Heenan that the hierarchy and clergy in Northern Ireland needed 'a spiritual kick in the pants' and that these men were ordained priests, not 'Political Agents'.[107] A Cheshire woman agreed and claimed 'for the first time in my life I am ashamed to be a Catholic' because the Church had not excommunicated IRA members.[108] Despite many frustrated people writing to the English hierarchy, the bishops did not publicly respond, as per an agreement between the Standing Committee of the Irish hierarchy and representatives of the Episcopal conferences in England and Wales, as well as Scotland, in January 1975.[109] As the clergy began to air their views in newspaper columns, radio interviews, and television programmes against perceived British government injustices, they became the face of the Irish Catholic Church for many

---

[101] Rafferty, *Catholicism in Ulster*, 268.
[102] William Philbin, *To You Simonides* (London, 1973).
[103] Rafferty, *Catholicism in Ulster*, 268.
[104] AAW, HE-1-1-2, F.F. to Heenan, 21 Nov. 1972.
[105] AAW, HE-1-1-2, A.T.P.M. to Heenan, 16 May 1972.
[106] AAW, HE-1-1-2, A.T.P.M. to Heenan, 16 May 1972.
[107] AAW, HE-1-1-2, C.B. to Heenan, 23 Oct. 1973.
[108] AAW, HE 1-1-2, I.B. to Heenan, 23 Nov. 1974.
[109] AAW, HE-1-1-2, H.M. to Heenan, 9 Jan. 1975.

abroad. However, the hierarchy still bore the brunt of public displeasure, as they were more readily accessible through institutional mechanisms of public address and leadership accountability.

Other cases of politicization of clergy were extreme, especially with Irish priests based in England. English Catholic parishioners grew even more concerned over priests aiding the IRA or even actively participating in the organization, particularly after the arrest of English-born, Catholic convert Fr Patrick Fell (see Appendix) in April 1973. Fell was the assistant priest at All Souls Church in Coventry and was arrested with six others after police uncovered a Provisional IRA bombing plot, though he pleaded not guilty to charges of arson and conspiracy.[110] The courts convicted Fell on all charges.[111]

Fell's superior, Archbishop George Dwyer of Birmingham, visited him annually while reaching out to the British government on issues of his incarceration.[112] When first imprisoned before their conviction, Fell and his six fellow conspirators faced solitary confinement as Category A prisoners for many months. In a show of ecumenism, Dwyer and the Church of England bishop, Laurence Brown, wrote to Home Secretary Robert Carr to petition for their release from their isolation, concerned for their physical and mental health. They asked that the prisoners 'have some form of association' but that this humanitarian request was 'no judgment on their guilt or innocence'.[113] In response, Carr issued special medical tests for the men, and the reports indicated that their overall wellbeing remained 'satisfactory'.[114] Throughout his incarceration, Sr Sarah Clarke (see Appendix) wrote to and visited Fell, sending him news of prison conditions across these islands and copies of the Vatican newspaper *L'Osservatore Romano*.[115] Clarke and her fellow sisters at La Sainte Union Convent in London petitioned British politician Lord Longford to advocate for parole for Fell.[116] Dwyer, with the Catholic Bishop of Leeds William Gordon Wheeler,[117] would continue to petition the Home Office on Fell's behalf on issues of access to the Mass, suspected abuse, and parole for the remainder of his eight-year imprisonment.[118]

---

[110] *An Phoblacht*, April 1973.   [111] *Times*, 19 Oct. 1973.

[112] BDA, GPD-L-C10, Patrick Fell to Dwyer, 30 Jan. 1972; BDA, GPD-L-C10, Joan Fell to Dwyer, 27 June 1973; BDA, GPD-L-C10, Patrick Fell to Dwyer, 3 March 1974.

[113] BDA, GPD-L-C10, George Dwyer and Lawrence Brown to Robert Carr, 16 July 1973.

[114] Wheeler was an enthusiastic supporter of the Second Vatican Council; BDA, GPD-L-C10, Robert Carr to Dwyer and Brown, 16 Aug. 1973.

[115] CTOMLA, Sr Sarah Clarke Papers, Box 21, Fr Patrick Fell to Clarke, 16 Aug. 1979, 23 Sept. 1979, 16 Oct. 1979, 10 March 1980, 11 May 1980, 5 Oct. 1980, 11 May 1981, 13 July 1981, 9 March 1982, 2 June 1982.

[116] CTOMLA, Sr Sarah Clarke Papers, Box 21, Clarke to Lord Longford, 19 May 1977.

[117] Wheeler's involvement in the conflict is discussed in depth in James Hagerty, *William Gordon Wheeler: A Journey into the Fullness of Faith* (Leominster, 2015), 253–60.

[118] Fell was sentenced to twelve years but was released in July 1982. BDA, GPD-L-C10, Dwyer to Roy Jenkins, 8 March 1974; BDA, GPD-L-C10, Dwyer to Merlyn Rees, 7 Oct. 1976; BDA, GPD-L-C10, Dwyer to William Whitelaw, 30 Dec. 1980.

Fell's incarceration sparked many worried English Catholics to petition the hierarchy, concerned over the growing radicalization of priests. An English Catholic wrote to Cardinal Heenan to express his concern that Irish priests had been 'setting a very bad example for Roman Catholics everywhere' and asking if Conway in Northern Ireland would condemn the IRA explicitly in his statements.[119] Heenan's personal secretary responded to the man that if Conway denounced Fell it would be 'unwise to add to the heavy burden' weighed on the priest.[120] Fears of the subversive Irish 'other' in English Catholicism were long held, fed by the rapidly growing working-class Irish community in Britain compared to the more decidedly middle-class English Catholics.[121] To many English Catholics, Irish priests in Britain appeared to be rhetorically, if not in reality, too closely aligned with the IRA's campaign of violence.

The Archbishop of Birmingham did not feel such qualms as acutely, however, and faced scrutiny when he suspended Fr Michael Connolly, a priest in his diocese who spoke at the funeral of Michael Gaughan, an IRA hunger striker who died in Pankhurst Prison on the Isle of Wight in June 1974.[122] Connolly allegedly referred to Gaughan as a 'great man' at his Requiem Mass in London near Kilburn.[123] In a letter to Connolly, Dwyer rebuked him, claiming: 'a priest must speak words of peace and reconciliation. Your actions can only foment bitterness and division'.[124] Connolly had made previously alleged comments supporting violence in Northern Ireland.[125] Gaughan was Connolly's cousin, and the priest appealed his suspension to Rome, requesting 'justice and a fair trial' outside of Britain.[126] His case was heard at the Sacred Congregation of the Clergy.[127] Connolly did not win his case, leaving Birmingham for the Republic later that year.[128] As these examples make clear, the most politicized clergy now refused to accept the English hierarchy's position on the conflict and this defiance became the most visible during the 1981 hunger strikes in Long Kesh/Maze Prison, as discussed in Chapter 3.

Some republicans admired the work done by clergymen who spoke out on social justice issues. Danny Morrison in conversation with the author recounted that some priests were 'much more in touch with the people' and did not 'live in big houses'.[129] He mentioned men including Murray, Faul, and Fr Des Wilson. Wilson had been living and working in West Belfast since 1966 and was assigned to Ballymurphy in 1975, one of the most impoverished areas of the city. More broadly, though, the priest questioned the actions of the Church, believing

---

[119]   AAW, HE-1-1-2, Y.A.K. to Heenan, 27 Nov. 1973.
[120]   AAW, HE-1-1-2, Heenan PS to Y.A.K., 30 Nov. 1973.
[121]   Harris, *Faith in the Family*, 35.
[122]   *An Phoblacht*, 5 July 1974; *Irish Post*, 24 Aug. 1974.
[123]   *Times*, 12 June 1974.   [124]   *Times*, 12 June 1974.
[125]   BDA, C.L. to Dwyer, 12 Dec. 1971.   [126]   *Times*, 13 June 1974.
[127]   *Irish Post*, 24 Aug. 1974.   [128]   *Evening Mail*, 22 Aug. 1974.
[129]   Interview with Danny Morrison, 29 April 2014.

'some Church policies and practices were damaging to people'.[130] Further, he thought that the clergy's great potential for social change was lost because of the strained relationship between the clergy and hierarchy. This assessment might have resonated with some of the clergy. For example, Wilson argued with Bishop Philbin over the need for clergy and hierarchy to be 'self-confident colleagues' and do away with some of the formality, where both clergy and hierarchy were enabled to freely speak their minds on all matters.[131] After many years battling official Church policy, Wilson avoided leaving the priesthood over his concerns by retiring instead in 1975 and relocating to live in his Ballymurphy community.[132] The hierarchy took his retirement as a means of protest, and he was forbidden use of any churches. Not many priests took this option, but by doing so Wilson was able to speak out against the hierarchy's actions and policies without risking retribution from his local bishop. This phase of the conflict brought to the surface many tensions in the Irish Church between the clergy and hierarchy, exposing a strain of anti-authoritarian and anti-clericalism which had existed in other European countries long before—for example the bishops in France and Belgium with worker-priests since the 1940s—but was new here.[133]

During the bloodiest years of the conflict, the clergy became more politically organized in an attempt to fight perceived injustices against Catholics in Northern Ireland. They spoke out in the media, wrote and distributed pamphlets, and visited prisoners, in addition to ministering to their parishioners. These clergymen and women then would remain militant until the 1990s, with a handful spurred on by their practice of liberation theology through their work and an attempt at experiencing the Bible through the eyes of the poor.[134] For some priests in the North, including McVeigh's and Wilson's diagnosis in oral history reminiscences, the Church needed to focus on the experience of the poor in order to create a just society. The actions of priests who followed the teachings of liberation theology further separated these clergy from the hierarchy during this period, whom many priests viewed as not focused or forceful enough against injustice.[135]

Internment

As we began to see in Chapter 1, internment without trial became one issue that politicized the clergy. Many Catholic families had family members or knew

[130] Des Wilson, *The Way I See It* (Belfast, 2005), 113.

[131] Wilson, *Way I See It*, 113–17.

[132] Interview with Fr Desmond Wilson, 1 Sep. 2014.

[133] Emma Bell, 'Disruptive religion: the case of the Catholic worker-priests (1943–1954)', *Journal of Management, Spirituality and Religion*, 4 (2007), 434.

[134] Interview with Fr Desmond Wilson, 1 Sep. 2014; Interview with Fr Joseph McVeigh, 14 April 2014.

[135] See survey results in McElroy, *Catholic Church*, 90–1.

someone who had been arrested and interned without trial. Some of the most radical priests viewed these people as 'political hostages'.[136] While many priests supported determined passive resistance by themselves and the laity, the bishops mainly condemned internment in press statements, while privately meeting with the British government to air their grievances about this breach of the rule of law and denial of natural justice. More radical priests however grew frustrated with the hierarchy's perceived lack of action, which further divided priests and bishops during this period.

A handful of priests began to visit the internment camps and prisons after the British government introduced the policy in August 1971. Regular visitors to Long Kesh included Fathers Brian Brady, Sean Cahill, Turlough Connolly, Denis Faul, Patrick Foy, Martin Kelly, John McKean, James McNally, Kevin McMullan, and Raymond Murray.[137] Some clergymen took a more radical position on internment and attempted to move internees across the border. Two men from Our Lady of Bethlehem Abbey, a Cistercian monastery in Portglenone, Co. Antrim, became directly involved in the protest against internment. On 19 November 1971, the RUC arrested Br Joseph Skehan and Fr Thomas O'Neill, along with two internees, after they were caught trying to help the men escape from the prison ship *Maidstone* and cross the border into the Republic. The RUC spent three days searching the monastery for explosives and weapons, ultimately finding nothing. When the courts found the monks guilty, they were prepared to go to jail but their abbot, Dom Aengus Dunphy, paid the alternative fine instead.[138]

Other priests wrote and distributed pamphlets on internment without trial. Nine priests who regularly visited sent their report, *Conditions in Long Kesh Internment Camp, The Maze, Northern Ireland*, to Prime Minister Edward Heath on 23 June 1973.[139] The priests decided to write the report after the suicide of Patrick Crawford, an internee in Compound Five. The priests had noted that the 'the stepping up of internment phases, changes in internment procedures, bad living conditions, unsatisfactory visiting facilities, and inadequate medical attention' had led to a deterioration in the morale and mental health of the internees.[140] After not receiving a reply from the Heath, merely a long letter from his private secretary, which the clergymen viewed as insufficient,[141] the priests issued a statement in which they asked Heath personally to respond to their concerns.[142]

---

[136] McVeigh, *Taking a Stand*, 101.
[137] CTOMLA, FDFP 1974, 'The Gardiner Committee' report on internment by Fathers Brady, Faul, and Murray, 4 Sep. 1974; CTOMLA, 'Au Tuaisceart', 'Conditions in Long Kesh internment camp, the maze, Co Down, Northern Ireland', 30 June 1973.
[138] Rafferty, *Catholicism in Ulster*, 267–8.
[139] The priests included Fathers Brian Brady, Sean Cahill, Turlough Connolly, Denis Faul, Patrick Foy, Martin Kelly, John McKean, James McNally, and Kevin McMullan.
[140] CTOMLA, FDFP 1973, *Conditions in Long Kesh Internment Camp, The Maze, Northern Ireland*, 20 June 1973.
[141] CTOMLA, FDFP 1973–74, R.S. to Brady, 14 Aug. 1973.
[142] CTOMLA, FDFP 1973–74, Press Release, 14 Sep. 1973.

Some priests went further and submitted evidence to the British government against the policy. Fathers Brian Brady, Denis Faul, and Raymond Murray drafted a memorandum to the Lord Gardiner Committee, a group set up 'to consider, in the context of civil liberties and human rights, measures to deal with terrorism in Northern Ireland'.[143] The Gardiner committee focused their findings on the policy of internment, and the priests, on their own authority, authored a report. Their memorandum included internee testimony, sample studies of anti-Catholic bias in the court system, the statement by nine priests, and their own conclusions and recommendations on internment.[144]

While attempting privately to sway politicians, Fathers Denis Faul and Raymond Murray also hoped to educate the public through their numerous pamphlets on internment during this period. *Whitelaw's Tribunals: Long Kesh Internment Camp, November 1972 to January 1973*, for example discussed the overall legal aspects of the policy and highlighted the harsh treatment of individual prisoners in internment camps.[145] The pair also distributed *Long Kesh: The Iniquity of Internment, August 9th 1971—August 9th 1974* in the same year, which similarly gave witness testimony, an overview of the legal situation, and individual internee stories to draw attention to the injustices of the policy.[146] Faul and Murray moved further to highlight the torture that occurred during internment in their 1974 pamphlet *The Hooded Men: British Torture in Ireland August, October 1971*.[147] When riots broke out at Long Kesh and the prisoners burned the camp, Faul and Murray wrote *The Flames of Long Kesh 15–16 October, 1974* to explain the situation and present the prisoners' grievances.[148] These writings circulated both within Northern Ireland but also in the Republic of Ireland, Britain, and the USA.[149] Faul corresponded with *Boston Globe* reporter Michael Barnicle, with whom he passed letters written by the internees and Faul's own reports on the conditions in the camps.[150] Faul and Murray worked to raise awareness of these issues and lobbied the International Red Cross, who cautioned the British government against internment in October 1971, December 1972, July 1973, and November 1974, after numerous visits to prisons in Northern Ireland.[151] The priests also maintained their connections with the Irish in America. In the 1979, Murray toured seven American cities including Boston, New York City, Washington D.C., and Phoenix to speak on Northern

---

[143] Lord Gardiner Committee Report, 1 Jan. 1975, http://cain.ulst.ac.uk/hmso/gardiner.htm
[144] CTOMLA, FDFP 1974, Memorandum to the Right Hon. Lord Gardiner, 4 Sep. 1974.
[145] Faul and Murray, *Whitelaw's Tribunals*, 1974.
[146] Denis Faul and Raymond Murray, *Long Kesh: The Iniquity of Internment, August 9th 1971–August 9th 1974*, 1974.
[147] Denis Faul and Raymond Murray, *The Hooded Men: British Torture in Ireland August, October 1971*, July 1974.
[148] Denis Faul and Raymond Murray, *The Flames of Long Kesh 15–16 October, 1974*, (Cavan, 1974).
[149] Interview with Mgr Raymond Murray, 11 Feb. 2014.
[150] CTOMLA, FDFP 1973–74, M.B. to Faul, 21 Nov. 1973.
[151] Faul and Murray, *The Flames of Long Kesh*, 12–15.

Ireland as, in Murray's opinion, it was 'difficult to break through to the media' because of 'the censorship' in Britain.[152]

Alongside their enlistment of the Red Cross, Faul and Murray regularly communicated with officials at Amnesty International, who asked the priests for periodic updates on the situation in Northern Ireland.[153] After the organization's conference on the abolition of torture in December 1974, the Secretary General asked Faul to help promote the findings.[154] Faul would continue his productive relationship with Amnesty International until the end of the conflict. Priests active in public and private campaigns to end internment demonstrated their determined stance, and willingness to move beyond Rome, to fight unethical policies.

Many in the Northern clergy felt that their hierarchy did not condemn internment strongly enough. Faul wrote a statement about the concern that many priests felt as their communities looked to them for guidance on how to react. He questioned why the Irish Episcopal Conference did not release an official statement on Church teaching towards the policy. Further, Faul believed 'the demands of justice must be stated before the words of peace find a receptive ground'.[155] Other Northern priests also wrote to Conway in this vein, urging him and the Irish bishops to speak out against British injustices. In his memoir, McVeigh suggested that if the hierarchy had taken a harder, more vehement, and public line on internment, it might have persuaded the Irish government to put more pressure on the British.[156]

In the face of inaction and intransigence, more vehement Irish and English priests began to petition hierarchy members in England to speak out on internment, since they felt that the Irish hierarchy was largely inactive. In March 1973, Cardinal Heenan spoke somewhat disingenuously on BBC radio about internment, communicating a belief that the British government was 'genuinely seeking a just solution to the problems in Northern Ireland'.[157] Fr Donal Gillespie based in Swansea wrote to Heenan, questioning his knowledge on the subject and pointing to internment without trial as an 'immoral, intrinsically evil and contrary to the teaching of the Church in *Gaudium et Spes*' policy.[158] The Vatican II constitution *Gaudium et Spes* urged the Church to take an active role in the world and to assume social responsibility in mediating conflict, as well as the promotion of social justice.[159] Heenan responded by touting his Irish heritage to

---

[152] Interview with Mgr Raymond Murray, 11 Feb. 2014.

[153] CTOMLA, Mgr Raymond Murray Papers, Box 4, B.B. to Murray, 10 July 1974.

[154] CTOMLA, FDFP 1974, M.E. to Faul, 17 April 1974.

[155] CTOMLA, FDFP 1972, 'The necessity for a statement of the Church's teaching on the immorality of internment', 1972.

[156] McVeigh, *Taking a Stand*, 109.

[157] AAW, HE-1-1-2, D.G. to Heenan, 20 March 1973.

[158] AAW, HE-1-1-2, D.G. to Heenan, 20 March 1973.

[159] Pope Paul VI, 'Pastoral constitution on the Church in the modern world', 7 Dec. 1965, http://www.vatican.va/archive/hist_councils/ii_vatican_council/documents/vat-ii_cons_19651207_gaudium-et-spes_en.html

contend that he was not on the side of the British government.[160] In June 1973, Fr Brian Brady sent Heenan the *Conditions* pamphlet. In a short note to Heenan, Brady asked the cardinal to help in ending internment.[161] Priests also wrote and distributed pamphlets to British and Irish government officials, MPs, and Members of Parliament—Ireland (TDs), in an attempt to change the policy. Faul petitioned MP Kevin McNamara of Hull North, providing him with pamphlets co-authored by himself and Murray.[162]

In addition to raising awareness on internment, priests gathered and distributed funds to help internees' families. Often, Faul and Murray's pamphlets included their addresses and stated that all proceeds from sales of the material went to help the wives and children of interned men.[163] Paul Fisher, the Direct of Public Projects at the Society for the Christian Commonwealth, met with Faul in Belfast, who agreed to act as Chairman for the Irish Relief Committee in North Ireland, and to receive the funds and redistribute them to 'suffering families of the Irish POWs' (Prisoners of War).[164] Faul also collected small but consistent donations from abroad, either personally distributing them in the community or depositing the funds with organizations like the Committee for Internees Dependents and the Armagh Political Prisoners' Dependents Fund.[165]

Some priests encouraged Catholics to peaceful protests through civil disobedience as a means to end internment. In some areas, Catholics held a rent and rate strike, refusing to pay their rent or their council tax until internment ended. This practice was a non-violent means of protest that took inspiration from that used by working-class Glaswegians from the 1890s to the First World War.[166] Faul supported this means of protest in his 1974 paper *The SDLP and the Rent and Rates Strike* in which he compared what members of the Social Democratic and Labour Party (SDLP) publicly stated in August 1971, to numbers on internment in May 1973, and statements by SDLP politician Austin Currie in January 1974. Countering political calls for Catholics to end their rent and rate strike now that the SDLP were part of the Northern Ireland Executive and had pledged to end internment, Faul retorted, 'promises do not release internees'.[167] He asked SDLP council members to either resign from their posts unless the British government released all internees, or to obtain an amnesty for all tenants in the strike on their arrears. As Gerald McElroy argues, the clergy's opposition to internment occurred

[160] AAW, HE-1-1-2, Heenan to D.G., 27 March 1973.
[161] AAW, HE-1-1-2, B.B. to Heenan, 23 June 1973.
[162] CTOMLA, FDFP 1972, Kevin McNamara to Faul, 2 May 1972.
[163] Faul and Murray, *The Flames of Long Kesh*, 2.
[164] CTOMLA, FDFP 1973–74, M.L. to B.M., 11 Dec. 1973; CTOMLA, FDFP 1973–74, Peter Fisher to Faul, 11 Dec. 1973.
[165] CTOMLA, FDFP 1973–74, J.M. to Faul, 10 April 1973; CTOMLA, FDFP 1973–74, Secretary of the Armagh Political Prisoners' Dependents Fund to Faul, 6 Aug. 1974.
[166] See Joseph Melling, *Rent Strikes: People's Struggle for Housing in West Scotland, 1890–1916* (Edinburgh, 1983).
[167] Denis Faul, *The SDLP and the Rent and Rates Strike* (1974), 1–2.

much sooner than that of the bishops and demonstrated a first fissure between the hierarchy and clergy on aspects of the conflict.[168] However, McElroy's assertion goes too far in this diagnosis, by ignoring some statements by the hierarchy on internment immediately after its introduction, as Chapter 1 has shown.[169]

In May 1972, Cardinal Conway paid a 'purely pastoral visit' to Long Kesh where he met internees, toured the hospital, and celebrated Mass with the prison chaplain, Fr Tom Toner (see Appendix).[170] It was the first time such a high level member of the hierarchy had visited the prisons in Northern Ireland since the conflict began. While this visit was delayed by nine months by the introduction of internment, Martin McCleery argues that the Church's opposition to the policy 'was reflective of the resentment to the measure that existed in the nationalist community'.[171]

Certain members of the Republic of Ireland hierarchy also spoke out on the policy. Cahal Daly, then bishop of Ardagh and Clonmacnois, gave a sermon in Cork on 29 July 1972 concerning injustices in Northern Ireland. Daly pointed to internment as one of the abuses of power used 'to crush human rights and liberties'.[172] In addition, Daly commented on sectarian murder, tarring and feathering, and intimidation, believing the 'bullets of the one side as of the other have no political labels', putting aside loyalist or republican identities to demonstrate 'we are only poor common weeping human beings'.[173] By highlighting these concerns, Daly attempted to establish the common humanity of all involved. Yet, as he shed light on the British government policy of internment, which mostly affected Catholics in Northern Ireland rather than Protestants, he sought to balance his statement with condemnations of atrocities by the republican and loyalist paramilitary groups.

In February 1974, Fr Edward Daly, best known for his involvement in helping victims of Bloody Sunday during the attack, became the bishop of Derry. By July of that year, he had met with then Secretary of State, Merlyn Rees, along with six senior members of staff, and the Chief Superintendent of the RUC, Frank Lagan. They talked over numerous topics, including policing, the British Army, the Community Relations Committee, and internment. Daly urged the 'complete ending of internment' so the hierarchy would be able 'to urge successfully co-operation with the security forces'.[174] Internment was the 'chief barrier to this' peaceful participation.[175] Daly recounted the meeting to Cardinal Conway in a letter, revealing that Rees 'did not impress' him nor did Rees have 'the charisma nor the ability of Callaghan or Whitelaw'.[176] Despite this poor account,

---

[168] McElroy, *Catholic Church*, 111–17.

[169] *Irish Catholic*, 19 Aug. 1971; CTOMLA, CCP, 18-8-1 1968–72 Press Releases, 21 Aug. 1971.

[170] CTOMLA, CCP, 18-8-1 1972 Press Releases, 5 May 1972.

[171] McCleery, *Operation Demetrius*, 60.

[172] Cahal Daly, 'The Way of the Cross in Ireland now', 29 July 1972 in Daly, *Violence in Ireland*, 113.

[173] Daly, *Violence in Ireland*, 114.   [174] DeDA, Edward Daly to Conway, 30 July 1974.

[175] DeDA, Edward Daly to Conway, 30 July 1974.

[176] DeDA, Edward Daly to Conway, 30 July 1974.

Daly also wrote to Rees outlining his views on ways to end internment after their meeting.[177] In April 1975, the pair met again at the Bishops' House in Derry for 90 minutes, where Daly reiterated 'the evil of internment'.[178] In his memoir, Daly remembers one comment from Rees, who wondered what his constituents in Leeds South would think of the proposal. For Daly, this comment highlighted the 'quandary in which Direct Rule ministers often found themselves—whether people in the North and their needs or people in their own English constituency and their needs had priority'.[179] British government officials were elected politicians in Britain. Therefore their actions in Northern Ireland, which many in Britain feared because of IRA bombings in England, could hurt their chances for re-election in their own district. The hierarchy worked with the British government privately to end internment through meetings with officials as well as publicly through their press statements. Importantly, they attempted to change British policy while also preaching restraint by the Catholic population.

When the British government announced that internment would end in 1975, Conway commented that he thought it was a 'wise decision' as the policy aroused 'very deep emotions'.[180] Further, Conway believed the end of internment would 'ultimately contribute powerfully to the cause of peace'.[181] However, it was too late for many clergy, who viewed the hierarchy's statements as lacking substance and felt they had lost credibility throughout the policy. In conclusion, while both the clergy and hierarchy spoke out against the British government policy of internment, priests worked to alleviate the suffering of both the internees and their families, as well as to report and record human rights violations. In public, the hierarchy spoke more moderately on the issue, while privately debating vigorously with the British government. In January 1978, the European Court of Human Rights condemned internment by claiming it was 'inhuman or degrading treatment' of the internees.[182] The policy had pushed many in the Catholic community towards republican paramilitary groups, as they felt powerless to fight this injustice. While some civil disobedience organizations maintained peaceful protests, the IRA's numbers grew significantly during this period, as a result of backlash against Bloody Sunday and internment.

Conclusion

In 1975, British government officials met to discuss the phasing out of SCS. The Gardiner Committee report in January 1975 recommended that the introduction

---

[177] TNA, CJ 4/1028, Edward Daly to Merlyn Rees, Aug. 1974.
[178] Daly, *A Troubled See*, 46–7.   [179] Daly, *A Troubled See*, 47.
[180] CTOMLA, CCP, 18-8-1 1975 Press Releases, 5 Dec. 1975.
[181] CTOMLA, CCP, 18-8-1 1975 Press Releases, 5 Dec. 1975.
[182] However, the Court dropped the charge of torture; McCleery, *Operation Demetrius*, 64.

of the policy was 'a big mistake' and should be ended.[183] A meeting held at Stormont on 26 September 1975 revealed that the British government had waited until cellular accommodation could be built in Long Kesh/Maze Prison before discontinuing the policy.[184] As of October 1975, 866 republican and 517 loyalist prisoners were held under SCS.[185] On 4 November 1975, Merlyn Rees announced that the government would end SCS for those convicted after 1 March 1976.[186] New offenders would now lose the right to their own clothes and would have to complete prison work. The first prisoner convicted after this date was Kieran Nugent, who began a blanket protest in September 1976 when he refused to wear the prison uniform after he was convicted without SCS. As we will see in Chapter 3, Nugent's protest would expand, lasting five years, and culminate in the 1981 hunger strike, with the death of ten men inside the prison. While protests against the injustice of internment now ended, a new battle began on SCS.

Increasingly during the period between July 1972 and September 1976, while the clergy and hierarchy agreed on denouncing bombings and sectarian murder, rejection of the policy of internment, and collaboration to prolong a ceasefire, their methods on each of these key issues differed. The clergy felt that the hierarchy did not condemn the British government vociferously enough, instead focusing their harsh words on loyalist and republican paramilitaries. Priests denounced the hierarchy's pronouncements as weak, further disturbed by the bishops' lack of comment on the British Army's use of rubber and plastic bullets. A handful of priests, including Fathers Raymond Murray, Denis Faul, and Brian Brady, spoke out against the British government in their pamphlets and speeches, rallying other clergymen to sign petitions against injustices, including internment and plastic ammunition. However, it should be noted that while many priests may have felt comfortable adding their name to a petition, only a small handful actively campaigned against British government policies after 1972. The notable exception remains the 1981 hunger strikes, which I will discuss in Chapter 3. It was far easier for most priests to offer a blanket condemnation of all violence, rather than to denounce specific republican and loyalist groups, in an effort to distance the Church from the violence.

However, the period did produce some members of the hierarchy who engaged more with the community, such as Cardinal William Conway and Bishop Edward Daly. Others, in contrast, retreated into themselves, like Bishop William Philbin, who found it difficult to relate to his parishioners. Between 1972–76, Conway and

[183] 'Report of a Committee to consider, in the context of civil liberties and human rights, measures to deal with terrorism in Northern Ireland', Lord Gardiner, 1 Jan. 1975, http://cain.ulst.ac.uk/hmso/gardiner.htm

[184] TNA, CJ 4/2214, Note of Meeting Held at Stormont Castle, Sep. 1975.

[185] TNA, CJ 4/2214, Kevin McNamara to Merlyn Rees, 22 Oct. 1975.

[186] English, *Armed Struggle*, 188–9.

Daly visited prisons, spoke at Requiem Masses for victims of sectarianism, condemned violence and met with British government and IRA members to bring about peace. While, individually their statements on the conflict sometimes condemned the British government, when speaking with the main Protestant church leaders or the hierarchy in the six counties as a whole, their statements were much more subdued. The following period between 1976–81, during the prison protests, would reveal a much more involved hierarchy, possibly because of the appointment of well know nationalist sympathizer Tomas Ó Fiaich to Archbishop of Armagh after the death of Conway in 1977.

After the end of the 1974–75 ceasefire, the conflict shifted from a short-term to a long-term engagement. From this period onwards, both the clergy and the hierarchy would re-orientate their efforts towards ecumenical relations with the main Protestant churches and government liaison. Increasingly after this period, church leaders of both faiths would join together to speak out against republican and loyalist violence.

3

'The Men of Violence', 1976–1981

In 1982, Pope John Paul II canonized Maximilian Kolbe; a Catholic priest who died in Auschwitz after taking the place of a condemned man.[1] When the Pope offered a reason for the canonization he paraphrased the Gospel of John 15:13: 'He gave his life for a brother.'[2] One year earlier, Robert 'Bobby' Sands quoted that same verse as the answer for his hunger strike in Northern Ireland's Long Kesh/Maze Prison, explaining: 'Greater love than this hath no man than that he lay down his life for his friend.'[3] Sands led the strike in an attempt to extract 'five demands' from the British government.[4] The prisoners had been working for these concessions since the beginning of their protests in September 1976. John Paul II made a failed attempt to save Sands by writing to Prime Minister Margaret Thatcher and sending his envoy to the hunger strikers. Ten prisoners died before the official end of the 1981 hunger strike, with each receiving a full Catholic burial on consecrated ground, despite protests. Archival documents reveal that between twenty and thirty members of the Irish clergy and Bishop Edward Daly and Cardinal Tomás Ó Fiaich reacted sympathetically to the hunger strikers. Unsurprisingly, the Vatican treated the deaths of the Provisional IRA and Irish National Liberation Army (INLA) hunger strikers in a very different way from Fr Kolbe's sacrifice, despite the mobilization of a similar scriptural interpretation.

Why was the Vatican reaction to the prison protests and 1980–81 hunger strikes so different from that of the Irish Catholic Church hierarchy and clergy in Northern Ireland? The three tiers of the Catholic Church acted in variance to each other because of their differing degrees of responsibility, physical distance from the conflict, and visibility on the world stage. Where some members of the Irish clergy could openly help the prisoners through their less constrained roles as prison chaplains, the actions of the Irish hierarchy were subject to intense media scrutiny. The Vatican acted independently from the Irish Catholic clergy and

---

[1] Chapter title reference: Pope John Paul II 1979 speech at Drogheda quoted in CTOMLA, Cardinal O Fiaich Papers 'Au Tuaisceart', Extracts from Papal statements and messages concerning Northern Ireland, 1969–87.

[2] Garry O'Connor, *Universal Father: A Life of Pope John Paul II* (London, 2005), 80.

[3] David Beresford, *Ten Men Dead* (London, 1987), 77.

[4] These demands included: the right not to wear prison uniforms, the right not to do prison work, the right to associate freely with other prisoners, the right to a weekly visit, letter, and parcel, and the right to organize educational and recreational pursuits, and full restoration of prison sentence returned.

hierarchy because of its global role and a desire not to isolate Irish Catholics or hunger strike supporters. This chapter examines these differences in order to highlight that there was no united Catholic Church in this instance and each tier of the Church acted in accordance with its own objectives and context. In addition, the further away individuals resided from Northern Ireland, the less positively they reacted to the prisoners' cause. Lastly, this chapter argues that the 1980–81 hunger strikes were a pivotal turning point in the relationship between the Church and republicans.

There is little consensus among historians when analysing the crisis of 1980–81. Scholars are divided over the value of 'human' sources and highly sensitive to their invested subjectivities, in contrast to officially generated archival documents. Some scholars prefer oral sources over archival ones, fearing a crucial loss of context when thoughts or conversations are translated onto paper. As Boston College's infamous oral history archive and other recent projects have shown, there are ethical and legal repercussions involved in publishing such material. Furthermore, the choice of who to interview, and their degree of confidence and candour, can lead scholars to very different conclusions.

What was the Catholic Church's reaction to the prison protests and hunger strikes in Northern Ireland and why? How did this response differ among varying tiers of Church leadership? How does the response fit into the wider context of Vatican diplomacy? This chapter will argue that the Vatican assumed a mediating role to the 1980–81 hunger strikes, in order not to isolate Catholics in Ireland from the Church. It attempted to accomplish these goals by discreetly contacting the British government and sending an envoy to the hunger strikers. In addition, the Vatican never excommunicated members of the IRA or other republican groups, despite the Pope's protestations against violence, especially in his Drogheda speech in 1979.

Throughout the prison protests the clergy did not always agree. In a handful of cases, the clergy became more involved in the lives of the prisoners because they were related to them. Yet many clergymen, as Fr Gerry McFlynn (see Appendix) notes, chose not to be involved in any aspect of the conflict and the priests discussed below were actually in the minority.[5] Consequently, there were very clear divisions of approach among the Church hierarchy. Women religious rarely worked with prisoners during the protests, with the exception of Sr Sarah Clarke in London.[6] This analysis allows for the exploration of ideas of masculinity and the hunger striking male body.

---

[5] Interview with Fr Gerry McFlynn, 6 May 2014.
[6] Sarah Clarke, *No Faith in the System: A Search for Justice* (Dublin, 1995), 28–31, 106–9.

1976–1978: The Blanket Protest

In 1972, the British government granted SCS to politically-motivated prisoners in Northern Ireland. However, this status was revoked on 1 March 1976 as such recognition was seen to fuel prisoners' belief they were engaged in a legitimate political struggle.[7] Six months later Kieran Nugent became the first Provisional IRA member sentenced under the new policy and he subsequently refused to wear prison uniform. In consequence, prison guards left Nugent in his cell without any clothes, so he covered his body with a blanket, thus beginning the blanket protest. Others, including female prisoners in Armagh, would later join the 'no wash' protest.

A small number of Irish priests became involved in an attempt to end the blanket protest. Fathers Denis Faul and Raymond Murray worked with the Relatives Action Committee (RAC), helping prisoners' families to 'keep the faith' when other clergymen and bishops ostracized them in their local parishes.[8] Murray was most active at Armagh Prison, which held mostly female inmates, where he was prison chaplain from 1971 to 1986.[9] Both Murray and Faul wrote extensively on civil and human rights issues, highlighting prison injustices and abuses of power in the system. Speaking in 2014, Murray repeatedly told me that priests like himself and Faul 'were on the ground', leading attempts to gain the public's attention and sympathy for the prisoners.[10] Along with Fr Piaras O'Duil, these three priests published numerous pamphlets on prison conditions beginning with the blanket protest, and continuing throughout the 'no wash' protests, and hunger strikes.[11]

There is no indication within existing archival records that the Irish Catholic Church hierarchy or the Vatican engaged in attempts to end the blanket protest at this point. A possible explanation for this lack of action stems from the minor media attention, and subsequent lack of wider public knowledge, concerning the protest.[12] Only later, when the protest became more severe and public

---

[7] 'The Gardiner Report', published in January 1975, recommended the phasing out SCS. On 4 November 1975, Secretary of State for Northern Ireland Merlyn Rees announced the end of SCS for those who committed crimes after 1 March 1976.

[8] The RAC was an organization of prisoners' relatives established in 1976 to defend political status of republican prisoners.

[9] Raymond Murray, *Hard Time: Armagh Gaol 1971–1986* (Dublin, 1998).

[10] Interview with Mgr Raymond Murray, 11 Feb. 2014.

[11] Denis Faul and Raymond Murray, *H-Block: The Caves of Long Kesh* (Armagh, 1978); Denis Faul and Raymond Murray, *Moment of Truth for Northern Ireland* (Armagh, 1980); Denis Faul and Raymond Murray, *Hunger Strikes: Search for Solutions* (Armagh, 1981); Denis Faul and Raymond Murray, *Hunger Strike 2: Why British rule has failed to solve prison problems* (Armagh, 1981); Piaras O'Duill, *H-Block: Can we remain silent?* (Dublin, 1980); Piaras O'Duill, *Hunger Strike: The Children of '69* (Armagh, 1981).

[12] The blanket protest was reported on much more in regional and national Irish newspapers. *The Times* published on the protests twice between 1 March 1976 and 1 March 1978; *Times*, 24 Nov. 1976; *Times*, 12 Sep. 1977. In the same period, *The Guardian* published four articles on the blanket protest; *Guardian*, 10 Nov. 1976; 23 Nov. 1976; 15 Aug. 1977; 3 Jan. 1978.

consciousness became more pronounced, did the hierarchy or Vatican take action and make statements concerning the prison situation.

1978–1980: The 'No Wash' or 'Dirty' Protest

In March 1978, the prison protests escalated to the 'no wash' or 'dirty' protest. This saw prisoners refusing to wash or 'slop out' their chamber pots, smearing their excreta on their cell walls. This proved the catalyst for more Irish Catholic clergy members becoming involved in raising awareness of the prison protests and conditions. Fr Joe McVeigh was one who began visiting the prisons. McVeigh was committed to liberation theology, a Catholic theological perspective which interprets the teachings of Jesus Christ in socio-economic and incarnational terms as requiring contestation of unjust economic and political conditions. In June 1978, McVeigh wrote a pamphlet in which he discussed how these ideas might be put into practice in the North. McVeigh acknowledged his views may be controversial to some, and wrote: 'Any talk of liberation is often considered dangerous and disturbing'.[13] However, McVeigh concluded, 'counter violence is counter productive', presenting further the Church's message of passive resistance.[14]

In addition to clergymen, by 1978 the Irish hierarchy was attempting to end the protests through meetings with British government officials, visiting the prisons, and public statements condemning prison conditions. The death of the conservative Cardinal William Conway, on 17 April 1977, paved the way for this change in approach. Pope Paul VI appointed President of Maynooth, Tomas Ó Fiaich, to the post of Archbishop of Armagh in August 1977. Friends and colleagues described Ó Fiaich, raised in the predominantly nationalist village of Crossmaglen, as a decidedly informal man who possessed a 'genuine love of people'.[15] The Dublin government initially welcomed his appointment, with the Taoiseach hosting a party in his honour.[16] In a features interview with *The Belfast Telegraph*, Ó Fiaich emphasized that he wanted complete separation of Church and state, appeared open to mixed marriages, and emphasized that he held 'the highest respect for the local Protestant clergy'.[17] Notably, on Irish unity, the new cardinal said: 'In the long run it is the people of the North who will be in charge. It doesn't

---

[13] Joe McVeigh, *Some Thoughts on Liberation Theology*, (Belfast, 1978), 3.

[14] McVeigh, *Some Thoughts*, 3.

[15] Billy Fitzgerald, *Father Tom: An Authorised Portrait of Cardinal Tomas Ó Fiaich* (London, 1990), 17–18.

[16] Later, no representative from the Dublin government would attend his appointment as cardinal, despite the Taoiseach Sean Lemass attending Cardinal William Conway's elevation ceremony in 1965. Official documents reveal that Irish government officials declined to send a delegation. Ó Fiaich would be the only appointee at the ceremony whose home country government did not send an official to the Holy See for the event. This snub resulted in many questioning the Dublin government's relationship with the new cardinal; National Archives of Ireland (NAI)/DFA/2009/120/206.

[17] *Belfast Telegraph*, 14 Oct. 1977.

matter what London or Dublin say. Basically it has to be solved here'.[18] This frankness on politics troubled many, including Cardinal Basil Hume of Westminster (see Appendix), who assured a Foreign Press Association luncheon that his Irish counterpart must have been 'misquoted or quoted out of context'.[19] Ó Fiaich's outspokenness would cause friction between himself and more conservative members of the Church establishment throughout the remainder of his tenure. Nevertheless, on 30 June 1979, Pope John Paul II appointed Ó Fiaich as the Cardinal-Priest of the S. Patrizio titular church in Rome.

Ó Fiaich had become involved in the prison protests before being made cardinal. After becoming archbishop in August 1977, prisoners' families spoke with Ó Fiaich and asked him to help their sons who 'were living in hellish conditions'.[20] Before his first visit to Long Kesh/Maze Prison in July 1978, Ó Fiaich met with the UK Secretary of State for Northern Ireland, Roy Mason.[21] Mason's dismissive attitude prompted Ó Fiaich to release a statement on 1 August. Firstly, Ó Fiaich said he was preparing a report on prison conditions for the Pope, which would include testimonies from prisoners who claimed to have been beaten. Secondly, he contended that non-conformity with prison regulations should not result in a loss of remission. Thirdly, Ó Fiaich argued these prisoners were no different from other, non-political prisoners and the authorities should not treat them as such. He concluded: 'One would hardly allow an animal to remain in such conditions, let alone a human being. The nearest approach to it that I have seen was the spectacle of hundreds of homeless people living in sewer pipes in the slums of Calcutta.'[22]

Ó Fiaich's words shocked the British establishment and Protestant leaders, with the Protestant community and *The Times* accusing him of supporting the IRA.[23] The NIO issued a statement attempting to discredit Ó Fiaich's claims by reminding the general public that these were conditions the prisoners had imposed upon themselves.[24] Perhaps the most important effect of Ó Fiaich's statement was that it placed the prison protests on the international news agenda, with the American press reporting excerpts of his speech.[25] Prior to his statement he had also given an interview to *The Irish Press*, in which he suggested that the British government should issue a letter of intent to withdraw from the North.[26] Despite his

---

[18] *Belfast Telegraph*, 14 Oct. 1977.
[19] NAI, DFA/2011/46/3, Telegram from London Embassy to Dublin, 19 Jan. 1978.
[20] Interview with Danny Morrison, 29 April 2014.
[21] TNA, CJ 4/2036/2, Note for the Record of the Meeting with Archbishop Ó Fiaich, 28 July 1978.
[22] *Irish Press*, 3 Aug. 1978.
[23] CTOMLA, 'Au Tuaisceart', Fr Clyne letter to Rev R.V.A. Lynas, 9 Aug. 1978; CTOMLA, 'Au Tuaisceart', Rev R.V.A. Lynas letter to Clyne, 17 Nov. 1978; *Times*, 3 Aug. 1978.
[24] TNA, CJ 4/2036/2, NIO Press Office Release in response to Ó Fiaich's statements on H block conditions, 1 Aug. 1978.
[25] TNA, CJ 4/2036/2, Reports of USA media reaction to Cardinal Ó Fiaich's statement, 2 Aug. 1978.
[26] *Irish Press*, 15 Jan. 1978.

condemnation of violence, these public statements meant republican prisoners, irrespective of personal beliefs, enjoyed good relationships with Ó Fiaich.[27]

Ó Fiaich's statements, and the international attention they generated, marked a new phase in diplomatic relations regarding the protests. Prior to the furore unleashed by Ó Fiaich's views, Mason had been working with the English and Welsh Apostolic Delegate, Archbishop Bruno Heim, on behalf of the British government. Mason was asked to make contact as Heim had told the British government that Pope Paul VI had received a petition with 200 signatures asking the Pope to show support for prison concessions. Heim reportedly told Mason: 'The Vatican's line had been to wonder why a humanitarian gesture could not be made by HMG', (Her Majesty's Government), to which Mason replied that the prisoners imposed such conditions on themselves.[28] Ó Fiaich's unexpected intervention increased the necessity for immediate action, especially as it had the support of the Irish Papal Nuncio, Archbishop Gaetano Alibrandi. The British government now felt they needed someone inside the Vatican to promote their perspective in relation to the prison protests. A further concern was the support the Provisional IRA received from Irish Americans which might now be increased. In a departmental circular on 10 May 1978, NIO private secretary J.D.W. Janes debriefed on Mason's lunch with Heim on 27 April:

> We have taken some steps to cultivate the Apostolic Delegate in the hope that this may help to ensure that the Holy See receive some accurate information and may therefore be restrained from making public condemnatory statements which could embarrass us internationally - an international embarrassment for example with Irish Catholics in the States can mean funds and arms for the PIRA.[29]

NIO officials hoped that if they could develop a relationship with Heim, who had been the English Apostolic Delegate since 1972, they could effectively give the Vatican a different version of the political landscape than that presented by the Irish Catholic hierarchy. Additional correspondence between NIO officials Thompson and Nielson revealed that by giving Heim diplomatic status, the British government believed he 'could be of value in balancing the information and attitudes fed to the Vatican by Mgr Alibrandi in Dublin'.[30] The British government had barely engaged with Heim before the protests began but it now became clear that they needed a voice within the Catholic hierarchy to promote their viewpoint to the Vatican.

A lack of clear engagement with the protests from the Vatican could be explained by 1978 being the extraordinary 'year of three popes.'[31] Pope Paul VI,

[27] Interview with Dr Laurence McKeown, 15 April 2014.
[28] TNA, CJ 4/2036/1, J.G. Pilling to J.D.W. Janes, 27 April 1978.
[29] TNA, CJ 4/2036/2, J.D.W. Janes Departmental Circular, 10 May 1978.
[30] TNA, CJ 4/2036/1, J.A. Thompson to Nielson, 10 March 1978.
[31] Peter Hebblethwaite, *The Year of Three Popes* (London, 1978), vii.

elected in 1963, died on 6 August 1978 after years of ill health. His successor, Pope John Paul I was elected by the College of Cardinals on 26 August but died thirty-three days later of a heart attack. Next came the Polish-born Karol Józef Wojtyla, elected on 16 October 1978, who chose the name Pope John Paul II to honour his predecessor.

Pope John Paul II would be proclaimed the 'Pilgrim Pope' for his extensive overseas visits during his lifetime.[32] He spent two days in Ireland in 1979 with the Irish press reporting everything from the colour of the blanket on his aeroplane's bed to the first glimpse of Ireland he would see from the aeroplane's windows, as this was the first visit of a Pope since the founding of the religion.

Biographer Garry O'Connor wrote that the Pope was seen proportionally by more people in Ireland than on any other of his foreign visits. More than 1,200,000 people heard his address at Phoenix Park, Dublin on 29 September. During his speech, he spoke of the persecution of the Irish (presumably by the British, although not explicitly stated) and related this struggle to his own native Poland's resistance against the Soviet Union and Communism. Crucially, the papal visit was meant to include a stay in Armagh, with Ó Fiaich extending an invitation. However, the visit was cancelled following the Provisional IRA's assassination of Lord Mountbatten and three others on a fishing boat in Sligo, and a bomb attack that killed eighteen soldiers at the Narrow Water in South Down.[33] If the Pope visited Northern Ireland, he could have jeopardized his own safety and the British press could have accused him of favouring a violent community. Nevertheless, at Drogheda, just thirty miles from the border, the Pope addressed an audience of 250,000 and beseeched the crowd, exclaiming:

> Now I wish to speak to all men and women engaged in violence. I appeal to you, in language of passionate pleading. On my knees I beg you to turn away from the paths of violence and to return to the ways of peace. You may claim to seek justice. Violence destroys the work of justice. Further violence in Ireland will only drag down to ruin the land you claim to love and the values you claim to cherish.[34]

At this address the Pope asked young people to reject the terrorists. He implored parents to teach their children about love and forgiveness. Finally, he invited those with political authority to 'show there is a peaceful, political way to justice.'[35]

The Provisionals responded to the Pope's speech by belittling his words. A Provisional IRA spokesman pointed out that the Pope was not in fact on his knees, but standing at a microphone to deliver the speech. An editorial for

---

[32]   As pontificate, he visited 129 countries; O'Connor, *Universal Father*, 218.

[33]   Liam Clarke, *Broadening the Battlefield: The H-Blocks and the Rise of Sinn Féin* (Dublin, 1987), 100.

[34]   Pope John Paul II, *Pilgrimage of Peace: The Collected Speeches of John Paul II in Ireland and the United States* (London, 1980), 18.

[35]   Pope John Paul II, *Pilgrimage of Peace*, 18.

An Phoblacht/Republican News stated: 'We know also that upon victory, the Church will have no difficulty in recognising us.'[36] A precedent had been set in the 1920s when the Vatican recognized the relationship between the Catholic Church and the IRA.[37] SF's director of publicity, Danny Morrison, saw the Pope's speech as one-sided and ignorant of loyalist violence.[38] Morrison highlighted that the Pope referred to the 'men of violence', which was the British government term for republican paramilitaries at the time.[39] By belittling the Pope and portraying him as a foreigner, the Provisionals distanced themselves from his message of peace and depicted him as out of touch with everyday Irish Catholics.

Morrison also insisted that the Provisional IRA, in contrast with earlier organizations, had become more anti-clerical and its members were often lapsed Catholics. Yet there exists little evidence to substantiate this claim. By the 1960s, Ireland had experienced two decades of rapid economic growth. This new wealth led to an increase in consumer growth and a decline in Church attendance.[40] Although the number of practising Irish Catholics remained higher than in most countries, attendance had begun to fall in the Republic from 94 percent in 1968 to 91 percent in 1974 and 87 percent by 1984.[41] Some have argued that the Pope suggested that materialism paved the way for violence through his Ireland speeches.[42] John Paul II believed economic growth led followers to turn away from the Church and seek instant gratification through material goods. To the outside world, the Pope's visit may have appeared as if 'Irish' and 'Catholic' still belonged together, as they had for centuries.[43]

The clergy, hierarchy, and Pope's actions demonstrate different ways of handling the prisons protests in Northern Ireland. Priests including Faul, Murray, Alec Reid, Oliver Crilly, John Murphy, and Tom Toner (see Appendix) saw the prisoners on a regular basis through their pastoral duties and consequently maintained direct relationships with the protestors, as discussed below. In comparison, Cardinal Ó Fiaich visited the protestors only a handful of times but made a powerful public statement in their defence and held meetings with British government officials.[44] The Pope did not visit Northern Ireland, but condemned violence generally and asked those committing crimes to stop.

---

[36] *An Phoblacht/Republican News*, 2 Oct. 1979.
[37] TNA, PCOM 8/349, Prison note concerning the condition of Terence MacSwiney by Dr W. D. Higson, 29 Aug. 1920.
[38] Interview with Danny Morrison, 29 April 2014.
[39] Interview with Danny Morrison, 29 April 2014.
[40] James S. Donnelly Jr, 'The troubled contemporary Irish Catholic Church', in Brendan Bradshaw and Dáire Keogh (eds.), *Christianity in Ireland: Revisiting the Story* (Dublin, 2002), 271.
[41] Louise Fuller, *Irish Catholicism since 1950: The Undoing of a Culture* (Dublin, 2004), 250.
[42] O'Connor, *Universal Father*, 220.
[43] Donnelly, 'Irish Catholic Church', 271.
[44] PRONI, NIO/12/68, 'Archbishop Ó Fiaich's Statement on Maze Prison', 1 Aug. 1978; TNA, CJ 4/3035, 'Note for the Record, Maze: The Dirty Protest', 28 Feb. 1980.

Although all three groups wanted to see an end to the violence, clergymen and the Irish hierarchy often also held nationalist beliefs. The Polish Pope, by contrast, was not motivated by Irish nationalism. In addition, many of the clergy involved in the protests were assigned to the prisons as their pastoral duty. They were able to visit the protestors because it was part of their employment. Other clergymen not appointed as chaplains to prisons did not develop these relationships with prisoners and would often condemn their actions.[45] Whereas the Irish hierarchy and the Pope carried more responsibility for a larger number of individuals, they could not actively protest about the treatment of the prisoners and lacked intimate knowledge of the prisoners' concerns.

1980 Hunger Strike

The prison protests came to a head in 1980. On 27 October, seven prisoners began a hunger strike with more joining in solidarity as it continued. With mounting public pressure, the British government acted. Secret Intelligence Service (MI6) officer Michael Oatley reopened talks with his Irish contact Brendan Duddy in mid-December. Duddy had indicated that Provisional IRA leaders may be willing to compromise on their demands. Thatcher approved an offer regarding concessions around mandated prison uniforms which Oatley took to Belfast on 18 December 1980. The Provisional IRA agreed to a British offer with the added pressure of striker Sean McKenna's impending death. However, by January 1981 it became clear that the British government would not meet the prisoners' demands.

In an effort to avert a hunger strike, some members of the Irish clergy continued to write numerous pamphlets and speak out against the conditions in the prison. The first elected chairman of the National H-Block/Armagh Committee, Fr Piaras O'Duill, wrote the pamphlet *H-Block: Can we remain silent?* to raise awareness of prison conditions and try to avert the 1980 hunger strike. Instead of calling on the prisoners to end their protest, he asked the public 'to demand that everything be done to resolve the problem'.[46] Faul and Murray quoted Pope John Paul II and his messages of non-violence in their own pamphlet *Moment of Truth for Northern Ireland,*[47] in which they attempted to discredit organizations like the Provisionals who claimed to protect the poor through violent means. By raising awareness about poor prison conditions and rallying against violence, the Irish clergymen attempted to strike a balance and not take one side explicitly. However, by supporting the prisoners' cause, something which these priests saw as

---

[45] F. Stuart Ross, *Smashing H-Block: The Popular Campaign against Criminalization and the Irish Hunger Strikes 1976–1982* (Liverpool, 2011), 49.
[46] O'Duill, *H-Block.*   [47] Faul and Murray, *Moment of Truth.*

synonymous with basic human rights, their intentions were automatically translated by unionists and conservatives as supporting the prisoners' violent methods for a united Ireland.

When their efforts failed to prevent the first hunger strike, the clergy attempted to act as mediators between the British government and the prisoners. Prison chaplains Murphy and Toner, as well as John Blelloch, the British civil servant in charge of the prisons, visited the strikers on 10 December 1980. They tried to explain to the protestors that reforms were already in place, indicating the 'civilian style uniform', should they choose to end their hunger strike.

The Irish hierarchy also attempted to end the 1980 hunger strike. Ó Fiaich met with two priests and two SF leaders to discuss possible resolutions to the conflict in early 1980. Additionally, Ó Fiaich discussed the prison situation with the new Secretary of State for Northern Ireland, Humphrey Atkins.[48] At a meeting with Atkins on 26 February, Ó Fiaich discussed a possible future meeting between the British government and SF, which secretly occurred. That September, with rumours of a hunger strike to begin the following month, Ó Fiaich and Bishop Edward Daly issued a press statement in an attempt to avert a crisis, in which they reflect that: 'too many lives have already been lost and we are fearful that if this problem remains unresolved, it may lead to further tragedy.'[49] Ó Fiaich wrote to Atkins the same day outlining a plan to avert a hunger strike and to end the prison protests altogether.[50] Ó Fiaich and Daly urged the British government to abolish the prison uniform in favour of civilian clothing in a final effort to prevent the strike. Two weeks later, Daly and Ó Fiaich travelled to London to speak with Cardinal Hume, the head of the Catholic Church in England and Wales.[51] Both Ó Fiaich and Daly felt better about the situation when the BBC lunchtime news announced that the British government would concede on civilian clothing.[52] However, their hopes deteriorated when they met with Atkins on 23 October. Atkins said the authorities would issue civilian-style clothing because they feared paramilitary prisoners would want to wear their paramilitary uniforms of khakis and black berets.[53] Ó Fiaich and Daly tried, in vain, to convince Atkins to allow the prisoners their own clothes.[54] Daly argued this concession would be sufficient to

---

[48] TNA, CJ 4/3044, Prisons and prisoners: Secretary of State for Northern Ireland, Humphrey Atkins; negotiations with the Prison Officers Association and the 'dirty protest', 1 Jan, 1979–31, Dec. 1980.

[49] CTOMLA, 'Au Tuaisceart', Cardinal Tomas Ó Fiaich and Bishop Edward Daly press release, 23 Sep. 1980.

[50] CTOMLA, 'Au Tuaisceart', Ó Fiaich to Humphrey Atkins, 23 Sep. 1980.

[51] Interview with Bishop Edward Daly, 2 June 2015.

[52] Edward Daly, *A Troubled See: Memoirs of a Derry Bishop* (Dublin, 2011), 109.

[53] Chris Ryder, *Inside the Maze: The Untold Story of the Northern Ireland Prison Service* (London, 2000), 205.

[54] Previously, the British government did not allow prisoners to wear their own clothes because of the prisoners' preference to wear military style uniforms.

end not only the hunger strike but 'the long-running blanket and dirty protests as well.'[55] Ó Fiaich and Daly released another press statement on 24 October to demonstrate their continued efforts, assuring the public that communication had not broken down between themselves and Atkins.[56] Despite their lobbying, the first hunger strike began on 27 October 1980.

However, Ó Fiaich was finally successful in helping to end the strike in December 1980. On 17 December, he publicly appealed both for Thatcher to intervene to end the hunger strike and for the prisoners to end their protest 'in the name of God'.[57] The next day, the republican prisoners called off their fifty-three-day hunger strike after Brendan Hughes refused to let fellow hunger strike Sean McKenna die. The cardinal's plea provided prisoners with an excuse and they released a statement 'saying they had come off the fast in response to the request of Cardinal Ó Fiaich.'[58]

Whereas the clergy met with the prisoners regularly, the hierarchy held high profile meetings with government officials. Yet the internal divisions among the hierarchy, notably between English and Irish, devalued their united front.[59] In November 1980, on a visit to Derry, Hume declared that hunger strikes were an act of violence.[60] In addition, Hume wrote a pastoral letter circulated throughout England and Wales denouncing the strike as suicide. The Church's stance on suicide was in flux in the years after the Second Vatican Council as it attempted to understand issues surrounding mental health.[61]

Ó Fiaich was also instrumental in showing the Vatican what could be done to help the situation. On 26 October, the day before the hunger strike began, Ó Fiaich dined with John Paul II and other cardinals in Rome. They discussed the impending strike and the Pope asked how he could intervene. Ó Fiaich urged the Pope to speak to Queen Elizabeth II the next day during her visit to the Holy See.[62] The next morning, the Pope raised the matter with the Queen, but to no avail. Any public statements on the subject by the Queen would have embroiled the monarchy in accusations of meddling in politics. Ó Fiaich met with the Pope privately and further explained the prison situation, mentioning the humiliating treatment the prisoners suffered.[63] When asked once again what he could do, Ó Fiaich hoped the Pope would discuss the hunger strike with Thatcher during her visit to the

[55]   Tom Collins, *The Irish Hunger Strike* (Belfast, 1986), 86–7.

[56]   CTOMLA, 'Au Tuaisceart', Cardinal Tomas Ó Fiaich and Bishop Edward Daly press release, 10 Oct. 1980; CTOMLA, 'Au Tuaisceart', Cardinal Tomas Ó Fiaich and Bishop Edward Daly press release, 24 Oct. 1980.

[57]   *Irish Times*, 18 Dec. 1980.

[58]   Padraig, O'Malley, *Biting at the Grave: The Irish Hunger Strikes and the Politics of Despair* (Belfast, 1990), 33.

[59]   *Irish Times*, 17 Nov. 1980; *Irish Times*, 17 Nov. 1980.

[60]   *Catholic Herald*, 21 Nov. 1980.

[61]   For more on these disagreements, see Margaret M. Scull, 'The Catholic Church and the hunger strikes of Terence MacSwiney and Bobby Sands', *Irish Political Studies*, Vol. 31 (2), 2016, pp. 290–7.

[62]   Collins, *Irish Hunger Strike*, 330.   [63]   Beresford, *Ten Men Dead*, 144.

Vatican scheduled for November. The Pope then asked Ó Fiaich for a briefing on the prison conditions and the prisoners' demands, which the cardinal provided.

Thatcher and the Pope communicated throughout the 1980 hunger strike: John Paul II sent Thatcher a telegram on 30 October, noting he was receiving 'disturbing news about the tension in the Maze Prison.'[64] The Pope said a hunger strike could cause 'both the tragic consequences which the agitation could have for the prisoners themselves and also the possible grave repercussions upon the whole situation in Northern Ireland.' He implored Thatcher to search out possible solutions before the consequences 'prove irreparable.'[65] The Pope reminded Thatcher that the deaths of prisoners during her term could taint the legacy of her political career.

Thatcher responded to the Pope on 13 November explaining that six of the seven hunger strikers were members of the Provisional IRA and convicted of serious crimes, including murder, arson, and theft. She acknowledged the Pope's fear that the hunger strike could cause further violence in Northern Ireland if not handled delicately and concluded that she 'very much welcome[d] the efforts of the clergy' in an attempt to end the strike.[66] Thatcher aimed to demonize the strikers by describing the violent nature of their crimes and reminding the Pope they were criminals, not martyrs. Although the prisoners faced appalling conditions including lack of clothes, unsanitary cells, and alleged beatings, Thatcher reminded the Pope that the prisoners had created these conditions by not adhering to universal prison rules. During a 45-minute meeting at the Holy See on 24 November, Thatcher said the Pope expressed that he 'had as little sympathy for the terrorists as I did'.[67] However, he pleaded with Thatcher to negotiate with the strikers. This meeting reflects the high-level political role which the Vatican played in attempting to resolve the conflict in Northern Ireland.

Following her return to London, Thatcher sent a telegram to the Pope on 29 November, highlighting the statement from the Irish bishops imploring the prisoners to end their strike,[68] and an additional plan proposed by priests in Northern Ireland to end the hunger strike.[69] Thatcher admitted she had not read the proposal in full, but asserted that such measures would give the prisoners too much power and 'justify terrorism.'[70] Nevertheless, she did not directly ask the Pope to publicly condemn the hunger strikers. Although writing private letters, Thatcher would have known that her letters would probably have been passed

[64] TNA, PREM 19/282, Pope John Paul II telegram to Thatcher, 30 Oct. 1980.

[65] TNA, PREM 19/282, Pope John Paul II telegram to Thatcher, 30 Oct. 1980.

[66] TNA, PREM 19/282, Thatcher telegram to Pope John Paul II, 13 Nov. 1980.

[67] Margaret Thatcher, *The Downing Street Years* (London, 1993), 390; TNA, PREM 19/282, Minutes by E.A.J Ferguson, 19 November 1980.

[68] *Irish Times*, 28 Nov. 1980.

[69] This proposal gave the prisoners three of their five demands; TNA, PREM 19/282, Thatcher to Pope John Paul II, 29 Nov. 1980.

[70] TNA, PREM 19/282, Thatcher to Pope John Paul II, 29 Nov. 1980.

to Ó Fiaich, while Atkins would also have been kept informed of the Pope's views. Thus the Vatican's position meant it played a much larger role in the relationship between the British government and the Irish hierarchy than seen in the public sphere.

On 30 November republican 'blanket man' Sam Millar wrote to the Pope. He asked: 'I am writing this note not to tell you about our conditions but to beg you to save the lives of my comrades who have been forced to hunger strike by the British government.'[71] Millar accused the Church of doing nothing, writing: 'Now that the Irish nation needs the Church we hear naught but a deadly silence. Why? ... You must speak out now, loudly; behind closed doors is no use. My comrades will die if you don't.' There is no public record of whether or not the Pope responded to this personal plea, but we do know the Pope did not make any public declarations concerning the 1980 hunger strike.

The Vatican's involvement in the 1980 hunger strike was limited to private discussions with Ó Fiaich and the British government. This is in contrast with the strike in 1981 when the Pope sent an envoy to meet the hunger strikers, which subsequently became public knowledge. During the 1980 hunger strike, the Pope had to balance the risk of being seen to endorse hunger striking with being accused of ignoring the plight of Catholics facing an apparent human rights violation, given that the prison conditions fell under the umbrella term of 'inhuman treatment'.[72] By speaking out in favour of the strikers, the Pope would have appeared to be endorsing terrorism. Conversely, the clergy and to an extent, the Irish hierarchy, could speak out in favour of protecting the prisoners without causing international turmoil. Two of the clergy had familial and personal relationships with the strikers: Fathers Brian McCreesh and Oliver Crilly. The Vatican remained constrained in their public declarations towards the strikers because they could easily offend Catholics and Christians on both sides of the issue. A year later, the Vatican held no such reservations, as Pope John Paul II publicly asked the British and Argentinian governments to end the Falklands War.

1981 Hunger Strike

The 1980 hunger strike did not result in the republican prisoners' five demands being met, so a second hunger strike led by Bobby Sands began on 1 March the following year. Instead of starting the strike on a block-by-block basis, INLA and Provisional IRA prisoners joined Sands one-by-one each week, adding to the

---

[71] Sam Millar to Pope John Paul II, 30 Nov. 1980, LHLPC in Richard English, *Armed Struggle: The History of the IRA* (London, 2004), 210–11.

[72] The use of 'human rights' had gained momentum during the Second World War; Kenneth Cmiel, 'The recent history of human rights', *The American Historical Review*, 109 (2004), 117–18.

strike's momentum.[73] Sands and his men demonstrated unyielding resolve. After the failure of the first strike, the prisoners saw only two outcomes: 'victory or death'. The strike finally ended on 3 October 1981 with ten men dead.[74] The remaining six prisoners who still refused food chose to stop their protest after their families specified that they would authorize medical intervention once the prisoners lapsed into comas.

Some Irish clergymen played a major negotiating role during this second hunger strike. Fr Brian McCreesh, the brother of striker Raymond McCreesh, had been attempting to improve prison conditions since the beginning of the protests. He was the only person in the family authorized to see his brother as Raymond refused the prison uniform and was therefore denied familial visits. Raymond only wore the uniform once, in February 1981, to tell his family he was joining the hunger strike.[75] McCreesh campaigned for support of the strikers and sent Thatcher a telegram on 17 May 1981, pleading for his brother's life. Thatcher's private secretary Clive Whitmore responded to McCreesh stating: 'You must be aware that these were conditions which the prisoners chose to impose upon themselves.'[76] In addition, McCreesh told a rally in Toome: 'My brother is not a criminal',[77] in direct response to Thatcher's 'crime is crime is crime, it is not political' speech.[78]

According to British government records, McCreesh even convinced his hallucinating brother not to receive food towards the end of his hunger strike.[79] On 16 May, the fifty-sixth day of his strike, Raymond began to hallucinate and asked for a glass of milk.[80] Although the family had already seen him once that day, the prison authorities called them back to discuss a 'major development'.[81] McCreesh spoke with his brother on the telephone. After a series of questions, he realized his brother was hallucinating and told Raymond he was on hunger strike in prison and not in a hospital in Scotland as he believed.[82] When visiting Raymond the next day, the family noticed a plaster on his arm and concluded that the medical personnel had drugged him.[83] Although no documentation exists to prove this

---

[73] During the 1980 strike, the first seven prisoners began their fast together, with further prisoners joining as the hunger strike continued.

[74] These deaths included Bobby Sands, Francis Hughes, Raymond McCreesh, Patsy O'Hara, Joe McDonnell, Martin Hurson, Kevin Lynch, Kieran Doherty, Thomas McElwee, and Michael Devine.

[75] R.K. Walker, *The Hunger Strikes* (Belfast, 2006), 117.

[76] TNA, PREM 19/504, Clive Whitmore telegram to Brian McCreesh, 20 May 1981.

[77] Walker, *The Hunger Strikes*, 118.

[78] At a press conference on 22 April 1981 in Saudi Arabia, Thatcher rejected any view there could be political reasons for republican violence; *Christian Science Monitor*, 22 April 1981.

[79] TNA, PREM 19/504, Bernard Ingham note to Clive Whitmore, 19 May 1981.

[80] TNA, PREM 19/504, Northern Ireland Office Press Notice, 'Case of Raymond McCreesh', 19 May 1981.

[81] Thomas Hennessey, *Hunger Strike: Margaret Thatcher's Battle with the IRA 1980-1* (Dublin, 2013), 230-3.

[82] TNA, PREM 19/504, Bernard Ingham note to Clive Whitmore, 19 May 1981.

[83] TNA, PREM 19/504, Brian McCreesh telegram to Margaret Thatcher, 17 May 1981.

theory, it was clear that Raymond did experience hallucinations. His family chose not to intervene medically and Raymond died on 21 May.[84] Potentially, Fr McCreesh's actions could have been used by the British government for propaganda purposes to blacken the name of the clergyman in hastening his brother's death. However, that was impossible because of the manner in which they acquired this information—namely through phone tapping. Thatcher's press secretary Bernard Ingham and private secretary Clive Whitmore concluded that the contents of this transcript could never be published, as the Provisional IRA would then know the government recorded their conversations.

In addition to McCreesh, Fr Oliver Crilly also met with his cousin, hunger striker Tom McElwee. Crilly remembered McElwee telling him he had experienced an image of Christ visiting his disciples in a thunderstorm and McElwee felt he, too, was caught in a storm. In a later interview, Crilly admitted: 'It would be very difficult for some people to even associate one of the hunger strikers ... [with] the scriptures'.[85] To those who condemned the violence outright, including many moderate Catholics and Protestants, these men were violent criminals who deserved this treatment. The strike troubled Crilly, his Christian convictions in conflict with his own nationalist sympathies, given that two of the strikers were his cousins.[86] His Irish nationalism, the politics of 'home', clashed with his Catholicism, the religion from 'Rome', because of the Church's mixed standing on hunger striking as suicide, and on the issues of violence and 'just war' more broadly.

Despite McCreesh's very personal connection, Faul remained the most influential priest on the 1981 hunger strikes. He had long championed the prisoners' cause during the blanket and 'no wash' protests. However, Faul saw the hunger strikes as a needless waste of life and felt compelled to help bring them to an end. He played a crucial role in bringing the families of the strikers together in an attempt to resist pressure from the Provisionals. Faul appealed to the strikers' families that their deaths would be fruitless, tangled up in a militant conflict much larger than themselves and used as pawns by their Provisional IRA superiors. Faul's own experiences during the 1980 hunger strike had left him feeling equally 'snubbed and deceived' by British actions and 'rejected and mauled' by the strikers' representatives.[87] The strikers had sent Faul a statement calling for him to stop pressuring their families and nicknamed him 'Denis the Menace.'[88] He was a man they respected but distrusted: distrusted because he frequently denounced violent republicanism but liked because he had done more than any other Church figure to advocate the prisoners' struggles. Faul wrote about the stories of many prison protestors in his diary, including that of hunger striker Francis Hughes,

[84] O'Malley, Biting at the Grave, 64.

[85] Prisons Memory Archive (PMA), Fr Oliver Crilly interview, July 2005, http://prisonsmemoryarchive.com/religion/

[86] Beresford, Ten Men Dead, 265–6.   [87] Ryder, Inside the Maze, 250.

[88] Ryder, Inside the Maze, 250–1.

who Faul believed 'suffers to draw attention to sufferings of his fellow prisoners.'[89] By recording the strikers' personal thoughts, Faul demonstrated his commitment to their cause. His personal musings could have also helped him decide whether the strikers would ever yield of their own volition.

In March 1981, Faul and Murray distributed their pamphlet *Hunger Strike 2: Why British rule has failed to solve prison problems*. The pamphlet attempted to provide justification for Sands' strike because of the numerous faults of the British government in Northern Ireland, mainly their use of internment and torture. Further, they claimed the 1980 hunger strike ended without deaths because of the actions of Catholic bishops and politicians, who spoke 'courageously against a tide of emotion'.[90] Murray and Faul's next pamphlet *Hunger strike: search for solutions* was published in May, after the death of Sands. This time they defended hunger striking as a legitimate form of protest, contending that: 'If a group of persons or even one man is suffering in silence and isolation and efforts to draw attention to their plight have failed, they have a sufficient reason for going on hunger strike.'[91] The priests denounced Cardinal Hume and his belief that hunger strikes were a form of suicide, arguing: 'Cardinal Hume has told us in letters about prisoners in Northern Ireland that he does not comment on affairs in another country. Why did he break his silence on this occasion?'[92]

Faul frequently visited Sands before his strike. In February 1981, writing to his republican contact outside the prison, Sands discussed a conversation in which Faul discouraged him from beginning his strike. Faul asked Sands for a six-month delay, reminding him of the work of Daly and Ó Fiaich to change the prison conditions. However, Sands remained critical of Faul's motives, believing a delay would coincide with the opening of a new prison, separating the prisoners and effectively ending the protests. Sands concluded: 'Anyway he now knows how determined we all are and more so me personally.'[93] Through their interactions with the prisoners, the priests realized they would not make any progress in having them attempt to end the protest.

Provisionals threatened Faul to 'keep his mouth shut' after the priest attempted to mediate the strike.[94] Even after the strike, republican Gerard Hodgins accused Faul of demonstrating 'his desire to destroy the IRA in 1981 by his treacherous about-turn in relation to the hunger strike'.[95] While criticizing Faul for persuading strikers' families to intervene in the strike, Hodgins noted: 'Nobody likes a turn-coat, even if he is a priest.'[96] In addition, *The Irish News* quoted Faul's

[89] CTOMLA, Fr Denis Faul Papers (FDFP) 1980–1981, Diary Entry, 30 April 1981.
[90] Faul and Murray, *Hunger Strike 2*.
[91] Faul and Murray, *Hunger Strike: the search for solutions*.
[92] Faul and Murray, *Hunger Strike: the search for solutions*.
[93] Beresford, *Ten Men Dead*, 77–8.
[94] CTOMLA, FDFP 1981–1982, Unknown letter to Faul, 5 Oct. 1981.
[95] *Sunday World*, 25 Jan. 1983.
[96] English, *Armed Struggle*, 211.

accusations against the RUC, announcing the organization would arrest 'any Catholic who used the word H-Block in a public place'.[97]

Nevertheless, Faul began to meet with the strikers' families in order to end the strike. As soon as a prisoner lapsed into a coma, his next-of-kin became his legal guardian and could medically intervene to save their life. Former Provisional IRA hunger striker Laurence McKeown, whose mother took him off hunger strike, relayed that the Catholic clergy attempted to guilt-trip families into intervening. McKeown said the clergy told prisoners' mothers and wives that good women would medically intervene.[98] Richard O'Rawe agrees with McKeown's assessment in his memoir, but excluded Faul's impact on the families in his chapter, describing the end of the strike.[99]

Faul continued to speak with the families while campaigning to expose alleged human rights violations in the prisons. He did this more so than any other cleric in Northern Ireland and had previously worked with the RAC. When Faul met with the families on 28 July in Toomebridge, he told them that the strikers would end their protest if the Provisional IRA leadership gave authorization. The families agreed that if the British government conceded on prison uniforms, they would end the strike. The same evening, Faul and the families travelled to Belfast to speak with SF leader Gerry Adams and convey their decision. However, the Provisional IRA council claimed they were never informed of the families' decision.[100] The strike lasted another two months before the families agreed to intervene without the prisoners' permission, due in part to Faul's influence. In an interview with *The Irish News* almost twenty years later, Faul said he believed Adams' lack of action indicated that the strike was for 'political reasons' outside the prison. He said: 'If these men died for votes, it would be a sad event. I mean, what was important— the votes or the lives?'[101] Another priest involved with bringing attention to the protests, McVeigh, told me in an interview that he campaigned for Sands during the Fermanagh South-Tyrone by-election in which SF put forward the prisoner as their candidate for MP. McVeigh canvassed for Sands because he hoped 'that my little contribution would make some difference'.[102] Sands won the election with a 1,000 vote majority.

Since the priests were not as well-known outside their own communities, they could voice their beliefs more freely. Murray and Faul could criticize Hume for his view that hunger striking was suicide but the Irish clergy were in a difficult position when it came to the burial of hunger strikers. Before the Second Vatican Council, Catholic theology stated that those who commit suicide cannot receive a

[97] *Irish News*, 5 Oct. 1981.   [98] Interview with Dr Laurence McKeown, 15 April 2014.
[99] Richard O'Rawe, *Blanketmen: An untold story of the H-block hunger strike* (Dublin, 2005), 233–8.
[100] O'Rawe, *Blanketmen*, 152.   [101] *Irish News*, 2 March 2005.
[102] Interview with Fr Joseph McVeigh, 14 April 2014.

Figure 3 'Bobby Sands' Funeral', *An Phoblacht/Republican News*, 7 May 1981
Source: Pacemaker Press

Catholic burial service on consecrated ground.[103] However, many Irish clergymen and bishops did not believe that hunger striking was suicide. During the funerals, McVeigh revealed that older hierarchy members would decide which priests could help with the services.[104] McVeigh knew the Sands family and that they would have wanted him to be involved in his funeral service. In the eyes of the Irish bishops, McVeigh was a radical priest who could have framed the Requiem Mass in terms of martyrdom. The more senior conservative members of the clergy and the hierarchy did attempt to control hunger striker funerals, but they could not contain the thousands of people who marched in funeral processions after the strikers' coffins (Figure 3). However, Danny Morrison has insisted that the Church's attitude towards funerals for hunger strikers was 'a disgrace', as while Catholic RUC men could be buried with the Union flag, republicans could not have the Irish tricolour on their coffins.[105] Conflict over the funerals between the Church and the IRA occurred on a micro-level as well, with Sr Genevieve

---

[103] Traditionally the Code of Canon Law 1184 was employed to prohibit funerals for individuals considered 'manifest sinners who cannot be granted ecclesiastical funerals without public scandal of the faithful'. Suicide was categorized as such; http://www.vatican.va/archive/ENG1104/_P4C.HTM
[104] Interview with Fr Joseph McVeigh, 14 April 2014.
[105] Interview with Danny Morrison, 29 April 2014.

O'Farrell arguing with IRA men who wanted to close St Louise's School on the Falls Road during the hunger strikers' funerals.[106]

The hunger strikes presented Ó Fiaich with a political, moral, and theological dilemma. He had warned of the possibility of such a strike for years. Ó Fiaich did not deny his support for Irish unity, but repeatedly denounced the use of violence as means to that end. When joining the priesthood, Ó Fiaich chose *Fratres in Unum*, 'Brothers in Unity,' as his episcopal motto, a phrase from the 113th Psalm: 'How good, how delightful it is for all to live together like brothers.'[107] Indeed, at his appointment as cardinal in 1979, he commented on his own republicanism. Ó Fiaich had never thought of deaths by hunger striking as suicide, for as an Irish history professor at Maynooth, he was well aware of the symbolic importance and historical resonances of hunger striking within Ireland. Hunger striking as a form of protest had always been used to raise awareness of disempowerment and grievances, although it is not a 'particularly Irish' form of protest.[108] The practice dated back to the fifth century, with W.B. Yeats chronicling the experience in his play 'The King's Threshold',[109] while suffragettes were the first to hunger strike in the twentieth century.[110] While many suffragettes ceased abstaining from food after the First World War, Irish republicans adopted the tactic after the 1916 Easter Rising. Most notable were the deaths of Irish Republican Brotherhood member Thomas Ashe after he was force fed in 1917, and the Lord Mayor of Cork, Terence MacSwiney's death, after a seventy-four-day hunger strike in October 1920.[111] In addition, the gospel strengthened Ó Fiaich's opinion: how could it be suicide to lay down your life for your friends, as the prisoners clearly believed they were doing?

Ó Fiaich again wrote to Thatcher in the days before Sands' death. After appealing to the strikers to end their protest, on 27 April Ó Fiaich sent a telegram revisiting earlier proposals by himself and Daly and highlighting the 'five-fold increase in the prison population' since 1968.[112] Although Thatcher responded the next day, she disregarded Ó Fiaich's proposals and reiterated the British government's firm position not to negotiate.[113] American cardinals were also contacting Thatcher, urging her to search for solutions, many from areas not heavily populated with Irish-Americans.[114] In a telegram sent on 13 May, Ó Fiaich urged Thatcher to concede to the demands on prison dress and work while also sending

---

[106] Rae, *Sister Genevieve*, 141–2.   [107] Fitzgerald, *Father Tom*, 63.

[108] For a wider history of hunger striking, see Ian Miller, 'Experiencing hunger striking: Remembering the Maze Prison hunger strikes', *Irish Review*, forthcoming. I am grateful to the author for providing me with an advanced copy.

[109] W.B. Yeats, *The King's Threshold*, I, i, 18–26.

[110] James Vernon, *Hunger: A Modern History* (Cambridge, MA., 2007), 61–71.

[111] TNA, PCOM 8/349, File on Terence MacSwiney.

[112] TNA, PREM 19/504, Ó Fiaich telegram to Thatcher, 27 April 1981.

[113] TNA, PREM 19/504, Thatcher to Ó Fiaich, 28 April 1981.

[114] See TNA, PREM 19/504, Cook telegram to Thatcher, 23 April 1981; TNA, PREM 19/504, Manning telegram to Thatcher, 25 April 1981.

a representative to speak with the prisoners' spokesmen. He wrote: 'In God's name, don't allow another death.'[115] Thatcher replied, declaring that she shared Ó Fiaich's concern for the loss of life, but she dismissed his idea of an official British government delegate negotiating with 'terrorists'.[116] She pointed out that representatives from Dublin's parliament, the European Commission on Human Rights, and the Pope's envoy had already attempted to negotiate with prisoners and all had failed.

On 27 May, Ó Fiaich received a telephone call telling him that Thatcher wished to see all church leaders in Belfast the following afternoon. Ó Fiaich had met Thatcher on one occasion, briefly and months earlier, before any of the deaths. However, Ó Fiaich had no desire to meet with Thatcher at this particular point, as hunger strikers had already started to die and he predicted further deaths could lead to increased violence. Ó Fiaich believed Thatcher wished to publicize their meeting and use it as a photograph opportunity to show unity between the British government and Catholic Church in Ireland. This was not the case, as shown by the seemingly immovable position of the British prime minister. Ó Fiaich also knew an agreement between the Church hierarchy and the British government would have left nationalist Catholics feeling isolated.

Ó Fiaich did meet with Thatcher at Ten Downing Street on 30 June 1981, at his own request, along with Bishop Patrick Lennon of Kildare and Leighlin. Prisoner Joe McDonnell was near death and Ó Fiaich hoped he could sway Thatcher to make concessions and possibly save McDonnell's life. However, Thatcher reiterated her position at the meeting.[117] She believed the hunger strike could end the next day if the Provisional IRA leadership gave orders to the strikers. In any case, she claimed 'she was not prepared to barter.'[118] The meeting delved into deeper issues concerning the status of Northern Ireland, with Ó Fiaich claiming that the territory was 'the most artificial division ever created.'[119] In the end, their meeting proved fruitless and McDonnell died on 8 July. In her memoirs, Thatcher recalled that she met with the cardinal in London as she hoped he could use his influence to end the hunger strike. She remarked that Ó Fiaich was not a bad person 'but he was a romantic Republican, whose nationalism seemed to prevail over his Christian duty of offering unqualified resistance to terrorism and murder.'[120] The cardinal asserted then that strikers did not act under Provisional IRA orders, while Thatcher was convinced otherwise.

The British press blamed the Irish hierarchy and the Catholic Church generally for the hunger strikes. Two weeks after Sands' death, an editorial in *The Times*

[115] TNA, PREM 19/504, Ó Fiaich telegram to Thatcher, 13 May 1981.
[116] TNA, PREM 19/504, Thatcher telegram to Ó Fiaich, 15 May 1981.
[117] *Irish Times*, 1 Aug. 1981.
[118] TNA, PREM 19/505, Clive Wainwright to Stephen Boys-Smith, 2 July 1981.
[119] TNA, PREM 19/505, Clive Wainwright to Stephen Boys-Smith, 2 July 1981.
[120] Thatcher, *Downing Street Years*, 392.

commented: 'The words and actions of some members of the [Catholic] Church have undoubtedly fed misinterpretations of what is happening in Northern Ireland.'[121] The editorial blamed the Church for giving deceased hunger strikers an aura of martyrdom. Even after the death of nine hunger strikers *The Times*, often seen as an unofficial mouthpiece of the British establishment, persisted in its condemnation. An editorial in late August read:

> It must be said with sadness that the gains the Provisionals are making out of their gruesome policy of suicide would be markedly less were it not that the Irish government and the Roman Catholic hierarchy... so conspicuously qualify their condemnation of this extension of terrorist violence by piling the blame on British ministers for allowing it to continue.[122]

This ambivalent stance of the Irish government and Irish Catholic hierarchy, *The Times* continued, 'articulate[d] and reinforce[d] the feelings of many Irishmen'[123] by giving the hunger strikers martyr status. Furthermore, elements of the British press claimed that Ó Fiaich backed the IRA. *The Daily Express* described Ó Fiaich as 'the Cardinal who is like a recruiting officer for the IRA.'[124] A popular, blatantly sectarian, outrageous cartoon published by *The Sunday Express* on 31 May showed Ó Fiaich as leading a group of marching Provisional IRA members, holding their rifles in the shape of a cross (Figure. 4). In the same issue an editorial characterized Ó Fiaich as 'Chaplain in Chief of the IRA.' Tom Collins has written that Cardinal Hume's assessment of the Irish hunger strikes as suicide increased English hatred towards Ó Fiaich and his opposing position. In part because Hume had claimed that the hunger strikes were sinful, the press then asked why Ó Fiaich had not similarly declared them suicide. Since Ireland has a tradition of hunger striking as a form of protest, and the Catholic ideology remained conflicted concerning suicide, Ó Fiaich chose not to respond.[125]

Instead, with McDonnell's death looming, Ó Fiaich and Daly threw their support behind the Irish Commission for Justice and Peace (ICJP). This was an organization established by the Church to campaign for human rights issues. However, neither the prisoners nor the British government had engaged with the ICJP, which included members from the hierarchy, clergy, and laity.[126] At the beginning of June, the ICJP issued a statement concerning possible solutions for resolving the hunger strikes.[127] The statement emphasized that women in Armagh

---

[121] *Times*, 27 May 1981.   [122] *Times*, 22 Aug. 1981.
[123] *Times*, 22 Aug. 1981.   [124] *Sunday Express*, 31 May 1981.
[125] For more on the Catholic Church's response to twentieth-century hunger striking, see Scull, 'The Catholic Church', 282–99.
[126] The ICJP consisted of the Auxiliary Bishop of Dublin, Dermot O'Mahony, Fr Oliver Crilly, and lay people Brian Gallagher, Jerome Connolly, and SDLP representative Hugh Logue.
[127] Irish Commission for Peace and Justice, *The H-Block Protest in the Maze Prison, Northern Ireland*, Statement issued 3 June 1981.

Figure 4 'Why can't the British show some Christian charity to someone carrying a cross?', *The Sunday Express*, 31 May 1981

Cummings/Daily Express/Express Syndication

prison already wore their own clothes, so this concession should be extended to male prisoners. The ICJP also argued there could be greater freedom of association within the prisons without permitting military activities pursued by some inmates. In addition, the ICJP declared penal work degrading and suggested that time could be used for educational pursuits or recreational activities.[128] The hierarchy in Ireland and England accepted and supported the ICJP's initiative. However, both the British government and the hunger strikers rejected the proposals.[129] At a press conference the ICJP discussed the details of their unsuccessful talks with the British government. The NIO released their own press statement and sent telegrams to the British embassies in Ireland and the USA, countering claims that: 'HMG have been in bad faith in their dealings with the ICJP'.[130]

In an interview with the author, Danny Morrison has claimed the ICJP involvement disrupted negotiations between himself and Gerry Adams on one side, and the British government on the other, during the 1981 hunger strike.

---

[128] *Irish Press*, 28 June 1981.
[129] TNA, FCO 87/1269, 'Statement on behalf of the protesting republican prisoners in the Maze prison', 28 June 1981.
[130] TNA, FCO 87/1269, Telegram from HMG to Ireland and USA Embassies, 10 July 1981.

Morrison dismissed the organization for including former SDLP MP Hugh Logue among its membership but no one from SF, causing republicans to distrust it.[131] He has also argued that the Catholic Church aligned itself with the SDLP, a more moderate and larger nationalist political group with mostly middle-class members. In any event, the ICJP made no progress between the prisoners and the British government as both parties dismissed the ICJP's initiatives to end the strike.

Perhaps the most notable aspect of the hierarchy's involvement in the second hunger strike was the fact that there was a clear divide among its members. As a result, although the Irish bishops played a less active role in the second hunger strike, members still met privately with officials and were criticized in newspaper editorials.[132] The hierarchy had more public influence than the clergy, but faced a greater backlash for their controversial decisions and failure to stop the deaths.

In Rome, John Paul II was drawn into the debate around the 1981 hunger strike far more than during the previous year. At the end of April 1981, the Pope sent one of his secretaries, Fr John Magee, to act as his personal messenger to the hunger strikers. Magee was an Irishman born in 1936 in the strongly nationalist border town of Newry. In 1962 Magee was ordained in Rome and later appointed the personal secretary of Pope Paul VI. Magee became a close friend of the Pope, and after his death was asked to remain the personal secretary of John Paul I. After the conclave elected John Paul II, the new Pope asked Magee to stay, explaining: 'I don't know anyone around here at the Vatican.'[133]

Prior to his prison visit, Magee discussed papal intervention in the hunger strike with Ó Fiaich via telephone. Ó Fiaich believed a visit would be too late and if an emissary should come from Rome in a wave of publicity and fail, it would damage the Church's position on the strike in Ireland. However, John Paul II and the Vatican's Secretary of State, Cardinal Agostino Casaroli, agreed that intervention would be worthwhile. The British Embassy to the Holy See was told of Magee's plan to visit and, to avoid loyalist demonstrations, all parties agreed not to announce his presence until after he arrived in Belfast. However, it was rumoured that the British government chose to alert the press to Magee's movements, to avoid charges of conspiracy with the Church, and journalists flocked to Heathrow airport when his flight landed en route to Belfast.[134] Ó Fiaich was also annoyed that the police met Magee at Belfast airport as he believed this security would associate the envoy too closely with the British authorities. Escorted in a bulletproof limousine to Fr John Murphy's home, Magee's arrival was heavily

[131] Interview with Danny Morrison, 29 April 2014.
[132] Interview with Bishop Edward Daly, 2 June 2015; TNA, FCO 87/1258, 'Media and Catholic Church Reaction to Sands' Death 1981 Hunger Strike 1981'; TNA, CJ 4/3639, 'Note for the Record', 28 Jan. 1981; TNA, CJ 4/3710, 'Catholic Church and 1981 Hunger Strike'.
[133] Beresford, Ten Men Dead, 123–4.
[134] TNA, PREM 19/504, Neville Gaffin to Sanders, 28 April 1981.

tracked by journalists peering in the ground floor windows of the house. Magee went to the prison twice, visiting Sands three times. The first visit was on the fifty-eighth day of Sands' strike, when he 'was in an advanced state of starvation.'[135] Magee also met with Hughes, McCreesh, and Patsy O'Hara, making a personal plea on behalf of the Pope and beseeching them to negotiate and to end the dispute. Before he left, unconfirmed reports say that Magee offered Sands prayers and a large gold cross as a gift from the Pope.[136]

Magee also met with Atkins while in Northern Ireland and explained that he came as the Pope's personal, not political, representative 'on a mission of peace.'[137] Magee reminded Atkins of the Pope's speech at Drogheda, where he denounced violence, including those who commit violence against themselves. In addition, Magee gave Atkins a full report of his conversation with Sands. Magee said he had enquired about how to end Sands' strike with the prisoner replying: 'Don't ask me that.'[138] Magee had then asked Sands how the strike could be postponed, in order to begin negotiations and then gave the Secretary of State Sands' terms for negotiation. Sands said he would suspend his fast for five days if a NIO representative would meet with him to discuss 'the whole question' with two priests and three other prisoners also present.[139] Although Atkins emphasized to Magee his acceptance of the Pope's message of non-violence, in addition to his personal respect for John Paul II, he explained that the British government could not negotiate. To do so would be to damage the control of the prison system and 'would threaten innocent lives.'[140] Magee hoped the prisoners would react positively to the Pope's plea. At the end of their meeting, Atkins explained he could not meet with Magee again, as that 'would risk creating the impression that some form of negotiation' had occurred.[141]

Magee's indication of the Pope's displeasure towards those who commit violence against themselves could indicate his personal beliefs on hunger striking as a form of suicide and therefore a mortal sin.[142] If the Pope personally disagreed with the Irish clergymen and hierarchy concerning the theological issue of hunger striking as suicide, he could not publicly do so because he would thereby isolate many Catholic nationalists. In addition, a public dismissal of the hunger strikes by the Pope could lead to international outrage amongst, in particular, the Irish

---

[135] Clarke, *Broadening the Battlefield*, 149.   [136] O'Malley, *Biting at the Grave*, 188.

[137] TNA, PREM 19/504, Summary of Conversation between Humphrey Atkins and John Magee by R.A Harrington, 29 April 1981.

[138] TNA, PREM 19/504, Summary of Conversation between Humphrey Atkins and John Magee by R.A Harrington, 29 April 1981.

[139] TNA, PREM 19/504, Summary of Conversation between Humphrey Atkins and John Magee by R.A Harrington, 29 April 1981.

[140] TNA, PREM 19/504, Summary of Conversation between Humphrey Atkins and John Magee by R.A Harrington, 29 April 1981.

[141] TNA, PREM 19/504, Summary of Conversation between Humphrey Atkins and John Magee by R.A Harrington, 29 April 1981.

[142] Achille Vander Heeren, 'Suicide' in *The Catholic Encyclopedia* (New York, 1912).

diaspora. However, since we only have a summary of the conversation between Atkins and Magee, we have merely an impression of the talk from the point of view of the British civil servant taking notes.[143] The potential release of the Pope's personal papers in the far distant future would perhaps enumerate John Paul II's opinion.

When Magee left Northern Ireland he issued a statement, assuring the public that the Pope 'will continue in seeking ways to help people in Northern Ireland, indeed in Ireland as a whole, to work out solutions to their communal problems in accordance with Christian teachings.'[144] In addition, Magee said: 'All life is sacred and must be preserved as a gift from God.' He continued, declaring violence of any kind 'must be condemned in the clearest terms as being against the law of God.' Magee's visit and pleas did not halt the hunger strike. In fact, *The Times* attacked the Pope for not openly condemning the hunger strikers and for failing to excommunicate IRA members.[145] The day after Sands' death, four British Catholics wrote to newspapers highlighting hunger strikes as a form of suicide and arguing that the strikers should not receive Catholic burials on consecrated ground. Fr John Mahoney, SJ eloquently outlined the debate within the Church over suicide in the post-Vatican II era, while Mrs Rosalind Ingrams from North London and Colonel J.H. Anderson from East Sussex condemned the Church for allowing the hunger strikers to receive Holy Communion and last rites despite their obvious death wish. Lastly, Mr P.R. Ellison of Lancashire was the most severe, calling on the Church to excommunicate Sands.[146] *The Guardian* quoted individuals who viewed the strikes similarly.[147] A spokesman for the Democratic Unionist Party (DUP) announced that the visit by the Pope's envoy was actually a direct effort to strengthen the strikers' determination. By blaming the Catholic Church, the British press could deflect or deny any wrongdoing on the part of the British government. In the event, the Pope did not release his own statement, perhaps seeing no benefit and potentially perceiving that it might cause more difficulties for those working to end the strikes.

The Vatican's attention to the Irish hunger strikes was abruptly displaced on 13 May 1981. At 5.17 p.m. in St. Peter's Square, the Pope was shot twice at close range by Mehmet Ali Ağca, a Turkish assassin. We do not know what would have happened had an attempt not been made on the Pope's life. However, by analysing the behaviour of the clergy and the hierarchy, it remains clear that direct negotiations with the strikers would not have ended the strike. Without the acceptance of their five demands, the prisoners would most likely have remained firm in their conviction. In addition, the Pope may have decided that sending an

---

[143] TNA, PREM 19/504, Summary of Conversation between Humphrey Atkins and John Magee by R.A Harrington, 29 April 1981.
[144] Beresford, *Ten Men Dead*, 125.   [145] *Times*, 29 April 1981.   [146] *Times*, 6 May 1981.
[147] *Guardian*, 7 May 1981.

envoy on multiple visits would have appeared one-sided. In the case of the 1981 hunger strikes, the Pope needed to balance his concern for the strikers with public perceptions of the Catholic Church. The Church was attempting to move away from the appearance of a Machiavellian approach to politics, from centuries of militancy from the Crusades through to Pope Pius XII's secret deal with Hitler.[148] Even through the *longue durée* lens of the Vatican's past relationship with Ireland and the 1155 Papal Bull *Laudabiliter*, there are examples of the Church's involvement with political violence.[149] A perception of a close association with the Provisional IRA and its violent methods now would only make matters worse.

Conclusion

Although the Pope used John 15:13 to justify his canonization of Maximilian Kolbe, he did not believe the same reasoning could be applied to the 1980–81 hunger strikers. As witnessed in his Drogheda speech in 1979, the Pope deplored violence and asked his followers to turn to Christ. John Paul II treated Kolbe's canonization and the 1981 hunger strike differently for a variety of reasons, most notably that Kolbe was an innocent Catholic priest persecuted in a concentration camp during the Second World War for his religion and righteousness, whereas Bobby Sands had been convicted of serious crimes. In addition, Kolbe saved a life, invoking Christ's sacrifice, while the hunger strike led to ten deaths before its end in October 1981.[150] Despite his meetings with Thatcher, the Pope was unable to influence the British government and the Vatican became more involved in the 1981 strike because the British government remained unrelenting in its policy towards the prisoners. Therefore, John Paul II changed his approach from speaking to the politicians to an appeal to the prisoners themselves. The Vatican's involvement resulted in heightened worldwide media attention for the strikers. In addition, the Pope faced public pressure to make a statement concerning the prisoners. Neither the Pope's telegrams to Thatcher nor Magee's visit to the strikers brought an end to the protest. If the Pope had made a public declaration in defence of the strikers' actions, he could have caused international outrage as his actions could appear to condone terrorists. However, the Pope urged restraint from Thatcher, reminding her of the Christian duty of forgiveness.

In the wider context of Vatican diplomacy, the Pope's reaction to the 1980–81 hunger strikes contrasts with other international interventions during his early papacy. On becoming Pope in October 1978, John Paul II attempted to heal the

---

[148] See John Cornwell, *Hitler's Pope: The Secret History of Pius XII* (London, 1999).

[149] In 1155, Pope Hadrian IV gave permission to English King Henry II to invade Ireland in order to 'proclaim the truths of the Christian religion'; Fitzgerald, *Father Tom*, 75.

[150] In addition, sixty-one individuals died outside the prison during the 1981 hunger strike because of the heightened community tensions, thirty-four were civilians; *Irish Times*, 3 Oct. 2016.

relationship between Polish people and Rome, writing to and meeting with the Italian Prime Minister Giulio Andreotti. In addition, extensive travelling during his papacy allowed him to address specific issues in each new country or region. During his visits to developing countries, the Pope championed the poor and admonished the wealthy. He led the Polish people in prayer during his first papal visit to his native country in 1978. His presence embarrassed the Communist government as workers united to sing about Christ, and the trip reinforced the Solidarity movement in 1980. The Pope often avoided sending envoys to other countries with politically fraught situations, instead visiting them himself. In contrast, by sending a papal envoy to Ireland in 1981, the Pope attempted to distance the Vatican from republican violence and manifested a 'hands off' attitude to the conflict.

On 28 May 1982, the Pope was again involved in a fraught diplomatic situation when he visited Britain during, coincidently, the time of the Falklands War. Church leaders in England had been organizing the papal visit for more than a year and the Catholic Church paid the majority of expenses. Rather than a state visit, John Paul II's trip was a pastoral one, meaning he did not intend to meet with state officials. Thatcher agreed with the designation of the visit as pastoral, stating: 'We recognised the difficulties which a visit at this time might cause him, however, and decided it would be best if none of the Cabinet met him personally.'[151] By doing so, the Pope could have appeared to favour the British cause, which would upset the predominantly Catholic Argentina. Alternatively, the British government's actions could be seen as a snub against the Pope, undermining his authority by not meeting him. However, before his visit the Pope communicated with Thatcher on 22 May: 'I urgently appeal to you to act decisively in order to secure an immediate cease-fire that will open the way to a peaceful settlement of the dispute.'[152] The Pope could not back out of his visit without appearing to make a political statement.

Instead, the Vatican quickly planned a short trip to Argentina on 11 June to balance the Vatican's political position and not seem one-sided.[153] Argentina welcomed the Pope with large rallies and cheering crowds. After greeting the Argentinean President Leopoldo Galtieri, the Pope gave a speech in which he denounced the war, claiming negotiation 'could and should have prevented it.'[154] Although the Pope had not intended for his Argentina trip to carry any political implications, Galtieri thanked him for his 'strengthening visit.'

The Pope's visits to Britain and Argentina, just a year after the 1981 hunger strikes, demonstrate the unique quality of the Vatican's response to the prison protests. Although the Falklands was an openly declared war, unlike the

---

[151] Thatcher, *Downing Street Years*, 230.   [152] Thatcher, *Downing Street Years*, 518.
[153] Paul Eddy, Magnus Linklater, and Peter Gillman, *The Falklands War* (London, 1982), 241–2.
[154] Eddy, Linklater, and Gilman, *Falklands War*, 242.

paramilitary campaigns in Northern Ireland, the Pope still rallied against violence. Instead of a papal envoy, he travelled to both Britain and Argentina to plead openly for an end to the war. In that instance, the British trip was planned long in advance, but the Argentina tour was hastily arranged so the Pope would not appear to take sides in the conflict. In contrast, sending a personal envoy to Ireland, the Pope demonstrated tacit support for negotiation without being seen to be directly interfering in the conflict.

At the other end of the Catholic Church, clergymen, specifically Fr Denis Faul, were able to influence the strikers' families by personally interacting with them and by demonstrating a long-term commitment to ending the prison protests. Whereas Faul, and to an extent Ó Fiaich, worked for many years to improve prison conditions, the Pope held only a few, albeit important, meetings and sent a personal envoy just once. In his defence, the Pope's vocation required him to look after 1.2bn Catholics worldwide and visit numerous nations every year on peace missions. One hunger strike, in a small European country, could not detract the Pope from his main duties of promoting Catholicism.

After the 1981 hunger strike ended, Thatcher claimed that the Provisional IRA regrouped and began a campaign of greater violence to try and achieve their ends.[155] When discussing a bomb outside the Chelsea Barracks which killed one person and injured many others, Thatcher wrote: 'To say that the people capable of this were animals would be wrong: no animal would do such a thing.'[156] During the 1981 hunger strike, Thatcher held true to her political credo: 'Never compromise unless you absolutely must.'[157] However, she miscalculated the consequences of her obstinacy. SF subsequently entered the electoral arena and the strikes pushed the British government into negotiations with the Irish government. These negotiations ultimately led to the major concessions made in the Anglo-Irish agreement in 1985.[158] In her memoirs, Thatcher admitted it was possible 'to admire the courage of Sands and the other hunger strikers who died, but not to sympathise with their murderous cause.'[159] She claimed she went as far as she could to involve the ICJP 'hoping that the strikers would listen to them.'[160] Thatcher suggested that the Catholic Church had falsely denounced the British government 'for going back on undertakings we had allegedly made in the talks we had with them.'[161] New British government archival files reveal that, while the British officials listened to the Daly and Ó Fiaich's suggestions on how to improve prison conditions and end the protest, they were

---

[155] Thatcher, *Downing Street Years*, 392.   [156] Thatcher, *Downing Street Years*, 393.
[157] McGarry and O'Leary, *Explaining Northern Ireland*, 247.
[158] The 1985 Agreement gave the Irish government an advisory role in the governing of Northern Ireland. It confirmed Northern Ireland's status would not be changed without the majority consent of the population. Although the arrangement did not end the conflict, it proved key to improving the relationship between the Irish and British governments.
[159] Thatcher, *Downing Street Years*, 391.   [160] Thatcher, *Downing Street Years*, 391.
[161] Thatcher, *Downing Street Years*, 391–2.

careful to note that these were only suggestions and not agreements.[162] One meeting note during the 1980 hunger strike suggested: 'the Church is not being particularly helpful'.[163]

After the 1980–81 hunger strikes, the relationship between the Catholic Church and republicanism became strained. The strikes were not the first time republicans had railed against the Church, but they significantly increased the hostility many republicans felt for the institution.[164] An Phoblacht/Republican News condemned Ó Fiaich as someone who 'cynically used his position to break the relatives and so end the hunger strike.'[165] Faul received similar treatment from republicans.[166]

The 1981 hunger strike ended on 3 October when the remaining six prisoners terminated their fast at their families insistence, despite failing to gain their demands. The strike's conclusion also marked an end to more than five years of prison protests. The hunger strike ended because of the combined pressure of the British and Irish governments. However it was the efforts of the Catholic Church, with the British government's hints of concessions, which led the families of strikers to intervene medically to save their loved ones.[167] Three days after the strike ended, the new Secretary of State for Northern Ireland, James Prior, announced that the British government would allow prisoners to wear their own clothes. The 1981 hunger strike won new supporters for the republican cause within nationalist Ireland. Whereas possibly only a few thousand people supported the Provisional IRA beforehand, the prison protests and more specifically the 1981 hunger strike, led thousands more back to their cause.

The prison protests exposed the fractured nature of the Catholic Church towards the conflict. The rigid hierarchical structure of the institution, where priests did not challenge their ecclesiastical superiors, had all but disappeared. The coming years would see a further dissolution in the unity of the Church as well as greater antagonism between militant republicans and the Church. This chapter has therefore argued that the 1981 hunger strikes should be seen as marking a key turning point in the conflict. The period after the hunger strike, where SF gained political momentum, and thereby pushed the Church further away from many of its parishioners, is the focus of Chapter 4.

---

[162] TNA, CJ 4/3036, 'Note for the Secretary of State's Further Meeting with Cardinal Ó Fiaich and Bishop Daly, 30 June 1980'; TNA, CJ 4/3039, 'Secretary of State's meeting with Cardinal Ó Fiaich 23 October in Northern Ireland Office London', 27 Oct. 1980.

[163] TNA, CJ 4/3039, 'Possible Developments on the Hunger Strike and Related Activity', 30 Oct. 1980.

[164] Gerard Murray and Jonathan Tonge, Sinn Féin and the SDLP: From Alienation to Participation (London, 2005), 162.

[165] An Phoblacht/Republican News, 26 Nov. 1981.

[166] An Phoblacht/Republican News, 26 Sep. 1981.

[167] Bernadette McAliskey, Freedom only comes if you take it! (New York, 1982).

4

'To Remind Catholics that Support for the IRA and SF was not Compatible with Membership of the Catholic Church', 1982–1990

The sympathy for the 1981 hunger strike created a surge in the political popularity of violent republicanism.[1] In the 1982 Northern Ireland Assembly elections, SF received more than 10 percent of the vote.[2] In the Westminster elections the following year, the party gained 13.5 percent, with the SDLP's quota falling to below 18 percent. At this stage, SF accounted for more than 43 percent of the Catholic vote.[3] The Irish Catholic hierarchy grew increasingly concerned about such support as it seemed to demonstrate many of their parishioners looked to militant republicans. However, the position of the Northern bishops had shifted with the arrival of Co. Antrim-born Cahal Daly in 1982. Daly had been based in the Republic of Ireland at Ardagh and Clonmacnois as bishop since 1967 but frequently commented on violence in the North. His eloquent writings on violence, his birthplace of Loughguile, and his extensive understanding of Catholic theology made him the obvious choice for the position of bishop of Down and Connor. With his introduction to the Northern hierarchy Daly employed meas-ured words, enriched with Catholic theology: 'to remind Catholics that support for the IRA and SF was not compatible with membership of the Catholic Church'.[4] However, Daly's sermons on political matters in West Belfast were often the subject of staged walkouts throughout the 1980s. The emphatic rejection of SF and militant republicanism in Daly's comments, sermons, and networks was counterbalanced by Cardinal Ó Fiaich's nationalist sympathies, creating a new dynamic in the Northern hierarchy which lasted until the cardinal's death in 1990.

This chapter interrogates the impact of Daly's introduction into the Northern hierarchy on conflict resolution and ecumenical efforts between 1982 and 1990. In addition, it analyses Church reaction to Irish prisoners in England, the entangled peace efforts and their coordination between the episcopal councils of Ireland,

---

[1] Chapter title reference: Rafferty, *Catholicism in Ulster*, 282.
[2] Rafferty, *Catholicism in Ulster*, 282.   [3] Rafferty, *Catholicism in Ulster*, 282.
[4] Rafferty, *Catholicism in Ulster*, 282.

Scotland, and England and Wales. I argue that, after the 1981 hunger strikes, the Church lost its ability to influence the grassroots political situation in Northern Ireland. This relative loss of support was part of a larger trend of the gradual separation between Church and state throughout the South, as demonstrated through the New Ireland Forum. In response, the hierarchy began to emphasize its pastoral role in the life of Irish Catholics, concentrating instead on ecumenical and entangled peace efforts to end the Troubles. As the conflict progressed, Bishop Cahal Daly filled his homilies for victims with messages of peace and reconciliation: homilies that often became formulaic.[5]

This chapter also examines a struggle between two prelates: Cardinal Ó Fiaich and Bishop Cahal Daly. Whether on issues of extradition or perceived British government injustices, the bishops' responses often differed. In effect, they represented both sides of a spectrum and balanced the hierarchy in the North. With Ó Fiaich's sudden death in May 1990, the hierarchy's viewpoint became markedly more conservative after Daly took his place as the new Primate of All Ireland.

The Church and Sinn Féin

After the 1981 hunger strikes, SF proved it could gain electoral support from the Northern Ireland Catholic community. Following the electoral victory of Bobby Sands and the pro-hunger strike candidates both in the North and South, the 'armalite and ballot box' strategy was born. Before the strikes, SF remained a minor political party with limited electoral success. As more Catholics cast their vote for a party linked with the Provisionals, the Catholic Church stood up and took notice of measurable Provisional IRA support. From 1982, the Church and especially the hierarchy, denounced the party. On rare occasions some bishops showed sympathy to the voters, but attempted to remind them of the party's incompatible support of violence. The battle between SF and the Catholic Church continued throughout the rest of the conflict.

During his New Year's Day address in 1983, Bishop Cahal Daly challenged SF to choose between the ballot box and the armalite. Daly asked why paramilitary groups did not openly set out their economic, social, and ideological policies and 'credible indications' of how they would realize these ideas.[6] The bishop's comments infuriated the Provisional IRA and, in a statement released in Dublin, they claimed the bishop's attack was hypocritical. They pressed Daly to give his opinion on the British presence in Northern Ireland and, if he said it was beneficial, they

[5] Funeral Mass for Colum McCallan, 18 July 1986; Funeral Mass for Martin Duffy, 22 July 1986; Funeral Mass for Patrick McAllister, 28 Aug. 1986; Funeral Mass for Raymond Mooney, 19 Sep. 1986; Funeral Mass for Roy Webb, 20 Sep. 1986 in Cahal Daly, *Addresses 1984–86*, (Belfast, 1986).

[6] CTOMLA, FDFP 1983–84, 'Dialogue for Peace: Address for World Day of Peace', 1 Jan. 1983.

would 'know where Dr Daly stood politically'.[7] Gerry Adams confronted Daly over what Adams saw as the 'Church's failure to play a leadership role in issues of justice'.[8] In his memoir Adams noted that unlike churches elsewhere, in South Africa or Latin America, in his opinion the Irish Catholic Church was detached from the most disadvantaged people.

The NIO felt Daly's comments were attuned with the Secretary of State Jim Prior's own policies. While the Secretary of State's office was content with most of Daly's speech, they believed he was 'unfair' concerning the effects that Northern Ireland's poor quality of housing had on community relations. Prior believed the bishop's knowledge of this issue was shaped by 'hearsay', especially because many unionists decried a new 'pro-Catholic' housing agenda.[9] To ensure Daly was better informed on housing, Prior's team arranged for a meeting of the bishop with the Housing Executive. An interesting point was made in the concluding remarks of the memo. It revealed plans for Prior to refer to Daly's evocation of persuasion over force in his address, but Prior worried that this might be giving Daly too much support in public and thus undermining his position in the Catholic community.

During a January 1983 recording of the RTÉ radio programme *This Week*, Cardinal Ó Fiaich announced he was 'not surprised' by the electoral success of SF but he believed only a small percentage of that vote was directly for the Provisional IRA,[10] as the SF campaign in some areas was much more aggressive than the SDLP's. These factors, combined with the party's youthful candidates and the protest vote, added to SF's recent success. Despite SF's open support for the Provisionals, the cardinal reflected it would not be proper for the Church to tell its parishioners which way they should vote. In the interview, Ó Fiaich accused SF of hiding their support for violence during their recent campaign for the Assembly elections. Danny Morrison, a Mid-Ulster Assemblyman at this time, criticized the cardinal for his 'disingenuous' attempt 'to claim that SF played down its principled support for the armed struggle until after the election result'.[11] Morrison claimed Ó Fiaich did a disservice to his intelligence by telling people they did not know what they voted for before this election.

The Irish government also rejected the cardinal's comments that people might be justified in voting for SF based on their 'local community activities'.[12] Ó Fiaich's remarks followed the Irish Defence Minister's call for the Church to condemn membership to the party after the death of two members of the Republic's security forces. Edward Moxon-Browne's 1986 article suggested 70 percent of SF voters polled that year agreed the 'use of violence can sometimes be justified to bring

[7] *Irish Press*, 4 Jan. 1983.
[8] Gerry Adams, *Hope and History: Making Peace in Ireland* (London, 2003), 14.
[9] TNA, FCO 87/1576, 'New Year's Address by Bishop Cahal Daly' memorandum, 14 Jan. 1983.
[10] *Irish Independent*, 3 Jan. 1983.   [11] *Irish News*, 4 Jan. 1983.
[12] *World Focus*, 22 Jan. 1983.

about political change'.[13] In an article for *World Focus*, journalist Patrick Bishop noted the growing annoyance of the state with the Church's interference in government affairs. However, what the journalist failed to address was the call on the Church to intervene had been initiated by the defence minister in the first instance.

The hierarchy continued to ask Catholics to 'think before voting SF' throughout 1983, lest their decision be construed as a vote for violence, which is 'one of the greatest dangers we all face'.[14] While the NIO welcomed this pronouncement, SF quickly responded that if British imperialism were to be removed from the area, then, 'Republican violence...would disappear'.[15] A plea by Ó Fiaich in May 1983 sought to clarify the hierarchy's stance, through appealing to Catholics after the murder of an RUC officer in Cookstown 'to refuse support of any kind to organisations which justify or use violence, bloodshed and murder as a means of achieving ends'.[16] The cardinal's comments followed a similar statement made by Bishop Edward Daly concerning sectarian murders in his diocese earlier that month. In his homily at the Requiem Mass of Alice Purvis, a woman shot by the Provisional IRA when she jumped in front of the intended target, her husband, a soldier in the British Army,[17] Daly stated:

> In conscience, as a follower of Jesus Christ and a member of the Catholic Church, I must state I could not offer support of any kind to any public representative who...in any way would attempt to excuse, justify or condone action such as this as part of a military campaign.[18]

By the end of 1983, it appeared three hierarchy members in Northern Ireland, bishops Cahal Daly, Edward Daly, and Cardinal Ó Fiaich, had agreed on a policy of unequivocal denunciation of SF. This coordinated effort stemmed from increased communication between the Northern dioceses and a more effective Catholic media office installed by Edward Daly in 1974. Catholics were, through a three-line whip, reminded to examine their consciences before choosing to vote for the party aligned with the Provisionals. On 9 June 1983, during the UK general election, Gerry Adams received 42.6 percent of the votes in West Belfast. In an article for *The Irish Times*, Fionnuala O Connor wondered if this result repeated the 'old maxim for Irish nationalists, religion from Rome, politics from home'.[19] After their parishioners went against the bishops' advice, the hierarchy regrouped, declaring the vote for SF was based on protest, not support of violence. In this instance, the line between the pastoral and the political was blurred, as it appeared

---

[13] Edward Moxon-Browne, 'Alienation: The case of the Catholics in Northern Ireland', *Journal of Political Science*, 14 (1986), 84.

[14] *Irish Times*, 5 May 1983.   [15] *Irish Times*, 5 May 1983.

[16] *Irish Independent*, 22 May 1983.

[17] McKittrick, Kelters, Feeney, and Thorton, *Lost Lives*, 943.

[18] *Belfast Telegraph*, 27 May 1983.   [19] *Irish Times*, 25 June 1983.

the bishops were defending the actions of their parishioners, having denouncing SF the week before. O Connor's article provided some understanding of the hierarchy's position on SF and highlighted the ways in which the bishops further isolated those within the Catholic community who supported the Provisional IRA.

The year 1984 opened with an intellectual attack on the Church after Ó Fiaich's interview on RTÉ radio. During the 15 January broadcast, the cardinal declared he could not judge another person's conscience but deemed SF to be 'morally wrong'.[20] However, he also stated people joined SF to become involved with agitating for local benefits and better housing. While he prefaced this statement, his words caused significant damage; the extent of which can be seen through politicians' statements and angry letters to the editor across national and local newspapers.[21] The SF President 'slammed' the cardinal for his views, believing while the Church equated SF with violence it did not do the same for the UDR after Thatcher had recently visited a barracks in Armagh.[22] Garret Fitzgerald's coalition Irish government denounced the cardinal's qualified stance without referring to him specifically. The Irish government released a statement in which it declared SF openly championed a campaign of violence and in these circumstances, 'ancillary political activities' could never 'provide grounds for support of any kind' for the party.[23] SF president Gerry Adams called the government's response 'hysterical', and he thought the government wished to make SF a 'scapegoat' for violence in Northern Ireland.[24] Further, the cardinal drew the ire of the SDLP party chairman, Sean Farren, who found it 'incomprehensible' that anyone could distinguish between the violent and peaceful activities of SF.[25] However, John Hume defended his former professor on the same programme two weeks later, arguing the prelate spoke 'pastorally'.[26] The DUP's Rev Ian Paisley declared Ó Fiaich's interview revealed 'the true aims and intentions of the Roman Catholic Church' were the same as the Provisionals.[27]

Ó Fiaich was the religious leader of a marginalized Catholic community. He attempted to understand those Catholics who felt frustrated by British Army and RUC harassment while SF potentially offered, seemingly, some understanding of their issues. Rather than further isolate this vulnerable group, the cardinal attempted to extend an olive branch to those in his community. Yet his words backfired and left many viewing the cardinal as, at best, ambivalent towards violence.

Private meetings between Irish government officials, clergy, and bishops revealed mixed reactions to Ó Fiaich's controversial interview. Bishop Cahal

---

[20] *Armagh Observer*, 19 Jan. 1984.   [21] *Belfast Newsletter*, 18 Jan. 1984.
[22] *Irish Press*, 19 Jan. 1984.   [23] *Corkman*, 20 Jan. 1984.
[24] *Irish News*, 19 Jan. 1984.   [25] *Belfast Newsletter*, 18 Jan. 1984.
[26] CTOMLA, 'Au Tuaisceart', Transcript of RTÉ Radio *This Week* with John Hume and Jim Dougall, 29 Jan. 1984.
[27] *Northern Constitution*, 4 Feb. 1984.

Daly met with Martin Burke of the Irish Department of Foreign Affairs. Daly felt Ó Fiaich would regret his words on the radio to the extent that they made it appear as if the cardinal supported SF. Daly reiterated the perspective that people voted for SF as a protest vote against the British government, not as a vote for violence—but SF promoted it as such.[28] Burke's other meeting with Fr John O'Connor, the Director of Down and Connor Relief Advisory Service, reiterated the cardinal would be embarrassed by the interview. O'Connor said he and his colleagues were not surprised the cardinal had 'put his foot in it' in regards to the RTÉ interview, and noted the cardinal was a sincere man but not taken 'too seriously in his own community'.[29] The cardinal's private secretary, Fr James Clyne, briefed another Irish government Department of Foreign Affairs officer, D. Ó Ceallaigh, that Ó Fiaich was upset about the reaction to his interview, especially Gerry Fitt's reaction. The cardinal and Fitt had had an acrimonious relationship since 1977, when Ó Fiaich was ordained as Archbishop of Armagh. On that occasion, Ó Fiaich had decided not to invite Westminster MPs, so he would not have to invite Rev Ian Paisley. Consequently, Fitt did not receive an invitation but John Hume, who was the cardinal's first MA student at Maynooth, did. Clyne explained this was probably why Fitt had attacked the cardinal ever since.[30] These meetings reveal that, privately, members of the Catholic Church were concerned over Ó Fiaich's statements but all agreed they did not accurately represent the cardinal's true sentiments.

Bishop Cahal Daly spoke at Queen's University Belfast three weeks after Ó Fiaich's interview, where he left no doubt about his views on the Provisionals and SF. He declared the Provisionals had no basis for their 'just war' claims and he also asked unionists to move away from their 'entrenched positions' and 'be flexible' to help with the deadlocked political situation.[31] Daly had long held this belief, combating the IRA's position since the early 1970s.[32] Despite this attempt, the Irish hierarchy failed in their efforts to demonstrate a united front.

The struggle between the hierarchy and SF continued throughout 1984. When four bishops from the USA visited Northern Ireland, they asked for a meeting with Northern politicians. While the Church claimed they had sent an invitation to every political party asking for two representatives to meet the bishops, only the SDLP and the Official Unionists agreed to this offer. SF asserted they had not received this message, and therefore the Derry spokesman for the group, Martin McGuinness, told the media of this failure and said he was 'keen' to meet the

---

[28] NAI, DFA/2014/52/40, Notes on 19 January 1984 meeting between Bishop Daly and Martin Burke, 23 Jan. 1984.
[29] NAI, DFA/2014/52/40, Notes on 18 January 1984 meeting between Fr John O'Connor and Martin Burke, 27 Jan. 1984.
[30] NAI, DFA/2014/52/40, Notes on meeting between Fr James Clyne and D. Ó Ceallaigh, 31 Jan. 1984.
[31] *Irish News*, 3 Feb. 1984.
[32] See Daly, *Violence in Ireland*; BDA, GPD-L-C2, Cahal Daly to George Dwyer, 8 Jan. 1972.

bishops.[33] McGuinness later claimed the American bishops had 'shunned' him during their visit, which the bishops denied.[34] While Bishop Edward Daly attempted to alleviate the misunderstanding, he repeated that the visiting bishops could not fit another meeting into their schedule.

The hierarchy had mostly spoken out against SF and refused to create dialogue with the rising nationalist party until the Provisional IRA laid down their weapons. It was not just the hierarchy who regularly battled with SF, but some priests and women religious like Sr Genevieve O'Farrell, because SF disagreed with her close relationship with the NIO and British government officials.[35] On the other hand, Fathers Des Wilson and Alec Reid believed a solution to the conflict could be found if the Catholic Church developed a process for conflict resolution. Reid began to convince politicians to seek dialogue with other political parties because of his friendship with Adams. In October 1982, Reid worked with republicans to help release two kidnapped men, Catholic Joseph Donegan and UDR member Sergeant Thomas Cochrane. While his efforts to bring both men safely home had failed, their deaths touched Reid and pushed him to re-double his efforts in bringing all nationalists together for peace.[36] Reid, Wilson, and Fr Gerry Reynolds (see Appendix) attempted to involve the Bishops' Conference by creating a formal meeting between SF and the hierarchy, but this plan did not come to fruition. Reid then approached SDLP deputy leader Seamus Mallon in 1985, who agreed to discussion between the parties. Yet these talks too were cancelled after the murder of a Catholic building contractor and father of six, Seamus McAvoy, whom the Provisional IRA claimed had sold building materials to the British Army.[37] In a letter to Adams, Auxiliary Bishop of Armagh Dr James Lennon, who had been privately working with Reid and Wilson to orchestrate the meeting, believed the talks between SF and the SDLP needed to wait until after the Anglo-Irish meetings concluded.[38] Building on their work as mediators between republicans and the British government during the 1974–75 ceasefire and the 1981 hunger strikes, these individual priests would bring SF together with the SDLP and the Irish government by the late 1980s and early 1990s.

The hierarchy continued publicly to condemn SF, although some in the priesthood attempted privately to persuade party members for a constitutional, rather than militant, solution to the conflict. While both Bishop Cahal Daly and Cardinal Ó Fiaich condemned violence, Daly's more outspoken words against SF demonstrated a different tactic towards the party. Whereas Daly dealt in passionate condemnations, the cardinal tried more quiet reasoning. Their fire and ice strategies often placed the men on opposite ends of the political spectrum. After SF's electoral

---

[33] *Belfast Telegraph*, 23 Oct. 1984.   [34] *Irish News*, 23 Oct. 1984.
[35] Rae, *Sister Genevieve*, 175–180.   [36] Adams, *Hope and History*, 16.
[37] McKittrick, Kelters, Feeney, and Thorton, *Lost Lives*, 1021.
[38] Adams, *Hope and History*, 37.

success, the bishops could no longer suggest the Provisional IRA was a minority group that lacked support. They appeared paralyzed in their desire to acknowledge the grievances of the Catholic working-class while also attempting to dissuade parishioners from supporting SF. Despite the problems faced by the Catholic Church as a whole, as the conflict continued individual priests like Reid and Wilson would play an important role in bringing SF towards the path to peace.

New Ireland Forum and Report

The New Ireland Forum was an assembly between 1983 and 1984 at which Irish nationalist parties and organizations discussed potential political developments that could alleviate the conflict. Taoiseach Garret Fitzgerald established the Forum, influenced by SDLP politician John Hume. Although unionists and SF initially dismissed the Forum, 317 submissions were received from the public. Clare O'Halloran notes the Forum 'attracted considerable if undefined popular support' but that it failed in its aims because it 'proposed concrete changes in the Republic without any compensatory guarantee of unity'.[39] Katy Hayward adds the Forum's stated desire for 'fundamental changes to the Irish state structures and constitution' to end the conflict proved too divisive for nationalist politicians North and South, including Charles Haughey.[40] The New Ireland Forum Report, published on 2 May 1984, listed three possible solutions to the conflict: a joint British/Irish authority; a unitary state; and a federal state. Two submissions came from the Irish Catholic Church: one individually from Dublin native Fr Brian Lennon SJ in October 1983 and a second from the Irish Episcopal Conference in January 1984.[41] O'Halloran argues that because the Catholic bishops were invited to submit to the Forum, unionists therefore equated nationalism with Roman Catholicism.[42] The Church's inclusion in the Forum also exacerbated unionist concerns. In addition, the Forum was the first time the bishops were publicly cross-examined by all the major nationalist parties 'about the effects [that] their religious positions had on politics', thereby challenging the relationship between Church and state.[43]

Murray and Faul denounced the Forum. In their pamphlet, *The Alienation of Northern Ireland Catholics*, the pair wrote they believed the Forum could not help Catholics who suffered discrimination as it excluded SF. The priests discounted

---

[39] Clare O'Halloran, *Partition and the Limits of Irish Nationalism: An Ideology Under Stress* (Dublin, 1987), 194.

[40] Katy Hayward, *Irish nationalism and European integration: The official redefinition of the island of Ireland* (Manchester, 2009), 192.

[41] Brian Lennon, *After the Ceasefires: Catholics and the Future of Northern Ireland* (Dublin, 1995), 10.

[42] O'Halloran, *Partition*, 201–4; 207.   [43] Lennon, *After the Ceasefires*, 42.

the standing of the Forum: 'besides no one in Northern Ireland talks about it, discusses it nor has any interest in it...It seems to be dismissed as a non-event'.[44] However many clerics from Protestant churches made contributions to the Forum, including the Methodist minister Rev Sydney Callaghan and members from the Church of Ireland.[45]

Despite Lennon's contribution through his oral submission on 4 October 1983, the New Ireland Forum overwhelmingly represented the views of the Irish hierarchy.[46] The Irish Episcopal Conference submitted their formal, written presentation in January 1984. This Forum provided the bishops with the opportunity to 'address their position in relations to issues which had become highly contentious'.[47] In its introduction, Ó Fiaich asserted the power of the churches, both Protestant and Catholic, to provide solutions in this field was 'strictly limited'.[48] Ó Fiaich thought it would be inappropriate for the hierarchy to make any recommendations regarding 'political structures' and thus the Church's involvement would remain limited. The bishops also expressed their resistance to divorce, which they described as 'an attack on society'.[49] They gave five key issues which they felt were relevant to people in a New Ireland which included morality, education, reconciliation, marriage, and violence in the North.[50]

Many in the media attacked the bishops' report. The *Galway Advertiser*, a regional newspaper, pounced on the submission as it held the 'expectation that Catholic moral teaching will be supported by legislation'.[51] While *The Church of Ireland Gazette* thought the bishops' submission revealed an 'absence of realism' and found particularly insulting the bishops' expectations that Roman Catholic canon law should be the authority on personal morality.[52] These negative regional and religious press reactions further illustrated a major shift in thinking; even twenty years previously it would have been commonplace for the Catholic Church to give its opinion on the workings of the state and societal morality without negative comment.

On 9 February 1984, the Irish Episcopal Conference gave their oral submission to the Forum. Four bishops gave evidence at Dublin Castle: Bishops Cahal Daly and Edward Daly from the North and Bishops Joseph Cassidy and Dermot O'Mahony from the South. Two lay people also joined the panel, Professor Mary McAleese of Trinity College Dublin and Dr Matthew Slater of

---

[44] Denis Faul and Raymond Murray, *The Alienation of Northern Ireland Catholics* (Armagh, 1984).

[45] NAI, 2014/52/29, Notes of Conversation with Martin Burke and Eric Elliott, 14 September 1983.

[46] Lennon does not include his own contribution to the Forum in his book despite discussing the Forum's merit; Lennon, *After the Ceasefires*, 28–9, 42.

[47] Louise Fuller, 'Political fragmentation in independent Ireland' in Oliver Rafferty (ed.), *Irish Catholic Identities* (Manchester, 2013), 317.

[48] *Irish Independent*, 13 Jan. 1984.   [49] *Irish Independent*, 28 Jan. 1984.

[50] *New Ireland Forum: Report of Proceedings Public Session, 9 February 1984* (Dublin, 1984), 1–5.

[51] *Galway Advertiser*, 19 Jan. 1984.   [52] *Irish Press*, 4 Feb. 1984.

Queen's University Belfast.[53] The bishops were questioned by a group of elected representatives from the political parties present, after their written submission caused 'controversy', with some newspapers claiming it 'displayed some alarming insensitivity to the rights of minorities'.[54]

In his opening statement, Bishop Cahal Daly reassured the Forum of the Church's desire to 'promote lasting reconciliation and justice and peace in Ireland'.[55] Further, the Church rejected a 'confessional state', a Catholic state for Catholic people, arguing 'the alliance of Church and state is harmful for the Church and harmful for the state'.[56] This was an argument that would never have been made during the creation of the Free State. As Katy Hayward has discussed, a large proportion of the New Ireland Forum proceedings involved acknowledging a Protestant, unionist, and 'British' identity and the role it could play in Ireland.[57] The Church recognized it needed to deemphasize its control over the Irish state in order to make unionists more comfortable with the prospect of a united Ireland. In his opening statement, Daly asserted the Church would resist any constitutional proposals to 'imperil the civil and religious rights and liberties cherished by Northern Protestants'.[58] On the issue of morality, Daly reiterated the Church did not want the moral teaching of the Gospel embedded in the constitution, but it was the Church's pastoral duty to 'alert the consciences of Catholics to the moral consequences of any proposed piece of legislation'.[59]

After each of the four bishop's statements, the appointed committee questioned them, with Cahal Daly facing one of the thorniest issues as presented by Seamus Mallon of the SDLP. Mallon referred to the written submission, where the bishops discussed political pluralism: 'It is clear that a political party which advocates misuse of political force in pursuit of its policies cannot claim acceptance merely on the basis of political pluralism'.[60] Here, Mallon clearly alluded to SF: at the party's last Ard Fheis, Gerry Adams declared armed struggle as a moral form of resistance. Responding to Ó Fiaich's January 1984 radio interview, Mallon questioned Daly on his support for SF; given SF's support for the Provisionals, was Daly not acting in opposition to the views of the Church? Daly responded that although people were driven to vote for the party out of frustration, they must realize that whatever their intentions, their vote would be interpreted as one for violence. When questioned on the subject, Bishop Edward Daly stated many in his community and especially young men could be caught up in the violence because of their frustrations over injustices. The argument concluded with Cahal Daly's

---

[53] McAleese was a lecturer in Criminal Law at Trinity College Dublin. She would go on to be the President of the Republic of Ireland from 1997 until 2011. Slater was a lecturer in education at Queen's University Belfast who specialized in integrated education.

[54] *Irish Press*, 20 Jan. 1984; *Irish Examiner*, 10 Feb. 1984.

[55] *New Ireland Forum*, 1.   [56] *New Ireland Forum*, 2.

[57] Katy Hayward, 'The politics of nuance: Irish official discourse on Northern Ireland', *Irish Political Studies*,19 (2004), 24.

[58] *New Ireland Forum*, 2.   [59] *New Ireland Forum*, 2.   [60] *New Ireland Forum*, 5.

Figure 5 *Sunday Independent*, 12 February 1984
Source: Jim Cogan Cartoons.

assertion that the armed struggle was both immoral and unjustified. However, he ended with a brief statement concerning his relationship with Ó Fiaich, declaring they were not divided in opinion. Both agreed it was 'morally wrong to support violence or to vote for political parties that support violence' but 'moral judgment' was 'distinct from pastoral analysis of the motives' which led people to vote SF.[61] Here Daly attempted some form of damage control to give the appearance of unity among the Irish bishops.

The bishops also spoke on divorce, Church-state relations, mixed marriages, reconciliation, ecumenism, and the Irish constitution. Cahal Daly believed in no way could the Republic's constitution 'be imposed on Northern Ireland Unionists'.[62] Therefore a united Ireland would require an adapted constitution. The bishops faced critical questioning from the political parties present, demonstrating a division between Church and state and the desire for this to become even more pronounced. *The Sunday Independent* reported on the 'drama' of the bishops' cross-examination, featuring a political cartoon (Figure 5) likening the event to a tennis match but one in which the bishop clearly controlled the rally.

---

[61] *New Ireland Forum*, 50. [62] *New Ireland Forum*, 39.

After the publication of the New Ireland Forum Report in May 1984, Margaret Thatcher dismissed the findings. Ó Fiaich denounced Thatcher's attitude in an interview on Irish radio, believing the Prime Minister did not possess a nuanced understanding of the situation in Northern Ireland.[63] However, the Forum helped to establish a nationalist consensus leading up to the Anglo-Irish Agreement in 1985.[64] Hayward acknowledges the Forum was 'one of the most visionary events for constitutional nationalism' as Irish nationalist politicians like Garret FitzGerald argued for the inclusion of the Protestant unionist identity and their 'sense of Britishness' would have to be acknowledged for a united Ireland to succeed.[65] Further, the Forum encouraged Fitzgerald's government to embrace a more pluralist state on his 'crusade' for constitutional reform.[66]

Irish Prisoners in Britain

Prison conditions in Northern Ireland continued to improve after the 1981 hunger strike. As a result, the clergy's focus shifted towards the situation of Irish people imprisoned in England. The cases of the Birmingham Six,[67] Maguire Seven,[68] and Guildford Four[69] demonstrate the activities of a handful of women religious and priests who worked to prove the innocence of these groups. While the hierarchy in Ireland spoke infrequently about the prisoners, the English hierarchy itself remained silent and seemingly aloof in respect of these detainees until 1986. It is likely that the reticence of the English hierarchy was a result of

---

[63] *Standard*, 4 Jan. 1985.

[64] While the Church played a role in the New Ireland Forum, the bishops' involvement in negotiations for the Anglo-Irish agreement was limited. Bishop Edward Daly wrote privately to the Taoiseach to congratulate him on the agreement but shied away from commenting on it publicly. NAI/ 2015/89/54, Edward Daly to Garret Fitzgerald, 17 Nov. 1985. Ó Fiaich worried that the nationalist community would be divided over the Agreement. NAI/2015/89/73, Meeting with Cardinal Ó Fiaich notes, 4 Nov. 1985. However, Faul and Murray voiced their concerns and how working-class nationalists would perceive it to Dublin government officials. NAI/2015/89/54, David Donoghue meeting notes, 2 Jan. 1986.

[65] Hayward, 'The politics of nuance', 24.

[66] The Irish government held a referendum in June 1986 to remove the constitutional ban on divorce in an attempt to improve relations in Northern Ireland. Archbishop Kevin McNamara of Dublin wrote of the Church's duty to explain the 'moral' aspects of new state legislation, including divorce, to Catholics but stressed the non-political nature of the Church. While the divorce referendum failed, the very fact it was held demonstrates the Irish government's willingness to further break ties with the Church.

[67] The Birmingham Six were Hugh Callaghan, Patrick Hill, Gerard Hunter, Richard McIlkenny, John Walker, and William Power. In 1975 they were sentenced to life imprisonment for Birmingham pub bombings.

[68] The Maguire Seven were Anne and Patrick Maguire, their sons Patrick and Vincent as well as Sean Smyth, Patrick O'Neill, and Giuseppe Conlon. They were charged with possessing nitroglycerine and creating bombs for the IRA. They were convicted in March 1976 and received a range of sentences.

[69] The Guildford Four were Paul Hill, Gerry Conlon, Paddy Armstrong, and Carole Richardson, individuals wrongly convicted in October 1975 for the Guildford pub bombings. They each received a sentence of life imprisonment.

greater pressures from the public; for the public needed to support these prisoners and favour acquittal before the hierarchy could publicly state their own position.

Individual members of the clergy and official prison chaplains helped prisoners held in the English prison system. One such person was Sr Sarah Clarke of the La Sainte Union order, a rural Galway woman who lived in a convent in Highgate, London. Clarke became involved in the campaign to help prisoners in England after attending a political rally in London at the age of fifty-three.[70] In her memoir, Clarke recounted many long waits in prison queues to deliver care packages to Irish men and women imprisoned throughout England. The Home Office refused Clarke visits to any Category A prisoners during her life because of her work as an advocate. Letters between government officials described the elderly nun as 'dangerous'.[71]

In the 1970s, Clarke founded the Relatives and Friends of Prisoners Committee (RFPC), which operated from bases in London and Belfast. The main objective of RFPC was to protect the rights of prisoners and their families. RFPC maintained a twenty-four-hour telephone service so that, when the security forces arrested Irish men and women in Britain, the RFPC could respond immediately. The RFPC also concentrated their efforts on the repatriation of Irish prisoners serving sentences in Britain. In June 1982, Clarke sent information to Lord Raymond Hylton, who then asked a question about the repatriation of prisoners in the House of Lords. Hylton had a keen interest in the Irish question and regularly corresponded with the Bishop of Arundel and Brighton, Cormac Murphy-O'Connor, providing his own proposals for a solution to the conflict.[72] RFPC also lobbied MPs, TDs, and British and Irish government ministers.

In November 1981, Pope John Paul II issued the encyclical *Familiaris Consortio*. Section four focused on 'Pastoral Care of the Family in Difficult Situations', which Clarke felt related to her work.[73] She wrote an impassioned letter, sending copies to Bishop Dermot O'Mahony, Cardinal Tomás Ó Fiaich, Archbishop Dermot Ryan in Dublin, Brian Lenihan, and the editors of *The Irish Times*, *Irish Press*, and *Sunday Press*, in which she highlighted over 800 prisoners serving time in British jails had been born in the Republic of Ireland. Clarke worried the hierarchy would excommunicate her but instead her letter's subsequent publication in *The Irish Times* on 1 March 1982 mobilized a dramatic response.[74] Ó Fiaich brought together the Irish Commission for Justice and Peace (now the Irish Commission for Justice and Social Affairs) (ICJP), with their English counterpart, to discuss the matter of prisoners.

---

[70] Clarke, *No Faith in the System*, 28–31.   [71] Clarke, *No Faith in the System*, 129–30.

[72] Arundel and Brighton Diocesan Archive (ABDA) Northern Ireland File, Raymond Hylton to Murphy-O'Connor, 14 Oct. 1981; ABDA, Northern Ireland File, 19 May 1981; ABDA, Northern Ireland File, 16 Nov. 1982; ABDA, Northern Ireland File, 5 Jan. 1983.

[73] Clarke, *No Faith in the System*, 113.   [74] Clarke, *No Faith in the System*, 114–15.

Fr P.J. Byrne, Secretary of the Irish Episcopal Commission for Emigrants, at the request of Bishop Eamon Casey, contacted Clarke about her work with prisoners. Byrne involved Fr Bobby Gilmore (see Appendix), leader of the Irish Chaplaincy Scheme, a group of priests who looked after Irish emigrants in Britain, to meet with Clarke in Dublin. Both organizations gave Clarke their support. Clarke also spoke at the annual general meeting of Ireland's Emigrant Chaplains but was deemed a Provisional IRA supporter by some hecklers when she discussed the Birmingham Six and Maguire Seven. A few months later, Clarke abandoned the Irish Chaplaincy Scheme as she felt disillusioned with the organization. Eventually, the Irish Chaplaincy Scheme created the Irish Commission for Prisoners Overseas (ICPO), which Clarke believed did 'good work' but not to the extent championed in 'the Holy Father's encyclical'.[75]

Fathers Brian Brady, Denis Faul, and Raymond Murray also worked with Clarke to campaign for the release of the Guildford Four, Maguire Seven, and Birmingham Six. The trio wrote to the Home Secretary to petition for the release of the prisoners and they attempted to involve the English hierarchy, chiefly Cardinal Hume. Clarke helped to organize campaigns to bring the cases to the court of appeal while Faul helped to connect the prisoners with lawyers.[76] Clarke commented in her memoir on the support given to her by Brady, Faul, and Murray, believing their backing allowed her to work with the prisoners as 'it was still a man's world at the time' and women religious usually worked in education.[77] Through the priests, who Clarke claimed were 'the closest we had to liberation theologians', she discovered human rights and liberation theology.[78] Despite this inclusion in her memoir, categorizations of her inspiration as 'liberation theology' may be a retrospective claim on Clarke's part, as her personal papers and literature of the time do not employ this terminology, unlike the contemporary writings of McVeigh and Wilson. Clarke noted women religious were often made to feel 'the lowest form of womanhood' but Brady, Faul, and Murray treated her 'as an equal'.[79]

Despite growing media interest in the cases of the Maguire Seven, Guildford Four, and Birmingham Six, Clarke felt the British media 'ignored elements of the cases' which she felt 'should have been reported on' including a letter from Cardinal Ó Fiaich to Home Secretary William Whitelaw in February 1985 asking him to reopen Giuseppe Conlon's case.[80] A BBC programme aired in July 1985, 'Surviving', produced by Jenny Morgan, which focused solely on Clarke's work with the Irish prisoners.[81] Clarke needed permission from her Mother Provincial and, after some initial confusion, she proceeded with the programme with no

---

[75] Clarke, *No Faith in the System*, 119.
[76] CTOMLA, FDFP 1985–86, E.O. to Faul, 29 Sep. 1986.
[77] Clarke, *No Faith in the System*, 141.   [78] Clarke, *No Faith in the System*, 141.
[79] Clarke, *No Faith in the System*, 141.   [80] Clarke, *No Faith in the System*, 147.
[81] Clarke, *No Faith in the System*, 148.

censorship from her Reverend Mother in England. Often Clarke would bring recently released or detained prisoners to her convent in order to regroup, supported by her fellow women religious and her Mother Provincial.

Fathers Faul and Murray had been working for the Birmingham Six since the 1970s, continuing to gather evidence and support their cause well into the late 1980s. Faul first met with Gerry Hunter's mother and then many of the other relatives of the imprisoned. While other advocates highlighted the allegations of abuse by police and false testimony, Faul and Murray drew attention to the 'weak' forensic evidence supplied in all three cases.[82] For his efforts to help these individuals, Faul received hate mail, condemning the priests' actions and railing about the prisoners' guilt.[83] In one example, an individual wrote: 'P.S.: The Birmingham 6 are guilty as hell. Their trial is a frame-up... The nitroglycerin didn't come from playing cards. Nobody knows that better than you.'[84] This anonymous author from Derry City demonstrates a closeness to the material. Unlike authors from outside the North, this person would have access to numerous newspaper articles reporting on the case.

The ICPO regularly campaigned for the release of these prisoners and aided their families. The Irish bishops founded the ICPO in May 1985, and organized a number of public meetings, petitions, and press conferences. The organization was composed of laity and clergy, funded by the bishops. The ICPO scheduled meetings for prisoners' families to gather and voice their concerns in Dublin in November 1986 and at Clonard Monastery, Belfast in March 1987.[85] The assistance of the ICPO demonstrated the institutional Church supported the Birmingham Six, Guildford Four, and Maguire Seven.

In addition to the ICPO, the National Birmingham Six Committee lead by Fr Bobby Gilmore also petitioned for the Six's release after the failed appeal in February 1988. Gilmore founded the organization in April 1988, with other local chapters created in Bolton, Sheffield, Oxford, Luton, Newport, and Southampton, as well as groups in the USA and the Republic.[86] Gilmore distributed information about the campaign's efforts to both Irish and English hierarchy members.[87] The campaign had two aims: to release the Birmingham Six and to secure their exoneration.[88] The Birmingham Six Campaign was another organization led by a priest, but was a quintessentially non-Church organization, with most members from the laity.

---

[82] *Irish Times*, 29 Oct. 1987.
[83] CTOMLA, FDFP 1987, J.K. to Faul, 8 April 1987; CTOMLA, FDFP 1987, M.M. to Faul, 10 May 1987; CTOMLA, FDFP 1987, Anonymous to Faul, Nov. 1987.
[84] CTOMLA, FDFP 1987, Anonymous to Faul, Nov. 1987.
[85] CTOMLA, FDFP 1986, Nuala Kelly to Faul, 23 Feb. 1987.
[86] Interview with Fr Bobby Gilmore, 23 May 2016.
[87] SDA, D47.2, Gilmore to Bowen, 19 July 1989.
[88] Liverpool Archdiocesan Archives (LAA), WOR 13/8, 'The Campaign' newsletter, Bobby Gilmore, 1988.

The Irish hierarchy, mainly through the voices of Cardinal Ó Fiaich and Bishop Edward Daly, championed repatriation and denounced the use of seemingly faulty forensic evidence during this period. In April 1983, Ó Fiaich spoke in Dublin at the Irish Episcopal Commission for Emigrants at the annual Congress of Irish Chaplains in Britain. He questioned the validity of forensic tests used in the case of the Maguire Seven.[89] The following year in his address to the same organization, Ó Fiaich asked why the Giuseppe Conlon and Maguire Seven case had not been reopened last year. There were 'doubts cast on forensic evidence' and support from several public figures, including Gerry Fitt, Sir John Biggs-Davidson, the MP Christopher Price, and 'the behind scenes' work of Cardinal Hume.[90] He asserted that many Irish hierarchy members had privately visited these prisoners in England, but because of their sheer number, after the introduction of the Prevention of Terrorism Act, there was a need for a group to aid these prisoners and their families. Ó Fiaich also singled out the case of prisoner Shane O'Doherty, who had renounced ties with the Provisionals years before.[91] Despite petitions from hierarchy members and politicians, he remained imprisoned in England.[92] The cardinal described how the prison system often moved O'Doherty to facilities across England, making it financially difficult for his family to visit. Repatriating him to a prison in Northern Ireland would ease his family's burden. Ó Fiaich remarked O'Doherty's case was just one example of many. Bishop Edward Daly and Bishop William Gordon Wheeler of Leeds had followed O'Doherty's case since 1980, when he and fellow prisoners at Wakefield Prison in West Yorkshire were refused Mass.[93] Daly voiced his outrage in an article for *The Irish News*.

Of the Irish hierarchy, Bishop Edward Daly was most preoccupied with the Birmingham Six. He had been corresponding and meeting with three of the prisoners, Paddy Hill, John Walker, and Hugh Callaghan, since the early 1980s. Daly felt his connection with Walker drew him to the case: 'I was deeply involved with that [the Birmingham Six appeal], because I knew one of them, John Walker, who's from Derry'.[94] In his memoirs, Daly recounts how long-term prisoners treated harshly other inmates who repeatedly announced their innocence. Such pleas of innocence 'cut little ice' with other inmates unless based in fact.[95] However, he noted many other prisoners with whom he visited championed the Birmingham Six's innocence, confirming Daly's faith in the innocence of the Six.

January 1987 marked a breakthrough in the Birmingham Six case, when British Home Secretary Douglas Hurd referred the case to the Court of Appeal.[96] The prisoners' solicitor Gareth Pierce asked Edward Daly to prepare an affidavit and give evidence on the particular Irish culture which surrounds funerals, whereby

[89] *Standard*, 22 April 1983.   [90] DeDA, Ó Fiaich Address, 26 April 1984.
[91] *Belfast Telegraph*, 8 April 1983.   [92] *Cork Evening News*, 2 March 1985.
[93] Shane O'Doherty, *The Volunteer: A Former IRA Man's True Story* (London, 1993), 223–6.
[94] Interview with Bishop Edward Daly, 2 June 2015.
[95] Daly, *A Troubled See*, 153.   [96] *Irish Times*, 15 Aug. 1987.

many Irish people attend funerals of paramilitaries but do not support the Provisionals. In November 1987, Daly attended a large portion of the appeal process and gave his statement in the early course of the retrial. He testified to the court that in Irish culture, it was normal for friends and family to travel long distances to comfort the family of the deceased.[97] When the judges announced their verdict—the appeal's dismissal—Daly wept. Outside the Old Bailey, Daly declared to waiting television camera crews that he had 'lost his faith in British justice years ago' and that 'I am devastated, just heartbroken'.[98] Cardinal Ó Fiaich announced the combination of this verdict and the Stalker-Sampson Report would shake whatever confidence 'the nationalist people of Northern Ireland may have in British Justice'.[99] Edward Daly became the most visible member of the Irish hierarchy to champion the Birmingham Six. While his testimony did not change the verdict, it demonstrated how fully the Irish hierarchy supported the prisoners.

Bishop Cahal Daly's memoir puts the Birmingham Six and Guildford Four in perspective, focusing on their positive outcomes. While recognizing that the imprisonment of these two groups was unjust, he states: 'it must be admitted that a judicial system which can find within itself the honesty and the courage to recognize its own unjust decisions'.[100] Despite the many years of appeals and the extended imprisonment of these individuals, Cahal Daly still praised the system for eventually recognizing its own miscarriage of judgment. Even in his memoirs, Cahal Daly could not fully condemn the British government. However, Cahal Daly did challenge the British government over these cases at the time. In a February 1988 sermon, Cahal Daly announced he was 'totally convinced' of the innocence of the Birmingham Six but warned, during the failed appeal, that their case should not become 'mere British-bashing'.[101] Daly noted if it were not for the Provisionals planting the bomb originally, the Birmingham Six's unfair imprisonment would never have occurred. Yet Daly did not include the fact that in their haste to find the culprits, the British government had used profiling and faulty forensic evidence to convict these prisoners.

Bishop Edward Daly continued to work for the Birmingham Six after their failed appeal. He petitioned Hurd to ask Her Majesty to bestow the royal pejorative of mercy, with Ó Fiaich joining him in this mission.[102] Their request was denied, but Daly continued to appear on television programmes, like *60 Minutes* in the USA, and to give interviews to newspapers in support of the Six. He

---

[97] *Guardian*, 6 Nov. 1987.   [98] *Irish News*, 29 Jan. 1988.
[99] LAA, Statements by the Bishop of Woolwich and Cardinal Tomas Ó Fiaich, 28 Jan. 1988.
[100] Cahal Daly, *Steps on my Pilgrim Journey: Memories and Reflections* (Dublin, 1998), 253.
[101] 'Justice and Law: The Birmingham Six and the Stalker-Sampson Report', 7 Feb. 1988 in Cahal Daly, *Addresses 1987–88* (Belfast, 1988).
[102] *Irish Press*, 2 Jan. 1989.

published a pamphlet describing his relationship with the Six, outlining their innocence.[103] Daly's media presence added to the onslaught of published material demanding another appeal. The Director of Public Prosecutions announced in November 1990 the Court of Appeal would once again examine the case. Daly attended yet again for a portion of the trial and, after ten days, the six men walked free. Daly's repeated efforts and unwavering support demonstrated the institutional Irish hierarchy's commitment to overturning these human rights abuses.

The Church also reacted to the continued imprisonment of the Guildford Four. At the March 1988 Irish Episcopal Conference at Maynooth, the bishops discussed these prisoners and their poor treatment in prisons throughout England. Carole Richardson, who was only seventeen years old at the time of her conviction, grew very ill in prison.[104] The bishops released a statement calling for the British government to re-examine the Guildford Four case.[105] Cardinal Ó Fiaich wrote to Home Secretary Douglas Hurd to request an appeal, but complained when he did not receive a reply and accused the British government of not taking their letter seriously.[106] Shortly afterwards, Cardinal Hume also looked to Hurd for an appeal, and when asked his thoughts on Hume's actions, the Archbishop of Canterbury Robert Runcie revealed he had done the same.[107]

In January 1989, during his World Day of Peace address in Armagh, Ó Fiaich called on Hurd again to announce a referral to the Court of Appeal for the Guildford Four.[108] When the British government decided to reopen the case, the ICPO and Ó Fiaich welcomed the decision, with the cardinal signalling out Cardinal Hume's influence and praising his efforts.[109] The court hearing for the second appeal of Guildford Four concluded on 19 October 1989. All four were released after the court quashed their convictions and the Church rejoiced at the news. Ó Fiaich claimed 'Justice demands that the convictions of the whole Maguire family circle, including the late Giuseppe Conlon, must now be quashed'.[110] Cardinal Hume was 'immensely grateful', declaring 'I think justice is going to be done'.[111]

The Maguire Seven received less attention from the Church. While they were included in most claims against British legal injustices, they received neither the same level of support as the Birmingham Six nor the Guildford Four from the Church.[112] The nature of their charges meant the Maguire Seven faced lesser jail

---

[103] LAA, 'The Birmingham Six- A Personal View', Edward Daly, Aug. 1988.

[104] NAI, DFA-2012-59-1716, 'The Guildford Four- trial, imprisonment and efforts to appeal sentences, 1975–82'.

[105] LAA, Meeting of the Irish hierarchy at Maynooth, 10–12 Oct. 1988.

[106] *Irish Times*, 19 Nov. 1988.   [107] *Guardian*, 22 Oct. 1989.

[108] *Irish Times*, 2 Jan. 1989.   [109] *Irish Times*, 17 Jan. 1989.

[110] *Irish Times*, 21 Oct. 1989.   [111] *Irish Independent*, 18 Oct. 1989.

[112] NAI, DFA-2014-38-127, 'Digest of Foreign News Coverage of Ireland, September 1976'; NAI, DFA-2012-59-1716, The Guildford Four- trial, imprisonment and efforts to appeal sentences, 1975–82'.

sentences. Yet privately Cardinal Hume had been working for the release of the Maguire Seven since 1978. In 1979, Hume privately petitioned the then Secretary of State for Northern Ireland, Merlyn Rees, for the early release of Giuseppe Conlon, one of the Seven who was gravely ill in prison. When the Labour government was defeated, Hume wrote to new Prime Minister, Margaret Thatcher.[113] Hume had expressed 'reservations' about the Maguire's conviction, but had not issued a call for a retrial.[114] Hume's decision to delay his public petition for a retrial of the Maguire Seven until overwhelming evidence supported their acquittal demonstrated his political awareness. If he had come out in support of the Maguire Seven while the tide of public opinion still favoured their imprisonment, he would have been seen to support criminals. In the case of the Maguire Seven, it was only after the general public and other figures, such as the leading liberal Law Lord, Baron Scarman, came out in favour of the Maguire Seven that Hume publicized his support.[115] The Maguire Seven won their appeal in 1991 after the courts accepted there had been poor handling of the forensic evidence used to indict them.

By the late 1980s, the Catholic Church across Ireland and England finally united to support the release of the Birmingham Six, Guildford Four, and Maguire Seven. The Church played a major role in drawing attention to their imprisonment but it was the prisoners' families who took on the majority of the burden of campaigning for their loved ones' freedom. The institutional Church, while divided on the extent to which they condemned the British government's mismanagement of these cases, held a unified front on this issue. With the aid of the English hierarchy, the Irish Church and laity were able to keep these issues at the forefront of British public consciousness through a media campaign that spanned television programmes, published books, and newspaper editorials.[116] The English and Irish bishops' support for the Maguire Seven, Guildford Four, and Birmingham Six demonstrated unity across the Catholic churches.

Concerted Peace Efforts

Throughout the conflict, the Church preached the message of peace. Yet this period witnessed a multifaceted and magnified effort for peace, as Irish bishops spoke in churches across Britain and vice versa. Many of these engagements

---

[113] Anthony Howard, *Basil Hume: The Monk Cardinal*, (London, 2005), 172–4.
[114] *Cork Evening News*, 2 March 1985.   [115] *Times*, 13 Oct. 1986.
[116] *Tablet*, 12 March 1988; *Times*, 30 Jan. 1988; *Guardian*, 6 May 1989; London campaign for the Birmingham Six group, *Justice Denied: The Case of the Birmingham Six*, (London, 1989); *Universe*, 29 Oct. 1989; *Universe*, 12 Nov. 1989; LAA, Fr Bobby Gilmore and The National Birmingham Six Campaign, 'The Campaign', 1988; LAA, Bishop Edward Daly, 'The Birmingham Six: A Personal View', 12 Aug. 1988; LAA, Meeting of the Irish hierarchy at Maynooth, 10–12 Oct. 1988.

encouraged ecumenism, as the Catholic Church hierarchy worked with their counterparts in Protestant churches. These ecumenical peace efforts across Britain, Ireland, and the USA were not limited to the bishops, with many in the clergy and laity participating as well. For example, some Catholic schools in Northern Ireland pushed for a greater incorporation of ecumenism in the curriculum throughout the 1980s.[117] The English and Welsh Catholic Church accepted a share of the responsibility to find a peaceful solution to the conflict because of the large Irish diaspora, as well as the Irish prison population in England.

One of the first instances of Catholic-Protestant peace measures within this period occurred at the annual Greenhills Ecumenical Conference in Drogheda. Fr Brian Lennon proposed an inter-church centre for political development as he preached the basic cause for injustice in Northern Ireland was 'the lack of a political structure that commands consensus of enough of its citizens'.[118] Cardinal Ó Fiaich also told delegates that while the 1981 hunger strikes may have led to increasing polarization between communities, the fact many ecumenical organizations survived indicated their value. This ecumenical conference had come together since 1973, under the joint chairmanship of Cardinal William Conway and Archbishop George 'Otto' Simms, but the period after the strikes, when sectarianism was at a high, demonstrated the necessity for such gatherings.[119] After this talk, both the Catholic and Church of Ireland hierarchies defended their record on ecumenical discussions, like those held at the Ballymascanlon inter-church summit, as they provided 'an important forum for the Churches'.[120]

In 1982, the Scottish, and English and Welsh hierarchies kept their plans for peace relatively quiet. A handful of the bishops were working on a campaign of prayer, which would include speaking tours of English bishops to the North. At a meeting in October, Ó Fiaich, Hume, and Archbishop Thomas Winning of Glasgow discussed a proposal for talks on Northern Ireland. The plan was to have a small gathering of English, Scottish, and Irish bishops with 'no particular agenda', a proposal initially put forward in 1979.[121] Representing the English and Welsh Catholic Church was Bishop Cormac Murphy-O'Connor of Arundel and Brighton, Bishop Augustine Harris of Middlesbrough, and Bishop James O'Brien, the auxiliary bishop in Westminster and Chairman of the English and Welsh Justice and Peace Commission. The Scottish hierarchy members who took part were Cardinal Gordon Gray, Archbishop Winning, and Bishop Francis Thompson of Motherwell. Cardinal Hume was initially to lead the delegation, but no explanation was given for his withdrawal.[122] In their correspondence

[117] Rae, *Sister Genevieve*, 181–5.   [118] *Irish Times*, 26 Jan. 1982.
[119] SDA, D47.2, 'Religion in Northern Ireland', Jan. 1986.
[120] *Irish Press*, 26 Jan. 1982; *Irish News*, 15 March 1985.
[121] ABDA, Northern Ireland File, Hume to Murphy-O'Connor, 25 Oct. 1982.
[122] *Irish Independent*, 4 Jan. 1983.

Murphy-O'Connor told Ó Fiaich he was 'delighted the Irish project' would go forward.[123] In response, Ó Fiaich wrote a 'warm welcome' awaited the English bishops.[124]

The first gathering took place in Armagh in January 1983. Cardinal Gray led the delegation of Scottish and English bishops to engage with members of the Irish hierarchy. However, the spokesperson for the Catholic Information and Press Office suggested the visit was purely 'private' and the bishops' meeting had 'absolutely nothing to do with the political situation in Northern Ireland'.[125] Officially, the bishops' talks were described as an exploratory meeting to improve communications between the three hierarchies. Talk quickly turned to the Troubles. Winning called for power sharing, declaring: 'People are being killed here—thousands of people—and yet they stop short of power sharing. From what I have heard the Irish people are desperately searching for a solution and if the Churches can do anything it will be done'.[126] The prospect of Scottish and English bishops recommending policy initiatives in Northern Ireland was unprecedented. Winning also said he would welcome a meeting with Rev Ian Paisley after the Free Presbyterian Church leader challenged the bishops to call on their flock to support the British Army.

The episcopal conferences of Ireland, Scotland, and England and Wales released a joint statement concerning their meeting in Armagh on 5 January 1983, noting they covered topics ranging from ecumenism, unemployment, the family and emigrants, and nuclear disarmament. The bishops unanimously decided 'in future there should be meetings held between the three hierarchies' and included topics for future gatherings.[127] Yet after the meeting, unionists challenged Ó Fiaich and the episcopal conferences to make a statement condemning the Provisionals, to which the cardinal responded: 'Hardly a week passes without my condemning the IRA. I do not know if condemnation from Scottish or English bishops carries particular weight'.[128]

In the weeks following the visit, the Scottish and English and Welsh hierarchies included prayers for Northern Ireland as part of all church services in their dioceses. Possibly inspired by their work, Cardinal Terence Cooke of New York released his own statement with ideas for a peaceful solution, for which he believed reconciliation fuelled by 'ecumenical efforts' between Protestants and Catholics would be the best path.[129] Cooke placed responsibility on the British government to create peace but was vague in how best to implement these resolutions.

---

[123] ABDA, Northern Ireland File, Murphy-O'Connor to Ó Fiaich, 18 Nov. 1982.
[124] ABDA, Northern Ireland File, Ó Fiaich to Murphy-O'Connor, 23 Dec. 1982.
[125] *Irish News*, 4 Jan. 1983.   [126] *Irish Independent*, 5 Jan. 1983.
[127] ABDA, Northern Ireland File, Episcopal Conference Statement, 5 Jan. 1983.
[128] *Irish Times*, 9 Jan. 1983.   [129] *Catholic New York*, 24 Feb. 1983.

The English and Welsh clergy also began initiating peace talks. Sr Katherine Christopher Warren helped organize a February 1983 course on Northern Ireland in Bath for those interested in ending the conflict. She wrote to Bishop Murphy-O'Connor asking him to include information on this event in his next *Ad Clerum*, a letter primarily addressed to ordained ministers, as the object of the course was to 'get people together who [were] truly concerned for Ireland'.[130] The impact of the Irish diaspora was also demonstrated through the Irish American clergy who attempted to bring a peaceful solution to the conflict. Fr Robert Johnson, the President of the National Federation of Priests' Councils based in Chicago, urged Hume to 'step up interdenominational dialogue already existing at the leadership level, and extend it to the grassroots level'.[131] While Hume's secretary Mgr George Leonard thanked the priest for his letter, he asserted 'initiatives have to begin in Northern Ireland and from the grassroots there'.[132] This rebuff, along with Hume's withdrawal from the bishops' gathering in Armagh in January 1983, could indicate the cardinal's thoughts on the value of multi-lateral efforts in bringing peace to the North.

Further collaboration occurred between the English and Irish bishops around the campaign for peace into 1984. Ó Fiaich approached Archbishop Derek Worlock of Liverpool (see Appendix), as well as his Anglican hierarchy counterpart Bishop David Sheppard, to journey to Northern Ireland and to speak on ecumenism during the forthcoming Week of Prayer for Christian Unity.[133] Worlock and Sheppard were close friends, who often worked together on issues in Liverpool, including campaigning to save the United Biscuits factory from closure and securing jobs in the area.[134] In January 1984, the pair gave a four-part sermon in both Church of Ireland and Catholic churches in Armagh and Belfast. Worlock discussed a shared sense of helplessness with the Northern Ireland people 'in face of events beyond your control' during his 'Meeting at the Foot of the Cross' homily in St Patrick's Cathedral, Armagh.[135] Years later Worlock hoped people would reflect on their visit as a 'breakthrough' for ecumenism.[136]

While Cardinal Hume had not joined the bishops for their January 1983 meeting in Armagh, his homily for the St Patrick's Day Mass in Westminster Cathedral the following year discussed the value of Irish emigrants in London. He paid tribute 'to the overwhelming majority of Irish in this country' stating their 'faith and qualities of mind, heart and spirit' made an important contribution 'to

---

[130] ABDA, Northern Ireland File, Warren to Murphy-O'Connor, 14 Jan. 1983.
[131] AAW, E5608, R.J. to Hume, 21 April 1983.   [132] AAW, E5608, G.L. to R.J., 5 May 1983.
[133] LAA, Ó Fiaich to Worlock, 14 Dec. 1983.
[134] Maria Power, 'Reconciling state and society? The practice of the common good in the partnership of Bishop David Sheppard and Archbishop Derek Worlock', *Journal of Religious History*, (2015), 5–6.
[135] LAA, 'Called to be one through the cross of Christ', Four Part Sermon in Northern Ireland by Worlock and Sheppard press pack, 24 Jan. 1984.
[136] LAA, Worlock to L.G., 30 Jan. 1984.

the life of this nation'.[137] Yet Hume could not ignore the conflict in Northern Ireland remarking so as he offered the Mass for St Patrick. Hume now challenged all leaders, including himself, to accept their responsibilities to bring about reconciliation, urging politicians and church leaders to work together. Although churchmen must speak out on issues that affect their flock spiritually and morally, for Hume governments and politicians needed to provide practical solutions.

The week of St Patrick's Day 1985 showcased the sometimes conflicting messages of the Irish Catholic hierarchy on the topic of peace. Ó Fiaich called for a United Nations peacekeeping task force in Northern Ireland during a television interview, broadcast on Channel Four's *Irish Angle* programme in March 1985. His comments were leaked the week before and outraged unionists, with Rev Ian Paisley labelling Ó Fiaich a 'Sinn Féin Cardinal'.[138] Then Bishop Joseph Duffy of Clogher added fuel to the fire that week when he called partition 'unjust' in his call for peace and reconciliation at a Co. Monaghan Association dinner in London.[139] However, on 15 March Bishop Cahal Daly's declaration in a Radio Ulster interview that the British Army's withdrawal from Northern Ireland would not solve the central problem in Northern Ireland, painted him as the more moderate prelate.[140]

The week's conflict continued at the annual Ballymascanlon inter-church summit, when the Presbyterian Moderator Rev Howard Cromie accused Ó Fiaich of making statements which 'gave comfort' to the Provisionals.[141] The accusation quickly turned into confrontation, with Ó Fiaich defending his remarks. Cromie continued, suggesting a call for the removal of British Army troops could only mean a withdrawal of all who considered themselves British. Despite the clash on the Thursday, the weekend concluded with church leaders uniting in prayer, with only a dozen Free Presbyterian Church members protesting outside.[142] As Christian church leaders gathered in Northern Ireland, Bishop Seamus Hegarty of Raphoe preached the St Patrick's Day Mass in Westminster Cathedral. Hegarty called on Irish emigrants in London to use their vote and petition their elected representatives for a 'meaningful political initiative'.[143] While not as controversial as remarks by some Irish bishops, it further underlined the notion that the Irish diaspora held a particular responsibility to help bring about a peaceful solution to the conflict. This week illustrated the different approaches by the Irish Catholic hierarchy in their petitions for peace. It demonstrated the difficulties faced by an ecumenical approach to reconciliation. The Irish, Scottish, and English and Welsh

---

[137] AAW, E5607, Text of Hume's St Patrick's Day Homily, 17 March 1984.
[138] *Irish Independent*, 14 March 1985.   [139] *Northern Standard*, 14 March 1985.
[140] *Irish Press*, 15 March 1985.   [141] *Irish News*, 15 March 1985.
[142] *Irish Press*, 18 March 1985.
[143] AAW, E5567, Sermon by Bishop Seamus Hegarty in Westminster Cathedral on St Patrick's Day, 17 March 1985.

hierarchies continued to meet throughout this period. In 1986 they again held a 'Day of Prayer for Peace in Northern Ireland' on St Patrick's Day.[144]

In conclusion, the bishops felt a need for an entangled approach to peace through the Irish, Scottish, and English and Welsh hierarchies joining together in calls for prayer and solutions to the conflict. Ecumenism also played a key role in these gatherings and conferences, as the leaders of the main Christian faiths in Ireland attempted to unify and intensify their message for reconciliation. These efforts would continue throughout the rest of the conflict, especially as bishops in England made statements calling for the release of wrongfully convicted Irish prisoners in Britain.

Remembrance Day/Enniskillen Bombing

The Remembrance Day bombing in Enniskillen on 8 November 1987 created a wave of revulsion towards the Provisional IRA's armed struggle. British and Irish politicians, Protestant church leaders, and even the band U2 spoke out against the bombings, with the Catholic Church leading the condemnations.[145] Even members of SF denounced the attack, demonstrating a division between the cell command structure of Provisional IRA units and the political wing of the movement. The bombing occurred near the town's cenotaph during a Remembrance Sunday service, killing ten civilians and one RUC officer, while injuring another sixty-three.[146] This bombing was different from others orchestrated by the Provisionals. It targeted civilians rather than members of the security forces and the Provisionals did not issue one of their customary warning calls.[147] The Provisionals later apologized for the bombing and Gerry Adams extended sympathy to the victims' families.[148] As Marianne Elliott has noted, it was difficult for Catholics to frame themselves as victims of the conflict when the Provisional IRA carried out such 'dreadful atrocities in their name'.[149] Many in the Catholic clergy and hierarchy condemned the attack; Fr Joe McVeigh, however, objected to the wording of the hierarchy's statement as explored below.[150]

Immediately following the attack, the Irish bishops released a statement to be read across all Masses on Sunday 15 November 1987. It read:

> There is in the Catholic community, North and South, a strong desire to find some way of collectively expressing our sympathy and solidarity with the Protestant community in this tragedy. During these days we ask people to come to

---

[144] CTOMLA, FDFP 1985–86, Ó Fiaich Ad Clerum, 10 March 1986.
[145] Irish Times, 9 Nov. 1987; Fermanagh Herald, 21 Nov. 1987.
[146] Bew and Gillespie, Chronology of the Troubles, 210.
[147] Ulster Herald, 14 Nov. 1987.　　[148] Guardian, 10 Nov. 1987.
[149] Elliott, Catholics of Ulster, 441.　　[150] McVeigh, Taking a Stand, 217–18.

week-day masses in large numbers, so that the whole population may be united in repentance, sorrow and prayer at this terrible time. Everything should be done to demonstrate Catholic revulsion at these crimes and to dissociate the Catholic community completely from those who carry out such deeds. There is no room for ambivalence. In the face of present campaigns of Republican violence the choice of all Catholics is clear. It is a choice between good and evil. It is sinful to join organizations committed to violence or remain in them. It is sinful to support such organizations or call on others to support them.[151]

While the bishops had used most of the statement's wording before, the call for Mass attendance and 'sin' was new. In a December 1981 RTÉ radio interview, when asked if membership of the Provisional IRA was a sin, Ó Fiaich had declared 'it depends on what you mean by membership' but 'certainly participation in evil deeds in which the IRA involves itself is a sin'.[152] A closer analysis of the bishops' motives in this 1987 statement is required. Fears of sectarian retaliation in light of the heightened national sentiment of emotional reaction played a role. In addition, a large crowd at these Masses would demonstrate public distance and disillusionment with the Provisionals. However, the next part of the statement disturbed some of the grassroots clergy:

We sympathise with the police forces North and South in their task of upholding the law in most difficult and dangerous circumstances. Many of their members have lost their lives...We call on our people to cooperate with the police in bringing the guilty to justice.[153]

The bishops also denounced safe houses in the Republic, used for Provisional IRA members on the run and the storage of weapons, stating those individuals who helped the Provisionals shared in their crimes. This hierarchy statement attempted to further distance the Catholic community from the Provisional IRA, and was meant just as much for Catholics as it was for Protestants who might read it. Strong condemnatory statements were offered, in the hope of diffusing tensions between communities. However, when Ó Fiaich apologized for the bombing on behalf of the Catholic community, many of his own parishioners were 'outraged that he should have so identified them with republican atrocities'.[154] In this instance, Church commentary on Enniskillen implicitly conflated Catholicism and Provisional IRA sympathy, linking, while also seeking to distance, everyday Catholics with terrorism.

---

[151] CTOMLA, Sarah Clark Papers (SSCP), Irish Catholic Bishops' Statement on kidnapping of John O'Grady and Enniskillen Bombing, 1987.
[152] CTOMLA, Cardinal Ó Fiaich Papers 'Au Tuaisceart', RTÉ Radio *This Week* interview with Kevin Healy and Ó Fiaich, 20 Dec. 1981.
[153] CTOMLA, Cardinal Ó Fiaich Papers 'Au Tuaisceart', RTÉ Radio *This Week* interview with Kevin Healy and Ó Fiaich, 20 Dec. 1981.
[154] Elliott, *Catholics of Ulster*, 473.

The Catholic clergy had varying reactions to the bishops' statement. Along with hundreds of other priests, McVeigh read out the bishops' statement at Mass that Sunday. However the priest disagreed with the bishops' wording in some parts, believing it 'contained all the flaws and weaknesses of previous episcopal pronouncements'.[155] When he read out the statement at Mass in Irvinestown, he clarified for his parishioners that three bishops had written it. Yet while McVeigh disagreed with some aspects of the statement, Fr Denis Faul hoped the bishops' words would cause the Provisionals to 'sit down and put an end to all their violence'.[156] For his reflections Faul received hate mail criticizing him personally and claiming the hierarchy's statement was '18 years too late'.[157]

Other bishops spoke out individually against the atrocity. Bishop Edward Daly called for an end to the Provisionals' campaign during an interview on Radio Foyle, where he asked people irrespective of their religion or politics to 'look at ourselves and say what I am doing in my own community to try to effect some kind of reconciliation'.[158] For Daly: 'To link the violence with any religious belief is the ultimate obscenity'.[159] He continued, reiterating the campaign of violence had advanced nowhere, and expressed his hope the Enniskillen Bombing would be a 'watershed' in the conflict, creating dialogue towards peace.[160] Bishop Cahal Daly echoed these sentiments at a Requiem Mass for Tommy McAuley, a Catholic murdered by loyalists in the aftermath of the bombing. Daly praised Gordon Wilson, who became a peace activist after his daughter's death in the atrocity, and called for Wilson's spirit to influence others towards reconciliation.[161] Wilson's tears moved even Adams, yet he criticized the bishops for ruling it sinful to join SF or the Provisional IRA. SF attacked the Irish bishops for what they perceived was a double standard. The local Maíre Drumm SF Cumann accused the bishops of silence concerning issues of RUC brutality and the 'morality of the British presence' in the North.[162] Even the Vatican became involved when Pope John Paul II sent a message of sympathy to Bishop Joseph Duffy of Clogher concerning the bombing. The Holy Father did not speak out on every attack, but claimed he was 'shocked and saddened' by this particular 'outrage', reiterating the Catholic Church's 'clear condemnation of violence'.[163]

The bombing damaged community relations, but the bishops reached out to Protestants in an attempt to bring the communities together. Bishop Joseph Duffy of Clogher concelebrated a cross-community service at St Michael's Church in Enniskillen. *The Fermanagh Herald* noted the bishop directed his words to

---

[155] McVeigh, *Taking a Stand*, 218.   [156] *Irish Times*, 11 Nov. 1987.
[157] CTOMLA, FDFP 1987, Anonymous to Faul, Nov. 1987.
[158] *Irish Times*, 12 Nov. 1987.   [159] *Irish Press*, 12 Nov. 1987.
[160] *Irish Times*, 12 Nov. 1987.   [161] *Irish Times*, 19 Nov. 1987.
[162] *Ulster Herald*, 28 Nov. 1987.
[163] CTOMLA, Cardinal Ó Fiaich Papers 'Au Tuaisceart', Extracts from Papal statements and messages concerning Northern Ireland, Telegram sent by the Cardinal Secretary of State on behalf of His Holiness Pope John Paul II to Bishop Joseph Duffy of Clogher, Nov. 1987.

Catholics: 'We have every reason to want to live here and to create a future for our children in the spirit of the Christian Gospel. With God's help, let us make a new beginning.'[164] However, a few days later, the Catholic Church was not represented at a special Remembrance Day Service on 22 November at St Macartan's Cathedral, with a spokesperson close to Ó Fiaich deeming it 'a local event'.[165] As Church archives remain closed for this period, we can only speculate this lack of an invitation to the event suggests that community divisions were too entrenched at that moment to allow for an ecumenical gathering.

Outside the institutional Catholic Church, ecumenical interactions grew with the creation of organizations like Enniskillen Together. The group consisted of Catholic and Protestant laity, as well as a few members of the Protestant clergy, and self-proclaimed atheists. Inspired by their Radio Ulster talk in January of that year, a woman of the group reached out to the well-known ecumenists Catholic Archbishop Worlock and the Anglican Bishop Sheppard of Liverpool. She asked for advice on how to bring Catholic clergy into their organization, as the group differed with priests on integrated education.[166] Worlock encouraged the woman to purchase a copy of *Better Together*, a book the archbishop co-wrote with Sheppard about the power of ecumenism and community organization.[167] The unwillingness of the Catholic clergy to make concessions on integrated education indicated a shift in the power and initiative of the laity, who began initiating peace gatherings of their own accord. No longer did the Church hold the same uncontested power in Northern Ireland as it did in the 1960s and 1970s, lay women and men no longer waited for Catholic priests to join in their movements.

In response to the hierarchy's handling of the Enniskillen Bombing, Fathers Wilson and McVeigh wrote an open letter to Irish Catholics. On 5 January 1988, the priests released a statement in which they expressed their opinion that the bishop's Enniskillen statement was 'politically motivated' but was presented as 'Catholic teaching'.[168] Wilson and McVeigh called on the bishops to condemn state violence. The priests also questioned the hierarchy's support of the RUC. The response the priests received from the public was less than enthusiastic, and on 7 January *The Irish Times* published an editorial entitled 'Excuses', describing McVeigh and Wilson's letter as a justification for the atrocity. This article, while establishing the clerical pair were atypical in their stance as priests, also claimed their open letter made 'it easier for Protestants to go on hating Catholics: perhaps, indeed, to go on killing them' because the letter 'minimised the culpability of the IRA'.[169] Despite their letter breaking with the hierarchy's

---

[164] *Fermanagh Herald,* 21 Nov. 1987.   [165] *Irish Times,* 21 Nov. 1987.
[166] LAA, A.T. to Sheppard, 17 Feb. 1988.   [167] LAA, Worlock to A.T., 18 March 1988.
[168] 'An open letter to Irish Catholics', 5 Jan. 1988 in *The Truth Will Set Us Free: Collected Statements 1988–1993,* Desmond Wilson and Joseph McVeigh, (Belfast, 1994), 1.
[169] *Irish Times,* 7 Jan. 1988.

stance, there remains no recorded episcopal sanction.[170] The response towards these two priests, who wished to open a debate about the role of violence, both paramilitary and institutional, was to isolate them and dismiss them as radicals.

The Irish Catholic Church's reaction towards the Enniskillen Bombing demonstrated that, while the hierarchy loudly condemned atrocities, few Catholics and Protestants were attentively listening. In other instances when Provisional IRA bombings became unpopular, SF spokesmen apologized but Edward Daly denounced these meaningless platitudes: 'We do not want apologies from the IRA or anyone else. We seek an end to the death and destruction which is destroying our city and our people.'[171] Ecumenical groups created by the laity, born out of the bombing, excluded the clergy who could not agree to integrated education. For the Provisionals, the Enniskillen Bombing proved attacking civilians was a step too far for many who otherwise supported a united Ireland. It emerged that another bombing almost took place at a Remembrance Day service in Tullyhommon, but did not detonate, proving the Enniskillen Bombing was not an isolated attack on the security forces gone wrong.[172] Only more outspoken, outsider priests questioned the bishops' unequivocal denunciations of republican violence, without mention of institutional, state-sanctioned brutality. In 2018 the Catholic Church rejected plans for a memorial on Church owned land to commemorate the victims, giving weak explanations as to their refusal.[173]

Extradition

By the late 1980s, after the signing of the Anglo-Irish Agreement, the topic of extradition became fiercely contested by the clergy and hierarchy. The Anglo-Irish conference between representatives of the British and Irish governments to discuss this agreement included extradition as a topic for conversation, but there was no formal agreement at this stage.[174] Extradition had long been on Margaret Thatcher's mind and she considered it an imperative to better Anglo-Irish relations.[175] The agreement paved the way for more legal cooperation between the two countries, leading to the possibility of sending republican paramilitaries who fled South after committing crimes back to the UK for trial.[176]

[170] Interview with Fr Joseph McVeigh, 14 April 2014; Interview with Fr Desmond Wilson, 1 Sep. 2014.

[171] *Irish Examiner,* 5 Sep. 1988.

[172] *Irish Independent,* 9 Nov. 1987; *Irish Independent,* 12 Nov. 1987; *Irish Examiner,* 11 Nov. 1987.

[173] *Irish News,* 4 May 2018, https://www.irishnews.com/news/northernirelandnews/2018/05/04/news/catholic-church-officially-rejects-enniskillen-bomb-victims-memorial-1321928/

[174] TNA, PREM 19/1551, Ref. A085/2721, Anglo Irish Relations: Northern Ireland, Oct. 1985.

[175] Charles Moore, *Margaret Thatcher: The Authorized Biography, Volume One: Not for Turning* (London, 2013), 602–7.

[176] CTOMLA, FDFP 1985–86, Joint Press Release summary of Anglo-Irish Agreement, 1985.

The Irish government planned to amend the 1965 Extradition Act in December 1987. While many in the British media and government championed extradition earlier in the conflict, the late 1980s witnessed the return of and an added emphasis upon this strategy.[177] Other groups called for extradition not just from the Republic, but from the USA as well.[178] Both grassroots clerical movements and the institutional Church opposed such measures, given the treatment of Irish prisoners in England and the quality of the evidence, through the use of supergrasses and faulty forensics. Despite pointed opposition from unionists, the British government, and British citizens, the bishops initially condemned extradition. These sentiments developed over time, with Cardinal Ó Fiaich believing extradition could be used to barter for better conditions in the North.[179] However, the cardinal's viewpoint set him apart from the rest of the Church.[180]

The ICPO voiced opposition to the Irish government ratification of the Extradition Act in its 1987 Annual Report. The Bishops' Commission for Emigrants, with acting chairman Bishop Eamon Casey of Galway, who founded the ICPO, commented it was 'quite clear if a tradition of justice' had not been established 'in a particular country, no Irish citizen should be extradited to that country'.[181] Casey noted until the question of alleged injustices towards Irish prisoners in Britain were addressed, extradition 'was out of the question'.[182] The ICPO also grew concerned over the Prevention of Terrorism Act, with 6,246 Irish people detained under its terms in Britain since November 1974 but less than 3 percent of those individuals charged. In addition, the Irish Council for Civil Liberties (ICCL) also opposed any plans for extradition. These organizations contained a mix of clergy and laity, and with the support of the Irish bishops, the Church maintained a united front against plans for extradition to Britain.

Before the Irish Extradition Act was amended in December 1987, Fr Joe McVeigh joined a town hall meeting to protest this decision that November. When speaking of the institutional Church's desire to reform the British justice system by 'bartering' with extradition, an opinion voiced by Cardinal Ó Fiaich, McVeigh claimed it was impossible to reform the 'unreformable'. McVeigh described extradition as immoral and rejected the cardinal's suggestion outright.[183] Fr Des Wilson also publicly disagreed with extradition, speaking at rallies across the Republic. He thought the chances that an Irish prisoner in a British prison would be maltreated were 'extremely high' and 'if the state can be protected

[177] *Daily Telegraph*, 13 Sep. 1982.
[178] LAA, 'Guth an Phobail: Reports from Occupied Ireland', Issue No. 9, Oct. 1983.
[179] *Irish Times*, 6 Nov. 1987.
[180] CTOMLA, 'Au Tuaisceart', J.D. to Ó Fiaich, 30 May 1988; CTOMLA, 'Au Tuaisceart', Ó Fiaich notes for Easter Week, 1986.
[181] *Irish Times*, 8 Oct. 1987.   [182] *Irish Independent*, 8 Oct. 1987.
[183] *Irish Times*, 6 Nov. 1987.

only by injustice then it is not worth protecting'.[184] Faul agreed with the cardinal, to a degree. Faul protested that no Irish person should be extradited for the purposes of prosecution and he called for the Irish government to include this proviso as he was concerned about the 'machinery' of the Act.[185] In a joint article for *The Irish Times*, Fathers Murray and Faul wrote about the treatment of Irish prisoners in British jails. They discussed the Prevention of Terrorism Act and how, two months earlier, the European Commission on Human Rights held that the Act was in breach of its Convention. Both noted the flaws with the British Court of Appeal, and the fact the British prison system kept many Irish republican prisoners in English jails, far away from their families in Ireland. They concluded by predicting 'miscarriages of justice' would occur should extradition be implemented.[186] In a rare show of support, a letter to the editor for *The Irish Times*, written by Stephen Preston from Drumbo, agreed with the priests about the treatment of Irish people by the British state. However, he viewed extradition as 'an inescapable necessity' and the priests would agree that just because a crime was committed on one side of the border and the person was from the other, they should not 'go scot free'.[187] While this letter demonstrates many in Northern Ireland did acknowledge the British government's poor treatment of Irish prisoners, they nevertheless did not think this justified stopping extradition.

In 1988, Fathers Raymond Murray and Denis Faul wrote and distributed the *British Justice is Flawed* pamphlet on the British justice system, highlighting their concern about the possibility of extradition from the Republic. On the seven-day detention policy for suspects, the priests accused the British government of prejudicing the public against the detainees. Therefore, when they were released, whether tried or not, the general public and any jury selected were predisposed to conclude guilt and therefore the outcome bound to be prejudiced. The priests suspected the British government and media would use this same process in the period when the Irish government extradited individuals back to Britain.[188] While the other aspects of the pamphlet discussing the British justice system were founded on quality data and known facts, this section on extradition was entirely speculative.

Remarkably, one Irish-born priest epitomized the Irish case against extradition. Fr Patrick Ryan, from Rossmore, Co. Tipperary and of the Pallottine order,[189] was extradited back to Ireland from Belgium, where he had gone on hunger strike to protest his impending extradition to Britain. Ryan was an Irish priest who was thought to be responsible for the coordination of republican paramilitary groups

---

[184] *Connacht Tribune*, 17 May 1989.   [185] *Irish Times*, 16 Nov. 1987.
[186] *Irish Times*, 7 Dec. 1987.   [187] *Irish Times*, 14 Dec. 1987.
[188] Raymond Murray and Denis Faul, *British Justice is Flawed*, 1988.
[189] *Nenagh Guardian*, 9 July 1988.

across England.[190] After three off-duty British soldiers were assassinated in the Netherlands in May 1988, Belgian police, operating on a tip-off, arrested known Provisional IRA-sympathizer Ryan in his home.[191] As an article in *Donegal News* reported, many Irish people believed Ryan would not receive a fair trial in Britain and therefore wanted the priest returned to the Republic. The article noted the propaganda battle surrounding Ryan's case was a 'perfect platform for those who are always ready to link the Catholic Church with the IRA and who harbour the terrifying illusion the present "troubles" are a Romanist plot to wipe out Northern Irish Protestants'.[192] His case echoed that of Fr Patrick Fell during the 1970s referred to in Chapter 2. Complicating the matter was Cardinal Hume's insistence Ryan was no longer a priest, as he had 'walked out of his religious order and ministry as a priest 14 years ago.'[193] For the Fianna Fáil-led Irish government, Ryan's case was a headache because of the public opposition against extradition, especially as the Guildford Four and Birmingham Six appeals gained momentum. Complicating this situation further was Ryan's own fierce denial of any involvement with republican organizations.[194] His story captured headlines across Ireland. Ryan was eventually brought back to the Republic, where he spoke at anti-extradition demonstrations across the country.[195] His case symbolized the failure of the Anglo-Irish Agreement in the assessment of Irish and British people alike.

Despite the opinion of Cardinal Ó Fiaich that extradition could be a bargaining tool for prison reform, many in the Irish Catholic Church warned against the practice and maintained a sharp opposition until the Irish government passed the 1987 amendment. As with abortion, divorce, education, condoms, and AIDS, the Church seemed out of touch with the tide of public opinion. The Irish Church now began facing opposition, and a conflict over the relationship between Church and state many western European Churches had experienced earlier in the twentieth century, particularly the 1960s.

Republican Paramilitary Funerals

Republican paramilitary funerals had always been a way to demonstrate power, with the Catholic Church officiating as the Provisional IRA marched alongside as pallbearers. Yet, in March 1987, after the Provisionals fired volleys over Gerry Logue's coffin—thereby desecrating consecrated Church grounds with a large crowd of mourners and televisions crews present to document the action—Bishop

---

[190] *Ulster Herald*, 3 Dec. 1988.
[191] TNA, CAB/128/91, Cabinet Meeting Conclusions, 1 Dec. 1988.
[192] *Donegal News*, 3 Dec. 1988.   [193] *Irish Press*, 1 Dec. 1988.
[194] *Irish Press*, 24 Oct. 1989.   [195] *Donegal News*, 29 July 1989.

Edward Daly's patience evaporated.[196] In a statement released on 26 March, Daly called the scene 'a cheap paramilitary propaganda stunt for the benefit of the media'.[197] Daly decreed from then on in Derry, Requiem Masses for republican paramilitaries 'would not be celebrated while the remains were present in the Church'.[198]

Requiem Masses for paramilitaries could no longer occur with the remains of the deceased present in Church grounds and, therefore, could not be official Church funerals.[199] This revised attitude towards paramilitary funerals in Derry increased the tension between the Church and the Provisionals. Unionists and constitutional nationalists alike welcomed Daly's decision, with the editor of *The Fermanagh Herald* deeming it 'necessary' Catholics 'not to confuse their faith with the ferocity of their politics'.[200] John Cushnahan of *The Irish Independent* also supported the ban and believed a 'majority of Catholics' agreed with Daly's stance.[201] While Cahal Daly did not implement the practice in his own diocese, he reiterated funerals were not ever to be occasions for republican propaganda coups: 'Paramilitary demonstrations and police saturation are an intrusion into family grief and are offensive to the Catholic Church's ministry to the dead and to the grieving'.[202] Yet subsequent events, including the fallout from the Gibraltar killings, would alter funerals from a relatively peaceful display to more violent affairs. The Church's attitude towards funerals divided it from some in the working-class community, as well as more rogue priests disagreeing with Daly's gag order. Fr Des Wilson declared Daly's ban 'contrary to Catholic Church law, and therefore illegal'.[203] Relatives were entitled to have the body present at the deceased's funeral unless the deceased had been formally excommunicated. Republican paramilitary funerals during this period demonstrate the widening gap between the Catholic Church and the reality of life and faith for many working-class Catholics.

After Logue's funeral, the Provisionals released a statement declaring it would no longer fire shots in Church grounds over coffins. Yet they challenged the British government, reasoning that as they brought weapons to the Church in defence, it was 'only a matter of time that the British forces engineer another Bloody Sunday situation'.[204] The RUC had surrounded the Church, but did not enter its precinct as the funeral occurred. Further, the Provisionals' statement

---

[196]   Daly, *A Troubled See*, 194.

[197]   Statement 26 March 1987 in Daly, *A Troubled See*, 195.

[198]   *Irish Press*, 27 March 1987.

[199]   *Irish Times*, 27 March 1987; However Daly recalls that it was not an unusual practice at this time for Requiem Masses to occur without the body present. In Derry city, no Requiem Masses were held on Sundays, so often the burial would take place on a Sunday with the Requiem Mass the following day. Daly, *A Troubled See*, 196.

[200]   *Fermanagh Herald*, 4 April 1987.   [201]   *Irish Independent*, 3 Nov. 1987.

[202]   *Irish Press*, 10 April 1987.   [203]   *Irish Press*, 27 March 1987.

[204]   *Irish Times*, 17 April 1987.

claimed any 'show of military strength on the streets would have resulted in the deaths of mourners', which is why they fired the shots on Church grounds.[205] Republicans viewed Daly's statement as supporting the RUC, with the Provisional IRA suggesting Daly was on the British government's side and therefore an agent of the state. Their view was not entirely anomalous, as two weeks before the then Chief Constable of the RUC, Sir John Hermon, praised the Church for its part as mediator in the violence following Provisional IRA member Laurence Marley's funeral in Belfast.[206] Martin McGuinness declared the bishops had 'deserted' Marley's family in their hour of need.[207] With Daly's declaration, the Provisionals claimed the Church became a tool for the British state to admonish the paramilitaries. Therefore, the Provisional IRA could dismiss the Church as a partisan organization.

The struggle between the Provisional IRA and the Church over Requiem Masses continued with the November 1987 funerals of Eddie McSheffrey and Paddy Deery in Derry. It was unclear if the coffins of the two individuals would be let into St Eugene's Cathedral following Bishop Daly's decision in March. Daly announced he would stand by his ruling after appeals made by the widows of McSheffrey and Deery for a Requiem Mass with the coffins present.[208] However, he expressed sympathy to the families and appealed to the RUC and British Army who had been 'insensitive' to the heightened amount of funerals that year.[209] Deery and McSheffrey's widows decided to defy the ban. The local SF organizers asked McVeigh to say a Mass in the grounds of the Cathedral if the clergy would not admit the coffins, to which he agreed. McVeigh's services were deemed unnecessary when the local Cathedral administrator, Fr Neil McGoldrick, permitted the coffins' entry.[210] The RUC surrounded the mourners, attacking the pallbearers and knocking the coffins to the ground as they made their way for burial. Daly was away in London for the retrial of the Birmingham Six while the Provisionals fired shots over the coffins inside Church grounds.[211] Daly felt the priests who admitted the coffins made 'the only decision possible under the circumstances', with thousands of mourners outside the Cathedral and a large media presence, all demanding entrance.[212] A workaround also appeared, as the funeral occurred on All Souls Day, meaning priests said Mass in churches across Ireland for all those who had died. To refuse these republican mourners entry would have been a propaganda coup, with two young widows standing by the coffins of their husbands rebuffed by the Church. The Church allowed admittance of the bodies to avoid such a display, and therefore appeared to go back on their word in the eyes of many unionists. In January 1988, the Derry diocese formally

---

[205] *Irish Times*, 17 April 1987.   [206] *Irish Times*, 9 April 1987.
[207] *Fermanagh Herald*, 18 April 1987.   [208] *Irish Independent*, 31 Oct. 1987.
[209] *Irish Times*, 31 Oct. 1987.   [210] McVeigh, *Taking a Stand*, 216–17.
[211] *Irish Press*, 4 Nov. 1987.   [212] *Irish Times*, 4 Nov. 1987.

lifted the ban, with SF welcoming the decision.[213] Daly's decree had backfired, forcing the Church into a corner, requiring it to recant, and weakening its negotiating position.

Tensions rose again over republican paramilitary funerals later on in 1988, with unforeseen consequences for community relations. The Special Air Service (SAS) shot three Belfast Provisional IRA members on 6 March who were allegedly on a bombing mission in Gibraltar. The plans for the funeral were well publicized, with the burial to take place in Milltown cemetery, close to the Falls Road. McVeigh attended the funeral, as he had known one of the deceased, Mairéad Farrell, and helped to carry her coffin along the route.[214] As the coffins were lowered into the earth, the mourners heard grenades explode around them and panic ensued, with many hiding behind the coffins for shelter.[215] Some began pursuing a man fleeing the scene, who shot at them as they ran, killing three. An RUC patrol appeared and apprehended the individual, Michael Stone, who claimed he acted as a lone loyalist vigilante. Stone was later charged for the murders, but no widespread condemnation of his actions by either Protestant or Catholic clergymen ensued. This lack of official condemnation, and the feeling in the nationalist community that the RUC could have prevented these deaths, led to an escalation in tension between the police and the Catholic community.[216]

Following the three murders at Milltown Cemetery, another funeral was held for one of the victims and violence ensued. A car travelling along the Falls Road approached the funeral party. Many in the crowd had also attended the funeral of the Gibraltar killings, and with tensions flaring they seized the car and the occupants, British Army corporals David Howes and Derek Wood.[217] Suspecting the individuals were loyalists, the crowd beat the men, with members of the Provisionals shooting them dead. Fr Alec Reid attempted to prevent the killings and to resuscitate one of the victims.[218] When that failed, Reid delivered the last rites. The famous image of Reid administering the last rites appeared in newspapers around the world, portraying a gruesome reality of the violence. It painted the republican people of West Belfast as savages and Catholic clergy as either passive observers, or, worse, condoning and complicit.

After this series of loyalist and republican deaths, the Church renewed its cries for a cessation of violence with increased vigour. Bishop Cahal Daly announced the activities of the Provisional IRA were 'killing the soul of those involved in it or actively supporting it'.[219] Daly had urged calm on all sides after the shootings at the funeral for the Gibraltar killings. After the murder of the two British soldiers,

---

[213] *Irish Press*, 20 Jan. 1988.   [214] McVeigh, *Taking a Stand*, 223.
[215] *Irish Times*, 17 March 1988.
[216] *14 Days*, BBC 1, 21 March 2013, http://www.bbc.co.uk/programmes/b01r7v48
[217] Kevin Rafter, 'Priests and peace: the role of the Redemptorist Order in the Northern Ireland peace process', *Études irlandaises*, 28 (2003), 165.
[218] *Irish Times*, 21 March 1988.   [219] *Irish Times*, 23 March 1988.

he extended his sympathy to their families, as well the people of West Belfast who had been 'so unjustly misrepresented to the world by the barbarous behaviour of a few'.[220] Yet Martin McGuinness chastised the hierarchy, claiming they had a pro-British agenda and Daly had 'no political credibility in west Belfast' as he had given 'moral succour and advice to the British war machine'.[221] Since Daly had not spoken out about Michael Stone's shootings, the Provisionals and SF painted him as a pro-British government supporter. The funeral for the Provisional IRA members killed at Gibraltar led an uncontrollable spiral of hate and destruction on both sides, giving the paramilitary republican movement the opportunity to further distance the Catholic Church from any part of peace negotiations.

Funerals for Sectarian Killings

The deadliest years of that conflict had passed, but sectarian murders remained high; one bishop, Cahal Daly, hoped to change that trend. Sectarian murders happened in every county, however Daly's diocese of Down and Connor, which contained Belfast, saw the most deaths. Daly personally intervened, making himself available to deliver the sermon for every Catholic murder victim in his diocese. During his eight years as the Bishop of Down and Connor, Daly spoke at the funerals of more than forty Catholics killed by sectarian violence.[222] Daly was a powerful orator, and wrote sermons against sectarian violence. *The Irish Independent* deemed Daly the 'most outspoken member of the hierarchy in his frequent and elegant condemnations of terrorist outrages'.[223] It is strongly probable that Cahal Daly's relentless condemnations of sectarian murders and of the Provisional IRA was one of the main reasons the Vatican chose him to become the next Archbishop of Armagh in 1990. Daly's words drew fresh attention to the issue, although the militant republicans' perception that Daly was in the British government's pocket damaged the effectiveness of his homilies in a wider context in creating peace.

Since he presided over almost every funeral for a Catholic sectarian victim, Daly travelled regularly throughout his diocese. While many of these murders occurred in deeply divided Belfast, a few happened in less central, urban districts like Kilkeel and Glengormley. These locations were dispersed across the diocese and presiding over these funerals ensured Daly remained deeply connected to all of the people suffering in his diocese. Before each Requiem Mass, Daly met with the victim's family, often in their home, so he could in his opinion 'speak out of their grief and to their heartbreak' in his sermon.[224] He mixed with his people in their time of

---

[220] *Irish Times*, 23 March 1988. [221] *Irish Times*, 4 April 1988.
[222] Daly, *Steps on my Pilgrim Journey*, 254. [223] *Irish Independent*, 7 Oct. 1989.
[224] Daly, *Steps on my Pilgrim Journey*, 254–5.

need but often drew ire for his condemnations of the Provisional IRA during these funeral homilies.

Bishop Cahal Daly used his homilies as a weapon against violence, especially republican violence. Despite the fact most of these were Catholic sectarian murders by loyalist paramilitaries, Daly condemned republican paramilitary violence in every Requiem Mass. To Daly, these sectarian murders fuelled the 'organisation and continuation' of the Provisional IRA campaign,[225] and the Provisionals' violence was a 'huge obstacle' to necessary dialogue for peace.[226] After the murder of twenty-two-year-old Catholic Jim Meighan, Daly appealed to both loyalist and republican paramilitaries to stop the killings, claiming 'grief is indivisible'.[227] UDA/UFF paramilitaries shot Meighan as he took his fiancée home to Prestwick Park in the Ballysillan area of North Belfast.[228] This funeral was just one instance during this time of Daly asking for the violence to end. He often made his homilies public, publishing them through the Catholic Press and Information Office, with many media outlets picking up his words. His sermon was particularly fiery following the assassination in 1989 of two retired Catholic RUC officers, Gabriel Mullay and Joseph Fenton, by the Provisional IRA.[229] Both were well-known Catholics and the IRA had deemed them traitors.[230] Daly severely chastised the Provisional IRA's political leaders. This homily, with its revulsion towards the Provisionals, displayed some of the most condemnatory language seen during Daly's tenure as bishop. He challenged the idea of 'legitimate targets', noting 'The IRA have neither the right nor the authority nor the legitimacy nor the mandate to kill anybody.'[231] In the months following, Daly announced SF carried the greatest blame for the carnage in Northern Ireland as they 'unequivocally supported' the IRA.[232] Daly's repeated denunciations of the Provisionals in these homilies at Requiem Masses led to the Provisional IRA in return denouncing the bishop as one-sided and pro-British government.[233]

In addition to condemning republication paramilitary violence in every homily, in about a quarter of the homilies surveyed during this period, Daly also blamed politicians for their inaction. When murdered father of two Terry McDaid was shot dead in his Belfast home, Daly warned politicians that people were impatient with the lack of progress and grew tired of 'talks about talks'.[234] Often these same sermons discussed problems with RUC tactics. The funeral for twenty-year-old

[225] Daly, *Steps on my Pilgrim Journey*, 254.   [226] *Irish Press*, 12 May 1987.

[227] 'Funeral Mass for James Meighan', 23 Sep. 1987 in Daly, *Addresses 1987–88*; *Irish Times*, 24 Sep. 1987.

[228] McKittrick, Kelters, Feeney, and Thornton, *Lost Lives*, 1091.

[229] 'Funeral Mass for Gabriel Mullaly', 1 March 1989 in Daly, *Addresses 1989–90*.

[230] McKittrick, Kelters, Feeney, and Thornton, *Lost Lives*, 1164.

[231] 'Funeral Mass for Gabriel Mullaly', 1 March 1989 in Daly, *Addresses 1989–90*.

[232] *Irish Independent*, 19 Jan. 1990.   [233] Interview with Danny Morrison, 29 April 2014.

[234] *Irish Independent*, 18 March 1988; *Irish Press*, 7 April 1987; *Ulster Herald*, 28 Nov. 1987; *Ulster Herald*, 10 Sep. 1988.

Billy Kane, shot by loyalist paramilitaries as he slept, sparked tensions between the deceased's loved ones and the security forces. Kane's family stated they would not attend the funeral if the police put on a 'show of strength' and Daly cautioned that deploying RUC forces in predominately nationalist areas needed to be kept 'under review'.[235]

The sheer volume of Daly's sermons for funerals meant that they often became formulaic. He gave homilies for twenty-nine Catholic sectarian murder related funerals between May 1987 and August 1990. By May 1987, Daly had presided over fifteen funerals since becoming the Bishop of Down and Connor in October 1982. Gary McCartan became his sixteenth Requiem Mass on 7 May 1987. Two UVF gunmen shot McCartan when he answered the door of his Ormeau Road home, although his father may have been the intended target.[236] In the homily for McCartan, Daly referred to the cycle of sectarian murders brought on by loyalist and republican paramilitaries. He inserted the loved ones who would miss McCartan, and mentioned ecumenism and reconciliation.[237] In the following twenty-eight Requiem Masses for sectarian victims during this period, Daly discussed ecumenism, reconciliation, and republican paramilitary violence in every one of them. He mentioned Pope John Paul II's appeal for peace at Drogheda in six of the homilies, which Daly used to demonstrate the full authority of the Catholic Church supported his message.

The large number of Catholic sectarian victims at this time caused Daly to re-use the same condemnatory and exasperated language towards the continued murders. While Daly referred to the role of politicians in every Requiem Mass, he never specifically named a political party. Interestingly, despite mentioning republican paramilitaries in every speech, Daly only discussed the environment created by the security forces, and their role in the conflict, in less than half of his homilies. More often than not, they included soft praise for the work the RUC had recently accomplished, as in the case of William Totten's funeral, with gentle reminders to further protect Catholics.[238] UVF paramilitaries shot Totten as he got into his car outside a friend's house on Cavehill Road. A detective told the inquest it had either been a 'random sectarian killing or a case of mistaken identity'.[239] The most venomous declaration against the security forces came during the homily for Jim McCartney, where Daly referred to them as 'oppressive'.[240] UVF gunmen shot McCartney as he worked the door of the Orient Bar on Springfield Road.[241] Therefore, many paramilitary republicans saw Daly as soft on the security forces,

[235] *Irish Press*, 19 Jan. 1988.
[236] McKittrick, Kelters, Feeney, and Thornton, *Lost Lives*, 1077.
[237] 'Funeral Mass for Gary McCartan', 11 May 1987 in Daly, *Addresses 1986–88*.
[238] 'Funeral Mass for William Totten', 14 June 1988 in Daly, *Addresses 1987–88*.
[239] McKittrick, Kelters, Feeney, and Thornton, *Lost Lives*, 1129–30.
[240] 'Funeral Mass for Jim McCartney', 13 March 1989 in Daly, *Addresses 1989–90*.
[241] McKittrick, Kelters, Feeney, and Thornton, *Lost Lives*, 1166.

Years	1987	1988	1989	1990
Number of Catholic Sectarian Murders per year	6	10	10	3
Number of Pope John Paul II's speech at Drogheda mentions	0	2	4	0
Number of Security Forces mentions	1	5	4	1

Figure 6 'Bishop Cahal Daly's Requiem Masses for Catholic Victims of Sectarian Murders'

further distancing the bishop from some Catholics who regularly faced threats from the security forces.

Daly's homilies condemned both republican and loyalist paramilitary violence, asked for reconciliation, challenged politicians for solutions, and drew on his faith from passages in the gospels and psalms, see Figure 6. The breakdown of content demonstrates Daly's homilies had become formulaic.[242]

Daly's condemnation of Provisional IRA violence at these funerals sparked a backlash from those in the Catholic community who supported republican paramilitaries. At the funeral for father-of-three Stephen McGahan, when he and two other Catholics where gunned down by loyalist paramilitaries outside of Avenue Bar, Daly asked the parishioners to pray for the victims and perpetrators. This statement inspired a walkout by a number of parishioners, who voiced their anger at the bishop's words. Outside St Patrick's Church on Donegall Street, twenty-one-year-old Eddie Kane thought the cardinal should 'have more to say for the Catholics. We feel very, very bitter and he only makes us feel more bitterness towards Protestants.'[243] In this instance, Daly's words backfired and rather than calm a grieving community, they inflamed their anger and alienation.

Bishop Cahal Daly's homilies at funerals for sectarian murders, combined with his extensive theological training, made him the clear choice by conservative Pope John Paul II for the next Archbishop of Armagh. Daly did not just meet with Catholics, but often met with the families of Protestant victims of Provisional IRA murders. As he could not preside over these funerals, Daly released statements condemning the Provisional IRA murders.[244] Further, when guaranteed there would be no military displays and when his visits could be seen as pastoral ones, he called on the homes of Provisional IRA members who had been killed.

---

[242] The statistical information here is from Cahal Daly's addresses, held in volumes at the Linenhall Library in Belfast. The information here is from *Addresses 1987–88* and *Addresses 1989–90*. In the 1990s the bishop donated this collection to the library. I have collated this data for this table.

[243] *Irish Independent*, 19 May 1988.

[244] 'Statement on Downpatrick Atrocity', 11 April 1990 in Daly, *Addresses 1989–90*.

Daly attempted to show compassion for grieving families of all religious and political persuasions, noting in his memoir:

> Yet there is a common human heartbreak, there are universal tears...and they have no political or religious colouring. Protestant tears and Catholic tears have the same colour; nationalist tears and loyalist tears are indistinguishable.[245]

By giving the homily for every Catholic victim of sectarian murder in his diocese, Daly drew focused attention to the issue. He constantly explained sectarian murders by loyalist paramilitaries fuelled Provisional IRA violence throughout the conflict. These sermons gave him a chance to decry militant republican and loyalist violence, as he believed they both created a cycle of never-ending killings—'an eye for an eye, a tooth for a tooth'.

Death of the Cardinal

On 8 May 1990, while leading a pilgrimage to Lourdes, France, Cardinal Ó Fiaich died suddenly of a heart attack aged sixty-six. This controversial nationalist stalwart had championed a softer approach to the republican movement, which made him unpopular with many moderate nationalists and most unionists, as well as the British government. Even in death, the cardinal generated controversy, as SF President and Vice President, Gerry Adams and Martin McGuinness respectively, attended Ó Fiaich's funeral. His untimely passing marked an absence in the Irish Catholic Church leadership, creating a vacuum of power for the next Primate of All Ireland. The staunch Irishman Ó Fiaich would be replaced by the soft-spoken, theologically driven Cahal Daly, dramatically altering the Church's involvement in the conflict.

Reactions in Northern Ireland to the news of the cardinal's death varied. Most in the Catholic Church mourned his loss.[246] Murray, by that time the administrator of St Patrick's Cathedral in Armagh, said immediately after news of the death reached him that Ó Fiaich 'was a warm hearted man who gave his priests tremendous leadership and freedom'.[247] Pope John Paul II deemed the cardinal a 'man of deep faith' who had 'a passionate love for his country'.[248] Bishop Cahal Daly was in Glasgow at the time for an ecumenical meeting, and recalled in his memoir hearing of Ó Fiaich's passing as 'impossible to take in' when his sister Shelia called to tell him the news.[249] Gerry Adams referred to Ó Fiaich as 'humane' and 'a friend to the prisoners' but above all 'an Irishman who never lost touch

---

[245] Daly, *Steps on my Pilgrim Journey*, 255.
[246] *Irish Catholic*, 10 May 1990; *Irish Times*, 9 May 1990; *Tablet*, 19 May 1990; *Universe*, 20 May 1990.
[247] *Irish Times*, 9 May 1990.   [248] *Irish Examiner*, 10 May 1990.
[249] Daly, *Steps on my Pilgrim Journey*, 258.

with his South Armagh roots'.[250] While Rev Ian Paisley welcomed news of the cardinal's death, referring to him as 'the mallet of Rome against the Protestants of Northern Ireland', Ulster Unionist Party (UUP) member Rev Martin Smyth remarked he mourned the passing of any person, but hoped Catholics would now have 'a more positive spiritual leadership and a less republican stance'.[251] Ó Fiaich's nationalism came from his Irish heritage and training, and those critical of the cardinal hoped a less fervent Irish nationalist would take his place. Cardinal Hume dismissed Ó Fiaich's critics, who had 'unjustly confused' the cardinal's 'dream of a united Ireland with sympathy for the IRA'.[252]

Ó Fiaich's funeral, like the man himself, was also controversial. The Auxiliary Bishop of Down and Connor, Anthony Farquhar, gave a Requiem Mass at St Pius X Basilica in Lourdes on 11 May and then travelled with the remains to Dublin the following day. Thousands lined the main road from Dublin to Belfast to wish the body farewell. The main service was held on 15 May 1990 at St Patrick's Cathedral, Armagh, with Bishop Cahal Daly as the chief celebrant. Taoiseach Charles Haughey, the Irish President Patrick Hillery, ten members of the Irish government, five cardinals, over sixty bishops, and 350 priests attended the Requiem Mass. Cardinals Basil Hume, John O'Connor of New York, Bernard Law of Boston, Adrian Simonis of Utrecht, and Francis Arzine, President of the Holy See's Council for Inter-Religious Dialogue, were also present. Members of the RUC, British and Irish Armies, and representatives from Protestant churches entered the Cathedral. Other notable attendees for the Requiem Mass included Lord Caledon, who attended to represent Queen Elizabeth II, and British Secretary of State, Peter Brooke. Controversially, Gerry Adams and Martin McGuinness of SF also sat in the pews.

Bishop Cahal Daly's funeral homily for Ó Fiaich touched upon his Irishness, scholarship, and devotion to reconciliation. Cahal Daly discussed Ó Fiaich's dominating and vivacious personality, and his ability to create lasting friendships with many. He noted 'this country has seldom witnessed such scenes of universal national mourning' for thousands of people saw the cardinal 'as a dear friend'.[253] While addressing the conflict, Cahal Daly discussed the cardinal's 'imperative need for reconciliation in Ireland' and felt warmed by the Protestants in attendance at the funeral.[254] The cardinal had opposed using violence to advance nationalist aims, despite his personal dreams of a united Ireland. Daly used this audience, with Adams and McGuinness in attendance, to state: 'May those committed to violence listen at last in death to this plea from the heart of that

---

[250] *Irish Times*, 9 May 1990.   [251] *Irish Times*, 9 May 1990.
[252] *Times*, 10 May 1990.
[253] 'Funeral Homily for Cardinal Tomás Ó Fiaich in St Patrick's Cathedral, Armagh', 15 May 1990 in Daly, *Steps on my Pilgrim Journey*, 383.
[254] Daly, *Steps on my Pilgrim Journey*, 389.

great Irishman who was Cardinal Tomás Ó Fiaich.'[255] At that point, the RTÉ and BBC cameras panned to the two SF leaders, focusing in on their expressionless faces. This direct statement to Adams and McGuinness foreshadowed the tumultuous relationship Cahal Daly would have with the republican movement as the next Archbishop of Armagh. With two Provisional IRA attacks on the day after the funeral, *The Irish Examiner* noted Daly's pleas 'fell on deaf ears'.[256] Overall, many praised Cahal Daly's Requiem Mass but disagreed with SF's presence. An article in *The Longford Leader* criticized the Church for allowing SF leaders to attend, for any 'non-Catholic would surely question how the Church could justify bestowing the Eucharist on such people'.[257] Former SDLP politician Austin Currie considered Adams and McGuinness' attendance at the funeral 'hypocritical'.[258] Even Ó Fiaich's funeral divided the public in the North.

The death of Ó Fiaich and his well-attended funeral marked the passing of an outspoken and engaging individual, delivering a blow to the Irish hierarchy. The institutional church had now lost three prelates in five years, with the deaths of the Archbishops of Dublin, Dermot Ryan and Kevin McNamara in 1985 and 1987 respectively. Ó Fiaich's sudden death shocked many as, at sixty-six years old, he was one of the younger members of the hierarchy. His nephew, John Ó Fiaich, noted cynically that his uncle 'was the only man in Ireland who could get the Taoiseach, the Secretary of Sate for Northern Ireland, Gerry Adams, and a representative of every church in the country under one roof, but he had to die to do it'.[259] His death left a power vacuum for the Church leadership and the loss of a guiding force in the Church through the conflict. His successor's relationship with the British government, media, and republican movement would be significantly different from Ó Fiaich's and, ultimately, mark a change in the Church's position in the conflict.

Conclusion

The premature death of Cardinal Ó Fiaich rocked the Church. With the emphasis of the contemporary Roman Catholic Church on conformity, Ó Fiaich's outspoken political beliefs set him apart. While he never strayed from the Vatican's line on contraception or divorce, he understood the pressure many of his parishioners faced when living under a government which allowed those practices to a degree. For pronouncement on these issues, he left the task to the former archbishops of Dublin, Dermot Ryan and Kevin McNamara. On theological matters,

---

[255] Daly, *Steps on my Pilgrim Journey*, 391–2.   [256] *Irish Examiner*, 18 May 1990.
[257] *Longford Leader*, 25 May 1990.   [258] *Irish Examiner*, 18 May 1990.
[259] *Irish Times*, 16 May 1990.

many clerics dismissed Ó Fiaich as a 'lightweight'.[260] Ó Fiaich's love was for the historical, especially the antiquarian history of Ireland, as demonstrated by his time as a lecturer and president of St Patrick's College, Maynooth. He passionately condemned Provisional IRA violence personally but left more formal presentations on the Church's attitude towards violence to Bishop Cahal Daly. Ó Fiaich's real successes were ecumenical, and he often welcomed Protestants into his Armagh home. He was chairman of the joint standing committee on mixed marriages at the annual Ballymascanlon inter-Church talks and kept 'good relations' with his counterparts in the main Protestant churches. Yet his open nationalist stance, and his view that people could vote for SF without supporting the Provisionals, generated mistrust. Many in the republican movement saw Ó Fiaich as offering a less prejudiced view towards their cause of a united Ireland: even if he denounced their methods.

This period demonstrates a balancing act among the hierarchy in Northern Ireland. Throughout the 1980s, Bishop Cahal Daly was not afraid to disagree with the cardinal and the republican movement perceived him as an ally of the British government. With the cardinal's death in May 1990, there was no overtly pro-nationalist hierarchy member. This therefore shifted the entire focus of the Irish hierarchy in Northern Ireland in favour of Bishop Cahal Daly's position. By the mid-1990s, the institutional Church rarely participated in communications between republicans and the British government for peace. Grassroots individuals and smaller groups, like the Clonard Monastery, took over this role.

---

[260] *Irish Times*, 9 May 1990.

5

'Let history judge who was to blame', 1990–1998

On 6 November 1990, Pope John Paul II appointed Cahal Daly the new Primate of All Ireland, after the sudden death of Tomás Ó Fiaich six months earlier.[1] This was no longer solely a Catholic issue. Protestant church leaders, community activists, and British and Irish government officials joined the Catholic Church in welcoming the appointment of Daly.[2] Even the UUP leader James Molyneaux released a statement of support.[3] Daly's appointment was noteworthy for another reason. At seventy-three, Daly was the oldest Primate to be appointed in Armagh for more than 170 years and had been written off by many as a possible successor to Ó Fiaich. For example, writing in *The Irish Times* three months earlier, Fr Enda MacDonagh had discounted Daly on account of his age and the fact he had suffered a heart attack in 1982.[4] Daly also appeared to be the complete opposite of his predecessor, in terms of both personality and physical appearance. Whereas Ó Fiaich was larger than life, with a thorough historical knowledge of the Church in Ireland, he was less known for his theological training. In contrast, Daly was petite, bird-like, with a complex and thorough understanding of theology, which he developed when he acted as the Irish theological expert for the Second Vatican Council. In addition, while both shared nationalist sentiments, Daly had endeared himself to moderates by acknowledging the position of the British government and of unionists in Northern Ireland at an early stage. This also had the effect of alienating the Provisionals, something he personally embraced. Popular support for the Provisional IRA may have been declining and Daly had been a long-standing vocal opponent to their methods. Upon his appointment, *The Irish Times* asked Daly whether he would use his new position to further a political agenda, in keeping with his frequent denunciations of the Provisional IRA and its actions. In response, Daly replied: 'A bishop is not a spokesman for any political party or political community. If a bishop is to be a minister for reconciliation—as he is called to be—he's got to understand and listen to both communities

---

[1] Chapter title reference: Fr Gerry Reynolds quoted in the *Universe*, 5 Nov. 1995.
[2] *Irish Times*, 7 Nov. 1990.   [3] *Irish Times*, 7 Nov. 1990.
[4] *Irish Times*, 22 Aug. 1990. *The Irish Times* later switched their position with an October report that the Pope was considering Cahal Daly for the position. *Irish Times*, 20 Oct. 1990.

and defend the rights of both communities.'[5] Nevertheless, Daly faced deep-seated resentment from militant republicans, and would face significant obstacles in his efforts to bring all sides to the negotiating table for peace.

This chapter will evaluate the changing role of the institutional Irish Catholic Church in the 1990s. The power of personalities is key to this evolution, and the switch from Ó Fiaich to Daly was a catalyst for change. As discussed in previous chapters, Daly had always condemned the Provisionals and had maintained a good relationship with constitutional nationalists and the British government. After the death of Ó Fiaich, the institutional Church, which had always been more moderate in its support for nationalism than Ó Fiaich, moved even further away from the republican politics of SF. Subsequently, the Catholic communities that did support SF became somewhat isolated from the institutional Church. Daly was well-known for his denunciation of the armed struggle and unwillingness to engage with militant republicans while their violence continued. While he was outspoken in encouraging peace and reconciliation, his previous denunciations had left him excluded from the negotiating table. As a former SDLP politician noted in trenchant terms, in an interview with the author, the institutional Church and Daly 'had nothing to do with the peace process, however much they claim they might have. I can guarantee it, I know about the peace process, I was there, they had nothing to do with it.'[6] However, Brian Feeney remains sympathetic to SF. On the other hand, it could be argued that Cardinal Daly promoted the idea of moderation, contributing to the general and growing feeling that compromise was inevitable. So it was left to individual clerics, rather than the Irish Catholic Church as a whole, to further the cause of peace through their own efforts in negotiation and mediation.

As discussed in previous chapters, since the early 1970s there had been a gradual breakdown in the hierarchical structure of the Irish Catholic Church and this allowed priests greater autonomy. For example, Fr Alec Reid, of the Clonard Monastery, had started his work of bringing together members of SF and the SDLP in 1986. By the early 1990s, the results of these efforts were visible, with SF entering into open talks with other parties to find peaceful, political solutions to bring about the end of the conflict.[7] The fragmentation of Catholic Church leadership was becoming clearer throughout the 1980s. Previously, Ó Fiaich had denounced paramilitary and state violence, while republicans perceived Daly as only condemning their armed struggle without commenting on that of the British Army or police forces. While some clergy sought to set up private peace talks, others were publicly denouncing the Provisional IRA for its violence. Tom Inglis argues that, by the 1990s, priests, bishops, and women religious were confident enough to allow their different perspectives to stand and no longer be seen to speak with one voice as they had done previously.[8] Private and public actions demonstrated a fractured Church with a less rigorous hierarchical structure, preventing clear lines of communication between the ranks as in earlier phases in the conflict.

For the Republic of Ireland, secularization had begun to impact on all sorts of issues and the Church was feeling a loss of deference to clerical authority by Catholics across the island. Divorce, abortion, contraception, and homosexuality were being more openly discussed in the government and society more generally, and there was pressure for the Church to engage in these debates. For example, the Church had commented on the AIDS crisis in the late 1980s, but by the early 1990s there was an expectation that the Church should publicly react to the spread of the disease by conceding to preventative measures.[9] A referendum asking whether abortion should be legalized in November 1992 ultimately led to a 'no' vote for abortion when there was an illness or disorder of the mother, but the bishops were nevertheless concerned that the electorate voted in favour of the right to travel to another country to procure an abortion, and the right to information about abortion services.[10] Pro-divorce lobbies were gaining momentum and this resulted in fundamental changes. The Fifteenth Amendment of the Constitution Act in 1996 removed the ban on divorce in the Republic.[11] The moral views of the Catholic Church were privileged in the Republic, so this increasingly formal separation between Church and state challenged the Catholic Church and was symptomatic of a diminishment of its influence over Catholic people. The culmination of this process, and a further source of delegitimization of the Church's moral authority, was the devastating revelations of the scale of clerical child abuse in 1994. While the Church's spiritual authority did not altogether disappear, as Inglis argues,[12] the scandal of clerical abuse altered the capacity of the Church to act as a mediator for peace in the conflict because its integrity, and therefore legitimacy, had been undermined.

The early 1990s saw the Provisional IRA tentatively begin discussions for peace. As Thomas Leahy argues, a variety of factors pushed SF and the Provisionals to consider peace, including SF's 'small but consistent electoral mandate', the Provisional IRA's ability to maintain the armed struggle, and political factors. These issues persuaded the Provisionals to consider dialogue and peaceful solutions by

---

[8] Inglis, *Moral Monopoly*, 241.

[9] *Irish Catholic*, 20 March 1990; *Universe*, 14 March 1993.

[10] Controversy around this issue was generated when the Dublin Supreme Court granted a fourteen-year-old rape victim the right to travel to Britain to terminate her pregnancy; *Catholic Herald*, 13 Nov. 1992; Inglis, *Moral Monopoly*, 220; Fuller, *Irish Catholicism since 1950*, 246.

[11] A 1992 referendum on divorce had failed; *Universe*, 4 Oct. 1992.

[12] Inglis, *Moral Monopoly*, 241–2.

the early 1990s.[13] This republican *glasnost* led to the use of priests and bishops as mediators between constitutional and militant republicans to a greater degree than ever before. In particular, this chapter will analyse the actions of Reid, Fr Gerry Reynolds, and Bishop Edward Daly. While sex abuse scandals challenged the institutional Church, by this point it was individual priests who furthered the peace process, by acting as intermediaries for militant republicans, constitutional nationalists, and the British government.

Declining Support for the Provisional IRA?

The portion of the Catholic community that supported the Provisional IRA faced strategic opposition from unionist and constitutional nationalists by the late 1980s and early 1990s. The Provisionals continued their armed campaign regardless and also increased punishment attacks on Catholics whom they deemed to have engaged in anti-social behaviour, such as theft, robbery, or joy-riding.[14] Individuals were 'brutally policed' through beatings, kneecappings, and punishment shootings. This practice was not new—there were 1,228 punishment shootings between 1973 and 1997.[15] SF President Gerry Adams lost his West Belfast seat in the 1992 UK general election, and Bew, Frampton, and Gurruchaga have argued that this was a major psychological blow to the party.[16] Nonetheless, votes for Adams remained consistent over these three elections in 1983, 1987, and 1992. However, by the 1992 election, there was a defection of Catholic support from SF to SDLP candidate Joe Hendron, in protest against Provisional IRA tactics and strategic voting by the Workers' Party and unionists was crucial to Adams' defeat. After the Enniskillen Bombing in 1987, the SDLP dropped its support of SF candidates in favour of UUP members for chairman positions on the Fermanagh District Council.[17] As Leahy notes, without 'sufficient electoral support', republican leadership needed to make more compromises in their negotiations with the British government.[18]

In addition to the punishment squads, Provisional IRA bombings which either explicitly targeted civilians, as seen in the Enniskillen Bombing, or those which inadvertently killed civilians, brought widespread revulsion towards the Provisionals' methods. The bombing of a Protestant fish shop on the Shankill Road in the heart of Loyalist Belfast at Saturday lunchtime on 23 October 1993 caused mass outrage from Catholics and Protestants alike. The UDA headquarters was

---

[13] Thomas Leahy, 'The influence of informers and agents on Provisional Irish Republican Army Military Strategy and British Counter-Insurgency strategy, 1976-94', *Twentieth Century British History*, 26 (2015), 141.

[14] English, *Armed Struggle*, 274–5.   [15] English, *Armed Struggle*, 274–5.

[16] Bew, Frampton, and Gurruchaga, *Talking to Terrorists*, 111.

[17] Leahy, 'The influence of informers', 141.   [18] Leahy, 'The influence of informers', 145.

located above the shop, making it a Provisional IRA target, but none of the organization's members were inside. The Shankill bombing, as it came to be known, killed nine Protestant civilians as well as the Provisional IRA bomber himself. Even Gerry Adams condemned the attack, saying: 'It was wrong. It cannot be excused.'[19] Cardinal Daly attacked the 'twisted mentality and perverse logic' of the Provisionals in a speech delivered the night after the atrocity. He said it was 'a sectarian mass murder of a degree of viciousness which brings shame to our city and our country and disgrace to any cause'.[20] Daly called for a suspension of Provisional IRA violence to demonstrate their commitment to peace talks but urged that dialogue should continue, for he understood how hard SDLP councilor and European MP for Foyle, John Hume, had worked for talks to begin at all.[21] As might be expected, Protestant church leaders themselves condemned the bombings, with Church of Ireland Archbishop Robin Eames predicting Northern Ireland would turn into a 'desert of hopelessness' if the paramilitaries continued fighting.[22] The Shankill bombing is just one example of both Catholics and Protestants criticizing the violence of paramilitaries by the early 1990s, weakening the perceived legitimacy of their actions and helping to pave, at a popular level, the path to peace.

The early 1990s witnessed renewed British public focus on the Provisional IRA following numerous bombings in England. The Scottish, and English and Welsh Catholic hierarchies worked to combat Irish xenophobia and discrimination against all Irish Catholics. The Warrington bombings on 20 March 1993, which killed three-year-old Jonathan Ball and fatally wounded twelve-year-old Tim Parry, heightened the feelings of anger and hostility felt in England.[23] The Warrington bombing is only one example of a Provisional IRA attack in England during this period, but it drew a wider emotive response because of the victims' young ages. Cardinal Hume of Westminster released a joint statement with Cardinal Daly which condemned the Provisionals' attack as 'utterly inhuman and barbaric' and appealed for 'an end to all such violence'.[24] It was symbolically important that the leaders of these two hierarchies stood together in a united front against the Provisionals. They also hoped their joint statement would reduce anti-Irish feeling in Britain by highlighting that their 'feeling of revulsion' was 'shared by the overwhelming majority of people in Ireland, as well as Britain, who bear no responsibility for such outrageous actions perpetuated by a very small faction'.[25] Daly wrote to Archbishop Derek Worlock of Liverpool, a diocese with a large Irish migrant constituency, to express his sympathy and share with him the disgust

---

[19] *Irish News*, 25 Oct. 1993 in English, *Armed Struggle*, 282.
[20] *Tablet*, 30 Oct. 1993.   [21] *Irish Times*, 25 Oct. 1993.   [22] *Irish Catholic*, 28 Oct. 1993.
[23] The Provisional IRA detonated bombs in litterbins on Bridge Street, a shopping and business area in the centre of town; English, *Armed Struggle*, 279.
[24] LAA, 'Joint Statement by Cardinal Hume and Cardinal Daly', 26 March 1993.
[25] LAA, 'Joint Statement by Cardinal Hume and Cardinal Daly', 26 March 1993.

most Irish now felt towards the Provisional IRA.[26] At an ecumenical service for 'remembrance, reconciliation and commitment' held at a Warrington Parish Church, St Elphin's, in April 1993, Worlock led the service with Anglican Bishop of Liverpool David Sheppard, with whom he had toured Northern Ireland and spoke on ecumenism in the 1980s. Baptist ministers also took part in the service.[27] Worlock condemned the violence and the Provisionals' token apology in his address and, significantly, also promoted the idea that most Irish people denounced the Provisional IRA's actions. Worlock stated that this bombing could be a turning point for the Provisionals, and praised Colin Parry who hoped his son would become 'a symbol for peace' and reconciliation.[28] Nevertheless Worlock still received angry letters from those who continued to believe that the Irish Catholic Church supported the Provisionals.[29] While this show of unity did not fully convince everyone in Britain, the Warrington bombing did bring the Irish and English and Welsh Catholic Churches together, as well as the churches of different Christian faiths, to condemn the Provisionals' violence, promote peace, and attempt to counteract anti-Irish sentiment.

Widespread revulsion for Provisional IRA methods by some parts of Northern Ireland's society and infiltration of their ranks by British Army intelligence convinced the IRA to talk peace. The Provisionals did not learn from the cross-community outrage that followed the 1987 Enniskillen Bombing and increased violence of this kind further isolated the paramilitaries from support. The Warrington bombing demonstrated how entangled the relationship between the Irish and English and Welsh Catholic Churches was when it concerned the conflict. A condemnation of the atrocity came quickly from Daly, and Worlock was also proactive in his attempts to quell any anti-Irish sentiment on English shores. At this point in the conflict, the English hierarchy commenting on the Troubles did not garner the same backlash as it had done in the 1970s and 1980s, although some English Catholics continued to ask their bishops to excommunicate IRA members. For its part, the institutional Catholic Church reiterated its condemnation of violence of any kind. Yet it was still Church individuals, rather than the institution itself, who were to do the most work to further the cause of peace.

---

[26] This letter was later sent to the media. LAA, 'Irish Cardinal condemns atrocity', Cathnews Press Release, 23 March 1993.

[27] LAA, Merseyside Churches' Media Service Press Briefing on Warrington Bombing, 6 April 1993.

[28] LAA, Address of Archbishop Derek Worlock at service of remembrance, reconciliation, and commitment, 7 April 1993.

[29] LAA, T.G. to Worlock, 12 April 1993; LAA, S.D. to Worlock, 11 April 1993; LAA, M.J. to Worlock, April 1993; LAA, A.S. to Worlock, 23 March 1993; LAA, B.O. to Worlock, 10 April 1993. One such letter wanted the British government to declare war on the Republic of Ireland because of the actions of the Provisional IRA. This missive appears to be a mass produced letter, and does not include any personal directive for the archbishop. LAA, R.H.S. to Worlock, 24 March 1993.

Community Relations

As the 1990s began, the Catholic and Protestant churches switched their attentions away from ecumenical endeavours and towards community relations. Discussions of differences in faith developed into practical projects aimed at bringing together a divided community. It is fair to say that the institutional Catholic and Protestant churches led some of these initiatives, but many of the most successful were lay driven. Maria Power has analysed this shift in the tactics of the churches and argues that as the churches in Northern Ireland negotiated the conflict, their emphasis moved from high-level theological discussion to the grassroots-orientated, experientially informed strategies of community relations.[30]

Institutionally-led activities focused on the actions of the leaders of both churches and received much publicity in the press and media. Conversely, the work of community-based organizations was less celebrated beyond their own neighborhoods but these organizations often crucially recruited both Protestant and Catholic clergy onto their boards. While ecumenical lay organizations have existed since the 1970s, there was a spike in spontaneous lay-led projects emerging in the early 1990s in reaction to shared, Christian-influenced outrage at paramilitary attacks and an overwhelmingly united urge to end the conflict.[31] Furthermore, many of these lay organizations were not focused around religion but did include religious figures from the community. This shift from ecumenism to interdenominational praxis reflected the breakdown of rigid hierarchical divisions and power relationships between the clergy and laity.[32] While peace movements led by the hierarchy still existed, this period saw the emergence of more dynamic organizations driven by ordinary members of the public. Of course, the institutional churches were clearly still working to have an impact on the conflict but they were now co-operating with lay Catholics and Protestants rather than dictating the course.

However, this was not a total change of direction for the churches. In 1993, as a sign of united Christian witness, the leaders of the Four Main Churches in Ireland travelled together to the USA to address a conference on peace in Northern Ireland and meet with ecumenical and business leaders with the hope of promoting investment in the North.[33] It was the first time that all four leaders had

---

[30] Power, *From Ecumenism to Community Relations*, 3–6; See also Maria Power, 'Providing a prophetic voice? Churches and peacebuilding, 1968–2005' in M. Power, *Peacebuilding in Northern Ireland* (Liverpool, 2011), 73–92.

[31] Between 1977 and 1992, five new ecumenical communities were founded. In addition to this existed the Corrymeela Community and the Christian Renewal Centre, founded in 1965 and 1974 respectively. Power, *From Ecumenism to Community Relations*, 118–19.

[32] Inglis argues that the laity played a stronger role in all aspects of Church life because of the declining number of priest vocations by this time. Inglis, *Moral Monopoly*, 257.

[33] *Irish Catholic*, 11 Feb. 1993.

co-operated together for an American tour.[34] Church of Ireland leader Archbishop Robin Eames, President of the Methodist conference Rev Derek Ritchie, and Moderator of the Presbyterian Church, Rev John Dunlop joined Cardinal Daly at the 'Living with Difference' conference in Boston, Massachusetts. The four men also visited Philadelphia, New York, and Washington D.C. during their stay.[35] However, the four leaders did not meet with Bill Clinton on their trip, despite the USA President's proposals to appoint a peace envoy to Northern Ireland, likely because of the President's position on abortion.[36] Nevertheless, considering the tumultuous relationship between the four church leaders in the 1980s, this joint trip demonstrated a palpable and proactive move in the direction of unity.[37] Individual priests were continuing to bring politicians together behind the scenes but these notable public and symbolic acts of ecumenism were important in supporting cross-community efforts. These leaders of the churches could not act as intermediaries in the same way as individual clerics because of their high profiles, but by publishing their weekly schedules in both religious and secular newspapers, and by holding such meetings, they could attract much-needed positive media attention to a fledgling peace process. As such, the USA visit demonstrated the church leaders' joint commitment to peace and ecumenism and a desire to end antagonism between their respective communities. In addition, the visit would not have occurred had it not been for the more conciliatory tone which Cardinal Daly brought to his role. His predecessor Cardinal Ó Fiaich had sometimes clashed with his Protestant counterparts over accusations that he appeared too sympathetic towards militant republicanism. Daly's long history of condemning the Provisionals and SF helped convince other church leaders of his true commitment to non-sectarian policy and peace.

By the early 1990s, long-standing lay organizations had altered their mission to fit with the changing nature of the conflict; this included the Corrymeela community and the Christian Renewal Centre (CRC). These groups wanted structures 'to be put in place to facilitate the long-term healing of past inequalities' through community relations and religious teachings. The Corrymeela community hoped to act as symbol for Protestant-Catholic unity, demonstrating that a love of Christ transcended community divisions and could lead to reconciliation through face-to-face contact.[38] Corrymeela emphasized its role as providing a practical support network for those participating in peace and reconciliation efforts even going beyond the conflict and addressing the core 'divisions rampant within society

---

[34] Representatives from the Four Main Churches travelled to Boston in November 1988, but that trip did not include the leader of each church; *Tablet*, 28 Oct. 1988; *Irish Catholic*, 4 Feb. 1993.

[35] *Catholic Herald*, 5 Feb. 1993.

[36] There was some indication that the leaders did not want to meet Clinton because of his stance on abortion; *Irish Catholic*, 11 Feb. 1993.

[37] *Irish News*, 15 March 1985.

[38] Power, *From Ecumenism to Community Relations*, 122.

which caused the violence'.[39] They held work camps for young people, family activity weeks, conferences and local cells, and involvement in schools. Yet Power argues their most important contribution was the impact on their own immediate community.[40] The community had evolved from its stance in the 1980s that focused solely on ecumenism in a Northern Ireland context and continued to foster relationships among individuals of different faiths that led to long-term transformation. The CRC based in Rostrevor, Co. Down, however, did not transform its mission until a leadership change in 2000. Instead it continued to practice its original message that prayer and renewal could transcend community differences.[41] Where Corrymeela focused on secular community-based efforts, the CRC rooted itself in Christ[42] and was mostly open to other local and international, evangelical charismatic groups.[43] Whereas Power notes that it remains difficult to assess the impact of these groups on the wider peace process, they both laid the foundations for compatible cross-community living.[44] Corrymeela and the CRC may have operated outside the institutional Catholic and Protestant churches but they still maintained a religious focus alongside grounded, pragmatic approaches to their efforts.

The early 1990s also witnessed the emergence of non-religious peace initiatives with a cross-community focus. These organizations had no religious basis but featured the involvement of Catholic and Protestant clergy who had chosen to take part. Some of these organizations had very specific aims but others, including Cooley's Stop Terror Oppression Pain (STOP), Initiative '92, and the Opsahl Commission, cast a broader net for peace. The Cooley Committee for STOP began after the 1991 murder of farmer Thomas Oliver by the Provisionals and was made up of members of the laity and the clergy.[45] The Provisionals claimed Oliver had acted as an informer for the Irish police.[46] In response to his death, Cooley residents organized a rally against the Provisional IRA on 4 August, with support from STOP, which saw thousands of people from both sides of the border in attendance.[47] *The Irish Independent* reported that these individuals gathered in Cooley 'to register their horror at what happened' and to protest against 'the

---

[39] Power, *From Ecumenism to Community Relations*, 123.

[40] Power, *From Ecumenism to Community Relations*, 124.

[41] Power, *From Ecumenism to Community Relations*, 131–3.

[42] This term comes from Colossians 2:7 and these groups emphasize grounding their practice in their faith in Christ.

[43] Charismatic groups believe in gifts of the faith. They often hold prayer meetings outside of churches, speak in tongues, and feature gifts of prophecy and faith healing; Power, *From Ecumenism to Community Relations*, 134.

[44] Power, *From Ecumenism to Community Relations*, 136.

[45] The committee included Brian Mckevitt, John Elmore, John Woods, Peadar McDonald, Eugene Begley, Bridie Magee, Rev Mervyn Kingston, Fr John McGrane, and Fr Sean McCartan; *Irish Press*, 20 Nov. 1991.

[46] *An Phoblacht/Republican News*, 25 July 1991.　　　　[47] *Irish Press*, 31 July 1991.

Mafia-type code' the Provisionals wished to impose on them.[48] Faul, a member of STOP, addressed the crowd at Cooley's Gaelic Athletic Association (GAA) ground who had gathered in defiance of Provisional IRA threats. *The Irish Press* reported cheers when Faul cried out: 'One man, Thomas Oliver, has delivered Cooley from evil. The Provisionals are finished here'.[49] The Auxiliary Bishop of Armagh, Gerard Clifford also spoke and said: 'There is no room for ambiguity here. You are either for peace or for violence'.[50] At the rally, Cooley community members made clear their view on Provisional IRA violence, agreeing a statement which addressed the organization directly: 'To you, the IRA, that you have no mandate to make demands from this community but the community demands from you that you stop'.[51] Nevertheless, the Provisionals did still hold some influence in the community. Dunleer native Siobhan Armstrong reported she knew that many more were 'afraid to come' to the rally and that the Provisional IRA had delivered letters warning locals not to attend.[52]

Cardinal Daly praised the estimated 10,000 people who attended the Cooley rally and the efforts of STOP. As the murder occurred in the Republic, this defiance in the face of Provisional IRA threats could have occurred because Cooley residents had neither been subject to the organization's intimidation and consequential actions nor had direct experience with British troops. Through this campaign, Thomas Oliver's name became a rallying call for all families who had lost loved ones as a result of Provisional IRA violence and in November 1991 STOP was granted the People of the Year award from Rehab group and televised on RTÉ for their bravery.[53] It is difficult to ascertain what impact the rejection of Provisionals' intimidation tactics in the South had in the North, but this event is important because it demonstrated an example of public defiance of the organization with visible support from the Catholic clergy.

One group that did publicly defy the Provisionals in the North was the Belfast-based Families Against Intimidation and Terror (FAIT). FAIT was a Northern Ireland pressure group to which Faul also belonged, formed by Nancy Gracey in 1990 following the shooting of her son by a paramilitary group.[54] FAIT achieved a major success when, with the assistance of Faul, they helped to negotiate the return of kidnapped Coagh father-of-five, Colm O'Neill. Faul pleaded for O'Neill's return at the Cooley rally and FAIT called the kidnapping 'an outrageous abuse of human rights.'[55] FAIT coordinator Jeff Maxwell appealed to the family to keep up the publicity because, as with previous kidnappings, a strong public response was the 'only hope' for the victims' return.[56] Faul called on Gerry Adams to bring O'Neill home and surmised that his Provisional IRA captors were most likely

[48] *Irish Independent*, 5 Aug. 1991.   [49] *Irish Press*, 5 Aug. 1991.
[50] *Irish Press*, 5 Aug. 1991.   [51] *Catholic Herald*, 9 Aug. 1991.
[52] *Irish Press*, 5 Aug. 1991.   [53] *Sunday Independent*, 24 Nov. 1991.
[54] Brewer, Higgins, and Teeney, *Religion, Civil Society, & Peace*, 78.
[55] *Irish Examiner*, 2 Aug. 1991.   [56] *Irish Examiner*, 2 Aug. 1991.

abusing O'Neill and forcing him to make 'ridiculous' tapes with 'no credibility',[57] detailing what information he had ostensibly passed on to the security forces. SF press officer Richard McAuley attempted to discredit FAIT in a 5 August letter to *The Irish Times*, causing others to write in rejecting his claims.[58] FAIT also worked with the Newry Hostage Support group in August 1991 in support of the two men who claimed sanctuary in the Cathedral—an incident that will be explored in greater detail.[59] FAIT worked throughout the 1990s condemning the intimidatory tactics of the Provisional IRA and petitioning Amnesty International on behalf of the victims' families.[60] Like STOP, it was not a religious organization but included both Protestant and Catholic clergy. Faul was a key figure within both STOP and FAIT and his tenacious personality helped to ensure public successes for both groups. Faul was ideally placed to assist these groups, given his own personal history with the conflict, and his long-standing role as a peace activist.

Like STOP and FAIT, Initiative '92 was a cross-community organization striving for peace and, again, Faul played a key role in the organization. Initiative '92 described itself as 'a citizens' inquiry' and was composed of civil activists, who established a commission which sat from 1992 to 1993.[61] These activists included academics, poets, authors, Protestant and Catholic clergy and bishops, politicians, and community organizers.[62] It also invited representatives from paramilitary organizations to speak as well as women and working-class Protestants, who Marianne Elliott argues were previously marginalized in these conversations.[63] Faul was the representative from the Irish Catholic Church while Bishop Samuel Poyntz stood for the Church of Ireland.[64] Initiative '92 held hearings across Northern Ireland, giving ordinary people the chance to voice their opinion on how a lasting peace could be achieved in Northern Ireland.[65] In February 1993, Faul proposed a consultative senate with new council boundaries to the commission, and named Co. Tyrone as an example where cross-community collaboration benefited everyone.[66] Faul was one of many who gave evidence to the group, in a similar fashion to the New Ireland Forum in 1984. Jesuit Fr Brian Lennon also gave evidence the commission.[67] Despite the many grandees who sat on the

---

[57] *Irish Times*, 2 Aug. 1991.   [58] *Irish Times*, 10 Aug. 1991.

[59] *Irish Times*, 29 Aug. 1991.

[60] *Irish Times*, 3 July 1992, 12 Jan. 1993, 25 Jan. 1994; *Tablet*, 8 Oct. 1994.

[61] *Irish Times*, 27 May 1992.

[62] Adrian Guelke, 'Civil society and the Northern Irish peace process', *Voluntas: International Journal of Voluntary and Non-Profit Organisations*, 14 (2003), 69–71.

[63] Marianne Elliott, 'The role of civil society in conflict resolution: The Opsahl Commission in Northern Ireland, 1992–93', *New Hibernia Review*, 17 (2013), 87–91.

[64] *Irish Times*, 27 May 1992.   [65] *Irish Press*, 25 Jan. 1993.

[66] *Irish Times*, 6 Feb. 1993.

[67] In his 1995 book, Lennon outlined his plan for peace, noting that for 'reconciliation and justice—to be real—must go together'. Lennon, *After the Ceasefires*, 9.

committee, the commission wanted to privilege the ordinary person above academics and politicians and to hear a wider range of voices on the conflict.[68] More than 500 individuals made submissions to Initiative '92 from a broad range of backgrounds and beliefs.[69] Chaired by Professor Torkel Opsahl from Norway, the group released a report of its findings in June 1993.[70] Dr Geraldine Smyth OP, who joined the Opsahl Commission in 1993 as the coordinator of the project in the dissemination phase, noted the project allowed people like herself 'to meet people across the whole spectrum of political, cultural, legal, educational, and religious worlds'.[71] Clem McCartney has argued that the group brought communities together to 'think and discuss options for the future', giving many confidence to engage in the political process.[72] However, the main conclusion of Opsahl was to call for another commission to continue conversation.[73] Although its impact may have appeared small at the time, with hindsight we can see that Initiative '92 and the subsequent Opsahl Commission generated engaged dialogue and provided an outlet for the involvement and investment of numerous key individuals in the peace process.

Whether through the institutional church or grassroots, cross-community organizations, individual clergy and bishops attempted to highlight and end Provisional IRA intimidation tactics and campaign for peace. At this point, individual clergy chose to work with cross-community organizations of their own volition, rather than following the lead of the institutional church. By the early 1990s, ecumenism had evolved in Northern Ireland. It was no longer enough for Protestants and Catholics to understand each other's theologies, but additionally to work together for peace. As the institutional Catholic Church would continue to lose credibility over the following years, the importance of these individual, grassroots organizations grew stronger. These community organizers emerged as the only real, untainted mechanisms for peace and greater community relations. They did not carry the baggage of the institutional Church, both with its previous attempts at mediating the conflict and with its loss of credibility through revelations of clerical child abuse during the 1990s.

---

[68] Marianne Elliott, *When God Took Sides: Religion and Identity in Ireland- Unfinished History* (Oxford, 2009), 19.

[69] *Irish Press*, 10 June 1993.

[70] Andy Pollak, ed. *A Citizen's Inquiry: The Opsahl Report on Northern Ireland* (Dublin, 1993).

[71] Dr Geraldine Smyth OP interview, 3 Dec. 2018.

[72] After the creation of the GFA, it needed to be ratified through an amendment. The core of the 'Yes' campaign consisted of those individuals involved in Initiative '92. Clem McCartney, 'The role of civil society', *Accord: Striking a Balance: The Northern Ireland peace process*, 89, (1999) http://cain.ulst. ac.uk/events/peace/docs/accord99.htm

[73] *Irish Press*, 10 June 1993.

Peace Talks: Clergy as Intermediaries

Throughout the conflict Catholic priests and many Protestant clergy had acted as negotiators between militant republicans and their political adversaries, whether they were constitutional nationalists or members of the British government. Priests were supposed to embody neutrality and had historically adjudicated between different Irish groups. For example, priests acted as mediators between the Officials and Provisionals in the early 1970s and again between the Provisionals and the British government to secure the 1974–75 ceasefire. Yet, by the early 1990s, some priests felt republican paramilitary and political parties had exploited their role as meditators to their own ends, with the claim of sanctuary at Newry Cathedral as one such example.[74] On the other hand they had achieved results: the Clonard Monastery and the private work of Reid had brought together Gerry Adams and John Hume, culminating in the Hume-Adams peace plan, for example. John Hume's personal relationship with Catholicism and Church leaders is a ripe avenue for extended exploration for a future project. Nevertheless, antagonism between the Church and militant republicans was high. Murray and Tonge have gone as far as to argue that the Church's criticism of armed struggle had actually pushed SF away from political solutions.[75] However, without the work of these priests, many potential avenues for dialogue may have failed or not even opened in the first place. Their efforts demonstrate that until the mid-1990s, nationalists still valued their services as mediators. Ultimately, it is fairly clear that the work of many priests culminated in the 1994 Provisional IRA ceasefire.

An early example of priests expressing displeasure at their role as neutral mediators being abused by republicans came at Newry Cathedral in August 1991. Two young Newry men, Liam Kearns and David Madigan, feared for their lives after the Provisionals accused them of anti-social behaviour and gave them until noon on 17 August to leave the country or 'face military action.'[76] Both men denied these allegations and, following an anti-IRA demonstration in Newry, sought 'the ancient right of sanctuary' at the cathedral.[77] Newry Catholics created the Newry Hostages Support Group, a lay organization with close ties to The Workers' Party, to demand the safety of Kearns and Madigan in an effort to stand up to Provisional IRA intimidation.[78] Punishment beatings and forced exile were common Provisional IRA tactics and the outspoken denunciation of their actions by the local Catholic community was an uncommon occurrence at this time.

Initially there was confusion around the actions of the clergy following Kearns and Madigan's claim of sanctuary. It was reported in the press and media that the priests attempted to remove the pair from the cathedral, which the clergymen

---

[74] *Irish Times*, 26 Aug. 1991.   [75] Murray and Tonge, *Sinn Féin and the SDLP*, 162.
[76] *Catholic Herald*, 23 Aug. 1991; *Irish Times*, 26 Aug. 1991.
[77] *Catholic Herald*, 23 Aug. 1991.   [78] *Irish Press*, 21 Aug. 1991.

fiercely denied.[79] However, the priests did say that it had become apparent Kearns and Madigan had ulterior motives and wished to use the space for political negotiations between The Workers' Party and SF. In a BBC Radio Ulster interview during the episode, Newry priest Fr Kevin Cullen claimed the Cathedral 'ended up becoming a place where the Workers' Party and SF are battling it out as to who has the right to say what and where' and that the bid for sanctuary actually had become a struggle about political territory.[80] Some in the press also accused local priests of passing messages between the Provisionals and the two men in an effort to resolve the dispute; a claim Cardinal Cahal Daly forcefully denied during an RTÉ Radio interview. All parties eventually reached a peaceful agreement and Kearns and Madigan were taken out of Newry to a secret location after twelve days. Priests were able to act as intermediaries in this situation for two reasons. Firstly, after Kearns and Madigan claimed sanctuary, priests were some of the few individuals trusted to enter the cathedral without ulterior motives. Secondly, the Catholic community that they served was now more openly opposed to the Provisionals, where earlier in the conflict there was fear of the organization. The Newry Cathedral sanctuary affair remains one example of priests maintaining their roles as intermediaries; a skill that would become even more necessary as peace talks progressed. Yet priests like Cullen also vocalized their disquiet, fearing that in this situation they were also used as political pawns in their work as mediators.

There was a spectrum of clerical responses to the Provisionals' armed struggle during the early 1990s. It is difficult to characterize this period as having one 'Church style'. While Reynolds and Reid privately worked as mediators, Faul publicly denounced SF throughout the early 1990s, proving that not every priest was in favour of dialogue. Faul criticized SF for their one-sided condemnations of loyalist paramilitaries without offering the same treatment to the Provisionals, calling SF's dialogue with other parties an 'alleged peace process' in March 1994.[81] Faul criticized Irish journalists for failing to call SF to account through condemnation of Provisional IRA violence 'when they say they do not speak for the IRA'.[82] He also argued that SF 'must have an opinion on the violation of human rights of every person in their constituency' by the Provisionals.[83] Faul continued to denounce SF and the Provisionals that April:

> Peace is a sacred thing meaning the relationship between men and men, based on respect for fundamental human rights and fundamental freedoms. The IRA doesn't understand that. Bombing airports and bombing people out of their jobs is not peace. We need to get some real proof of peace.[84]

---

[79] *Catholic Herald*, 30 Aug. 1991.   [80] *Irish Times*, 29 Aug. 1991.
[81] *Irish Times*, 9 March 1994.   [82] *Irish Times*, 9 March 1994.
[83] *Irish Times*, 9 March 1994.   [84] *Irish Times*, 4 April 1994.

For Faul, the lack of expressions of regret from the Provisionals, coupled with his view that SF only used terms like 'moving the peace process forward' for their own propaganda purposes made his involvement as an intermediary between republican organizations unlikely.[85]

While the institutional Church had less impact on the peace process during this time, individual clergy members played key roles in bringing together politicians to discuss peaceful solutions.[86] Priests acted as intermediaries for more major peace talks, most evidenced in the work of Tipperary-born Redemptorist priest Alec Reid during the Hume-Adams talks.[87] Reid was a member of the Clonard Monastery in West Belfast, and had been involved in helping republican prisoners during the 1970s and 1980s. As a priest, Reid felt 'the Church ha[d] a moral obligation to get stuck in when people [were] suffering and to try and stop it'.[88] Both Reid and his fellow Redemptorist priest, Fr Gerry Reynolds, had a long history of cross-community activities, often crossing the peace line to go on the Shankill Road and meet with Protestant families whose relatives were killed by the Provisional IRA.[89] The Redemptorist focus on the poor and emphasis on living with their community enabled many of these priests to help bring peace to this troubled area. Fr Christy McCarthy, who served as a Clonard rector from 1976 until his death in 1983, inspired Reid and Reynolds. McCarthy believed in empowering the Catholic laity so they could search for peace and reconciliation with Protestants themselves.[90] They stressed the importance of relating to their parishioners 'in all aspects of their daily lives'.[91] Redemptorist priests wanted to understand why their community would support a campaign of violence. The mission of their order, combined with their duty as Christians, pushed these religious men into the role of community leaders and advocates for peace.

Reid had a close relationship with Adams, and as such was able to steer Adams towards a peace dialogue.[92] Former SDLP politician Brian Feeney described Reid as a man Adams would 'go to' to help create dialogue.[93] As mentioned in Chapter 4, Reid was publicly recognizable as he was photographed attempting to help two British Army corporals after they were beaten to death by a republican mob during a 1988 funeral. Unknown until many years later, at the time the photograph was taken Reid was carrying a letter for Hume from Adams, outlining SF's plan for peace.[94] When Reynolds came to live at Clonard he recalled asking Reid what could be done about the violence. Reid's response was 'the only thing

[85] *Irish Times*, 4 April 1994.   [86] Brewer, Higgins and Teeney, *Religion*, xvi.
[87] English, *Armed Struggle*, 264.
[88] '14 Days', BBC 1, 21 March 2013, http://www.bbc.co.uk/programmes/b01r7v48
[89] Interview with Fr Adrian Egan, 22 Nov. 2007 in Brewer, Higgins, and Teeney, *Religion*, 43.
[90] Wells, *Friendship towards Peace*, 32–3.   [91] Fuller, *Irish Catholicism since 1950*, 226.
[92] English, *Armed Struggle*, 264.   [93] Interview with Brian Feeney, 26 May 2015.
[94] *BBC News*, 31 Aug. 2014.

that will resolve it is the dialogue'.[95] To create a line of communication between SF and other nationalist and unionist parties, Reid acknowledged that he needed to 'get the IRA to stop' their campaign of violence.[96] Adams told Reid the only way to stop the Provisionals was through a 'peaceful strategy', which could bring together SF, the SDLP, and the Irish government.[97] His early work with SF and the Provisionals meant Reid had the trust of these groups. As a non-political figure known for his desire to end the conflict, he was the perfect candidate to bring these organizations together.

The first task of individual priests who pursued peace was indeed to create dialogue. Adams had made his intentions known publicly during the BBC radio programme *Behind the Headlines* on 31 August 1985, saying he would ask the SF National Executive to invite the SDLP for talks on their shared 'pan-Nationalist interests'.[98] Yet it was Adams' private connection with intermediary Reid which ensured that meaningful dialogue began. By that time, Reid had created the Clonard Church Ministry with other priests, as a special peace-making ministry within the Redemptorist Order. As Adams stated, the tradition of the Redemptorists of offering sanctuary allowed for the creation of such a ministry.[99] In response to the lack of institutional Church support for dialogue with political parties, as demonstrated in previous chapters, the Redemptorists at Clonard placed themselves as intermediaries for SF and other parties. Redemptorist Fr Stephen Mahoney first wrote to John Hume, asking if the SDLP leader would meet with priests at Clonard in 1985. Hume did not initially agree to the meeting, but after Reid wrote to him in May 1986, he came to Clonard to speak with Reid, Reynolds, and Fr Seamus Enright about the Redemptorists' efforts for peace.[100] The Clonard priests facilitated a meeting in September 1986 between Hume and Adams in the hopes that through dialogue the men could create a 'common nationalist policy of aims and methods for resolving the conflict and establishing a just and lasting peace'.[101] In the beginning, the monastery's involvement remained secret from other leaders in SF and the Provisionals. Relations between militant republicans and the Catholic Church were fraught, especially after the hunger strikes.[102] Through Reid, however, Adams and Hume were able to secure a private backchannel. Negotiations with the SDLP would give SF legitimacy in the

---

[95] Interview with Fr Gerry Reynolds in '14 Days', 21 March 2013.

[96] Interview with Fr Alec Reid, '14 Days', 21 March 2013.

[97] Interview with Fr Alec Reid, '14 Days', 21 March 2013.

[98] Hume accepted to have talks with the Provisional IRA Army Council in 1985, but the discussion lasted only a few minutes when the Provisionals insisted the talks were filmed. Hume was wary of being used for propaganda purposes, but Murray argued the public offer for talks was the first step by SF towards constitutional politics; Murray, *John Hume and the SDLP*, 162–4.

[99] Adams, *Hope and History*, 41.

[100] 'A Letter to John Hume', 19 May 1986 in Martin McKeever, *One Man, One God: The Peace Ministry of Fr Alec Reid C.Ss.R.* (Dublin, 2017), 112–29.

[101] Adams, *Hope and History*, 41–3.

[102] Murray and Tonge, *Sinn Féin and the SDLP*, 162.

political arena. The secret talks also benefitted the SDLP, who faced criticism from unionists for talking to SF while the Provisional IRA's armed struggle continued.[103] Reid knew that the parties shared the same goal of a united Ireland, even if their methods for achieving that dream were different.[104] Reid wrote to John Hume of the SDLP and insisted that by connecting with Adams he would give the SF leader authority on which to speak to the Provisionals. Hume accepted this proposal and met Adams at Clonard. These initial talks, held in the neutral, safe, private space of Clonard and away from the media, built trust between the politicians.

After a series of meetings and letters between the pair, they agreed to a series of formal talks between their two parties at the start of January 1988. However the violence did not stop. While the formal talks between the two parties had ended, Hume and Adams met four times during 1989 in rooms made available to them at the Clonard Monastery by Reid.[105] Along with Clonard, Hume and Adams also met at other Redemptorists operated establishments including St Gerard's, Liguori House in Dublin, and St Joseph's Monastery in Dundalk. All of these locations were kept secret.[106] As the peace negotiations progressed, the SF leadership met with a Fianna Fáil delegation at St Joseph's Monastery with Reid acting as a key contact between the Irish government and SF throughout. Adams recounted that Reid's work in keeping the party leaders away from the 'media spotlight' gave them the 'opportunity for some private dialogue'.[107] In this instance, their shared Catholicism afforded Hume and Adams access to this retreat. Reid used his relationship with Adams to connect the two party leaders in his drive to end the conflict. Without the trust he shared with Adams, dialogue between the SDLP and SF may have never occurred at this time.

The media often hindered opportunities for open dialogue and criticized those priests who acted as mediators for SF. While the Newry Sanctuary claim had highlighted some priests' displeasure in their role as mediators, the Clonard priests never voiced such an opinion. Reid had a complicated relationship with the media because of his work as a mediator. In some instances, he wrote for major newspapers, making a plea for peace, while in the tense negotiations in the months preceding and following the Provisional IRA declaration of a ceasefire, he backed off from making public statements. In November 1990, Reid wrote for *The Irish Times* and stated: 'I believe, that, even now, the violent, tragic dimensions of the conflict could be ended within any given six month period provided the situation were handled properly'.[108] At this point in the peace talks, such an assessment seemed naively optimistic as the possibility of any political or

[103] P.J. McLoughlin, *John Hume*, 142.
[104] Murray and Tonge, *Sinn Féin and the SDLP*, 162.
[105] English, *Armed Struggle*, 264.   [106] Adams, *Hope and History*, 75.
[107] Kevin Rafter, *Martin Mansergh: A Biography* (Dublin, 2002), 180–8.
[108] *Irish Times*, 29 Nov. 1990.

government organization publicly negotiating with SF seemed remote.[109] Reid's article attempted to place the onus on the Catholic Church to act as a catalyst for peace talks and to explain why many in his diocese were prepared to 'use military force' for a united Ireland, including republican paramilitaries who ignored the Catholic Church blanket condemnations of violence.[110] In his West Belfast community, Catholics were marginalized and felt both that their state and Church was not helping to alleviate their real concerns of unemployment, poverty, and discrimination. Yet Reid's comments also spoke directly against the aims of the SDLP. Gerard Murray noted that while constitutional nationalists accepted SF as a 'permanent part of the political landscape', they sought to end justifications like Reid's for Provisional IRA violence.[111] Reid proposed that the Church act in a pastoral capacity to end the conflict and 'enter into direct communication and dialogue with the Republican movement . . . to persuade it to abandon the gun and to follow the way of peaceful politics'.[112] For Reid, the Church needed to create these lines of communication between republican movements, and the best way for him to spread this message was via the public forum of a newspaper article.[113] While he could also speak from the pulpit, that reached only a small number of his immediate Catholic community. Yet years later, in the months before and after the fragile beginnings of the 1994 Provisional IRA ceasefire, Reid avoided the limelight, emphasizing the need to be 'discreet' because of the fragile nature of the truce.[114] His partner in these negotiations, Reynolds, waited a year before speaking to the media, at which point the ceasefire seemed much more stable. Reynolds continued to emphasize the role of religion in the peace process and said: 'Dialogue creates peace, which is from the Holy Spirit. It was done and blessed by God'.[115] Since the 'democratic process had broken down', Reynolds felt he and Reid needed to 'intervene directly to bring an end to the political killing' which meant 'talking to the combatants'.[116] At certain points during this period, Reid and Reynolds did speak with the media to aid their cause, but they also understood the value of discretion during delicate moments.

Reid acted as Gerry Adams' main intermediary with nationalist parties, both North and South, from 1986 onward. As a priest, Reid was counted on to be politically neutral and therefore trusted by both constitutional and militant nationalists. After Reid facilitated the meetings of Hume and Adams in the late

---

[109] In October 1990, the British government was willing to privately woo the Provisional IRA away from violence with former MI6 Michael Oatley meeting with SF's Martin McGuinness. A private chain of dialogue between the British government and militant republicans was held open by intermediary Brendan Duddy and an MI5 officer known as 'Fred' between Oct. 1990 until Nov. 1993; English, *Armed Struggle*, 267.

[110] *Irish Times*, 29 Nov. 1990.   [111] Murray, *John Hume and the SDLP*, 166–7.

[112] English, *Armed Struggle*, 267.

[113] Reid also wrote for *The Irish Independent* about his experiences of living on the peace line; *Irish Independent*, 26 March 1988.

[114] *Catholic Herald*, 9 Sep. 1994.   [115] *Universe*, 5 Nov. 1995.

[116] *Universe*, 5 Nov. 1995.

1980s, he mediated between Northern nationalists and the Irish government. With Adams' blessing, Reid approached Fianna Fáil leader Charles Haughey to open up a channel of communication between Fianna Fáil and SF, as both were united in opposition against the Anglo-Irish Agreement.[117] When Reid attempted to bring SDLP into these discussions, the party abstained as it disagreed with calls for immediate British withdrawal from Northern Ireland. From 1986 onward, Adams utilized Reid as his intermediary with Haughey. When, in October 1988 talks took place in Duisburg, West Germany between the four main Northern Ireland constitutional political parties, the Alliance Party, UUP, DUP, and SDLP, Reid attended. The priest was able to relay the viewpoints of SF in relation to political progress.[118] P.J. McLaughlin argues that by approaching Hume and Haughey, Reid attempted to create an alternative strategy for militant republicans and to put an end to the violence.[119] Through these meetings, Reid argued, the nationalist parties on both sides of the border could create a common nationalist policy that would establish 'a just and lasting peace'.[120] Reid's ability to speak on behalf of SF demonstrated the trust Adams' placed in him, but also his functional neutrality. His vocation combined with his regular preaching of non-violence meant the other political parties present could also trust his motives for a political solution.

While Reid acted as a mediator between SF and the SDLP, he continued to facilitate discussion between republicans and the Irish government. The Irish government used Reid as a backchannel in the 1980s, and they revisited this relationship in 1992.[121] The visit of Republic of Ireland President Mary Robinson to West Belfast in the summer of 1992 sparked rumours of a dialogue between the Irish government and nationalists, with Reid at the centre. He believed Robinson's June 1993 visit 'made a very significant contribution' to the 'search for peace'.[122] In December 1993, Reid briefed the Taoiseach, Albert Reynolds, on the stance of the Provisionals ahead of the Downing Street Declaration.[123] By this point in the peace process, Adams was visiting Hume at his house in Derry, and the Clonard Monastery was required less and less for meetings.[124] Nevertheless, Reid's role as a mediator remained crucial in paving the way for peace and he continued to act as a private channel between SF and the Irish government.

Protestant clergy also approached SF to create a way for peace. Former Presbyterian Moderators Rev Jack Weir and Rev Godfrey Brown sought a meeting with Adams in March 1992. With SF politician Tom Hartley and Adams talked

[117] Murray, *John Hume and the SDLP*, 170–1.
[118] Murray and Tonge, *Sinn Féin and the SDLP*, 171.
[119] McLaughlin, *John Hume*, 142.
[120] Letter from Reid to Hume in Gerry Adams, *Hope and History*, 42.
[121] McLaughlin, *John Hume*, 156.   [122] *Irish Times*, 26 June 1993.
[123] *Catholic Herald*, 8 April 1994.   [124] English, *Armed Struggle*, 271.

with Brown and Weir over tea at Councillor Marie Moore's home in West Belfast.[125] The Northern Ireland media attacked the Protestant ministers when they released details of the meeting, but out of this talk dialogue grew between SF and leaders of the Methodist Church and Church of Ireland. It was not just Catholic clergy, but Protestant ministers too who reached out to include SF in political talks, another area for potentially more fruitful research.

Priests acted as mediators between republicans and other organizations by creating opportunities for private dialogue. It was individual priests like Reid and Reynolds, not the institutional Church, who took on the role of advocates of a negotiated settlement. Adams noted that Reid's writings on peace and his ideas for the SF/SDLP talks in 1988 became the basis of the Hume/Adams initiative of 1993.[126] After years of conflict, Hume saw SF as trapped into supporting armed struggle. By communicating directly to Hume, with the help of Reid, Adams could create conditions for SF to enter 'democratic constitutional politics'.[127] Gerard Murray and Jonathan Tonge argue that, in 1987, Adams' position as leader of SF would have been 'untenable' if those around him knew the extent of his talks with Hume and then the British government.[128] Even before Hume, Reid had privately encouraged members of SF to abandon armed struggle. By involving Irish nationalist parties North and South, Reid 'hoped to demonstrate the viability of an approach which would bring together the various strands of Irish nationalism in a common, peaceful strategy'.[129] McLaughlin notes that these original ideas were Reid's, but Hume was able to run 'with this idea' through Hume's own involvement and that of Dublin and Washington D.C.[130] As the conflict continued, Adams argues, Reid's deep faith in the Holy Spirit and his ability to follow up with his backchannels kept SF, the SDLP, and the Irish government on the path to peace.[131] Both sides of the nationalist community needed a private, discreet communicator who believed in non-violence but supported a united Ireland. As a priest and a nationalist, Fr Alec Reid was the perfect candidate.

In an effort to act as mediators, both Reid and Reynolds were fully engaged with their communities. Reid integrated with the republican community on all sides, attending events with high profile nationalist sympathizers and politicians, including attending Adams' *Selected Writings* book launch in September 1994.[132] To show solidarity with victims of republican violence, Reynolds attended the funeral of Ulster Democratic Party (UDP) chairman Ray Smallwoods, who was murdered by the Provisional IRA outside his home in Lisburn. The UDP was a small loyalist

---

[125] Adams, *Hope and History*, 126.   [126] Adams, *Hope and History*, 120.
[127] Murray, *John Hume and the SDLP*, 173.
[128] Murray and Tonge, *Sinn Féin and the SDLP*, 163.
[129] McLaughlin, *John Hume*, 221.   [130] McLaughlin, *John Hume*, 222.
[131] Adams, *Hope and History*, 178.   [132] *Irish Times*, 16 Sep. 1994.

party in Northern Ireland and the political offshoot of the UDA.[133] Reynolds described Smallwoods as 'a great man' and his death as 'a tragic loss'.[134] During the peace process, UVF leader Gusty Spence noted: 'Alec Reid was particularly close to the Provos, didn't agree with their tactics or whatever but was a very, very, close confidant of Adams. Whenever I was speaking to Alec, I knew I was speaking directly to Gerry Adams.'[135] In order to work as effective mediators for peace, these priests needed to be trusted and well-informed actors recognized by both Catholic and Protestant communities.

Bishop Edward Daly's role as a mediator between the Provisionals and the British government began in 1991. His discussions with SF's Martin McGuinness and Mitchel McLaughlin continued until the bishop suffered a stroke in early 1993.[136] Daly invited McLaughlin to his home to speak, and felt encouraged that there was an 'openness' towards ending the violence which the bishop had not felt previously.[137] In June 1992, Daly publicly revealed during a BBC radio interview that he was meeting with SF as dialogue was a tool for breaking down barriers.[138] Daly said: 'For years Sinn Féin had talked to no one but each other... that way no one learns and no one moves'.[139] Both Daly and the Derry SF leadership needed to overcome the previous bad feeling between parties, as evidenced by Daly's 1988 refusal to allow Provisional IRA funerals in churches. Daly also acted as a go-between for the Provisionals and SDLP, keeping in constant contact with Hume for whom he had 'enormous admiration'.[140] Many Protestant church leaders praised Daly's efforts with SF in his capacity as an individual, but the Presbyterian Moderator Rev John Dunlop warned there would be 'considerable dangers' for official Catholic Church negotiations, as that was 'the politicians' job'.[141] Catholic politicians like the SDLP's Seamus Mallon called Daly's actions 'wise and prudent', as 'the more people who talk to SF and tell them how counterproductive their campaign is, the better.'[142] With the support of other Christian leaders and constitutional nationalists, Daly could publicly negotiate with SF and diplomatically bridge the divide between militant and constitutional nationalist movements.

British Prime Minister John Major and Taoiseach Albert Reynolds issued the Downing Street Declaration on 15 December 1993, in which the heads of government affirmed the right of the people of Ireland to self-determination. At the same time, they stated that Northern Ireland would be transferred from the UK to the Republic of Ireland only if a majority of its population supported such a move.[143] Even after this joint British-Irish government plan, the Provisionals

---

[133] Bew and Gillespie, *Chronology of the Troubles*, 152.
[134] Bew and Gillespie, *Chronology of the Troubles*, 15 July 1994.
[135] Brian Rowan, *How the Peace Was Won* (Dublin, 2008), 94.
[136] Daly, *A Troubled See*, 238–9.   [137] *Catholic Herald*, 9 Sep. 1994.
[138] *Tablet*, 13 June 1992.   [139] *Tablet*, 13 June 1992.
[140] *Catholic Herald*, 9 Sep. 1994.   [141] *Tablet*, 13 June 1992.
[142] *Tablet*, 13 June 1992.
[143] This point would later become a key point of the GFA; English, *Armed Struggle*, 271–3.

continued their violent campaign causing Cardinal Daly to declare: 'The blunt message to the IRA must be "stop killing or stop talking peace".'[144] Unlike Bishop Edward Daly who had a stroke in February 1993 and retired from his position in October of that year, Cardinal Cahal Daly repeatedly condemned the Provisionals' violent methods until late August 1994. Initially, Cardinal Daly had asked for time to allow the Provisional IRA to respond to the declaration, speaking at a January 1994 Mass at St Patrick's Cathedral in Armagh.[145] For the cardinal, the Downing Street Declaration demonstrated that the British government had 'made significant movement towards recognising the legitimacy of Irish republicanism ... and towards recognising the legitimacy of the aspiration towards a united Ireland.'[146] However, as the killing continued and SF called for 'clarification on the terms', Daly had had enough.[147] By mid-1994, the cardinal started to believe that now was the time for republicans to seize the moment and end the fighting.[148] Unlike Edward Daly, Cahal Daly refused talks with SF until the Provisionals ended their armed struggle. Perhaps the eventual opening of Church archives for this period will potentially reveal whether this was a coordinated effort between the bishops. Even if this was not the case, the Dalys balanced the role of the hierarchy in mediating between all sides and censoring militant republicans. In effect, the bishop acted as carrot to the cardinal's stick.

Priests acted as mediators for republican movements during the late 1980s until the mid-1990s, helping to establish plans for peace. For his work as a mediator, Reid won widespread admiration. In December 1994, the Tipperary Peace Convention gave its Peace Award to Reid, the Presbyterian minister Rev Roy Magee, and the former Irish government advisor Dr Martin Mansergh for their joint efforts in bringing about the ceasefires.[149] Mansergh had suggested the use of Magee as an intermediary for loyalist paramilitary groups, and understood the importance of Protestant and Catholic clergymen in peace negotiations.[150] Many in the republican movement trusted Reid. For example, Danny Morrison acknowledged Reid's importance in the peace process even beyond the 1994 ceasefire, noting Reid along with Rev Harold Good, a former President of the Methodist Church in Ireland: 'verified independently that the IRA had decommissioned'.[151] The long-time friendship between Presbyterian minister Rev Ken Newell and Reynolds also aided the peace process, as their relationship had 'huge public implications' about what it meant to be 'Christian in Northern Ireland'.[152] While individual priests like Reid and Reynolds could act as a go-between for

---

[144] *Irish Times*, 26 April 1994.   [145] *Catholic Herald*, 28 Jan. 1994; *Tablet*, 29 Jan. 1994.
[146] *Tablet*, 26 Feb. 1994.   [147] *Tablet*, 26 Feb. 1994.
[148] *Irish Times*, 8 May 1994. Daly reiterated his pleas for peace up until the days before the Provisionals declared a ceasefire on 31 Aug. 1994. *Irish Catholic*, 2 June 1994; *Irish Times*, 30 Aug. 1994.
[149] *Irish Times*, 29 Dec. 1994.   [150] Rafter, *Martin Mansergh*, 180–5, 211.
[151] Interview with Danny Morrison, 29 April 2014.
[152] Wells, *Friendship Towards Peace*, 7.

the militant and constitutional republican movements, Bishop Edward Daly's talks with SF in 1992 and 1993 lent gravitas to the peace process. His status and willingness to meet demonstrated that the Church as an institution backed the process, paving the way for more public discussions between republicans and unionists as well as the British state. What is clear here is that these priests and bishops acted as individuals driven by the palpable sense of the duty of Christians to strive for peace. Gone were the days when the Irish hierarchy could only make statements condemning violence; action was now required. The beginning of the 1994 Provisional IRA ceasefire marked a new phase in the evolution of the priests as mediators. The 1991 Newry Cathedral sanctuary claim was the last 'grand stand' of institutional Church involvement in peace talks, with the key dialogue taking place more privately in Clonard Monastery or the Bishop's House in Derry. Newspaper headlines changed from references to the Church to instead itemizing the names of individual priests, bishops, or cardinals, demonstrating the power of personalities in these peace talks. In this way, the peace process appeared to transcend the religious divide, and it was these individuals' actions, not their institutional affiliations, which were presented as leading to peace. Yet the headlines on the revelations of clerical child abuse, in which the Church featured prominently, demonstrated that while the peace process might be attributable to the laudable efforts of individuals, the institution itself was tarnished. By the early 1990s, it was only a few, very trusted priests who could facilitate dialogue between republicans.

Clerical Child Abuse

The reputation of the Irish Catholic Church was catastrophically undermined with the revelations of clerical child abuse in the early 1990s. By this period, the Catholic Church no longer enjoyed unequivocal moral authority over its parishioners.[153] For many, the Church's moral stance now appeared hypocritical, as some of its most trusted leaders had committed these vile crimes, and acts of violence against the most innocent within society. Bishop Eamonn Casey's love child revelation in 1992 caused many to question the Church's judgment, but it was the child abuse allegations, made famous with the Fr Brendan Smyth case, that had the most impact.[154] In 1991, after the abuse of four siblings in the Falls Road area was reported to police, the RUC arrested Smyth. Upon his release on bail, the priest, who was a member of the Norbertine religious order, fled to the Republic.[155] He remained on the run for the next three years, mostly residing at

---

[153] Inglis, *Moral Monopoly*, 242.
[154] Chris Moore, *Betrayal of Trust: The Father Brendan Smyth Affair and the Catholic Church* (Dublin, 1995), 15.
[155] Moore, *Betrayal*, 143–70.

Kilnacrott Abbey. This severely delayed the extradition process of Smyth, as requested by the RUC, and ultimately brought down the Fianna Fáil-Labour coalition in the Republic.[156] While individual priests' mediation with the Provisionals and the uncovering of clerical abuse were largely separate developments, it is conjectured that the accusations of clerical abuse weakened the Church's position as moral authority in Ireland as whole.

The problem of clerical abuse in the Catholic Church spread across continents.[157] The Catholic Church in the USA faced reports of clerical child abuse in the early 1990s, mainly concerning Cardinal Joseph Bernardin, of Chicago.[158] Victims also reported abuse in Boston, recently highlighted in the 2015 film *Spotlight*.[159] A 'particularly high number of abuse cases' were reported in respect of the Canadian Catholic Church.[160] In September 1993, Bishop Christopher Budd, of the English and Welsh Catholic Church, apologized for priest child abuse at the National Conference of Priests in Birmingham.[161] Even Pope John Paul II spoke out on the issue in a letter to the American hierarchy, claiming priests who had sexually abused children would face damnation.[162]

Faith and trust in the leadership of the Irish hierarchy was first compromised though in 1992 when the story broke that Bishop Eamon Casey, of Galway, had a child with divorcee Annie Murphy and had paid for his son Peter to be hidden away in America with more than £70,000 of diocesan funds.[163] The affair began in the summer of 1973, when Casey served as Bishop of Kerry. Casey revealed he had attempted to persuade Murphy to put their child up for adoption, but Murphy refused.[164] While there is little evidence to demonstrate that the Casey scandal had any impact on the Church's role in Northern Ireland, it showed that the cracks in the Church's rigid moral authority had begun to appear. After news of Casey's affair broke, the Irish hierarchy, and some in the Catholic media, rallied around the bishop. An article in *The Universe* called the bishop 'a pioneer of peace and justice' and spoke of his prominence with Trócaire, a Catholic charity established in 1973, which worked toward economic reformation so that the wealthiest countries would bear a greater burden and make sacrifices to benefit the poor.[165] Trócaire distributed funds to some of the poorest countries in the world and fought injustices, especially through organizing boycotts of South African goods during Apartheid.[166] As details of Casey's actions became public, the media

---

[156] *Irish Press*, 22 Dec. 1994; *Irish Independent*, 17 Nov. 1994.

[157] See Paul Dokecki, *The Clergy Sexual Abuse Crisis: Reform and Renewal in the Catholic Community* (Washington, DC, 2004); Marie Keenan, *Child Sexual Abuse and the Catholic Church: Gender, Power, and Organizational Culture* (Oxford, 2011).

[158] *Catholic Herald*, 11 Sep. 1992; *Catholic Herald*, 25 June 1993.

[159] *Guardian*, 21 April 2010.   [160] *Guardian*, 17 Sep. 1993.

[161] *Universe*, 12 Sep. 1993.   [162] *Catholic Herald*, 25 June 1993.

[163] *Catholic Herald*, 15 May 1992.   [164] *Tablet*, 16 May 1992.

[165] Kenny, *Goodbye to Catholic Ireland*, 279; *Universe*, 17 May 1992.

[166] Kenny, *Goodbye to Catholic Ireland*, 280.

called the bishops' judgment into severe question.[167] However, Murphy found herself being shamed as *The Universe* stated: 'There's more than one victim when women kiss and tell'.[168] While *The Universe* pinned the blame with Murphy, *The Tablet*, *Irish Catholic*, and *Catholic Herald* reported on the affair in a much more even handed manner.[169] The Church's reputation was not hurt by Casey's affair, but the bishop's actions were another factor of a Church in turmoil. He was seen as a man who made a mistake, as other men had done before. The issue of celibacy had long been debated within the Church, and a *Sunday Press* survey conducted after the news broke on Casey's affair indicated that seven out of ten Catholics thought celibacy should no longer be compulsory for priests.[170] However, when those abused began accusing the Church of paedophilia in 1994, the reaction was far from ambivalent.

Even before the Smyth case was made public in 1994, the institutional Irish Catholic Church was on the offensive. After the BBC made allegations about a child-abusing priest in Birmingham, the Catholic Church Press Office Director Jim Cantwell spoke to reporters at *The Universe*: 'We know now that child sexual abuse is to be found at all levels of society and among all age groups...Not surprisingly, but unfortunately, it's also found among priests and religious.'[171] Yet Cantwell assured the public that any 'allegation concerning a priest is immediately investigated and, if found to have substance, the priest is removed from his post'.[172] Smyth's actions prove this was not the case. Since the late 1960s, fellow Norbertine priest Fr Bruno Mulvihill had alerted two abbots, a bishop, and two papal nuncios to Smyth's abuse, but nothing was done.[173] The watershed moment in the Smyth case came on 6 October 1994, with the UTV Counterpoint documentary programme *Suffer the Children*, which revealed clerical abuse throughout Ireland.[174] Journalist Chris Moore's subsequent book, co-written with Kevin Hegarty and published the following year, included copies of letters, conversation summaries, and research notes concerning the cover-up by many in the Norbertine community of Smyth's crimes.[175]

In a letter to Moore, Smyth's Abbot, Kevin Smith, admitted 'many errors in dealing with his wrongdoing'.[176] As early as 1968, Smyth's previous abbot initiated psychiatric treatment for the priest, which continued on several occasions. On two occasions, Smyth was assigned parish work in North America, but his abbot failed to notify the relevant diocesan bishop of Smyth's propensity to molest children, which Smith noted was a 'grave error'.[177] Smith also allowed the priest to work in

---

[167] *Tablet*, 23 May 1992.   [168] *Universe*, 24 May 1992.
[169] *Tablet*, 16 May 1992; *Irish Catholic*, 14 May 1992.   [170] *Catholic Herald*, 29 May 1992.
[171] *Universe*, 29 Aug. 1993.   [172] *Universe*, 29 Aug. 1993.
[173] *Irish Independent*, 13 Oct. 1994; *Irish Times*, 4 May 2012.
[174] *Irish Times*, 6 Oct. 1994.   [175] Moore, *Betrayal*, 194–223.
[176] *Irish Independent*, 13 Oct. 1994.   [177] *Irish Independent*, 13 Oct. 1994.

hospitals, although numerous accounts of his abuse were reported.[178] Even after the airing of the Counterpoint documentary, it appeared as if Smith would not leave his post.[179] Finally, at the end of October 1994 and after much public outcry, Abbot Smith resigned his position as head of the Norbertine Order.[180]

Many condemned the Irish hierarchy for their lack of action in discovering and preventing Smyth's actions. The Irish Catholic Church faced accusations of a cover-up, which Cardinal Daly fiercely denied. In numerous statements, Daly repudiated that the Church had prevented Smyth's extradition from the Republic to the North, and that he had personally failed to inform the RUC of Smyth's actions.[181] After the premiere of the UTV Counterpoint documentary, Cardinal Daly spoke on the radio programme *This Week* in which he claimed the abuse scandal brought him to tears.[182] In an insightful op-ed in *The Irish Times'* Fintan O'Toole said of the cardinal:

> For a man who carries such a weight of public authority, and who has learned over many years in the cockpit of violent confrontation to be guarded in expressing his feelings, the sudden revelation of those emotions was dramatic. Dramatic but appropriate—for it acknowledged, in a way, that more abstract language could not have done, the sheer scale of the crisis that faces both the Catholic Church and Dr Daly himself.[183]

For O'Toole, the darkness of child abuse in the Church was always present and taken for granted by Irish Catholic pupils, who often also faced corporeal punishment by the religious brothers and sisters who taught them. While O'Toole acknowledged sexual abuse was very different than corporeal punishment, to him, the two could easily go hand in hand. The Church operated in the murky waters of moral authority, and in the case of Smyth, appeared to act above the law. Others wrote in to *The Irish Times*, acknowledging the validity of O'Toole's sentiments.

In a December 1994 statement, Cardinal Daly revealed the background to Smyth's case. Daly said on 23 February 1990, a young person told a social worker at the Catholic Family Welfare centre in Belfast of Smyth's abuse over a number of years. The social worker then informed the RUC, and the family made a formal complaint on 7 March. Daly stated he thought it was right and proper that allegations against Smyth were passed to the police. Daly also claimed that in a March 1990 meeting, Abbot Kevin Smith accepted 'full responsibility' for Smyth's actions.[184] Yet after the family wrote to Daly in February 1991 and August 1992 to admonish him that nothing had been done to extradite Smyth from the Republic,

---

[178] *Irish Times*, 17 Oct. 1994.   [179] *Irish Press*, 15 Oct. 1994; *Irish Times*, 18 Oct. 1994.
[180] *Catholic Herald*, 28 Oct. 1994.   [181] *Irish Times*, 30 Nov. 1994; *Tablet*, 10 Dec. 1994.
[182] *Irish Times*, 21 Oct. 1994.   [183] *Irish Times*, 21 Oct. 1994.
[184] *Irish Times*, 8 Dec. 1994.

only then did the cardinal put pressure on the abbot to take firm action to deal with Smyth. But the inaction continued, and Daly said in December 1994:

> At no time was I aware nor was I made aware of Fr Brendan Smyth's long previous history of paedophile crimes...I have never had any knowledge of ministerial placements of Fr Smyth at any period of his ministry, neither was I instrumental in any such placement.[185]

Daly repeatedly stated that as a Norbertine, Smyth was not under his jurisdiction, but that of his abbot.[186] Further, that as Archbishop of Armagh, Daly had no control of affairs outside his diocese.[187] Inglis argues in *Moral Monopoly* that while the level of control and supervision of bishops over religious orders is much less than over parish priests, bishops are still in many ways 'responsible'.[188] Nevertheless, Daly apologized for Smyth's behaviour and that his actions had gone unchecked.[189] However, questions remained. While the first report against Smyth was made on 7 March 1990, it took until 8 March 1991 for the RUC to interview him.[190] In his 1991 letter to the victim's family, Daly acknowledged that there had been 'complaints before' about Smyth.[191] In addition to Cardinal Daly, the spokesperson for the Irish Bishops' Conference, Bishop Thomas Finnegan, ensured the Church would 'fully accept our obligations in regard to civil law and the need to cooperate with civil authorities' in the handling of all future abuse cases.[192]

The Smyth abuse case forced the Irish hierarchy to admit wrongdoings, which consequently impacted upon the Church's ability to project any sort of moral authority. With hindsight, Danny Morrison recounted that while republicans had lost their faith in the Church after the hunger strikes: 'amongst the faithful the scandals were devastating' and former hunger striker Laurence McKeown agreed.[193] Surveys of Catholics in the Republic over the following years reported a major lack of confidence in the Church as a moral leader. One poll commissioned by *The Sunday Independent* and the RTÉ *Late Late Show* put weekly Mass attendance at just 64 percent, down from 82 percent in 1988/89.[194] Media attitudes agreed with the loss of Church influence, for as journalist Mick MacConnell concluded, the abuse scandals 'proved to be the straw that broke the camel's back'.[195]

---

[185] *Irish Times*, 8 Dec. 1994.
[186] As a member of an order, Smyth's superior was his abbot. Despite his role as Primate of All Ireland, Cardinal Daly did not control religious orders.
[187] *Irish Press*, 6 Dec. 1994.   [188] Inglis, *Moral Monopoly*, 45.
[189] *Tablet*, 10 Dec. 1994.   [190] *Irish Press*, 6 Dec. 1994.   [191] *Irish Times*, 6 Oct. 1994.
[192] *Irish Catholic*, 24 Nov. 1994.
[193] Interview with Danny Morrison, 29 April 2014; Interview with Dr Laurence McKeown, 15 April 2014.
[194] Fuller, *Irish Catholicism since 1950*, 250–3.   [195] *Kerryman*, 22 Dec. 1995.

Over the course of his life, Smyth abused 117 Irish children, with the extent of his abuse in the USA unknown.[196] The Smyth case was a watershed moment for the Irish Catholic Church, with many individuals now criticizing the institution for its inability to protect children. The Church appeared hypocritical, denouncing homosexuality, divorce, abortion, and the violent conflict in Northern Ireland, while one of its own, and indeed many others, abused children. As the 1990s continued, more victims stepped forward with allegations against other priests, revealing that the problem was systematic and widespread.[197] Attempts to pass off Smyth as 'one bad apple in a good bunch' proved unfounded. Yet despite the decline in the Church's 'moral monopoly' over Ireland in the early and mid-1990s, many Irish people still regularly attended Mass and baptized their children, indicating that complete secularization was not inevitable.[198] While individual priests acted as mediators between republican groups during this period, the institutional Church was embroiled in conflict surrounding clerical child abuse. As Louise Fuller argues, the Church's 'inability to deal publicly with these crises' exacerbated the situation.[199] Robert Tobin adds the Church's 'loss of public influence' in the early 1990s directly relates to the 'revelations of sexual misconduct among its clergy'.[200] Cardinal Daly's installation as leader of the Church, combined with the revelations of abuse, caused the Church's role in the conflict to move from the institutional to individual clerics who personally created opportunities for peace.

Increased Sectarian Attacks

The mid- to late 1990s witnessed an increase in sectarian attacks. Many loyalist paramilitaries viewed the peace process as a threat to the union with organizations including the Orange Order feeling particularly under siege. Clergymen and women worked to ease community tensions through mediation, often on a grassroots level, with individual clerics or small groups living among their parishioners. While the bishops could still denounce these attacks and call for justice, it was the everyday actions of priests and women religious which helped to bring resolution.

A group of sisters lived on the peace line in Belfast and experienced the day-to-day turmoil of the conflict and the marching season first hand. Among their

---

[196] *Irish Times*, 4 May 2012.

[197] *Tablet*, 24 June 1995; *Catholic Herald*, 2 Dec. 1994.

[198] The Church's continued control over education illustrates this phenomenon; Inglis, *Moral Monopoly*, 223–44.

[199] Fuller, *Irish Catholicism since 1950*, 253.

[200] Robert Tobin, 'The evolution of national and religious identity in contemporary Ireland', in Jane Garnett, Matthew Grimley, Alana Harris, William Whyte, and Sarah Williams (eds.), *Redefining Christian Britain: Post-1945 Perspectives* (London, 2007), 282.

number was Sr Anne Kilroy, a Loreto sister who lived on Springfield Road as part of the ecumenical Cornerstone Community.[201] Cornerstone regularly visited the bereaved on both sides of the peace line.[202] In 1994, Sr Kathleen Keane, of the Little Company of Mary, moved to house along the road from Sr Anne.[203] Her semi-detached house connected with the peace wall with her front door opening on the Catholic side of the divide and her back door on to its Protestant neighbour. During this period a pedestrian gate between the two sides was only open during daylight hours unless there was trouble—which regularly occurred. Those wanting to cross the line when the pedestrian gate was closed would have to take a long detour, unless Sr Kathleen was home. Then they could knock on her back door and ask to pass through the kitchen and hallway and out of the front door on to the Springfield Road.

Sr Anne noted that the marching season was a 'very traumatic' time.[204] One year Cornerstone led the negotiations between the Orange Order and the Springfield Road residents but the attempt was derailed due to a graffiti sprayed on the nearby school reading: 'The unholy trinity: the Orange Order, the RUC, and the Cornerstone Community'.[205] Sr Anne felt this was a 'slap in the face' as Cornerstone had tried to remain neutral.[206] The sisters' presence on the peace line may have allowed them to witness the divide between these fractious communities first hand but religious involvement with the conflict was at times even more of a polarizing element.

Loyalists regularly picketed Catholic churches in an attempt to protect parade marching routes. A picket of Our Lady in Harryville, Ballymena, was described as 'a blatant act of sectarian discrimination designed to pressurise not just the Mass-goers but the Garvaghy Road residents and indeed the whole nationalist population' by SF North Antrim councillor James McCarry.[207] The picket of Saturday evening Mass-goers at Harryville began in September 1996 when nationalists objected to Orange Order marching in Dunloy. It continued until May 1998.[208] Despite their openly aggressive stance towards the Catholic Church by this point, SF councilors still regularly used sectarian attacks and demonstrations on church buildings as a rallying cry for the nationalist cause. Some Catholics in these areas boycotted Protestant businesses in response which then added to the increased tension between communities.[209]

[201] Belfast Telegraph, 16 Sept. 2010, https://www.belfasttelegraph.co.uk/news/northern-ireland/through-the-eyes-of-sister-kilroy-28559268.html.
[202] Sr Anne Kilroy interview in 'Sisters of the Troubles', BBC News World Service, 25 March 2018.
[203] Tablet, 21 March 2018, http://www.thetablet.co.uk/features/2/12814/the-untold-story-of-the-role-of-catholic-nuns-during-the-troubles-.
[204] Sr Anne Kilroy interview in 'Sisters of the Troubles', BBC News World Service, 25 March 2018.
[205] Sr Anne Kilroy interview in 'Sisters of the Troubles', BBC News World Service, 25 March 2018.
[206] Sr Anne Kilroy interview in 'Sisters of the Troubles', BBC News World Service, 25 March 2018.
[207] An Phoblacht/Republican News, 2 July 1998.
[208] Times, 27 May 1998.   [209] Observer, 22 Sept. 1996.

In fact, Catholic and Protestant churches often became a point of attack and parishioners sometimes watched helplessly as their places of worship went up in flames. In Drumcree, the actions of the Orange Order increased sectarian tension. After one attack on St Coleman's Roman Catholic Church at Annaclone, Co. Down, the parish priest Fr Frank Kearney said: 'There are good community relations here, so it saddens me to see this type of destruction to a house of God, which is a very sacred thing to most people of whatever denomination'.[210] Ten Catholics churches in the North were devastated by fire in coordinated attacks in the first half of 1998.[211] Loyalists even carried out arson attacks on Protestant churches in an attempt to provoke a sectarian backlash against Catholics, as seen by the 1997 attack on Mountpottinger Baptist Church in East Belfast.[212] In other instances, Catholic rioting in response to loyalist violence resulted in damage to Protestant churches, as in the case with the Methodist Sacred Heart Church.[213] In a show of ecumenism Catholic priests worked to raise funds to repair the church. Churches were regularly unlocked and unguarded and therefore became an obvious and easy target for sectarian violence.

The Drumcree standoff became a focal point of sectarian violence and tension during the 1990s. Despite the rising tensions the Orange Order continued to insist they should be allowed their march to and from the Drumcree Church mostly through a Catholic area. As Claire Mitchell notes, the striking image of UUP leader David Trimble holding hands with Rev Ian Paisley at the 1995 march highlighted the longstanding relationship between unionism, Protestantism, and the Orange Order.[214] The Catholic hierarchy made few public statements on the standoff, mirroring their Protestant counterparts who also continually failed to speak out against this violence. Angry republicans particularly singled out Church of Ireland Archbishop Robin Eames for his inaction.[215]

When the bishops did speak out on Drumcree it was to call for police reform. After violence during the July 1996 marches Cardinal Cahal Daly demanded a 'genuinely independent' public inquiry 'covering all the aspects of the events from the Chief Constable's first and second decisions, through the Orange Order protests and the nationalist protests, [and] the behaviour of the RUC in respect of each of these protests'.[216] Daly hoped for genuine reform of the RUC in 'recruitment, training, and police culture' so that both communities might trust the organization again.[217] This, Daly felt, could lead to the Provisionals reinstating their ceasefire. As such the cardinal praised Northern Ireland Secretary Sir Patrick Mayhew's announcement of a parades review in 1996. However, after

---

[210] *Times*, 17 April 1997.   [211] *Guardian*, 3 July 1998.
[212] *Irish Catholic*, 24 April 1997.   [213] *Irish Catholic*, 29 Aug. 1996.
[214] Mitchell, *Religion, Identity, and Politics*, 50.
[215] *An Phoblacht/Republican News*, 18 May 1995, 17 Aug. 1995, 16 July 1998, 30 July 1998, 22 Oct. 1998.
[216] *Tablet*, 27 July 1996.   [217] *Tablet*, 27 July 1996.

this appeal was made, the Catholic hierarchy made few other calls for action against the parades.

Anger at the perceived inaction of Catholic Church hierarchy on this issue was not limited to the North. A seventeen-year-old man in Lancashire wrote to Bishop Terence Brain in Salford and asked why his diocese did not offer support to those in Drumcree facing regular intimidation by loyalists. Bishop Brain responded:

> . . . it is not true that the Church has not spoken out in defence of the Catholic community in Northern Ireland. Over the Drumcree issue the Catholic community in Northern Ireland has been very quiet, deliberately, because it has made the Protestant community face the reality of their situation without the excuse of the Catholics criticising and thus becoming a distraction from the essential questions. It doesn't need us to tell them they were wrong. This time they know in their heart of hearts they were wrong and many of them will now begin to take steps to putting their house really in order.[218]

Brain urged the young man to control his anger over the Drumcree standoff and to ask his parish priest why he had not discussed the issue in his homily. Brain wrote: 'It requires much more discipline to control the anger, but when we can do that we have found the way to be able to dialogue and find solutions, so don't fall out with us, talk about it.' This direct approach, albeit to one individual, suggests continued support from the English Catholic hierarchy for their Irish counterparts.

At times during the Drumcree standoff the RUC prevented Catholic parishioners from attending Mass. Catholic clergy attempted to mediate between the Garvaghy Road residents and the police. However one anonymous self-proclaimed Catholic reader of *The Irish Catholic* wrote to defend the RUC, citing that SF was behind the 'peaceful' protest meant to antagonize the Orange Order and the police were left with few options.[219] In response Malachy Foots from Dundalk challenged the first writer, asking: 'Does this suggest that the Garvaghy Road Residents Coalition chairperson, a Jesuit priest, and the local parish priest were part of the writer's theory of a Sinn Féin or IRA plot?'[220]

Despite the tension between communities, Catholic clergymen and women were still able to provide opportunities for ecumenism with their Protestant counterparts. One such occasion was at the Annual Glenstal Ecumenical Conference where Rev Brian Kennaway, minister of the Crumlin Presbyterian Church and member of the Orange Order, announced he would like to see the Order's philosophy change 'from being anti-Catholic to being pro-Protestant'.[221] While this may appear to be a lesson in semantics, Fr Tom Stack championed it as a

---

[218] SaDA 873, Bishop Terence Brain to R.N., 16 July 1998.
[219] *Irish Catholic*, 31 July 1997.   [220] *Irish Catholic*, 14 Aug. 1997.
[221] *Irish Examiner*, 27 June 1997.

small victory in his weekly *Irish Catholic* column as it was the first time a member of the Orange Order had attended the conference, especially one held at a Benedictine monastery.[222] Equally, parish priest Fr Andrew Dolan brokered the Bellaghy agreement between Catholic residents in Bellaghy, Co. Derry and the Royal Black Institution, a Protestant fraternal society.[223] Another was Fr Oliver Crilly, who sat on the three-person North Review of Parades Committee with Presbyterian minister Rev John Dunlop in 1996.[224] Crilly was encouraged by the 'frankness' with which the ninety-three community groups discussed the parades issue and argued that no one group should be demonized in the dispute.[225] Fr Eamon Stack, Secretary of the Garvaghy Coalition and a negotiator in the dispute, did not share Crilly's hope for a peaceful resolution and thought it unlikely.[226] However, when the Orange Order called off or rerouted some of its most contentious 12 July marches that year, the subsequent unrest in response was noticeably muted, proving that negotiations had made some headway. Archbishop Eames said: 'This tremendous spirit of relief is bound to carry the [peace] process forward.'[227] Each July between 1995 and 2000 saw the dispute drawing international attention as it was the catalyst for sparking further protests throughout Northern Ireland.

The increase in sectarian community tension on the streets during this period occurred alongside the peace process negotiations in the corridors of power. While the work of individuals like Reid, Reynolds, and Wilson occurred behind the scenes, many women religious and priests dealt with this everyday violence by attempting to put an end to disputes themselves. It was often a parish priest or a sister living among their parishioners who worked to mediate these marches, boycotts, pickets, and arson attacks. Without their day-to-day actions, the peace process may not have stayed on track and the signing of the GFA may have been delayed or even scuppered.

Peace Process and the Good Friday Agreement

Just after 11 a.m. on 31 August 1994, the Provisional IRA announced a 'complete cessation' of military operations.[228] With this announcement, bishops in Ireland, Scotland, and England championed the path to peace. Cardinal Daly understood trust was required for peace to work, Cardinal Hume acknowledged the Provisional IRA ceasefire was 'not an opportunity to be missed', and Archbishop

---

[222] *Irish Catholic*, 3 July 1997.   [223] *Irish Catholic*, 5 Sept. 1996.
[224] *Strabane Chronicle*, 10 Aug. 1996.   [225] *Irish Catholic*, 3 July 1997.
[226] *Irish Catholic*, 19 June 1997.   [227] *Times*, 14 July 1997.
[228] 'Irish Republican Army (IRA) Ceasefire statement, 31 August 1994', http://cain.ulst.ac.uk/events/peace/docs/ira31894.htm

Winning of Glasgow noted it was a time 'to walk the path of reconciliation and peace'.[229] While the Catholic Church across these islands were united in their hope for peace, the Irish Church in particular continued to face other difficulties within their own ranks. Further clerical child abuse scandals involving priests came to light as more victims came forward to share their stories and the wider trust in the authority of the church was hugely undermined as a result.[230]

Decommissioning was one of the major issues of the peace process in which the Church became involved during the 1994 Provisional IRA ceasefire. As Irish-American Catholics increasingly became aware of the situation in Northern Ireland, the American Church hierarchy stepped up their involvement. On a visit to Northern Ireland in November 1995, Bishop Raymond Boland of Kansas City outlined paramilitary decommissioning as one of his three concerns about how long-term peace would be achieved.[231] Preaching at the rededication of St Mary's Church, Stewartstown in Co. Tyrone, Cardinal Daly argued against opponents of decommissioning, noting all sides needed to overcome this 'road-block' to ensure peace.[232] He reiterated this message at a Mass held in Coventry Cathedral, urging all sides to begin peace talks and remove the obstacle of decommissioning: 'Given that the prize at the conclusion of the talks is nothing less than the decommissioning of all weapons, the taking of the gun forever out of Irish politics'.[233] Cardinal Daly's message throughout this period was clear: do not let decommissioning stand in the way of peace talks as with increased all-party meetings and negotiations decommissioning would naturally occur.

Clergymen and women were also working to further a resolution on decommissioning. However, Fr Joe McVeigh questioned the British government's motives on the issue, arguing that Mayhew used decommissioning as an excuse to delay all-party talks.[234] Irish Taoiseach Albert Reynolds agreed with McVeigh, citing that the British government had not set Provisional IRA decommissioning as a prerequisite to talks prior to the Downing Street Declaration.[235] Privately, Rev Bob Beresford, a Catholic Deacon, conferred to the Irish government that while the impasse over decommissioning was largely a 'symbolic' issue, it was of great importance nonetheless.[236] Fearing a collapse of the peace process if the British government insisted on pushing through proposals for an international commission on arms disposal at the Anglo-Irish summit in September 1995, Reid secretly summoned two Irish government officials to Clonard Monastery to discuss the issue. The Sunday Independent reported that the republicans' message from that

---

[229] Universe, 4 Sept. 1994.   [230] Inglis, Moral Monopoly, 225–8.

[231] The other two issues were the weakness of John Major's British government and the uncertainty of David Trimble's tenure as UUP leader; Irish Catholic, 23 Nov. 1995.

[232] Tablet, 26 Aug. 1995.   [233] Tablet, 23 March 1996.

[234] Irish Catholic, 6 July 1995.   [235] Guardian, 25 Aug. 1995.

[236] SDA, D47.2 Ireland 'Department for International Affairs' Current Northern Ireland Matters by Rev Bob Beresford, 26 Oct. 1995.

meeting was clear: stop this commission or there will be 'bodies in the streets'.[237] No transcript of the meeting has been made public to confirm these threats. Nevertheless, Reid was instrumental in coordinating the meeting and helping to keep SF engaged with peace process.

The seventeen-month Provisional IRA ceasefire came to an end at 7:01 p.m. on 9 February 1996, with the bombing of Canary Wharf in the London Docklands. The blast killed two people, injured more than 100, and caused around £100 million worth of damage.[238] Cardinal Daly described the bomb as an 'outrage' which would likely see the peace talks 'recklessly thrown away'.[239] Mgr Denis Faul said the bombing demonstrated that SF and 'the IRA do not understand politics and cannot handle it'.[240] Claire Mitchell has claimed the Provisionals breaking the ceasefire 'reinforce[d] ideas of Catholic dishonesty', therefore weakening the overall Catholic negotiating power in the peace process.[241]

Despite fears to the contrary peace negotiations did resume. However, under this new cloak of violence, the institutional Catholic Church played a much smaller role. The negotiations moved firmly into the political arena where Catholic priests and women religious had no footing, unlike some Protestant clergymen who held elected political positions in Northern Ireland.[242] Those grassroots women religious continued to work to bring politicians together as well as personally advocate for peace. Another secular effort came from Dr Joseph Liechty and Dr Cecelia Clegg in the form of the 'Moving Beyond Sectarianism' project which emerged in the mid-1990s from the Irish School of Ecumenics.[243] In an interview with the author, Dr Geraldine Smyth OP, who acted as a supervisor on the project which focused on the role of Christian religion in sectarianism in Northern Ireland, spoke of the difficulty she faced when some individuals asked her to separate her ecumenical efforts from her peace building efforts. She noted difficulties remained in this period:

> Some Protestant Church people will find it much easier to engage with peace building and reconciliation at a social level. But they don't want to bring theology and Church belonging into it because many of them had a certain suspicion of ecumenism which is quite understandable as some of the ecumenism they saw around them in Ireland, and historically, was the 'return to Rome' model.[244]

Dr Smyth tried to assuage such suspicions by assuring her Protestant counterparts that other models of ecumenism existed allowing Catholics and Protestants to learn about one another's differences. She asserted: 'Don't ask me to leave my faith

---

[237] *Sunday Independent*, 10 Sept. 1995.
[238] Ed Moloney, *Voices from the Grave: Two Men's War in Ireland* (London, 2010), 488.
[239] *Tablet*, 17 Feb. 1996.   [240] *Tablet*, 17 Feb. 1996.
[241] Mitchell, *Religion, Identity, and Politics*, 115.   [242] See Bruce, *God Save Ulster*.
[243] Liechty and Clegg later published *Moving Beyond Sectarianism: Religion, Conflict and Reconciliation in Northern Ireland* (Dublin, 2000).
[244] Dr Geraldine Smyth OP interview, 3 Dec. 2018.

outside the door and just be involved in secular peace building'.[245] However, suspicions continued, with the misunderstandings around different types of ecumenism remaining. At the same time as these grassroots efforts, the involvement of US President Bill Clinton pulled the peace process into the realm of international politics.

The issue of how to bring paramilitary organizations into peace talks and preventing future violence through the disposal of weapons pressed hard on the minds of Catholic religious leaders. American Senator George Mitchell chaired the international body on arms decommissioning, which published six principles on disarmament in May 1996 recommending that 'participants in all-party negotiations should affirm their total and absolute commitment'.[246] The committee worked through 1995 and 1996, and initially received a mixed reaction. The Provisional IRA feared once it turned over its weapons it would lose its main source of power, and the peace process could crumble, maintaining the status quo. However, the Auxiliary Bishop of Dublin, Dermot O'Mahony, noted 'it would be a tragedy if the substance of the [arms decommissioning] report was abandoned'.[247] Cardinal Daly stressed the importance of decommissioning and the Mitchell Principles the night before cross-party talks in June 1996. The British government excluded SF from the talks because the Provisionals had not declared their intent to decommission. Daly supported the decision of the Irish and British governments to appoint Senator Mitchell as chair for the talks as he was 'the best possible guarantee for unionists as well as for nationalists that this delicate problem will be handled fairly, impartially, and effectively'.[248] Throughout this period Reid continued to act as mediator for republicans, writing to Mitchell explaining the republican viewpoint on the principles and the conditions necessary for the Provisionals to establish another ceasefire.[249] As talks on the Mitchell Principles continued, Faul took a more realistic approach, arguing not for the focus on the decommissioning of weapons but on the need 'to decommission minds, hearts, and wills'.[250] It was not only the removal of weapons but of attitudes towards each other that had to change in order to secure a lasting peace.

The Provisional IRA had claimed the Docklands Bombing as a 'one off' event,[251] but the bombing in central Manchester on 15 June 1996 proved this to be false. The second attack led clergymen and women to become divided over whether to support SF's admission into the peace talks. Fr Gerry Reynolds, of the Clonard Monastery, condemned the bombing but suggested if the British government admitted SF to the talks 'that would end the violence'.[252] Faul argued the

---

[245] Dr Geraldine Smyth OP interview, 3 Dec. 2018.   [246] *Irish Times*, 21 May 1996.
[247] *Irish Catholic*, 1 Feb. 1996.   [248] *Tablet*, 15 June 1996.
[249] 'Letter by Fr Alec Reid to Senator George Mitchell', 18 Nov. 1996 in McKeever, *One Man, One God*, 188–96.
[250] *Tablet*, 19 Oct. 1996.   [251] *Irish Times*, 12 Feb. 1996.
[252] *Tablet*, 22 June 1996.

opposite; that SF should only be admitted to the peace talks only if the Provisionals made a statement renouncing violence before an independent witness such as the Pope or President Clinton. Faul wanted the British government and the media to isolate SF and the Provisional IRA, arguing that denying them coverage would 'bring them to heel'.[253] These two opposing views within the Church highlighted internal division but also demonstrated a 'carrot and stick' policy. If the Church appeared too willing to support SF after these bombings, they would be seen as complicit, while if they went too far the other way they could push SF into a corner and the violence would continue. The Provisionals once again declared a ceasefire in July 1997. Cardinal Daly urged that peace talks begin quickly under the terms set out in the Mitchell Report.[254] All parties including SF entered peace talks in earnest, although the issue of decommissioning would cause the DUP to later walk out.

Negotiations eventually led to the signing of the GFA on 10 April 1998. Scholars have largely overlooked the role of the Church in the lead up to this event.[255] This can be explained by the relatively unsuspecting roles played by individual clergymen and women who helped bring the parties to the table and continuously encouraging negotiations from the sidelines. In terms of the hierarchy, Archbishop Sean Brady (see Appendix) welcomed the signing of the Agreement: 'Our prayers have been answered'.[256] Brady asked all sides to 'become participants in the work of reconciliation, of building trust, and healing hurts'.[257] Yet some clerics were more cautious, including Fr Kevin Browne, Rector of Clonard Monastery, instead opting to a 'wait and see'.[258] Clonard had witnessed the violence since the late 1960s and so caution appeared a sensible approach. Browne encouraged his parishioners to continue to pray for peace. Conversely, religious women, both Protestant and Catholic, rejoiced at the news of the Agreement, with Dr Geraldine Smyth OP reflecting years later on the significance of the signing being on Good Friday.[259] Baroness May Blood, a Protestant woman who lived and worked on the peace line in Belfast and who often met with Catholic sisters, noted: 'When it was announced there was euphoria because I have to tell you nobody actually thought it was going to come about'.[260] Rev Lesley Carroll, a Presbyterian minister who also worked on the peace line, reflected twenty years later that for the GFA to work 'there had to be substantial network of all sorts of relationships, up, down, across, diagonally

---

[253] *Tablet*, 22 June 1996.   [254] *Irish Catholic*, 24 July 1997.
[255] See Siobhán Fenton, *The Good Friday Agreement* (London, 2018); McKittrick and McVea, *Making Sense of the Troubles*; English, *Armed Struggle*.
[256] *Fermanagh Herald*, 15 April 1998.   [257] *Fermanagh Herald*, 15 April 1998.
[258] *Times*, 11 April 1998.
[259] Dr Geraldine Smyth OP interview in 'Sisters of the Troubles', *BBC News World Service*, 25 March 2018.
[260] Baroness May Blood interview in 'Sisters of the Troubles', *BBC News World Service*, 25 March 2018.

across society' and that politicians had failed to understand the importance of those relationships.[261] Without these networks, which women were a part, Carroll believes the peace would not have succeeded.

The subsequent overwhelming referendum result in support of the GFA saw further statements of elation from members of the church. The Catholic and Church of Ireland bishops of Clogher welcomed the result, noting voters North and South had shown faith in the Agreement.[262] Fr Joe McVeigh, at that time an organizer of The Centre for Human Rights in Belfast, said: 'The Agreement is about making radical changes in Irish society' and that this societal change was necessary for a lasting peace.[263] In an article for *An Phoblacht/Republican News*, McVeigh warned that in light of the Agreement and subsequent referendum, it was 'now time for the leaders of the churches in Ireland to take a stand for human rights and equality'.[264] One way McVeigh claimed the leaders could do this would be through confronting British Prime Minister Tony Blair to 'stop the provocative Orange marches in Catholic/nationalist districts', as there churches needed to lead the way in laying the ground for reconciliation.[265] The referendum confirmed that the people of Ireland wanted peace, but the Church, McVeigh believed, would need to help make that peace a lasting one.

The Agreement was clearly a positive step but many issues of the conflict were still unresolved and open for debate, discussion, and disagreement. Despite the tumultuous political period following the Agreement, years later, Cardinal Cahal Daly privately reflected to Mgr Raymond Murray that within the framework of the Agreement: 'There is firm hope of justice and equality and hope of a peaceful future'.[266] Individual clergymen and women played a role in issues around decommissioning, the 'disappeared', and reconciliation efforts.[267] Yet gone were the days when the institutional Church leaders were called upon to rally the masses for peace. Catholics and Protestants could make up their own minds about the future of peace in Northern Ireland. It was now time for their clergymen and women to stand beside them rather than lead.

Conclusion

Only a few months after the signing of the GFA, the Real IRA, a splinter faction of the Provisionals, placed a car bomb on Omagh's Lower Market Street. Detonated at 3:10 p.m. on 15 August 1998, the blast killed twenty-one people at the scene

---

[261] Rev Lesley Carroll interview in 'Sisters of the Troubles', *BBC News World Service*, 25 March 2018.
[262] *Fermanagh Herald*, 27 May 1998.   [263] *Fermanagh Herald*, 3 June 1998.
[264] *An Phoblacht/Republican News*, 25 June 1998.
[265] *An Phoblacht/Republican News*, 25 June 1998.
[266] CTOMLA, Mgr Murray Papers, Box 22, Cahal Daly to Murray, 14 Jan. 2003.
[267] McKeever, *One Man, One God*, 53–7.

with nine more succumbing to their wounds over the following weeks. The bombing highlighted the continuing deep community divisions and drew outcry from Protestant and Catholic Church leaders alike.

The funerals of the Omagh bombing victims proved to be places of public political reconciliation. Irish President Mary McAleese, SF leaders Gerry Adams and Martin McGuinness, and UUP First Minister David Trimble attended the service for twelve-year-old James Barker. Bishop Seamus Hegarty, of Derry, denounced those who built the bomb, calling on them to repent and to 'give up their immoral trade in destruction and death—not temporarily or conditionally, but permanently'.[268] The funerals offered Catholic and Protestant church leaders an opportunity to once again show a public united front against violence.[269] When meeting with relatives of the victims, Adams commented to An Phoblacht/Republican News that he was 'totally horrified' by the bombing.[270] The funerals offered SF the opportunity to position themselves as separate from the gruesome 'other' republican groups who must be contained in the post-GFA political landscape.

Catholic leaders worked in small ways to bring communities together after this attack. Christian Brothers organized a football match between Catholic boys at their schools and Protestant students from the Omagh Academy, for example. However, the gesture was met with skepticism and resistance by parents and their children and the Brothers appeared out of touch.[271]

In the aftermath of the bombing the Four Main Churches once again rallied together to plea for peace.[272] However, the reputation of Irish Catholic Church as mediator had undoubtedly been affected by the clerical child abuse scandal. In an interview with the author, former SDLP member Brian Feeney speculated that in his view British politicians and officials were now less keen to heed the advice of church leaders.[273] Specifically the Catholic Church no longer held unimpeachable standing, as allegations and accusations of abuse and subsequent cover-ups abounded after the revelations of the Smyth case. As my concluding chapter contends, by 1996 the role of the institutional Catholic Church was greatly diminished and had been replaced almost entirely with grassroots, community-based organizations in which the Catholic laity, alongside their Protestant neighbours, worked together to end the conflict. However, the nature of the conflict had also changed. Individual priests or bishops were no longer needed to bring together political parties and paramilitaries for dialogue as these introductions had already been made. Speaking publicly with Adams in the mid-1990s was no longer political anathema for nationalist or unionist politicians.

[268] Guardian, 20 Aug. 1998.   [269] Fermanagh Herald, 19 Aug. 1998.
[270] An Phoblacht/Republican News, 20 Aug. 1998.   [271] Tablet, 26 June 1999.
[272] Tablet, 9 March 1996.   [273] Interview with Brian Feeney, 26 May 2015.

The Catholic Church also faced a changing society in the Republic of Ireland; a country now on the long road to secularization. The full extent of the brutality of the Magdalene Laundries and Mother and Baby Homes run by nuns had begun to be made known in 1993. The total control that the Church had over moral issues had begun to alter, and adapted to look much more like the more tenuous relationship between Church and state that had pervaded since partition in Northern Ireland. Birth control, homosexuality, and AIDS were much less taboo subjects and in 1996 the Republic of Ireland voted to make divorce legal.[274]

A key theme of this period is the overwhelming power of personalities in bringing together individuals from different sides of the conflict. On one hand, it was small, everyday actions that prevented an escalation of the conflict 'into total civil war', as Sister of Mercy Sr Mary Delargy reflected twenty years later.[275] On the other hand, key clerical figures operated around political frameworks to make a real difference. While Reid and Reynolds could work privately in mediating between republicans and nationalist political parties, Faul publicly condemned the Provisional IRA and worked with those who defied them. This balance was necessary to bring about peace. After Faul spent years denouncing the Provisionals, it would have been hypocritical for him to help mediate the peace talks in the same way as Reid and Reynolds. Unlike Faul, in the early 1990s, Reid and Reynolds avoided the media, realizing their words could be misconstrued and damage the fledgling peace process.

Admiration for Reid and his work as a mediator continued into the twenty-first century. Former Provisional IRA member Tommy McKearney remarked in a 2013 documentary: 'I have no doubt that Fr Alec Reid, acting as an intermediary, as a conduit, facilitated the developments that took place'.[276] Journalist Eamonn Mallie also highlighted his importance, writing: 'When Reid brought the message, people knew that there was a validity and authenticity attached to it and that was his great strength and his great value and worth to the evolving peace process'.[277] Reid had the confidence of militant republicans and constitutional nationalists, facilitating meetings between SF and other political parties discreetly. Through his vocation and his words, all sides knew he condemned violence but could nevertheless understand the motives of those in the armed struggle. Unlike some Protestant clergymen, he did not hold political office. He was motivated solely by his convictions and accountable only to his abbot and his God. Reid's trustworthiness and steadfastness made him the ideal mediator between constitutional and militant nationalist parties. Also, speaking in 2013,

---

[274] Inglis, *Moral Monopoly*, 225–8.
[275] Sr Mary Delargy interview in 'Sisters of the Troubles', *BBC News World Service*, 25 March 2018.
[276] Interview with Tommy McKearny in *14 Days*, BBC 1, 21 March 2013.
[277] Interview with Eamonn Mallie in *14 Days*, BBC 1, 21 March 2013.

Adams said: 'Would we have got a peace process without him? Yes. But not of the particular type and certainly not at the time'.[278] In his work as a quiet peacekeeper known for helping those on all sides, who lay over two British Army soldiers in an attempt to save them, Reid excelled in bringing very different individuals together for peace.

---

[278] Interview with Gerry Adams in *14 Days*, BBC 1, 21 March 2013.

Conclusion
'The Church Needs to do a Reality Check'

When Pope Francis looked out on to the sparse crowds at Dublin's Phoenix Park, during his August 2018 papal visit to Ireland, he would have seen quite a different scene than that which greeted his predecessor almost forty years earlier.[1] Pope John Paul II's famous 1979 address at the same venue was to an audience drawn from as far afield as Belfast and Derry, as well as from Cork and Galway, with the numbers reported to have reached 1.25 million. Despite drastic changes in the level of violence between 1979 and 2018, neither Pope crossed the British border in Ireland, revealing times had not changed enough to risk a papal visit to the North. Pope John Paul II's popularity saw him dubbed as almost being the 'fifth Beatle', with the media reporting on everything from the colour of the blanket in his plane to what his first glimpse of the Emerald Isle would be as he glanced out of his aeroplane window. Francis, by contrast, was met with speculation over how the social-media savvy prelate would respond to accusations of clerical abuse cover-ups, the legacy of the Magdalene laundries, and Mother and Baby homes across the island. These questions hung heavy in the air, a sickly perfume over every speech and interview, both before and after Francis' visit as part of the World Meeting of Families.[2] Welcoming Francis at Dublin Castle, the openly gay Taoiseach Leo Varadkar referred to the 'people kept in dark corners, behind closed doors' whose cries for help went unheard.[3] The results of Gladys Ganiel's survey suggests Francis did not do enough to address claims of clerical child sex abuse.[4] It appeared as if the Pope was visiting a different island all together, leading many to wonder if this may be the 'end' of Catholic Ireland.

The paltry attendance and less than reverent welcome for Pope Francis was part of a series of events revealing the decline in Catholic Church influence. In 2015, a

[1] Chapter title reference: *RTÉ News*, 24 May 2015, http://www.rte.ie/news/vote2015/2015/0523/703227-same-sex-marriage-referendum-no-reaction/

[2] https://www.bbc.co.uk/news/world-europe-45310821, 26 Aug. 2018.

[3] *Irish Times*, 25 Aug. 2018, https://www.irishtimes.com/news/social-affairs/religion-and-beliefs/taoiseach-tells-pope-francis-there-must-be-zero-tolerance-for-those-who-abuse-1.3607797?mode=sample&auth-failed=1&pw-origin=https%3A%2F%2Fwww.irishtimes.com%2Fnews%2Fsocial-affairs%2Freligion-and-beliefs%2Ftaoiseach-tells-pope-francis-there-must-be-zero-tolerance-for-those-who-abuse-1.3607797

[4] Gladys Ganiel, 'Surveying the Papal Visit to Ireland: The Francis Effect?', Oct. 2018, http://qpol.qub.ac.uk/wp-content/uploads/2018/10/Gladys-Ganiel-Paper-on-Pope-Francis.pdf

referendum in the Republic of Ireland legalized gay marriage to the shock of Catholic Church leaders. In an RTÉ interview discussing the landslide result, the Archbishop of Dublin, Diarmuid Martin said: 'The Church needs to do a reality check'.[5] Some in the media claimed the vote symbolized a revolution rather than a referendum. Martin agreed. 'It's a social revolution that didn't begin today,' he said, 'it's a social revolution that's been going on'.[6] In 2018, Republic of Ireland citizens also voted decisively to repeal the Eighth Amendment, lifting restrictions against abortion. The campaign on both sides was fierce but Irish Catholic bishops backed a 'No' vote. Bishop Kevin Doran suggested those Catholics who voted 'Yes' needed to confess their sin.[7] Some priests had threatened to withhold Communion from those in their congregations who planned on voting 'Yes'.[8] However, on the other side of the ecumenical aisle, a Church of Ireland bishop hailed the result as 'an exhilarating challenge in presenting the faith in a fresh way to a changing nation.'[9]

These votes supporting both abortion and gay marriage are potent examples of the loss of the Church's moral influence. Indeed, following the 2015 vote Cardinal Pietro Parolin, the Vatican Secretary of State, called the result in Ireland a 'defeat for humanity'.[10] Writing in *The Irish Times* in June 2018, Fintan O'Toole said: 'If Catholic Ireland is a culture of obedience to a male hierarchy, it is indeed over—and has been for some time. The referendum produced for the church leadership something much worse than defiance: mere indifference.'[11] This erosion of Church authority had a long genesis, reaching a crescendo in the mid-1990s as discussed in Chapter 5, with numerous accusations of clerical child abuse and the institutional Church's palpable loss of influence in the peace process. The #Repealthe8th campaign, empowered by social media and non-violent protest, vociferously and effectively challenged this last bastion of the Church's moral influence over abortion in the South.[12] The 'social revolution' diagnosed by Archbishop Martin continues.

The focus of activists and the media will undoubtedly shift across the border and Northern Ireland will be forced to confront its position as the only part of the United Kingdom not to recognise the 1967 Abortion Act. The pro-life DUP will

---

[5] *RTÉ News*, 24 May 2015, http://www.rte.ie/news/vote2015/2015/0523/703227-same-sex-mar riage-referendum-no-reaction/

[6] *RTÉ News*, 24 May 2015, http://www.rte.ie/news/vote2015/2015/0523/703227-same-sex-marriage-referendum-no-reaction/

[7] *Irish Mirror*, 28 May 2018, https://www.irishmirror.ie/news/irish-news/bishop-kevin-doran-tells-rtes-12609994

[8] *The New York Times*, 26 May 2018, https://www.nytimes.com/2018/05/26/world/europe/ireland-abortion-yes.html

[9] *Irish Times*, 28 May 2018, https://www.irishtimes.com/news/social-affairs/religion-and-beliefs/bishop-says-yes-vote-on-abortion-presents-exhilarating-challenge-1.3511604

[10] *Guardian*, 26 May 2015.

[11] *Irish Times*, 2 June 2018, https://www.irishtimes.com/opinion/fintan-o-toole-catholic-ireland-is-now-a-religious-rust-belt-of-half-empty-churches-1.3513677

[12] The 1967 Abortion Act has never been applied in Northern Ireland; http://www.bbc.co.uk/news/magazine-35980195

hope to gain support from conservative Catholic voters on the issue.[13] At the time of writing, SDLP councillors in Newry, Mourne, and Down have reaffirmed 'their pro-life position'.[14] In June 2018, SF delegates voted to support women having access to abortion within the first 12 weeks of pregnancy.[15] The argument over abortion in Ireland is not over, even though the Church has been side-lined. In the North, the Catholic Church has long been a bogeyman for unionists. However, claims that Irish Catholics did whatever their priests told them to do, and that 'Home Rule' equalled 'Rome Rule', now prove defunct with the equal marriage and eighth amendment referenda. With this new legislation, the South proves much more secular than the North. Now that the Church can no longer truly act as a barrier to unity, what new excuse can unionists use? Furthermore, will Ireland continue to be seen as a 'Catholic' country, even with the dramatic decline of Church influence? Time will tell.

What makes this change even more important is that traditionally in Ireland there exists a longstanding notion that the 'Celtic' people are inherently religious, with the Emerald Isle 'the island of saints and scholars'. Yet in reality this is profoundly untrue today. As Perry Share, Hilary Tovey, and Mary Corcoran argue, this turnabout occurred 'as the outcome of many complex social factors'.[16] The post-famine era had seen the Irish Catholic Church rapidly develop to a position where it dominated almost every aspect of life. In addition, when the British left the twenty-six counties in 1921, a vacuum emerged in several areas allowing the Catholic Church to step in as the natural arbiter of the fledgling Irish Free State's education and health care systems. This provided an opportunity to organize its followers in a way of life where the Church was central to the community. As Fintan O'Toole noted, 'the "cradle to grave" attention of European social welfare was created in Ireland by the Church'.[17] However, by 1998 the Church was no longer an omnipotent presence in the working lives of the Catholic populations on either side of the border. Its role now was predominantly to offer comfort and a sense of community to those who continued to attend services as part of their faith. At a November 2018 symposium entitled 'The end of Catholic Ireland?', Gladys Ganiel discussed the decline in the number of people who self-identified as Catholic in Northern Ireland between the late 1970s and 2016; and identified a similar drop in the number of those claiming to regularly attend mass between 1968 and 2012. It is true to say Ireland has been 'one of the

---

[13] *Belfast Telegraph*, 4 June 2018, https://www.belfasttelegraph.co.uk/news/northern-ireland/paisley-to-reveal-letter-from-priest-urging-catholics-to-vote-for-dup-36973640.html

[14] *Irish News*, 7 June 2018, http://www.irishnews.com/paywall/tsb/irishnews/irishnews/irishnews//news/northernirelandnews/2018/06/07/news/sdlp-councillors-in-newry-mourne-down-reaffirm-their-pro-life-position–1349727/content.html

[15] *BBC News*, 16 June 2018, https://www.bbc.co.uk/news/uk-northern-ireland-44507054

[16] Perry Share, Hilary Tovey, and Mary P, Corcoran, *A Sociology of Modern Ireland*, 3rd edition, (Dublin, 2007), 403.

[17] Fintan O'Toole, *The Lie of the Land: Irish Identities* (London, 1998), 67.

most religiously sensitised nations in the western world' during the last two centuries.[18] The revelation of clerical abuse scandals across the island damaged the reputation and moral authority of the Catholic Church. Those who still speak to that faith are practicing a form of 'extra-institutional religion'.[19] While 'Irish Catholic' still may be a dominant ethnic identifier, the practice of that faith outside of the institutional Church stems from a radical minority. Questions around the downfall of 'Catholic Ireland' are one thing but individuals identifying as Catholic remains strong throughout the island.

Indeed, the actions of individuals were vital in shaping the direction of the institutional Catholic Church throughout the Northern conflict. This work documents the way in which the personal views, political preferences, and strategic behaviours of individual cardinals impacted disproportionately on the Church's engagements with the peace process, with particular republican parties and with the British state. This helped to create significant changes in the role of the Catholic Church over the period of the conflict. At any moment of the conflict, the personality of the Archbishop of Armagh mattered greatly to the reaction of the Church as an institution.

Furthermore, the sustained and co-ordinated actions of certain individuals echoed and refracted within the larger Church. Individual priests, women religious, and bishops shared the goal of lasting peace but their methods varied depending on their analysis of the impediments to a just solution. The hierarchical structure of the Church made the intervention of bishops particularly influential though the institutional Catholic Church's actions and words varied greatly during the conflict and often depended on the prelate's leadership. Only a handful of priests gained an equivalent status: Fr Denis Faul during the 1981 hunger strikes, for example. At times these disparate personalities created tensions within the institutional Church and their impact should not be underestimated.

The approaches of four archbishops of Armagh throughout the conflict illustrate this theory. The actions of William Conway, Tomás Ó Fiaich, Cahal Daly, and Sean Brady impacted on the peace process in different ways during their respective tenures as the Primate of All Ireland. Their upbringings, family backgrounds, political viewpoints, and personalities both helped and hindered their interactions with Protestant church leaders, the Holy See, as well as British and Irish politicians, and government officials. Historians have not interrogated closely enough the contextual settings impacting Catholic religious leaders' abilities to create a dialogue for peace. Both Conway and Daly were careful to not offend their Protestant counterparts, while Ó Fiaich embraced his staunch nationalist sympathies. The gradual evolution from ecumenism to community relations,

---

[18] Donald Akenson, *Small Differences: Irish Catholics and Irish Protestants, 1815–1922* (Dublin, 1991), 16.

[19] Ganiel, *Transforming Post-Catholic Ireland*, 229–30, 251–2.

as an example of the local politics being prioritized over general religious precepts, influenced these leaders in their abilities to govern the Church and intervene between the warring parties. Access to personal papers, as well as reviewing their public statements, has added greater nuance to our understanding of each Catholic Church leaders' words and actions.

Individual personalities mattered outside the hierarchy as well. As demonstrated in Chapter 5, while Fathers Alec Reid and Gerry Reynolds arranged private meetings between militant and constitutional republicans, Fathers Denis Faul and Raymond Murray publicly denounced the peace process until the Provisional IRA agreed to lay down arms. The majority of priests in the North condemned republican violence but not state violence and remained aloof of efforts to secure peace. By focusing on the personalities of the key Catholic clerics, again enriched with access to personal papers and key interviews, this study can highlight the difficulty in identifying a coherent institutional and united Church vision for a peaceful solution.

As with most large, multinational organizations, it is clear the Catholic Church is made up of disparate identities, diverse theological priorities, and conflicting positions despite representations of the contrary by the media and some politicians. Clerical dissension occurred throughout the conflict, possibly because of changes in hierarchical jurisdiction, as discussed earlier, on class and moral authority. These different perspectives have always existed among clergy members, but individuals have often remained silent in deference to the hierarchy's position, thus maintaining the perception of unanimity. However, the conflict witnessed public and publicized tension between the hierarchy and members of the more outspoken clergy. Differing approaches of individuals working towards peace fractured the unity of the Irish Catholic Church in such a defining period of British and Irish history.

As important as acknowledging the impact individuals can have on events, it is the necessity to see the Troubles in the broader context of the Catholic Church beyond Ireland. Indeed, the role and actions of the Irish Catholic Church during this tumultuous time cannot be properly analysed or understood in isolation. Scholarship on the conflict has long been focused on the six counties, regularly ignoring the impact of the conflict in the rest of the United Kingdom, Republic of Ireland, and beyond. That is why this study is so important and opens up further avenues for research. By bringing in the experiences of the English and Welsh Catholic Church we can build on the traditional story and view the conflict through a new lens. Future studies could expand this remit further, bringing in more on the Catholic Church in Scotland and the USA, and perhaps even incorporating the views and interaction of the Catholic Churches elsewhere in Europe at a time of global political and societal tensions. Comparing this study with the actions of Catholic Church leaders during Apartheid in South Africa, the civil rights movement in the United States, or in response to events during the

Cold War will expand our understanding of the interconnected nature of power structures and the Catholic Church.

Using a comparative, entangled history approach to the literature on religion during the conflict not only highlights the relative lack of previous academic engagement with the English and Welsh Church, but significantly broadens our understanding of this period. Despite remaining silent on Irish matters after the partition until the 1970s, the English and Welsh Catholic Church influenced public perceptions with increasing frequency in the 1980s. The English and Welsh Catholic Church was in a position to influence British public perceptions of the Irish Catholic Church on issues including the excommunication of IRA members. British press reports citing disagreements between the Irish and English and Welsh Catholic Church hierarchies added to the compromised united position in mediating for peace. By drawing extensively on relevant, previously under-researched English diocesan archival material, this study shows that the mid-1980s witnessed the Scottish, English, and Welsh hierarchies assuming more active roles in attempting to find a solution to the conflict. It is perhaps surprising no study has taken this approach before now when taking into consideration the considerable Irish diaspora in Britain. Irish priests in England, Wales, and Scotland often came to the aid of those requiring support in their districts. For example, Fr Bobby Gilmore's role in leading the national Birmingham Six campaign, Sr Sarah Clarke who faced criticism from the British government for her work with Irish prisoners, and Fr Gerry McFlynn for his continued work with the Irish Commission for Prisoners Overseas. Through interviews with Irish priests who served in England and scrutiny of memoirs written by Irish clergy based abroad we can begin to integrate this aspect of the contemporaneous experience into the literature.

All of this strengthens the argument that while the Vatican influenced Catholicism during the conflict, it was profoundly refracted through a regional lens with religion and politics in constant and creative dialogue. A Vatican-directed Catholic Church, with its stringent theology, rules, and regulations should have resulted in Church leaders across these islands 'singing from the same hymn sheet'. In reality, this study illustrates how each Church is refracted through a national lens, and impacted by the personality, lived experience, history, politics, and identity of individual Church leaders.

What cannot be ignored when trying to make sense of the role played by the Catholic Church during the conflict is the sharp decline in clerical legitimacy as the twentieth century came to an end. In 1968 the Irish Catholic Church sought to maintain a rigid authoritarian hierarchical structure. By the 1990s this had mostly collapsed. In 1968, Catholic communities held religious leaders in high esteem. A generation later a string of horrifying scandals and revelations saw this respect seriously eroded. In the early years of the conflict priests had resumed their historic role as mediators between nationalist groups, and between nationalists and unionists. Many unionists, British government officials and, to an extent, British Army leaders, appreciated the authority Catholic clerics held to negotiate with a measure of 'neutrality'. Priests became intrinsically and symbolically linked with meditating the conflict in the global consciousness. The iconic image of Fr Edward Daly waving a white handkerchief on Bloody Sunday was seen around the world. Many nationalists and unionists alike respected those few priests who became involved in attempting to mediate the conflict for their objective and tenacious advocacy for peace.

It was the revelations of clerical abuse in the 1990s which led to a profound loss of trust from the Catholic community. Cover-up accusations, especially in the Fr Brendan Smyth case, severely damaged the institutional Church's reputation. This study has not sought to prove a direct correlation between the loss of Catholic Church influence in the peace process with the revelations of clerical abuse. However, it does suggest the two things were not mutually exclusive. By 1994, priest mediators were no longer essential facilitators to dialogue as Gerry Adams and John Hume could speak publicly about an end to violence without detriment to their careers, parties, or the peace process.

When it came to politics during the conflict, the Catholic Church had a preference for constitutional nationalism and the Catholic middle class over-whelmingly voted for the SDLP. This has changed, despite the long opposition of the Catholic Church to SF. Since the GFA there has been a massive growth in Catholic middle-class support for SF's peace strategy as witnessed by their rise in electoral power. As a result, we now see a collapse in the support for the Church's 'traditional' party in the SDLP.[20] Catholic middle-class support for SF impacts the narrative by showing the influence of the Church hierarchy on the people in their pews, and the unwillingness of the population to take any heed to church pronouncements from the pulpit, or otherwise, on politics, LGBTQ issues, and women's reproductive rights.[21] In 2018, the *Observer* reported a rise in the number of women from Northern Ireland travelling to England for an abortion.[22] This trend may change now as the Republic of Ireland changes its laws to allow women from the North to access abortion facilities across the border.[23] The Church and its parishioners continuously clash over these issues, as they become increasingly irrelevant to the non-spiritual lives of the Church's flock. Therefore, the

---

[20] In the 2017 Westminster general election, the SDLP lost their remaining parliamentary seat with SF gaining three additional seats. https://www.bbc.co.uk/news/election-2017-40188101, 9 June 2017.

[21] An October 2018 Amnesty International poll showed nearly three-quarters of people in Northern Ireland want abortion to be available in cases of rape and incest and when the foetus will not survive outside the womb. https://www.amnesty.org.uk/press-releases/northern-ireland-nearly-34-public-support-abortion-law-change-new-poll-0, 18 Oct. 2018.

[22] *Observer*, 21 July 2018, https://www.theguardian.com/world/2018/jul/21/women-travelling-from-northern-ireland-to-england-for-abortions

[23] *Irish Times*, 7 Aug. 2018, https://www.irishtimes.com/news/politics/women-from-northern-ireland-will-be-allowed-access-abortion-in-republic-harris-1.3589111

well-observed decline in religious observance among Catholics is not just explained by age but also class. So, as discussed previously, the decline in mass attendance may not reduce the number of those who self-identify as Catholics, but does demonstrate a massive decline in clerical legitimacy and authority. The island of Ireland was slow to adopt the ethos of the Second Vatican Council. Perhaps what we see today is a truer adherence to the principles of Vatican II, as priests and women religious work alongside the laity rather than dictating to them.

An uncertain future holds across these islands as the relationship between Britain and Ireland continues to evolve. The slippery landscape of politics in Northern Ireland is one still focused on retribution. As Máire Braniff notes: 'we have had civil society almost impotent and neutered in [its] attempts to advance any form of reconciliation at a political elite level. And we've had grassroots experience of reconciliation that is not mirrored anywhere else across the political spectrum.'[24] So where do the Churches fit in today and what role can they play in reconciliation of post-GFA Northern Ireland?

Many people across this island feel emboldened to engage in reconciliation without Church leaders; even if their efforts go by the term 'community relations' rather than ecumenism. One such cross-border, cross-community example begins in Donegal with the Newtowncunningham Community Outreach Project, which received two years funding to turn an Orange Hall into a space which can 'rebuild some relationships shattered by the conflict'.[25] The aims of the project to offer education, training, and skills development in 'an inclusive model of engagement between traditions and minority communities' echoes 'reconciliation' even if it does not use that term.[26] Whereas Church leaders were involved at some level with projects including Initiative '92, the Opsahl Commission, STOP, FAIT, and others, some more recent initiatives are firmly secular in nature.

Today, many Church leaders continue to act as independent agents, letting their faith guide them in organizations co-ordinated by Church figures and the laity. One such example is the 'Healing through Remembering' project, a cross-community organization which hopes it can contribute to a better future for all in Northern Ireland through remembering the conflict and in dealing with the legacy of the past. Dr Geraldine Smyth OP serves on the board of this organization and the majority of its members are both religious and secular Protestants and Catholics.[27] Another example is the 4 Corners Festival, an annual festival started by two Christian Church leaders in 2013 which examines a new theme each year.

[24] Dr Máire Braniff Keynote Lecture at the 'Agreement 20' conference, *Slugger O'Toole*, https://sluggerotoole.com/2018/04/09/maire-braniff-the-spirit-promise-of-1998-agreement-has-been-firmly-cast-aside-agreement20. 9 April 2018.

[25] *Donegal News*, 17 Dec. 2018, https://donegalnews.com/2018/12/orange-hall-to-be-hub-for-cross-community-project/

[26] *Donegal Now*, 10 Dec. 2018, https://donegalnews.com/2018/12/orange-hall-to-be-hub-for-cross-community-project/

[27] http://healingthroughremembering.org/

In 2019, the festival will focus on the theme of reconciliation. Two of the co-chairs, Fr Martin Magill and Rev Steve Stockman, have asked: 'It has been said that the Eskimos have fifty words for snow. Should we in Northern Ireland have fifty words for forgiveness?'[28] These religious individuals, one Catholic one Protestant, are partners to assist both sides on a difficult path to forgiveness. However, with no apparent resolution of tension in sight, it is likely this winding, pot-holed road will continue for quite some time.

Margaret M. Scull

20 December 2018

[28] *Belfast Telegraph*, 13 Dec. 2018, https://www.belfasttelegraph.co.uk/opinion/rev-steve-stockman-and-fr-martin-magill-if-the-eskimos-have-50-words-for-snow-does-northern-ireland-need-50-words-for-forgive-37621282.html

Important Figures

(*Pertains to individuals interviewed by author)

Fr Brian Brady (1927–1987)

He resided in the Andersonstown area of Belfast. Brady was ordained to the priesthood in 1953. He taught at St Joseph's College of Education in Belfast and later became Head of the Religious Education Department. Brady worked with Fathers Denis Faul and Raymond Murray during the 1970s to raise awareness of British government policy towards Irish internees and prisoners. In the late 1970s Brady moved to New York but returned to Ireland in 1984, acting as the parish priest for Drumbo until his death.

Archbishop Sean Brady (b. 1939)

Born in Drumcalpin, Co. Cavan, Brady was one of three children. Brady entered Maynooth College in 1957, before being ordained into the priesthood in 1964. In 1967 Brady earned a doctorate in canon law at the Pontifical Lateran University, Rome, before returning to Ireland to work at St Patrick's College in Cavan until 1980. Between 1980 and 1993 Brady worked first as vice-rector, and then rector, of the Pontifical Irish College in Rome. In December 1994, Pope John Paul II appointed Brady the Coadjutor Archbishop of Armagh, to work alongside Archbishop Cahal Daly. Upon Daly's retirement in 1996, Brady took over as Archbishop of Armagh and Primate of All Ireland, serving in this role until his own retirement in 2014.

Fr Patrick 'Pat' Buckley* (b. 1952)

Born in Tullamore, Co. Offaly in May 1952, Buckley knew from a young age that he wanted to join the priesthood.[1] The eldest of seventeen children, Buckley began his priestly training in September 1970 at Holy Cross College, Clonliffe.[2] He was ordained to the priesthood in 1976 and spent his early ministry in Bridgend, Wales working as an assistant priest.[3] In 1978 he moved to Belfast, working in three ministries over the next decade. Buckley would later become embroiled in controversy as a priest in Belfast when he performed weddings for couples where one of the partners was divorced.[4] He went on to found his own church after leaving the Catholic Church in the late 1980s.

---

[1] Buckley, *Thorn in the Side*, 5–13.   [2] Buckley, *Thorn in the Side*, 18.
[3] Buckley, *Thorn in the Side*, 35.
[4] Interview with Bishop Pat Buckley, 30 October 2017.

Sr Sarah Clarke (1920–2002)

Sarah Clarke was an Irish sister living in England, who worked tirelessly to visit and assist Irish prisoners in English prisons. Born in Galway, Clarke's political involvement began in 1970 when, at the age of fifty-three, she attended her first political rally.[5] Over the years she campaigned for the Birmingham Six, Guildford Four, and Maguire Seven, constantly declaring their innocence and fighting to prove a miscarriage of British justice. The British government banned Clarke from visiting Category A prisoners and she spoke in parliament on behalf of Irish prisoners wishing to be moved to prisons back home. Unlike many women religious in England who ignored the conflict, Clarke's Irish heritage pushed her towards this cause.

Cardinal William Conway (1913–1977)

William Conway was the leader of the Northern bishops at the outbreak of violence. Born in Belfast, he was the eldest son of a house painter and small business owner and Conway went on to study at Queen's University Belfast. He was ordained in 1937, studying in Rome during the Second World War. After briefly teaching at St Malachy's College in Belfast, Conway took on a lectureship at Maynooth, where he remained until 1958. He served as Auxiliary Bishop of Armagh under Cardinal John D'Alton before assuming the role of Archbishop of Armagh in 1963.[6] The arrival of Conway and Bishop William Philbin to the Northern episcopate in the 1960s marked a shift in the hierarchy. Both men were intellectuals and 'religiously orthodox' who had participated in the Second Vatican Council.[7] Unlike their predecessors, Philbin and Conway were politically reserved. Conway has been described as 'cautious and correct', a man who publicly worried about the 'ultra-left and neo-Marxist' element within the civil rights movement.[8] By the outbreak of violence he was aged and battled cancer, mostly confining him to Armagh by the mid-1970s until his death in 1977.

Fr Oliver Crilly

He was born near Bellaghy, Co. Derry and was the second cousin of Francis Hughes and Tom McElwee, two men who joined the 1981 hunger strike in Long Kesh/Maze Prison.[9] He earned a BA degree in Celtic Studies and an MA in the Irish language. In 1980 Crilly was appointed to the Irish Commission for Justice and Peace. In 1981, Crilly was the Director of the Irish Catholic Church's Commission for Communications, responsible for the Church's publishing headquarters in Dublin.

Cardinal Cahal Daly (1917–2009)

Cahal Daly was born to a schoolteacher and housewife in Loughguile, Co. Antrim. He trained for the priesthood at Maynooth before lecturing at Queen's University Belfast for

---

[5] Clarke, *No Faith in the System*, 28–9.
[6] Surprisingly, there is no monograph written on Conway's life.
[7] Elliott, *Catholics of Ulster*, 471.   [8] O Connor, *In Search of a State*, 172 and 281.
[9] Beresford, *Ten Men Dead*, 265–6.

twenty years. Daly served as a theological expert on the Second Vatican Council before becoming the Bishop of Ardagh and Clonmacnois in 1967. His diocese was located in the South but that did not hinder Daly from writing frequently on the conflict and regularly pleading for Christian unity. In 1982 Daly was installed as the Bishop of Down and Connor and suffered a heart attack that same year. He was a stark contrast to his predecessor, both physically, personally, and theologically. Where Ó Fiaich spoke of 'Irish' Catholics, Daly pontificated to 'Catholics'.[10] Marianne Elliott describes Daly as 'the most anti-republican of all the clerical voices' despite his nationalist beliefs.[11] His appointment in 1990 came as a surprise because of his advanced age of seventy-three years. Daly took a noticeably harder line against the Provisional IRA and at times this caused accusations of British government favoritism. He stepped down as Archbishop of Armagh on his seventy-ninth birthday in 1996. Maria Power's upcoming monograph tracing Daly's life, utilizing archival and interview sources, will greatly demystify the objectives and intellectual influences of this priest-theologian.[12]

Bishop Edward 'Eddie' Daly* (1933–2016)

Edward Daly was relatively young when he took up his position as Bishop of Derry in 1974. Daly was born in Ballyshannon, Co. Donegal but raised in Belleek, Co. Fermanagh to shopkeeper parents.[13] He attended St Columb's on a scholarship before studying for the priesthood at the Irish College in Rome. Daly served as a curate at St Eugene's Cathedral during the 1960s and early 1970s, where he gained global fame as the priest waving the white handkerchief while helping to move Bloody Sunday victim Jackie Duddy out of the line of fire. Before his appointment as the Catholic Bishop of Derry, Daly briefly took a position as RTÉ's religious programming advisor where he developed a greater under-standing of media strategy. As bishop, Daly frequently condemned internment as well as paramilitary and state violence. His banning of Provisional IRA military funerals in the late 1980s earned him republican ire.[14] Daly counted SDLP MP John Hume as a close confidant, and allowed republicans to use the bishop's house as a peace meeting place in the early 1990s.[15] His efforts in mediating the conflict were cut short in 1992 when, after suffering a stroke, he stepped down from his position in 1993.

Bishop Neil Farren (1895–1980)

Neil Farren was seventy-five years old at the outbreak of violence, having served as Bishop of Derry for twenty-nine years. Educated at Maynooth, he became Derry's youngest bishop when appointed at the age of thirty-nine. Previously the President of St Columb's College in Derry, he had spent most of the 1960s campaigning for a second university in the city. Farren was markedly conservative during the conflict, and his presiding over the Requiem Mass for the Bloody Sunday victims was one of the few instances where he was involved in a funeral for a victim of the conflict. He stepped down as the Bishop of Derry in 1974.

---

[10] Elliott, *Catholics of Ulster*, 298.   [11] Elliott, *Catholics of Ulster*, 474.
[12] Maria Power's upcoming work is provisionally titled *A Just Peace: Cardinal Cahal Daly and the Conflict in Northern Ireland.*
[13] Daly, *Are You a Priest?*, 13–15.   [14] Daly, *A Troubled See*, 193–202.
[15] Interview with Bishop Edward Daly, 2 June 2015.

Mgr Denis Faul (1932–2006)

A mixture of Irish history, ecclesiastical training, and lived experience influenced Denis Faul profoundly. Born in the village of Louth, Co. Louth, he received his education from St Patrick's College, Armagh before studying for the priesthood at Maynooth. After a year studying theology in Rome, Faul joined the faculty at St Patrick's Boys' Academy. In his spare time, Faul worked with Mgr Raymond Murray and Fr Brian Brady. Between 1972–84, the three men jointly wrote more than thirty books and pamphlets documenting human rights abuses in the North. Faul famously worked to end the 1981 hunger strike in Long Kesh/Maze Prison by convincing the families of the hunger-striking prisoners to agree to intravenous feeding once their family member had lapsed into a coma. Throughout the rest of the conflict, Faul repeatedly condemned the Provisional IRA and believed that SF could not campaign for peace while the Provisionals continued their armed struggle. In 1995, Cardinal Cahal Daly appointed Murray and Faul honorary prelates on the same day, bestowing on them both the title of 'Monsignor' (Mgr).[16] Upon his death in 2006 of cancer, some republicans attended his funeral to pay their respects.

Fr Patrick Fell (1940–2011)

Born in England in 1940, Fell converted to Catholicism as a young adult and went on to become a Catholic priest. In the 1970s Fell was accused and later convicted of being a commander of the Coventry Provisional IRA active service unit. Fell never admitted to being a Provisional IRA volunteer and pleaded not guilty to the charges. In June 1984 he was successful in his action to find the British government guilty of violating the European Convention on Human Rights. The British government had denied the right of legal representation to prisoners facing internal prison disciplinary charges. Upon his release Fell served as a parish priest in rural Frosses, Co. Donegal.

Fr Robert 'Bobby' Gilmore* (b. 1938)

Ordained in 1963, Gilmore worked as a missionary in the Philippines from 1964–78 before acting as the Director of the Irish Chaplaincy Scheme in Britain from 1978–92. He aided Irish prisoners' rights in Britain, leading the National Birmingham Six Campaign to victory.[17] He was a founding member of Migrant Rights Centre Ireland.

Cardinal John Carmel Heenan (1905–1975)

Born in Essex to Irish parents, he studied at St Ignatius College in Stamford Hill, Durham. He was ordained to the priesthood in 1930, working in Brentwood until 1947. In 1951, Pope Pius XII appointed Heenan Bishop of Leeds. From Leeds he moved to Liverpool, becoming the Archbishop of Liverpool in 1957. He rose quickly up the ranks of the English hierarchy, becoming the Archbishop of Westminster in September 1963, a position he held until his

---

[16] https://www.irishnews.com/lifestyle/faithmatters/2018/10/18/news/monsignor-raymond-murray—a-life-dedicated-to-the-rhyme-of-hope-and-history-1461075/

[17] Interview with Fr Bobby Gilmore, 23 May 2016.

death in 1975 at the age of seventy. Pope Paul VI created him cardinal in 1965. Heenan participated in the Second Vatican Council and took a moderately conservative stance to many of the reforms proposed.

Cardinal Basil Hume (1923–1999)

Born George Halliburton Hume to wealthy parents in Newcastle upon Tyne, his mother was a French Catholic and his father an aristocratic English Protestant. He became a novice at the Benedictine Monastery of Ampleforth Abbey in North Yorkshire in 1941, adopting the name 'Basil' before being solemnly professed in 1945. Hume was ordained a priest in 1950 and returned to the Abbey to teach modern languages until becoming the abbot in 1963. On 9 February 1976, Pope Paul VI appointed Hume as the Archbishop of Westminster and made him a cardinal that same year. Hume famously became involved in the debate over hunger striking as suicide during the 1980–81 hunger strikes.

Fr Gerry McFlynn*

Before moving to England in the 1980s, McFlynn worked in parishes in north Belfast. For more than two decades McFlynn has been a part of the Irish Commission for Prisoners Overseas and currently manages their London office.[18] As part of his work McFlynn visits Irish prisoners in English and Welsh prisons. In addition, McFlynn writes letters of support for court appearances and parole hearings, liaises with prisoners' families, and conducts advocacy work in relation to issues like repatriation, deportation, health and legal matters, discrimination, and ill-treatment.

Archbishop John Charles McQuaid (1895–1973)

Born in Cootehill, Co. Cavan in 1895 to middle class parents, he entered the novitiate of the Holy Ghost Fathers in Kimmage, Co. Dublin in 1913. McQuaid received BA and MA degrees in classics from University College Dublin before being ordained a priest in 1924. He went on to attend the Gregorian University in Rome to receive a doctorate in theology. In 1925 he began work at Blackrock College in Dublin, ending his career there as the President from 1931–39. McQuaid heavily campaigned for 'special position' of the Catholic Church in the 1937 Irish constitution before his appointment as Archbishop of Dublin in 1940, a position he held until 1971.

Fr Joseph 'Joe' McVeigh* (b. 1945)

McVeigh started life in Co. Fermanagh: 'I was born in Ireland yet all the trappings of the state in which I grew up were British'.[19] His upbringing was surrounded by unionist neighbours '(otherwise decent people)' who 'appeared to undergo a personality

---

[18] Interview with Fr Gerry McFlynn, 6 Nov. 2018.
[19] McVeigh, *Taking a Stand*, 15.

transformation in the summer months'.[20] These experiences of discrimination, his personal desire for a united Ireland and his understanding that Christianity 'proclaims the message of social justice' pushed McVeigh into his role as an outspoken priest against the British state.[21] Wilson and McVeigh frequently met with republicans in an effort to mediate the conflict. They preached liberation theology or 'sharing the people's lot': 'putting the social Gospel of Jesus Christ into practice in situations of oppression and taking the side of the poor'.[22] To insiders and outsiders alike, they were radical in their thinking and practice, most notably, when McVeigh struggled to read out the Irish bishops' authored statement concerning the Enniskillen Bombing.[23] While in the minority, McVeigh and Wilson drew media and public attention, forcing the Church to respond to these priests' statements and actions.

Fr Anthony 'Tony' Mulvey (1926–2010)

Mulvey was an Omagh native and son of a nationalist MP.[24] Based in Derry at St Eugene's Cathedral since the early 1950s. Bishop Edward Daly described Mulvey as knowing the Derry parish 'like the back of his hand' and that Mulvey had 'a powerful social conscience'.[25] In 1960, he co-founded the Credit Union in Derry in collaboration with John Hume and Paddy Doherty. Hume, Doherty, and Mulvey went on to co-create the Derry Housing Association (DHA) in 1965.[26] Along with Fr Bennie O'Neill, the administrator of St Eugene's Cathedral, Mulvey protested RUC demonstrations on Derry's streets during the initial outbreak of the conflict.[27]

Fr John Murphy (1929–2016)

Murphy was ordained in 1959 originally for the diocese of Salford in North England, returning to his native Co. Antrim in the early 1960s. He served as deputy prison chaplain at Long Kesh/Maze Prison from 1976 until the prison's closure in 2000. Republican prisoners referred to Murphy as 'Silver' or 'Silvertop' in their comms to each other.[28] Murphy passed in August 2016.

Mgr Raymond Murray*

Murray was born in Newtownhamilton, Co. Armagh and studied for the priesthood at Maynooth. Murray worked with Fr Denis Faul and Fr Brian Brady to raise awareness of British injustices in the North, concerning the issues of internment, Diplock courts, and strip-searching through a publicity campaign of pamphlet writing. Between 1972–84, the three men wrote more than thirty books and pamphlets documenting human rights abuses in the North. Between 1967–1986 he served as the Catholic chaplain for Armagh prison.

---

[20] McVeigh, *Taking a Stand*, 15.   [21] McVeigh, *Taking a Stand*, 13.
[22] *An Phoblacht/Republican News*, 18 March 2010.
[23] Interview with Fr Joseph McVeigh, 14 Feb. 2014; McVeigh, *Taking a Stand*, 218–219.
[24] Daly, *Are you a Priest?*, 1.   [25] Daly, *Are You a Priest?*, 103–4.
[26] Daly, *Are You a Priest?*, 123.   [27] Prince and Warner, *Belfast and Derry*, 193.
[28] Beresford, *Ten Men Dead*, 74.

From 1985–93, Murray served as an Administrator at St Patrick's Cathedral under Cardinal Tomás Ó Fiaich and Cardinal Cahal Daly.

Sr (Mary) Genevieve O'Farrell (1923–2001)

Born into a large and devout Catholic family in County Offaly, she joined the Daughters of Charity of St Vincent de Paul at the age of eighteen. After joining St Louise's Comprehensive School in West Belfast in 1958, serving as Principal of the school from 1963 until 1988. Republicans criticized Sr Genevieve for being too friendly with the British 'occupying force' and too quick to receive their praise and accolades. She accepted an OBE in 1978 for her work which upset many Catholics in her community, who would have refused such an honour from the British establishment.[29]

Cardinal Tomás Ó Fiaich (1923–1990)

Born Tom Fee in the nationalist area of Cullyhanna, he lectured on Irish history at Maynooth. He was a surprise appointment for archbishop, and in 1979, Pope Paul VI created Ó Fiaich a cardinal. Throughout his tenure as archbishop, Ó Fiaich courted controversy with his firm nationalist stance and undeniable desire for a united Ireland.[30] His 'slums of Calcutta' comment on prison conditions during the 'no wash' protest in Long Kesh/Maze Prison put him at odds with Margaret Thatcher, and he worked to end the 1980-81 hunger strikes by mediating between the prisoners and the British government.[31] His sudden death at the age of sixty-six in May 1990 paved the way for a very different man to lead the Irish Catholic Church.

Bishop William Philbin (1907–1991)

Born in Kiltimagh, Co. Mayo in 1907, Philbin attended Maynooth and was ordained in June 1931. Most of his ministry was spent lecturing on theology as a professor at Maynooth. Pope Pius XII appointed him Bishop of Clonfert in 1953 and in 1962 he became the Bishop of Down and Connor. Philbin attended the Second Vatican Council and was succeeded by Bishop Cahal Daly upon his retirement in 1982.

Fr Alec Reid (1931–2013)

Reid was born in Nenagh, Co. Tipperary and was professed as a member of the Redemptorist Congregation of priests and brothers in 1950, before his ordainment to the priesthood seven years later. Reid moved to Clonard Monastery to work alongside the local people in the early 1960s, where he remained until his death in 2013.[32] In 1988 Reid delivered the last rites to two British Army soldiers after they drove into a republican funeral cortege and were beaten to death by the crowd.

---

[29] Rae, *Sister Genevieve*, 175–6.   [30] FitzGerald, *Father Tom*, 76–80.
[31] FitzGerald, *Father Tom*, 82–3.   [32] *Guardian*, 24 Nov. 2013.

Fr Gerry Reynolds (1935–2015)

Reynolds was born to a farming family near Limerick.[33] After four years of secondary education in St Munchin's College, Limerick and the final year at the Redemptorist St Clement's College, Reynolds joined the Redemptorist community. He took his vows in 1953 before receiving a BA degree from University College Galway in 1956 and then seeking ordination to the priesthood in 1960.[34] From 1969 to 1975, he worked with the Catholic Communication Institute and edited the monthly pastoral magazine *Intercom*. His ecumenical activities began around this period and continued for the rest of his life.[35] Reynolds arrived at Clonard Monastery in 1983, where he remained until his death in 2015.[36] Reynolds was well known for his ecumenical activities with Presbyterian minister Rev Ken Newell.

Dr Geraldine Smyth OP* (b. 1948)

An expert on Ecumenics in its theological, psychological, and socio-political dimensions, and deeply committed to reconciliation and peacebuilding. She has written and lectured widely on such topics. With an interchurch family background, she grew up on Belfast's Falls Road, and as a Dominican Sister she was involved in education in Dominican schools in Portstewart and Belfast during the conflict, and in various leadership roles in her Order. She was coordinator of the work of the Opsahl Commission, 1993–94; and twice Director of the Irish School of Ecumenics, Trinity College Dublin, where she is currently an Adjunct Professor. Smyth carries the Commemoration portfolio on the Board of the Northern Ireland organisation, Healing through Remembering. On the staff of the Irish School of Ecumenics since 1994, Smyth holds a first-class degree in English from the University of Ulster; Masters and Ph.D degrees in Theology from Trinity College Dublin; an Honorary Doctorate from Queen's University Belfast for services to reconciliation; and a Diploma in Transpersonal Psychotherapy and Psychosynthesis. Smyth is a member of the Dominican Order, was Prioress of her international congregation from 1998 to 2004, currently serves on its Council, and lives in a Dublin community.[37]

Mgr Tom Toner (1936–2012)

Toner was an Irish priest educated at St Malachy's College, Belfast. He completed his theological studies at Maynooth and was ordained in 1962. Toner served as a Catholic chaplain in Long Kesh/Maze Prison from 1962 until 1982. Republican prisoners referred to Toner as 'Index' in their comms to each other.[38] After the 1980–81 hunger strikes, Toner became a parish priest in Belfast for St Agnes' Cathedral and then St Teresa's Church on Glen Road. In 1998, he established the Belfast Cathedral partnership between St Anne's and St Peter's.[39]

---

[33] Wells, *Friendship towards Peace*, 40–1.   [34] Wells, *Friendship towards Peace*, 41–2.
[35] Wells, *Friendship towards Peace*, 41–6.   [36] *Irish Independent*, 6 Dec. 2015.
[37] Interview with Dr Geraldine Smyth OP, 3 Dec. 2018.
[38] Beresford, *Ten Men Dead*, 47.
[39] http://www.catholicbishops.ie/2012/11/14/homily-bishop-patrick-walsh-requiem-mass-monsignor-tom-toner-rip/

Fr Desmond 'Des' Wilson* (b. 1925)

Wilson was born in 1925 on the Ormeau Road in Belfast and 'lived during eight papacies and six episcopacies in Down and Connor'.[40] He trained at Maynooth and in 1975 acted as a curate in St John's Parish near the Falls Road when he asked Bishop William Philbin for 'retired status'.[41] Wilson disagreed with direction of the Church under Philbin's leadership, and was all but ostracized from the ordained clergy until Cahal Daly brought him 'back into the fold' in 1983.

Archbishop Derek Worlock (1920–1996)

Worlock was born in London in 1920 to Anglican parents who converted to Roman Catholicism when he was child. Worlock was a student at St Edmond's College from 1934 to 1944 and was ordained to the priesthood in 1944 at Westminster Cathedral. In 1965, Worlock was appointed the Bishop of Portsmouth before becoming the Archbishop of Liverpool in 1976. He worked with Anglican Bishop Derek Sheppard on ecumenical initiatives both in Liverpool and Northern Ireland.

---

[40] *Irish Catholic*, 31 July 2014.   [41] Interview with Fr Desmond Wilson, 1 Sep. 2014.

Bibliography

Government Archives

The National Archives (TNA), Kew, United Kingdom
CAB 128 Cabinet: Minutes.
CAB 129 Cabinet: Memoranda.
CJ 3 Home Office and Northern Ireland Office: Registered Files, 1958–73.
CJ 4 Home Office and Northern Ireland Office: Registered Files, 1930–85.
FCO 87 Foreign and Commonwealth Office: Republic of Ireland Department: Registered Files, 1972–85.
PCOM 8 Prison Commission: Registered Papers, Supplementary Series I, 1876–1958.
PREM 15 Prime Minister's Office: Correspondence and Papers, 1970–74.
PREM 19 Records of the Prime Minister's Office: Correspondence and Papers, 1979–97.

The Public Records Office of Northern Ireland (PRONI), Belfast, United Kingdom
CAB/9/B/312 Disturbances in Northern Ireland, 1969–73.
NIO/12/68 Northern Ireland Office: Protest Action Arising from Claim to Special Category Status – Policy and General Matters (1978).

Church and Diocesan Archives

Archdiocesan Archives of Westminster (AAW), London, United Kingdom
AAW, Cardinal John Carmel Heenan Papers, He 1–475.
AAW, Cardinal Basil Hume Papers, E5567.

Arundel and Brighton Diocesan Archives (ABDA), Brighton, United Kingdom
ABDA, Northern Ireland File.

Birmingham Diocesan Archives (BDA), Birmingham, United Kingdom
BDA, Archbishop George Dwyer Papers, GPD-L-C1-C10.

The Cardinal Tomás Ó Fiaich Memorial Library and Archive (CTOMLA), Armagh, United Kingdom
CTOMLA, Sr Sarah Clarke Papers, Boxes 20 and 21, Binders 1–4.
CTOMLA, Cardinal William Conway Papers, 1968–72.
CTOMLA, Cardinal William Conway Papers, Letters Troubles, 1969.
CTOMLA, Cardinal William Conway Papers, 18–8–1 1968–72, Press Releases.
CTOMLA, Anne Cooney Papers.
CTOMLA, Mgr Denis Faul Papers, 1970–2000.
CTOMLA, Mgr Raymond Murray Papers, Boxes 1–5.

CTOMLA, Cardinal Tomás Ó Fiaich papers, 'Au Tuaisceart'.
CTOMLA, Cardinal Tomás Ó Fiaich papers, NP2: Six Transcripts of Radio Interviews and diverse news cuttings.
Newspaper Cuttings Service for Cardinal Tomás Ó Fiaich, 1982–86.

Derry Diocesan Archives (DeDA), Derry, United Kingdom

DeDA, Bishop Edward Daly Papers.

Dublin Diocesan Archives (DDA), Dublin, Republic of Ireland

DDA, Archbishop McQuaid Papers.

Liverpool Archdiocesan Archives (LAA), Liverpool, United Kingdom

LAA, 'Disasters, Wars and Conflicts' Box: Northern Ireland, WOR 13/8.

Salford Diocesan Archives (SaDA), London, United Kingdom
SaDA, 636.
SaDa, 831.
SaDA, 873.
SaDA, Bishop Holland Pastoral statements.

Southwark Diocesan Archives (SDA), London, United Kingdom
SDA, Bishop Michael Bowen Papers, D47.2.

Other Archives

Conflict Archive on the Internet (CAIN), University of Ulster, Northern Ireland, United Kingdom
Lord Gardiner Committee Report, 1 January 1975, http://cain.ulst.ac.uk/hmso/gardiner.htm

Prisons Memory Archive (PMA), Queen's University Belfast, United Kingdom
Crilly, Fr Oliver, interview by Prisons Memory Archive, July 2005. http://prisonsmemoryarchive.com/religion/
Murray, Mgr Raymond, interview by Prisons Memory Archive, July 2005. http://prisonsmemoryarchive.com/armagh-stories/

Interviews
Bishop Pat Buckley interview, 30 October 2017.
Bishop Edward Daly interview, 2 June 2015.
Dr Brian Feeney interview, 26 May 2015.

Fr Bobby Gilmore interview, 23 May 2016.
Fr Gerry McFlynn interview, 2 May 2014 and 6 November 2018.
Dr Laurence McKeown interview, 15 April 2014.
Fr Joseph McVeigh interview, 14 April 2014.
Danny Morrison interview, 29 April 2014.
Mgr Raymond Murray interview, 11 February 2014.
Dr Geraldine Smyth OP interview, 3 December 2018.
Fr Desmond Wilson interview, 1 September 2014.

Newspapers/Media Outlets

An Phoblacht/Republican News, The Armagh Observer, BBC News, The Belfast Newsletter, The Belfast Telegraph, Boston Irish Echo, Catholic Herald, Catholic New York, Catholic News Service, Chicago Tribune, The Christian Science Monitor, Connaught Telegraph, Corkman, Cork Evening News, Cork Examiner, Daily Chronicle, The Daily Express, Daily Herald, The Daily Mail, The Daily Telegraph, Donegal News, Evening Herald, Evening Mail, Evening Press, The Fermanagh Herald, Fermanagh News, Galway Advertiser, The Guardian, The Irish Catholic, Irish Central, The Irish Independent, The Irish Mirror, The Irish News, The Irish Post, The Irish Press, The Irish Telegraph, The Irish Times, Kerryman, Longford Leader, Manchester Guardian, National Catholic Reporter, Nenagh Guardian, The New Statesmen, Newry Reporter, Northern Constitution, The New York Times, The Observer, RTÉ News, Slugger O'Toole, Southern Star, Standard, Strabane Chronicle, The Sunday Express, The Sunday Independent, The Sunday Times, The Sunday Tribune, The Tablet, The Telegraph, The Times, Ulster Herald, The Universe, Western People, World Focus, Yorkshire Post

Booklets and Pamphlets

Daly, Cahal, *Dialogue for Peace* (Dublin, 1983).
Daly, Cahal, *Renewed Heart for Peace* (Dublin, 1984).
Daly, Cahal, *Addresses 1984–86*, held at the Linenhall Library (Belfast).
Daly, Cahal, *Addresses 1987–88*, held at the Linenhall Library (Belfast).
Daly, Cahal, *Addresses 1989–90*, held at the Linenhall Library (Belfast).
Faul, Denis, *The SDLP and the Rent and Rates Strike* (Armagh, 1974).
Faul, Denis, *The Stripping Naked of Women Prisoners in Armagh Prison 1982–83*, (Armagh, Easter 1983).
Faul, Denis, *The Stripping Naked of Women Prisoners in Armagh Gaol: November 1982 – January 1984*, (Armagh, 1984).
Faul, Denis and Murray, Raymond, *Conditions in Long Kesh Internment Camp, The Maze, Northern Ireland* (Armagh, 20 June 1973).
Faul, Denis and Murray, Raymond, *Long Kesh- The Iniquity of Internment, August 9th 1971– August 9th 1974* (Armagh, 1974).
Faul, Denis and Murray, Raymond, *The Flames of Long Kesh 15–16 October 1974* (Cavan, December 1974).
Faul, Denis and Murray, Raymond, *The Hooded Men: British Torture in Ireland August – October 1971* (Armagh, July 1974).
Faul, Denis and Murray, Raymond, *Whitelaws Tribunals: Long Kesh Internment Camp November 1972 to January 1973* (Armagh, 1974).
Faul, Denis and Murray, Raymond, *The Triangle of Death: Sectarian Assassinations in the Dungannon-Moy-Portadown Area* (Armagh, April 1975).
Faul, Denis and Murray, Raymond, *H-Block: The Caves of Long Kesh* (Armagh, 1978).
Faul, Denis and Murray, Raymond, *Moment of Truth for Northern Ireland* (Armagh, 1980).

Faul, Denis and Murray, Raymond, *Hunger-Strike: The Search for Solutions* (Armagh, May 1981).
Faul, Denis and Murray, Raymond, *Hunger Strike 2: Why British rule has failed to solve prison problems* (Armagh, March 1981).
Faul, Denis and Murray, Raymond, *Rubber and plastic bullets kill and maim* (Armagh, August 1981).
Faul, Denis and Murray, Raymond, *Plastic Bullets: Plastic Government* (Armagh, October 1982).
Faul, Denis and Murray, Raymond, *Second International Tribunal of Inquiry into Deaths and Injuries by Plastic Bullets* (Armagh, October 1982).
Faul, Denis and Murray, Raymond, *The Alienation of Northern Ireland Catholics* (Armagh, 1984).
St Patrick's College, Maynooth, *Kalendarium: Collegii Sti Patritii*, (Dublin, 1940–41).
St Patrick's College, Maynooth, *Kalendarium: Collegii Sti Patritii*, (Dublin, 1975–76).
McAliskey, Bernadette, *Freedom only comes if you take it!* (New York, 1982).
McVeigh, Joseph, *Some Thoughts on Liberation Theology* (Fermanagh, June 1978).
McVeigh, Joseph and Wilson, Desmond, *The Truth Will Set Us Free: Collected Statements 1988–1993*, (Belfast, 1994).
O'Duill, Piaras, *H-Block: Can we remain silent?* (Dublin, 1980).
O'Duill, Piaras, *Hunger Strike: The Children of '69* (Armagh, April 1981).

Journals and Magazines

Doctrine and Life (1968–94)
The Furrow (1968–94)
Spare Rib (1972–93)

Speeches

Daly, Cahal, *Violence in Ireland and Christian Conscience: From Addresses given by Cahal B. Daly Bishop of Ardagh and Clonmacnois* (Dublin, 1973).
Pope John Paul II, *Pilgrimage of Peace: The Collected Speeches of John Paul II in Ireland and the United States* (London, 1980).
Pope John Paul II, *The Pope in Ireland: Addresses and Homilies* (Dublin, 1979).

Memoirs/Diaries

Adams, Gerry, *Hope and History: Making Peace in Ireland* (London, 2003).
Buckley, Pat, *A Thorn in the Side* (Dublin, 1994).
Clarke, Sarah, *No Faith in the System: A Search for Justice* (Dublin, 1995).
Daly, Cahal, *Steps on my Pilgrim Journey: Memories and Reflections* (Dublin, 1998).
Daly, Edward, *A Troubled See: Memoirs of a Derry Bishop* (Dublin, 2011).
Daly, Edward, *Mister, Are You a Priest?* (Dublin, 2000).
Faulkner, Brian, *Memoirs of a Statesman* (London, 1978).
Hayes, Maurice, *Minority Verdict: Experiences of a Catholic Public Servant* (Belfast, 1995).
Hume, John, *Personal Views: Politics, Peace and Reconciliation in Ireland* (Dublin, 1996).

McCann, Eamonn, *War and an Irish Town* (London, 1993).

McNamara, Kevin, *Law and Morality* (Dublin, 1986).

McVeigh, Joseph, *Taking a Stand: A Memoir of an Irish Priest* (Cork, 2008).

Morrison, Danny (ed.), *Ten on Ten: Memories of the 1981 Hunger Strike* (Dublin, 1991).

Murray, Raymond, *Hard Time: Armagh Gaol 1971–1986* (Dublin, 1998).

O'Doherty, Shane, *The Volunteer: A Former IRA Man's True Story* (London, 1993).

Philbin, William, *To You Simonides* (London, 1973).

Pope John Paul II, *Gift and Mystery* (New York City, 1996).

Sands, Robert, *The Diary of Bobby Sands* (Dublin, 1981).

Sands, Robert, *One Day in My Life* (Dublin, 1983).

Thatcher, Margaret, *The Downing Street Years* (London, 1993).

Wilson, Desmond, *A Diary of Thirty Days: Ballymurphy–July–December 1972* (Belfast, 1973).

Wilson, Desmond, *The Chaplain's Affair*, (Belfast, 1999).

Wilson, Desmond, *The Way I See It*, (Belfast, 2005).

Reports

Faith in the City: A Call for Action by Church and Nation, The Report of the Archbishop of Canterbury on Urban Priority Areas (London, 1985).

Hickman, Mary and Walter, Bronwen, *Discrimination and the Irish Community in Britain: A Report of Research undertaken for the Commission for Racial Equality* (London, 1997).

New Ireland Forum: Report of Proceedings (Dublin, 1984).

Pollak, Andy (ed.) *A Citizen's Inquiry: The Opsahl Report on Northern Ireland* (Dublin, 1993).

Books

Akenson, Donald, *Small Differences: Irish Catholics and Irish Protestants, 1815–1922* (Dublin, 1991).

Appleby, R. Scott, *The Ambivalence of the Sacred: Religion, Violence, and Reconciliation* (Maryland, 2010).

Aveyard, S.C., *No Solution: The Labour Government and the Northern Ireland Conflict, 1974–79* (Manchester, 2016).

Baum, Gregory and Wells, Harold (eds.) *The Reconciliation of the Peoples: Challenge to the Churches* (New York, 1997).

Beresford, David, *Ten Men Dead* (London, 1987).

Bew, John, Frampton, Martyn, and Gurruchaga, Iñigo, *Talking to Terrorists: Making Peace in Northern Ireland and the Basque Country* (London, 2009).

Bew, Paul, *Ireland: The Politics of Enmity 1789–2006* (Oxford, 2007).

Bew, Paul, Gibbon, Peter, and Patterson, Henry, *Northern Ireland 1921/2001: Political Forces and Social Classes* (London, 2002).

Bew, Paul and Gillespie, Gordon, *Northern Ireland: A Chronology of the Troubles 1968–1999* (Dublin, 1993).

Bew, Paul and Patterson, Henry, *The British State and the Ulster Crisis: From Wilson to Thatcher* (London, 1985).

Bourke, Richard, *Peace in Ireland: The War of Ideas* (London, 2003).

Boyce, D. George, *Nationalism in Ireland* (London, 1982).

Brewer, John D., and Higgins, Gareth I., *Anti-Catholicism in Northern Ireland, 1600–1998* (London, 1998).

Brewer, John D., Higgins, Gareth I., and Teeney, Francis, *Religion, Civil Society and Peace in Northern Ireland* (Oxford, 2011).

Bruce, Steve, *God Save Ulster! The Religion and Politics of Paisleyism* (Oxford, 1986).

Cadwallader, Anne, *Lethal Allies: British Collusion in Ireland* (Cork, 2013).

Chiffolo, Anthony, *Pope John Paul II: In My Own Words* (New York, 2002).

Clarke, Liam, *Broadening the Battlefield: The H-Blocks and the Rise of Sinn Féin* (Dublin, 1987).

Collins, Tom, *The Irish Hunger Strike* (Dublin, 1986).

Comerford, R.V., *Ireland: Inventing the Nation* (London, 2003).

Coogan, Tim Pat, *On the Blanket: The H-Block Story* (Dublin, 1980).

Coohill, Joseph, *Ireland: A Short History* (Oxford, 2005).

Cornell, John, *Pontiff in Winter: Triumph and Conflict in the Reign of John Paul II* (New York, 2005).

Cornwell, John, *Hitler's Pope: The Secret History of Pius XII* (London, 1999).

Craig, Mary, *Pope John Paul II* (London, 1982).

Dillon, Martin, *God and the Gun: The Church and Irish Terrorism* (London, 1997).

Dokecki, Paul, *The Clergy Sexual Abuse Crisis: Reform and Renewal in the Catholic Community* (Washington, D.C., 2004).

Dunne, Derek, *The Birmingham Six* (Dublin, 1988).

Eddy, Paul, Linklater, Magnus, and Gillman, Peter, *The Falklands War* (London, 1982).

Elliott, Marianne, *The Catholics of Ulster: A History* (London, 2000).

Elliott, Marianne, *When God Took Sides: Religion and Identity in Ireland, Unfinished History* (Oxford, 2009).

Ellmann, Maud, *The Hunger Artists: Starving, Writing and Imprisonment* (London, 1993).

English, Richard, *Armed Struggle: The History of the IRA* (London, 2003).

Fitzgerald, Billy, *Father Tom: An Authorised Portrait of Cardinal Tomas Ó Fiaich* (London, 1990).

France, John, *The Crusades and the Expansion of Catholic Christendom, 1000–1714* (London, 2005).

Freedman, Lawrence, *The Official History of the Falklands Campaign, Volume II: War and Diplomacy* (London, 2004).

Fuller, Louise, *Irish Catholicism since 1950: The Undoing of a Culture* (Dublin, 2002).

Gallagher, Eric and Worral, A.S., *Christians in Ulster* (Oxford, 1982).

Ganiel, Gladys, *Transforming Post-Catholic Ireland: Religious Practice in Late Modernity* (Oxford, 2016).

Gibson, Brian, *The Birmingham Bombs* (London, 1976).

Hagerty, James, *Cardinal John Carmel Heenan: Priest of the People, Prince of the Church* (Leominster, 2012).

Hagerty, James, *William Gordon Wheeler: A Journey into the Fullness of Faith* (Leominster, 2015).

Hanley, Brian and Millar, Scott, *The Lost Revolution: The Story of the Official IRA and the Workers' Party* (Dublin, 2009).

Harris, Alana, *Faith in the family: A lived religious history of English Catholicism, 1945–82* (Manchester, 2013).

Harris, Mary, *The Catholic Church and the Foundation of the Northern Irish State* (Dublin, 1993).

Hastings, Max and Jenkins, Simon, *The Battle for the Falklands* (London, 1983).

Hayward, Katy, *Irish nationalism and European integration: The official redefinition of the island of Ireland* (Manchester, 2009).

Heaney, Seamus, *North* (London, 1975).

Hebblethwaite, Peter, *The Year of Three Popes* (London, 1978).

Hennessey, Thomas, *The Evolution of the Troubles 1970–72* (Dublin, 2007).

Hennessey, Thomas, *Hunger Strike: Margaret Thatcher's Battle with the IRA 1980–1981* (Dublin, 2013).

Hoppen, K. Theodore, *Ireland since 1800: Conflict and Conformity* (London, 1989).

Hopkins, Stephen, *The Politics of Memoir and the Northern Irish Conflict* (Liverpool, 2013).

Horn, Gerd-Rainer, *The Spirit of Vatican II: Western European Progressive Catholicism in the Long Sixties* (Oxford, 2015).

Howard, Anthony, *Basil Hume: The Monk Cardinal* (London, 2005).

Inglis, Tom, *Moral Monopoly: The Catholic Church in Modern Irish Society* (Dublin, 1987).

Keenan, Marie, *Child Sexual Abuse and the Catholic Church: Gender, Power, and Organizational Culture* (Oxford, 2011).

Kelley, Kevin, *The Longest War: Northern Ireland and the IRA* (London, 1988).

Kenny, Mary, *Goodbye to Catholic Ireland* (Dublin, 2000).

Keogh, Dermot, *The Vatican, the Bishops and Irish Politics 1919–1939* (Cambridge, 1986).

Kerr, Gordon, *Timeline of the Popes: A History from St Peter to Francis* (Newport, 2013).

Larkin, Maurice, *Religion, politics and preferment in France since 1890: Le Belle Époque and its legacy* (Cambridge, 1995).

Lennon, Brian, *After the Ceasefires: Catholics and the Future of Northern Ireland* (Dublin, 1995).

Liechty, Joseph and Clegg, Cecelia, *Moving Beyond Sectarianism: Religion, Conflict, and Reconciliation in Northern Ireland* (Dublin, 2000).

MacDonagh, Oliver, *States of Mind: A Study of Anglo-Irish Conflict 1780–1980* (London, 1983).

Maguire, Mairead Corrigan, *The Vision of Peace: Faith and Hope in Northern Ireland* (New York, 1999).

Marwick, Arthur, *The Sixties: Cultural Revolution in Britain, France, Italy and the United States, c.1958–c.1974* (Oxford, 1998).

McAllister, Ian, *The Northern Ireland Social Democratic and Labour Party: Political Opposition in a Divided Society* (London, 1977).

McCleery, Martin, *Operation Demetrius: and its aftermath: A new history of the use of internment without trial in Northern Ireland 1971–75* (Manchester, 2015).

McDaid, Shaun, *Template for Peace: Northern Ireland, 1972–75* (Manchester, 2013).

McElroy, Gerald, *The Catholic Church and the Northern Ireland Crisis 1968–86* (Dublin, 1991).

McGarry, John and O'Leary, Brendan, *Explaining Northern Ireland: Broken Images* (Oxford, 1995).

McKeever, Martin, *One Man, One God: The Peace Ministry of Fr Alec Reid C.Ss.R,* (Dublin, 2017).

McKittrick, David, Kelters, Seamus, Feeney, Brian, and Thorton, Chris, (eds.), *Lost Lives: The stories of the men, women and children who died as a result of the Northern Irish Troubles* (Edinburgh, 1999).

McLoughlin, P.J., *John Hume and the revision of Irish nationalism* (Manchester, 2010).

Melling, Joseph, *Rent Strikes: People's Struggle for Housing in West Scotland, 1890–1916* (Edinburgh, 1983).

Mitchell, Claire, *Religion, Identity, and Politics in Northern Ireland: Boundaries of Belonging and Belief* (Aldershot, 2006).

Moloney, Ed, *Voices from the Grave: Two Men's War in Ireland* (London, 2010).

Moore, Charles, *Margaret Thatcher: The Authorized Biography, Volume One: Not for Turning* (London, 2013).

Moore, Chris, *Betrayal of Trust: The Father Brendan Smyth Affair and the Catholic Church* (Dublin, 1995).

Mullin, Chris, *Error of Judgment: Truth About the Birmingham Bombings* (Dublin, 1997).

Murray, Gerard, *John Hume and the SDLP* (Dublin, 1998).

Murray, Gerard and Tonge, Jonathan, *Sinn Féin and the SDLP: From Alienation to Participation* (London, 2005).

O Connor, Fionnuala, *In Search of State: Catholics in Northern Ireland* (Belfast, 1994).

O'Connor, Garry, *Universal Father: A Life of Pope John Paul II* (London, 2005).

Ó Dochartaigh, Niall, *From Civil Rights to Armalites: Derry and The Birth of the Irish Troubles* (Basingstoke, 1997, 2005).

O'Halloran, Clare, *Partition and the Limits of Irish Nationalism: An Ideology Under Stress* (Dublin, 1987).

O'Malley, Padraig, *Biting at the Grave: The Irish Hunger Strikes and the Politics of Despair* (Belfast, 1990).

O'Rawe, Richard, *Afterlives: The Hunger Strike and the Secret Offer that Changed Irish History* (Dublin, 2010).

O'Rawe, Richard, *Blanketmen: An untold story of the H-block hunger strike* (Dublin, 2005)

O'Toole, Fintan, *The Lie of the Land: Irish Identities* (London, 1998).

Power, Maria, *From Ecumenism to Community Relations: Inter-Church Relationships in Northern Ireland 1980–2005* (Dublin, 2006).

Prince, Simon and Warner, Geoffrey, *Belfast and Derry in Revolt: A New History of the Start of the Troubles* (Dublin, 2011).

Prince, Simon, *Northern Ireland's '68: Civil Rights, Global Revolt and the Origins of The Troubles* (Dublin, 2007, 2018).

Rae, John, *Sister Genevieve* (London, 2001).

Rafferty, Oliver, *Catholicism in Ulster: 1603–1983: An Interpretative History* (London, 1994).

Rafter, Kevin, *Martin Mansergh: A Biography* (Dublin, 2002).

Robbins, Keith, *England, Ireland, Scotland, Wales: The Christian Church 1900–2000* (Oxford, 2008).

Ross, F. Stuart, *Smashing H-Block: The Rise and Fall of the Popular Campaign against Criminalisation, 1976–1982* (Liverpool, 2011).

Ross, Kristin, *May '68 and its afterlives* (Chicago, 2002).

Rowan, Brian, *How the Peace Was Won* (Dublin, 2008).

Ruane, Joseph and Todd, Jennifer, *The Dynamics of Conflict in Northern Ireland: Power, Conflict and Emancipation* (Cambridge, 1996).

Ryder, Chris, *Inside the Maze: The Untold Story of the Northern Ireland Prison Service* (London, 2000).

Sandal, Nukhet A., *Religious Leaders and Conflict Transformation: Northern Ireland and Beyond* (Cambridge, 2017).

Sanders, Andrew and Wood, Ian S., *Times of Troubles: Britain's War in Northern Ireland* (Edinburgh, 2012).

Share, Perry, Tovey, Hilary, and Corcoran, Mary P., *A Sociology of Modern Ireland*, 3rd edition, (Dublin, 2007).

Taggart, Norman, *Controversy, Conflict, Co-operation: The Irish Council of Churches and 'the Troubles' 1968–1972* (Dublin, 2004).
Tanner, Marcus, *Ireland's Holy Wars: The Struggle for a Nation's Soul 1500–2000* (London, 2001).
Vernon, James, *Hunger: A Modern History* (Cambridge, MA., 2007).
Walker, R.K., *The Hunger Strikes* (Belfast, 2006).
Wells, Ronald, *Friendship towards Peace: The Journey of Ken Newell and Gerry Reynolds* (Dublin, 2005).
White, Barry, *John Hume: Statesman of the Troubles* (Belfast, 1984).
Whitehead, A.N., *Process and Reality* (New York, 1978).
Wright, Frank, *Northern Ireland: A Comparative Analysis* (Dublin, 1987).

Journal Articles

Bell, Emma, 'Disruptive religion: the case of the Catholic worker-priests (1943–1954)', *Journal of Management, Spirituality and Religion*, 4 (2007), 432–42.
Berman, David, Lalor, Stephen and Torode, Brian, 'The theology of the IRA', *Studies*, 22 (1983), 137–44.
Bourke, Richard, 'Antigone and after: "ethnic" conflict in historical perspective', *Field Day Review*, 2 (2006), 168–94.
Bourke, Richard, 'Languages of conflict and the Northern Ireland Troubles', *Journal of Modern History*, 83 (2011), 544–78.
Bruce, Steve, 'Secularization and the impotence of individualized religion', *Hedgehog Review*, 8 (2006), 35–45.
Bull, Peter, 'Shifting patterns of social identity in Northern Ireland', *Psychologist*, 19 (2006), 40–3.
Cmiel, Kenneth, 'The recent history of human rights', *The American Historical Review*, 109 (2004), 117–35.
Elliott, Marianne, 'The role of civil society in conflict resolution: The Opsahl Commission in Northern Ireland, 1992–93', *New Hibernia Review*, 17 (2013), 86–102.
Hanna, Erika, 'Photographs and the "Truth" during the Northern Ireland Troubles', *Journal of British Studies*, 54 (2015), 457–80.
Hayward, Katy, 'The politics of nuance: Irish official discourse on Northern Ireland', *Irish Political Studies*, 19 (2004), 18–38.
Kirby, Dianne, and Rafferty, Briege, "Sisters in the 'Troubles', *Doctrine and Life*, vol. 67 (2017), 2–12.
Kocka, Jürgen, 'Comparison and beyond', *History and Theory*, 42 (2003), 39–44.
Kowalski, Rachel, 'The role of sectarianism in the Provisional IRA campaign, 1969–1997', *Terrorism and Political Violence*, 30 (2018), 658–83.
Leahy, Thomas, 'The influence of informers and agents on Provisional Irish Republican army military strategy and British counter-insurgency strategy, 1976–94', *Twentieth Century British History*, 26 (2015), 122–46.
Loughran, Christina 'Armagh and feminist strategy: campaigns around Republican women prisoners in Armagh Jail', *Feminist Review*, 23 (1986), 59–79.
McBride, Ian, 'The shadow of the gunmen: Irish historians and the IRA', *Journal of Contemporary History*, 46 (2011), 686–710.
Moxon-Browne, Edward, 'Alienation: the case of the Catholics in Northern Ireland', *Journal of Political Science*, 14 (1986), 74–88.

Ó Dochartaigh, Niall, '"Sure it's hard to keep up with the splits here": Irish American responses to the outbreak of conflict in Northern Ireland 1968-1974', *Irish Political Studies*, 10 (1995), 138-60.

Pernau, Margrit, 'Whither conceptual history? From national to entangled histories', *Contributions to the History of Concepts*, 7 (2012), 1-11.

Power, Maria, 'Reconciling state and society? The Practice of the common good in the partnership of Bishop David Sheppard and Archbishop Derek Worlock', *Journal of Religious History*, 40 (2016), 545-64.

Prince, Simon, '5 October 1968 and the beginning of the troubles: flashpoints, riots and memory', *Irish Political Studies*, 27 (2012), 394-410.

Prince, Simon, 'The Global Revolt of 1968 and Northern Ireland', *The Historical Journal*, 49 (2006), 851-75.

Rafferty, Oliver, 'The Catholic Church and the nationalist community in Northern Ireland since 1960', *Éire-Ireland*, 43 (2008), 99-125.

Rafter, Kevin, 'Priests and peace: the role of the Redemptorist Order in the Northern Ireland peace process', *Études irlandaises*, 28 (2003), 159-76.

Reichley, James, 'Faith in politics', *Journal of Policy History*, 13 (2001), 157-80.

Rosland, Sissel 'Victimhood, identity, and agency in the early phase of the troubles in Northern Ireland', *Identities: Global Studies in Culture and Power*, 16 (2009), 294-320.

Ruane, Joseph and Todd, Jennifer, 'Path dependence in settlement processes: explaining settlement in Northern Ireland', *Political Studies*, 55 (2007), 442-58.

Ruane, Joseph and Todd, Jennifer, 'The roots of intense ethnic conflict may not in fact be ethnic: categories, communities and path dependence', *European Journal of Sociology*, 45 (2004), 209-32.

Scull, Margaret M., 'The Catholic Church and the hunger strikes of Terence MacSwiney and Bobby Sands', *Irish Political Studies*, 31 (2016), 282-99.

Walker, Breifne, 'The Catholic Church in Ireland- - adaptation or liberation?', *The Crane Bag*, 5 (1981), 74-8.

Weinstein, Laura, 'The significance of the Armagh dirty protest', *Éire-Ireland*, 41 (2006), 11-41.

Chapters in Books

Akinwale, Anthony, 'The decree on priestly formation, *Optatam Totius*', in Matthew Lamb and Matthew Levering (eds.), *Vatican II: Renewal with tradition* (Oxford, 2008), 229-57.

Brady, Sean, 'Why examine men, masculinities and religion in Northern Ireland?', in Lucy Delap and Sue Morgan (eds.), *Men, Masculinities and Religious Change in Twentieth-Century Britain* (Basingstoke, 2013), 218-51.

Bruce, Steve, 'History, sociology and secularisation', in Christopher Hartney (ed.), *Secularisation: New Historical Perspectives* (Newcastle, 2014), 190-213.

Donnelly Jr, James S., 'The troubled contemporary Irish Catholic Church', in Brendan Bradshaw and Dáire Keogh (eds.), *Christianity in Ireland: Revisiting the Story* (Dublin, 2002), 271-86.

Fitzduff, Mari, 'Just enough to hate - not enough to love: Religious leaders in Northern Ireland', in Timothy D. Sisk (ed.), *Between Terror and Tolerance* (Washington, 2011), 145-68.

Fuller, Louise, 'Political fragmentation in independent Ireland', in Oliver Raffety (ed.), *Irish Catholic Identities* (Manchester, 2013), 307–20.

Hurley, Michael S.J., 'Northern Ireland and the post-Vatican II ecumenical journey', in Brendan Bradsaw and Dáire Keogh (eds.), *Christianity in Ireland: Revisiting the Story* (Dublin, 2002), 259–70.

Kenny, Mary, 'Introduction', in Sean O'Keeffe (ed.), *3 Days in September* (Dublin, 2004), 11–18.

McCartney, Clem, 'The role of civil society', in Clem McCartney (ed.), *Accord: Striking a Balance: The Northern Ireland peace process* (London, 1999).

Power, Maria, 'Providing a prophetic voice? Churches and peacebuilding, 1968–2005', in Maria Power (ed.) *Building Peace in Northern Ireland* (Liverpool, 2011), 73–92.

Tobin, Robert, 'The evolution of national and religious identity in contemporary Ireland', in Jane Garnett, Matthew Grimley, Alana Harris, William Whyte, and Sarah Williams (eds.), *Redefining Christian Britain: Post-1945 Perspectives* (London, 2007), 278–88.

Theses

Peoples, Matthew Terence, 'The Catholic Church and the Northern Ireland Conflict', (University of Ulster unpublished MA Thesis, 2002).

Film

14 Days, BBC 1, 21 March 2013, http://www.bbc.co.uk/programmes/b01r7v48

Bloody Sunday: The Story, 12 January 2009, https://www.youtube.com/watch?v=MQsr1buOCbc

Audio Recording

'Sisters of the Troubles', *BBC World Service: The Documentary Podcast*, 25 March 2018, https://www.bbc.co.uk/programmes/p0623s43

Index